The Tragedy of Bukharin

The Tragedy
of Bukharin

Donny Gluckstein

Pluto Press
LONDON • BOULDER, COLORADO

First published 1994 by Pluto Press
345 Archway Road, London N6 5AA
and 5500 Central Avenue
Boulder, CO 80301, USA

Copyright © 1994 Donny Gluckstein

The right of Donny Gluckstein to be
identified as the author of this work has been
asserted by him in accordance with the
Copyright, Designs and Patents Act 1988

British Library Cataloguing in Publication Data
A catalogue record for this book is available
from the British Library

ISBN 0 7453 0772 8 (hbk)
ISBN 0 7453 0773 6 (pbk)

Library of Congress Cataloging in Publication Data
Gluckstein, Donny, 1954–
    The tragedy of Bukharin / Donny Gluckstein.
    p. cm.
    Includes index.
    ISBN 0-7453-0772-8 (cloth). — ISBN 0-7453-0773-6 (pbk.)
    1. Bukharin, NIkolai Ivanovich, 1888–1938. 2. Communists—Soviet
Union—Biography. 3. Statesman—Soviet Union—Biography. 4. Soviet
Union—Politics and government—1917–1936. 5. Communism.
I. Title
HX313.8.B85658   1993
947.084'092—dc20
[B]   93–34928
                                                                          CIP

Designed and Produced for Pluto Press by
Chase Production Services, Chipping Norton
Typeset from author's disk by
Stanford Desktop Publishing Services, Milton Keynes
Printed in Finland by WSOY

Contents

Preface		vi
Acknowledgements		vii
Introduction		1
1	World Economy and Imperialism	4
2	Left Communism	18
3	War Communism	32
4	The Bridge of Philosophy and Culture	58
5	The New Economic Policy	78
6	The Russian Peasantry	96
7	The Hammer of Trotskyism	109
8	'Enrich Yourselves'	130
9	The Market and Transition to Socialism	156
10	The Comintern and Disaster: World Bukharinism	171
11	The NEP in Crisis	199
12	Was Bukharin the Alternative to Stalin?	217
	Notes and References	253
	Index	285

Preface

The disappearance of the USSR presents contemporary writers of history with a problem of terminology. In the absence of an appropriate word to cover all the various nationalities, the term Russia has had to be used to denote the entire area once covered by the Soviet state.

It was the custom of Soviet politicians frequently to emphasise particular words. In order to distinguish between these and words stressed by the present author, in quoted material emphasis in the original is given in *italics,* while emphasis that I have added is shown in ***bold italic*** type.

Acknowledgements

Many people have helped in the preparation of this book. Particular thanks are due to Lynda Aitken, Tony Cliff, Lindsey German, Chris Harman, Mike Haynes, Derek Howl, Penny Packham, John Rees, Chanie Rosenberg, Ahmed Shawki and Ian Wall.

Introduction

While this book concerns a figure from the past, it is also about some of the central questions of our time. The fragmentation of the once mighty USSR and the utter failure of its command economy have led to a re-examination of the origins of the Stalinist system. However, this re-examination has been stamped by the ideology of the West's triumphant Cold War warriors. Instead of Stalin's monstrous distortion of history we have a new, equally pervasive and false orthodoxy whose central belief is the need for market relations in economic life.

As their system lurches from crisis to crisis, capitalists try to extinguish any hope of liberation from its poverty, exploitation and oppression. The rewriting of the USSR's history serves this purpose. It is not only Stalinism that is being thrown out but the tradition of the 1917 revolution. The workers' state that the Bolsheviks established represents the best attempt up to now to replace the dictatorship of capital, and its profit motive, with workers' power and socialism.

Writings on Nikolai Ivanovich Bukharin have played a significant role in this rewriting of Soviet history. After the publication of Stephen Cohen's influential biography of Bukharin in 1971 a different approach to the post-1917 period arose. Supporters of the new trend included historians like Moshe Lewin and Alec Nove. They wrote works which denounced not only Stalin's destruction of Bolshevik party democracy but also the violence of forced peasant collectivisation and forced industrialisation in the towns.[1] While attacking Stalin in this way, these academics also wished to distance themselves from the Trotskyist tradition which posed revolutionary socialism as the alternative to Stalinism.

Bukharin's writings from 1924 to 1929 provided the solution they were looking for. Bukharin was a prominent Bolshevik who had participated in the October revolution and edited *Pravda*, the party newspaper. After Lenin's death in 1924 he vigorously promoted the further development of market relations. In doing so he clashed with Trotsky and his followers in the left opposition. Bukharin also crossed swords with Stalin when the latter embarked on his counter-revolution in the years 1928 and 1929. In the eyes of academics like Cohen this endowed Bukharin with the political credibility necessary to be the champion of the new creed of market socialism.

This political current grew in importance in the mid-1980s when market socialism was adopted by the Soviet regime. The intention of Gorbachev and his allies was straightforward. The Soviet establishment wanted a change of economic policy that would not disrupt its position of privilege. It needed an authoritative figure who could justify the turn to market-based capitalism from within the Communist Party tradition. Once again Bukharin fitted the bill. His works were republished and a host of laudatory articles appeared in the press. However, the love affair between the Soviet establishment and the ghost of Bukharin came to an abrupt end with the attempted coup of August 1991 and its aftermath. The memory of Bukharin had served as a sort of bridge across which members of the Russian state capitalist ruling class could travel to the market. Once over this bridge, people like Yeltsin had no further use for Bukharin or the Communist legitimacy he had provided.

Bukharin is too important a historical and political figure to be used and abused in this way. He is much more than a mere political cypher for market socialists. His theoretical arguments touched on many of the issues of today. Bukharin's work on the interaction of capital and the state constitutes an important element of contemporary Marxist theory. He developed the concept of state capitalism which, in a context he never envisaged, explains the character of the Stalinist system that grew up in the 1930s. However, Bukharin was more than a theoretician; he actively shaped events in the period between the 1917 revolution and Stalin's counter-revolution in 1928-9.

It is an axiom of Marxism that being determines consciousness, rather than the reverse. Bukharin was not a pure theorist aloof from developments around him. It is therefore impossible to evaluate his ideas while ignoring the times in which he lived. The converse is also true. These times cannot be understood without knowledge of his individual contribution. A study of Bukharin's career between 1917 and his disgrace in 1929 can therefore help us understand how the great hopes of the Russian revolution could have been replaced by the horrors of Stalinist counter-revolution.

The general reasons for the long-term problems of the Russian revolution – the backwardness of the country, the physical destruction of the small working class, international isolation – are well known. Trotsky's battle against the rising tide of Stalinism is also effectively documented. Yet the complex process of degeneration which took place in the period up to 1929, and which involved retreat on the economic, political, social and ideological fronts, is not so well served by historians. It is here that a study of Bukharin, who above all came to represent the revolution's degeneration, as opposed to its original revolutionary spirit (expressed by Trotsky and the left opposition) and its final defeat (represented by Stalin), is so useful.

While this book will argue that many of Bukharin's theories are invaluable to Marxists, it will also be sharply critical of many of his ideas and actions. There is much to be learnt from Bukharin, both positive and negative. He had such a brilliant mind and was so dedicated to the cause of socialism that even his most serious errors are instructive. Thus, in spite of Bukharin's at times vitriolic campaigning against the left opposition, in 1938 Trotsky, its leader, could write: '*Bukharin has thirty years of revolutionary work to his credit.*'²

1 World Economy and Imperialism

The First World War, which began in August 1914, was a conflict which dwarfed all previous ones. To Rosa Luxemburg it proved capitalism to be: 'Shamed, dishonoured, wading in blood and dripping with filth ... an orgy of anarchy ... so it appears in all its hideous nakedness.'[1] It was the first 'total war' in which not just troops but the entire physical resources of economies – finance, industry, workers – were thrown into the fray. States confronted each other as gargantuan integrated machines of destruction.

This fratricide between workers on behalf of their own capitalist classes could have been prevented, or at least cut short, by the mobilisation of the international workers' movement. Alas, almost all the parties of the Second International, led by the 'Pope of Marxism', Karl Kautsky, abandoned their previous anti-war stance and became chauvinists supporting the war effort of their own governments. The collapse of the Second International exposed the hollowness of its 'official Marxism' but left the tiny handful who had not succumbed to war fever politically disarmed. The weapons of Marxism would have to be resharpened. This task was tackled from various directions, for example in Luxemburg's *Junius Pamphlet*, Lenin's *Imperialism*, and Trotsky's *War and the International*. Bukharin's *Imperialism and World Economy* was arguably the most important contribution to this literature.

At the outbreak of war Bukharin was in exile. Born into a middle-class Muscovite family in 1888, he had become involved in revolutionary politics at an early age. In 1905 he played a prominent part in the Moscow student movement and later in the local Bolshevik organisation. By 1914 he had made the acquaintance of Lenin, helped Stalin to complete a pamphlet on the national question and found time to write a masterful critique of the marginalist economics of the Austrian school of Böhm-Bawerk, *The Economic Theory of the Leisure Class*. Imperialist war and the collapse of the Second International presented a still greater theoretical challenge. His answer, *Imperialism and World Economy*, was written in the most difficult circumstances. After its completion in Sweden, Bukharin was jailed. The manuscript was confiscated by the military censor on arrival in Russia in 1917, lost, found again, then seized by right-wing opponents. Finally it was rescued and published after the Bolshevik revolution. This book went far beyond a simple defence of the tradition of Marxism to achieve brilliant insights into the future development of capitalism.

Bukharin's target was less the obviously reactionary nonsense of the jingoists[2], than the politically more damaging arguments of the Second International socialists Rudolf Hilferding[3] and Kautsky. They justified their abandonment of principle by suggesting that the war was an aberration, an accident out of character with 'normal' capitalist development. Socialism could only be pursued in times of peace. Until then workers should get on with fighting their foreign brothers for the sake of the fatherland. According to this view imperialism and war were peripheral features of capitalism, mere temporary policies which would go as easily as they came. Kautsky wrote that imperialism is 'not an "economic phase" ... I believe we have every reason to maintain this distinction ... Imperialism is a particular kind of capitalist policy.'[4]

Kautsky believed imperialist competition ran counter to capitalist economic trends and insisted that wars would rapidly become a thing of the past. They would be superseded by the true, normal and peaceful development of capitalism towards 'ultra-imperialism'. Fighting would be banned because it interfered with the making of profits: 'It is the capitalist economy which is extremely threatened by conflicts between its states. Every far-sighted capitalist today must call to his comrades: Capitalists of the world, unite!'[5] Kautsky might have been forgiven if the outbreak of war had caused him to rethink his position. But such was his faith in the long-term peaceful development of the system that he had his article on ultra-imperialism, written before August 1914, published a month after the war had begun. A subsidiary argument put by Kautsky, but developed in greater detail by the English Liberal economist J.A. Hobson, was that imperialism was concerned with little more than relations between advanced capitalist countries and agrarian colonies. The 'scramble for Africa' at the end of the nineteenth century was cited as a prime example of this.

Bukharin's book demolished these arguments in a novel fashion. Although Marx originated the concept of world economy, Bukharin was the first to give it such emphasis.[6] The first chapter set out his general approach: 'the problem of studying imperialism, its economic characteristics and its future, reduces itself to the problem of analysing the tendencies in the development of world economy.'[7]

This argument about world economy had major political consequences. It showed the reformist belief that winning control of national governments could decisively influence events was being rendered ever more utopian by economic development. The power of capitalism organised on an international scale could subvert national governments which attempted major change. If national reformism made less sense, international socialism became even more relevant. World economy meant that the global cooperation of workers was not an abstract concept but now a real possibility. Its material preconditions had been nurtured in the womb of capitalism itself. Such socialism could not be achieved by tinkering with the system on a national basis, but only by overthrowing it on an international scale, a task made still more urgent by the monstrous carnage of seemingly perpetual war.

Bukharin's discussion of the multinational character of modern capitalism did not lead him to accept Kautsky's idea of a peaceful and stable ultra-imperialism. Bukharin stressed that world economy was 'characterised by its highly anarchic structure'.[8] The capitalist contradictions that existed within national economies did not disappear, they were reproduced on a bigger scale: 'This anarchic structure of world capitalism is expressed in two facts: world industrial crises on the one hand, wars on the other.'[9]

Shifting his discussion from world economy to its component parts, Bukharin discerned what he called the 'nationalisation of capital'. This was brought about through concentration and centralisation of capital. Concentration occurred when an enterprise expanded or took control of more and more stages of production, from acquisition of raw materials to selling the finished commodity. Through centralisation, small capitalists were swallowed up by larger ones, leading to the formation of giant trusts, cartels and monopolies. 'There is going on a continuous process of binding together the various branches of production, a process of transforming them into one single organisation.'[10]

These new forms were rooted in and operated through the national framework. Thus there was 'a very strong tendency towards transforming the entire national economy into *one gigantic combined enterprise under the tutelage of the financial kings and the capitalist state*'.[11] This discovery was important. It showed that capitalism was not identified exclusively with private ownership of the means of production. Capitalism could take many forms without losing its essential exploitative character. This aspect of Bukharin's work cannot be overemphasised. As one writer puts it: 'Bukharin is the only one of the three major Marxist students of imperialism (Luxemburg, Bukharin, Lenin) of the time who points out the importance of the state in the process of economic organization.'[12]

For Bukharin therefore, 'national economy' now took the form of 'state capitalist trusts'.[13] The aims of capitalist economy and capitalist state were not only linked, as in the past, but *organisationally intertwined*. Following his insight to its logical conclusion, Bukharin foresaw a future where 'state and private monopoly enterprises merge into one entity';[14] in other words, full-blown *state capitalism*. Bukharin was the first to give a rigorous definition of this term[15] and he laid so much stress on it that he confidently predicted: 'the future belongs to economic forms that are close to state capitalism.'[16]

If the world was tending towards state capitalism then relations between national blocs of capital would also change. Capital's close links with the state added a new twist to methods of competition. They now included armed struggle. Far from national capitals heading towards peaceful ultra-imperialism, 'Those groups find their final argument in the force and power of the state organisation, first of all in its army and navy.'[17] Bukharin analysed imperialism by demonstrating each link in the chain connecting capitalist development to the appearance of total war on a world scale.

Turning directly to Kautsky's ultra-imperialism, Bukharin recognised 'the great stimulus to the formation of an international state capitalist trust given by the internationalisation of capitalist interests'. But he added, 'significant as this process may be in itself, it is, however, counteracted by *a still stronger tendency* of capital towards nationalisation, and towards remaining secluded within state boundaries.'[18] Competition between units of capital would ensure that there was no possibility of long-term peaceful development on either the economic or the military front.

Bukharin's remarkable ability to abstract from immediate events to discern general lines of development makes his work on imperialism as relevant today as it has ever been, while other accounts are now of chiefly historical interest. Nevertheless, there were flaws which marred his attempts to translate the insights of his book into immediate political practice.

The first problem was the work's one-sidedness. Bukharin carried his arguments too far. For example, although his realisation that capitalism worked in a framework of world economy was inspired, he took this contention to the point of insisting that it had a uniform impact everywhere. According to *Imperialism and World Economy*, the globe was neatly divided into advanced industrial countries (all state capitalist trusts) and backward countries (all totally agrarian): 'entire countries appear today as "towns", namely, the industrial countries, whereas entire agrarian territories appear to be "country".[19]

This ignored the unevenness of development within countries. Even the most industrialised possessed an agrarian sector of some size. Equally, while in most countries the majority were peasants, places such as Russia or China did possess a small but potentially significant industrial sector. This mistaken division of the world into 'town' and 'country' would play an important role when Bukharin came to lead the Comintern in the late 1920s. Having analysed the most advanced forms of capitalist development, Bukharin presumed that this set the parameters for all social and political issues. Social conflict was reduced to the 'relations between two classes – the class of the world proletariat on the one hand and the world bourgeoisie on the other'.[20] Given Bukharin's later attack on Trotsky for 'ignoring the peasantry', this was ironic.

A tendency to over simplification was also evident in Bukharin's analysis of domestic developments. Brilliant as his discovery of state capitalist trusts was, it was a gross exaggeration to claim, even in the exceptional situation of wartime, that 'every one of the capitalistically advanced "national economies" has turned into some kind of "national" trust.'[21]

Cohen rightly points out Bukharin's problem here:

> His defenders would later argue that his writings on modern capitalism had to be understood as abstract analysis (similar to that presented by Marx in the first volume of *Capital*), as a 'chemically pure' model designed not to correspond to every aspect of reality, but to reveal transitional tendencies in contemporary bourgeois society. It was a reasonable qualification, one that Bukharin now and then added. For the most part, however, he gave every indication of meaning his theory, at least in broad outline, to be read literally.[22]

Bukharin believed that state capitalist trusts would only be affected by crises from outside. This led him to ignore the inner contradictions that still existed in capitalist countries. In an article written soon after the completion of *Imperialism and World Economy* he put it plainly: 'The process of organisation gradually removes the anarchy of separate components of the national-economic mechanism.'[23] Here capitalism was treated as a system of organisation rather than a system of antagonistic social relations. Through a new method of organisation, all internal contradictions could be projected to the outside.

It is interesting to contrast Lenin's pamphlet *Imperialism the Highest Stage of Capitalism* with Bukharin's work. Although influenced by

Bukharin, Lenin's work was far less theoretically ambitious. Its focus was more restricted to the period in which it was written, in contrast to the broad canvas of capitalist development given by Bukharin. For this reason Lenin's pamphlet has far less immediate relevance for socialists today. If it lacked the daring innovations of *Imperialism and World Economy*, such as the concept of state capitalism, its method was often more dialectical.[24]

Bukharin began with the latest stage of capitalism, portraying it as a uniform structure, and then proceeded to deduce the nature of all its component national parts from this:

> a system of *collective capitalism* is created ... The separate capitalist disappears: he becomes a *Verbandskapitalist* [federated capitalist], a member of an organisation: he no longer *competes* but instead *cooperates* with his 'compatriots'; for the center of gravity in the competitive struggle is carried over into the world market, whereas within the country competition dies out.[25]

By contrast, Lenin described an uneven and contradictory process of development. This meant that while giant corporations might project their competitive struggles on to an international level, previous forms of capitalism and their contradictions did not suddenly vanish at home:

> On the contrary, when monopoly appears in *certain* branches of industry, it increases and intensifies the anarchy in capitalist production *as a whole* ... At the same time the monopolies, which have grown out of free competition, do not eliminate the latter but exist above it and alongside it, and thereby give rise to a number of very acute antagonisms, friction and conflicts.[26]

In spite of its blemishes, *Imperialism and World Economy* was a brilliant piece of work which opened the way to Bukharin's insights regarding the state.

The Imperialist State

The savagery of the First World War pointed to the true character of capitalist states more clearly than ever before. Many had believed the state existed, in the words of Hammurabi's Babylonian code, 'to safeguard the law of the land and to destroy what is wicked and evil so that the strong may not harm the weak'.[27] Far from preventing violence and protecting the weak, the state showed itself to be the supreme perpetrator of violence. More and more workers came to see that the state was not neutral. It sent millions to their deaths and abolished civil liberties for the rest. All this was done in the name of empire and for the sake of profits.

Wartime conditions undermined the mystique surrounding the state and helped Bukharin to a new breakthrough. In *Imperialism and World Economy* he had linked capitalism with aggressive state policies and the tendency of giant capitalist enterprises to encroach upon the state. In his article 'Towards a Theory of the Imperialist State', he traced the same process from the opposite side, observing the state encroaching on capitalist production. In doing so, he rediscovered the Marxist theory of the state.

In a letter to Lenin, who at first strongly disagreed with his arguments, he did not claim any originality but summed up his viewpoint in these terms:

> The whole first section can perhaps be reduced in my opinion to these absolutely indisputable and orthodox Marxist positions: 1) Every state is the organisation of the ruling class; 2) socialism is not state organisation; 3) the dictatorship of the proletariat is a workers' state, where the ruling class is the proletariat. It is a necessary stage towards socialism.[28]

This may have been orthodox Marxism, but at that time it was political dynamite.

Lenin and Bukharin argued over the inclusion of the article in *Sotsial Demokrat*, the Bolshevik theoretical journal. Lenin argued that only the second section (on the imperialist state rather than the state in general) was acceptable and should be published.[29] Lenin later recognised the value of Bukharin's work as is clear from his study of it while preparing his pamphlet on *State and Revolution* in 1917. In a footnote to the 1925 Russian edition of his article, Bukharin quotes his first meeting with Krupskaia, Lenin's wife, on his return to Russia: 'V.I. asked me to tell you that he no longer has any disagreements with you on the question of the state.' Cohen makes a great deal of this, stating that in *State and Revolution* the 'arguments and conclusions were Bukharin's'.[30] Cohen is only correct insofar as this comment applies to the opening section of Bukharin's article. On its later discussion of state capitalism Lenin and Bukharin never agreed.

By returning to Marx's theory of the state, Bukharin had refuted the most cherished belief of the Second International. Even Kautsky's most radical statement, *The Road to Power* of 1909, had insisted that 'the special task' of the proletariat is to 'attain a dominant position in the state'.[31]

Capturing the existing capitalist state was the means; nationalisation the goal. Socialism itself was conceived of as the state replacing private action in what might be called the complete 'statisation' of social life.

Against this, Bukharin affirmed that the basic function of all previous states was *'to preserve and expand the exploitation of the oppressed classes'*.[32] They should not be taken over but smashed. This viewpoint, pure heresy from a Kautskyite perspective, gave socialism a different meaning. The long-term aim was not nationalisation of private property (though this would be one phase of the proletarian dictatorship) but the disappearance of the state after a period of rule by a workers' state: 'Thus, the society of the future is a society *without* a state organization.'[33] The contrast between Bukharin's ideas and those of the Second International was graphic confirmation of Luxemburg's contention that 'people who pronounce themselves in favour of the methods of legislative reform *in place of and in contradistinction to* ... socialist revolution, do not really choose a more tranquil and slower road to the *same* goal, but a *different* goal'.[34]

Bukharin's article predicted that the tendency outlined in *Imperialism and World Economy* would continue to its end, 'the logical limit of which is state capitalism'.[35] It followed that 'Such a structure of the ruling classes is accompanied by a corresponding change in the "state machine": the state power becomes the supreme organization of the finance-capitalist bourgeoisie, who constitute a homogeneous group.'[36] Although the notion of a homogeneous capitalist class was one-sided and Bukharin was premature in suggesting that his highly abstract prediction might materialise 'in the near future',[37] his argument was superb.

He was concerned to prevent his argument being misused. It might be taken to mean that with one state owning and controlling *all* the means of production then capitalism would cease to exist. With competition at an end the worker 'would become a slave' living on state rations rather than wages.[38] Everything that Marx wrote about in his *Capital* would have disappeared. Bukharin feared that this theoretical hypothesis could be used to suggest that existing capitalism was less of an enemy than this potential new menace.[39] Alas, it is precisely this misrepresentation of Bukharin's views that has been made by Cohen, his American biographer, who thereby turns him into some sort of modern social democratic Cold War warrior. He says that 'Bukharin foresaw, however idiomatically, the advent of what came to be called the totalitarian state ... a third kind of modern society, neither capitalist nor socialist.'[40] Cohen recognises that 'Bukharin never acknowledged that such an outcome was a real possibility but it lingered in his mind all his life.' He concludes that 'it was a liberalizing element in his Bolshevism.'[41]

Cohen is wrong. Bukharin not only explicitly rejected the real possibility of a 'post-capitalist society [that] might bring another crueler system of exploitation',[42] *he showed why it was impossible.* Even if a great concentration of capitalist forces were to come about, capitalism would not have disappeared unless a single world state had been created:

> we would ... introduce some new designation for the type of relations now being formed only in one event - that is, if *a single world economy* were in existence ... [But] a single world economy represents an impossible hope, and insofar as the anarchy of the *world* market remains, the categories of value and wages are also preserved - with the single difference that now the position of the separate enterprises has been taken by the state enterprise ... The pressure of the world market remains.[43]

With a few minor qualifications, this constitutes an accurate description of the Stalinist system and explains its demise in the face of the competitive pressures of world capitalism. An alternative to either capitalism or socialism could be conceived only in the abstract. It could not appear in practice. Bukharin insisted it was *capitalism* that was preparing what he called a terrifying 'New Leviathan',[44] and gradually 'placing the whole of economic life under the iron heel of **the militaristic state**'.[45]

Bukharin's theory of the state had great strengths. But there were shortcomings which were already visible in *Imperialism and World Economy*. He wrote that the state 'was only an expression of economic connections',[46] or 'an *exact* expression of the interests of finance capital'.[47]

The problem was that this ignored the fundamental distinction Marx made between the economic base and superstructure, which he identified as 'the guiding principle' of his studies: 'The totality of [the] relations of production constitutes the economic structure of society, the real foundation, on which arises a legal and political superstructure.'[48] In a situation of social change:

> it is always necessary to distinguish between the material transformation of the economic conditions of production, which can be determined with the precision of natural science, and the legal, political religious, artistic or philosophic - in short, ideological forms in which men become conscious of this conflict and fight it out.[49]

It was a major achievement of Bukharin that he re-established the link between capitalism and the state, but this should not have blurred the distinction between economics and politics. Alas, it did; the result was that he saw ideological and political change as a direct and automatic reflection of economic change. This had consequences for his political practice.

Bukharin developed a particular view of socialist revolution. He believed that since capitalism was overcoming internal difficulties by developing on the international plane, a revolutionary crisis could only occur when external contradictions resulted in war. Not only did this ignore other forms of crisis which could lead to revolution, it led Bukharin into the ultra-left trap of posing political tasks in either/or terms. Either the working class smashed imperialism outright or the growth of state capitalism would immediately cause its complete annihilation as an independent force:

> *either the workers' organizations, like all the organizations of the bourgeoisie, grow into the general state organization and become a simple appendage of the state apparatus, or, alternatively, they outgrow the confines of the state and explode it from within.*[50]

The real world was more complex than this view suggested. The First World War did indeed explode one state from within – that of tsarism. But in the rest of the advanced capitalist world there was a multitude of different outcomes, ranging in intensity from dual power in Germany and Austria, to factory occupations in Italy, to mass strikes in Britain, and so on. Under such circumstances the slogan 'either explode the state or all is lost' was insufficient. The role of a Marxist is not to set tasks that have been abstractly drawn up at a desk, but to use the tools of analysis to lead the concrete struggles forward.

In the same way that Bukharin collapsed the superstructure into the economic base, he simplified the connection between workers' consciousness and reality. He wrote that in the fully developed imperialist state, 'the process of exploitation is not hidden by any secondary forms: the mask of a supraclass institution that looks after everyone alike is torn away from the state.'[51] If this were true, change in consciousness would not come about through the interaction of workers' self-activity and the surrounding world. Instead a change in the external situation of the class would mechanically lead to its ideas being altered:

> So long as imperialism allowed only its 'progressive side' to be seen (the 'peaceful' expansion of prewar times), imperialist attitudes necessarily grew up within the proletariat. But now imperialism has displayed its aggressive side; and the more it does so, the greater is the burden it imposes on the international proletariat. Whereas the

imperialist bourgeoisie sees vital necessity in continuation of the imperialist policy, the proletariat sees an equal necessity in the destruction of imperialism, and of capitalist production along with it.[52]

This quotation raises the issue of Bukharin's attitude to the working class, and indeed to all classes. Just as the capitalist class was seen as integrated into a single state capitalist trust, so other classes tended to be described as though each formed a single undifferentiated bloc. The entire working class was presented as either the complete victim or the triumphant destroyer of capitalism. There were no gradations in between. For example, the influential *ABC of Communism,*, written in 1919 with Evgeny Preobrazhensky, talked of how workers were 'trained and tamed, just as wild beasts in a menagerie ... so that they may resemble domestic animals who will work like horses, and eat humble pie'.[53] In *Imperialism and World Economy* the workers were described as 'bondsmen ... the white slaves of the predatory imperialist state'.[54] A few pages later Bukharin portrayed the working class as free from the chains of bourgeois ideology:

The war severs the last chain that binds the workers to the masters, their slavish submission to the imperialist state. The last limitation of the proletariat's philosophy is being overcome: its clinging to the narrowness of the national state, its patriotism ... The masses of the people, aroused to political life and originally tame and docile, raise their voices ever higher.[55]

Thus in 1918, during the debate on Soviet Russia's ability to fight Germany, Bukharin thought the working class was endowed with almost superhuman qualities which would overcome any obstacle.

For Bukharin, proletarian revolution was a consequence, an almost automatic reflex that followed upon material change. However, this ignored many difficult problems such as the uneven level of class consciousness among workers and the influence of capitalist ideology.

One test of theory is how far it rises above the immediate circumstances to become of lasting value. Here Bukharin's achievement was immense. Another equally important test is how effective theory is in assisting immediate revolutionary practice. Here he was far less successful. One example of where a fundamentally correct general analysis completely failed to translate into a useful practice was the debate on national self-determination in Berne.

The National Question

As a member of the 'Baugy Group' of self-declared '*extreme Lefts*'[56] Bukharin presented a set of theses to the Berne Bolshevik Conference of February 1915 which argued: 'The slogan of "self-determination of nations" is first of all *utopian* (it cannot be realized *within the limits* of capitalism) and *harmful* as a slogan which *disseminates illusions*.'

Bukharin's starting point was the *general* existence of world economy and imperialism, which therefore determined a common position for *all* – a position that could only be one of absolute rejection of the nation:

> The imperialist epoch is an epoch of the absorption of small states by the large state units ... It is therefore impossible to struggle against the enslavement of nations otherwise than by struggling against imperialism, *ergo* – by struggling against imperialism, *ergo* – by struggling against finance capital, *ergo* against capitalism in general. Any deviation from that road, any advancement of 'partial' tasks, of the 'liberation of nations' *within* the realm of capitalist civilization, means [a] diverting of proletarian forces from the actual solution of the problem.[57]

Lenin, attending the same congress, strongly disagreed with Bukharin's denial of the right of self-determination. He believed that in proposing this position Bukharin was committing a far greater error than Luxemburg, who took a similar line. She was a revolutionary from Poland, an oppressed nation. Her rejection of the slogan of self-determination on principle was a mistake, because it ignored the fact that socialists in oppressor countries must fight to wean workers from the imperialist ideology of their rulers by insisting on the rights of oppressed countries to break away. For Bukharin to reject self-determination was worse, because he was a revolutionary from Russia, an oppressor country. He was therefore playing into the hands of the Great Russian chauvinism, a major imperialist force. Although Lenin appeared less formally internationalist than Bukharin or Luxemburg, he was more realistic. As Cliff puts it: 'the positions of oppressed and oppressor nations being different, their attitude to the same question must be different.'[58] It might appear wrong in formal logic for internationalists to articulate their tactics differently just because they lived in different countries. But only in this way was a correct *general* internationalism related to *concrete* conditions.

Bukharin did not differentiate between oppressor and oppressed; he explicitly claimed that self-determination would be politically harmful even to the 'working masses of a Great Power'.[59] Lenin's answer to this was: 'In the internationalist education of the workers of the oppressor countries, emphasis must necessarily be laid on their advocating freedom for the oppressed countries to secede and their fight for it. Without this there can be *no* internationalism'.[60]

Lenin called Bukharin's position 'imperialist economism' because it drew political conclusions regarding revolution and national self-determination directly from economics:

> To imagine that social revolution is *conceivable* without revolts by small nations in the colonies and in Europe, without revolutionary outbursts of the politically non-conscious proletariat and semi-proletarian masses against ... national oppression etc. - to imagine all this is to *repudiate social revolution*. So one army lines up in one place and says, 'We are for socialism,' and another, somewhere else, says, 'We are for imperialism,' and that will be a social revolution!'[61]

Bukharin's flawed approach to strategy is also apparent in his general 'Theses on the Tasks and Tactics of the Proletariat' of 1915. His analysis of the capitalist state was invaluable and his suggestion that '*Social democracy must forcefully underline its hostility, in principle, to state power*' was the best answer to the reformism of Kautsky. But how was this to inform practical activity? To Bukharin it meant virtually repudiating struggle for immediate partial demands: 'the center of gravity of the proletarian struggle must shift from the sphere of struggle in favor of general democratic demands to the sphere of socialist demands of the proletariat - socialist in the narrow sense of the word'.[62]

Unfortunately no copy of Bukharin's speech at the Berne Conference survives, but Lenin's notes on it indicate the tenor:

> The petty bourgeoisie is not as it was in 1905. It is allied to big capital. No need to call on it ...
> What is new in the situation?
> *Before* reforms
> *Now* the conquest of power by the proletariat
> One of the mistakes of the Central Organ is to call upon the democratic bourgeoisie in a number of countries where partial gains are impossible.[63]

Like Bukharin, Lenin accepted that in the current situation major reforms were not on offer from the big bourgeoisie. But in no way was this *objective* situation alone a sufficient basis for deciding tactics. How did it affect the *subjective* consciousness of the masses? He argued:

Capitalism in general, imperialism in particular, turns democracy into an illusion – though at the same time capitalism engenders democratic aspirations among the masses, creates democratic institutions, aggravates the antagonism between imperialism's denial of democracy and the mass striving for democracy. Capitalism and imperialism can be overthrown only by economic revolution. They cannot be overthrown by democratic transformations, even the most 'ideal'. But a proletariat not schooled in the struggle for democracy is incapable of performing an economic revolution.[64]

Bukharin's ultimatum – 'either socialism or imperialism!' – ruled out such struggles.

During the First World War Bukharin produced his finest work. His intellectual daring and readiness to think ideas through to their utmost limit meant that he made an outstanding contribution to Marxist theory in the areas of imperialism, state capitalism and the state. His theoretical contribution here went beyond that of any of his contemporaries. A sign of this is that the relevance of his work has in no way diminished with the passage of time. But for a rounded approach, the necessarily high level of abstraction required to solve complex theoretical problems had to be combined with an ability to relate concretely to circumstances. At the level of theory Bukharin performed magnificently, but he could not match this with skill in practical politics.

Bukharin's one-sidedness and ultra-leftism were mitigated by two things. First, there was the extreme situation of war. This itself was a very 'one-sided' expression of capitalist development that rendered many daring predictions redundant as soon as they were uttered. Second, and more importantly, Bukharin was not acting as an individual and should not be judged as such. He was a valued member of an organisation of revolutionaries, a part of the collective leadership. As such, his contribution was used effectively to rebuild Marxism out of the ruins of the Second International and to help the Russian revolution to victory.

2 Left Communism

First Evaluation of the Russian Revolution

In February 1917 (according to the old Julian calendar employed in Russia before the revolution) Russia was engulfed in a revolution which toppled the Romanov dynasty and threw society into a state of ferment. Although a bourgeois Provisional Government was established, it was challenged from the first by councils of workers' and soldiers' delegates – the soviets. When the tsar fell, Bukharin was in New York editing a revolutionary newspaper – *Novy Mir* – whose contributors included Trotsky. Overjoyed at the news of the revolution, he immediately embarked on the long and hazardous journey back to Russia via Japan and Siberia, suffering arrest by Mensheviks on the way.

After his arrival in April, Bukharin was based in Moscow and was quickly elected one of the local Bolshevik leaders. A demonstration on 26 May by local Bolsheviks against the death sentence passed by the Austrian government on the socialist leader, Friedrich Adler, was evidence of his distinctive internationalist influence. One writer says: 'During the Russian revolution hardly any other city witnessed a similar movement, one whose focus was so distant from the immediate concerns of the Russian worker.'[1]

From the first, Bukharin threw his weight behind the struggle for workers' power. Unlike many Bolshevik leaders such as Stalin and Kamenev, he had no hesitation in supporting Lenin's *April Theses*, which called for 'All Power to the Soviets'. Bukharin's worth was recognised by his promotion to the Central Committee. In October 1917, when certain Moscow leaders, like their Petrograd counterparts, Zinoviev and Kamenev, drew back from insurrection, Bukharin had no such doubts.[2]

On 25 October the Bolshevik revolution triumphed and the immensely difficult job of building a new society began. A sign of Bukharin's importance in the new government was his mission to present the Bolshevik case to the Constituent Assembly. Although the call for the Assembly to be convened had been a Bolshevik demand, the parlimentary-style elections, which occurred in November, could not reflect the swiftly changing mood of the population. Furthermore, through their soviet organisations elected at workplaces, workers had gone beyond the bounds of capitalist institutions. The Constituent Assembly, the last symbol of bourgeois parliamentarism, would be dispersed by the new Soviet government. Those market socialists who would make of Bukharin a prophet of 'pluralism' and bourgeois democracy forget that, even in later years, as a revolutionary he was never duped by the phoney political 'equality' of capitalism. To the last he believed that in the parliamentary system:

> all the people apparently participate in elections, but under this pretence is hidden the domination of capitalism ... under the cloak of universal suffrage, the power is found to be entirely in the hands of the great forces of capitalism.
>
> Under the parliamentary system each citizen casts his vote into the ballot box once in four or five years, and the field is then clear for the members of Parliament, Cabinet Ministers and Presidents, to manage everything without any reference to the toiling masses. Gulled and exploited by its officials, the toilers have no part whatever in the administration of the capitalist state ...
>
> In the Soviet Republic, born of the dictatorship of the workers, the administration rests on an altogether new basis ... not only because the country is administered by the workers and peasants, but above all because the Government of the Soviets is in constant relations with the organised masses, and in this way, at all times, the greater part of the population joins in the administration of the State.[3]

Bukharin's speech to the Constituent Assembly showed how inspired he was by the prospects opening up after the Russian revolution:

> Comrades, we must now remember our responsibility. We must not forget that at present human history is living through a moment of breakthrough such as has never existed in the history of human society – not in the time of the Thirty Years' War, nor in the days of the Great French Revolution, nor in the times of the bourgeoisie's liberation wars, has there been such a move forward as at present. Comrades, we are now laying down the foundations of human life for a millenium.[4]

This responsibility was to tax the brain, nerve, muscle and sinew of every Bolshevik to the utmost limit. It faced Bukharin with the imperative need to relate his theories to an exceptionally difficult and complicated specific case, a workers' revolution that had occurred in one of the most economically backward of the Great Powers. Bukharin was entering a field of debate that had been well trodden by Russian socialists over the decades. His most influential statements on this subject would be made in the mid-1920s, when he polemicised against Trotsky's theory of permanent revolution. Here it is only necessary to sketch his early views.

Bukharin shared with other Bolsheviks the absolute conviction that without international revolution the Soviet experiment was doomed. In works of this period, he made innumerable statements to the effect that 'the final victory of the Russian revolution is unthinkable without the victory of the international revolution'; and 'a lasting victory of the Russian proletariat is impossible without proletarian revolution in Europe.'[5] If he stood out at all it was because of the almost exclusive emphasis he placed on this international dimension. As Mike Haynes states: 'From 1917 to the early 1920s he distinguished himself by the strength of his desire to throw the full weight of the revolution behind international revolution.'[6] This emphasis stemmed from Bukharin's evaluation of the motive forces of the Russian revolution.

Bolsheviks also agreed about the primary role of the workers. Their successive strikes, demonstrations and mass activity had weakened the urban foundations of the old regime and brought it crashing down. Where Bolsheviks disagreed was over the significance of the peasantry, without whom the October revolution could not have succeeded. The peasant revolt began in February. By the summer of 1917, Provisional Government offices were flooded with reports to the effect that: *'Uezd* and *guberniia* [units of local government] commissars are powerless to end the anarchy.' But the peasants themselves did not think anarchy was the right word. As one of their number from Tambov said: 'You think that this is done by hooligans and vagrants and drunk ragamuffins, but you are a little mistaken. This is not vagrants and ragamuffins, but people drunk from hunger.'[7] What was the social significance of this vast peasantry, despised as the 'dark people' by the upper classes, yet comprising a majority of Russians and constituting a key factor in the revolution?

Bukharin's views were outlined in an article called 'The Russian Revolution and its Destiny', written shortly after his return. In it he gave a potted history of Russian development in the twentieth century. Until 1905, he said, Russia was dominated by feudal relations. But after 1905 capitalism grew quickly. Agriculture was transformed through the actions of 'a peasant bourgeoisie and capitalist landowning entrepreneurs'[8] and there was a rapid growth of large capitalist firms resulting in modern forms of finance capital. During the war this became state capitalism. Clearly Bukharin was squeezing Russia into the framework of his theory of modern imperialism. His certainty on this score was underlined by the debate on the the party programme at the Seventh Bolshevik Congress of March 1918, where he sought to delete the whole of the old theoretical section (which dealt with capitalism as a broad and varied system of production). He wanted only capitalism's imperialist phase to be mentioned. This was because, as his pamphlet 'The Programme of the Communists' (Bolsheviks) stated: 'In every capitalist country small capital has practically vanished of late. It has been eaten up by the big sharks of capitalism.'[9]

In the congress Bukharin was defeated by Lenin, who argued that reports of the death of the petty bourgeoisie and small capitalists were greatly exaggerated. Bukharin's version of Russian development, he said, left too little room for the petty bourgeoisie or for the peasantry.

However, Bukharin stuck to his guns. The existence of these middle layers could not be denied, but he thought they could be eliminated from the equation. Earlier he had written:

> In the struggle between the bourgeoisie (which now wants to crush the revolution and carry the war to a 'victorious conclusion') and the workers (who want to put an end to the war and restore order to the enfeebled economy of Russia), the situation is complicated by those petty bourgeoisie and sections of the peasantry who drag along behind finance capital ... However the experience of life itself is more and more opening the eyes of the semi-proletarian elements in towns and countryside, and they begin to understand that outside of the struggle between the people and the bourgeoisie there is no salvation.[10]

He pictured peasants as almost neatly divided into semi-capitalist or semi-proletarian socialist camps. This was the exact opposite of his position in the mid-1920s, when the peasantry would be treated as a largely undifferentiated mass.

By the late summer of 1917 it was becoming clear that the peasantry was not behaving as the tail of either the bourgeoisie or the working class. Its members were subdividing the land, thus reducing the number of both rich and very poor peasants. This made Bukharin's initial view untenable. So at the August 1917 congress of the Bolsheviks, he outlined a different perspective:

> I conceive of a new advance in the revolution passing through two
> distinct stages: the first stage – with the participation of the peasantry
> who are trying to get the land; the second stage – after the peasantry
> fall away satiated, the phase of proletarian revolution when the
> Russian proletariat is supported only by proletarian elements and the
> proletariat of Western Europe.[11]

This vision of more or less separate stages in the development of revolution would be resurrected in the mid-1920s when Stalin and Bukharin were in alliance against Trotsky. Ironically, it was Stalin who, at the 1917 congress, reproached Bukharin for his rigidity:

> According to him, during the first stage we go towards peasant
> revolution. But how could it not meet up and overlap with the
> workers' revolution? It cannot be that the working class which forms
> the vanguard of the revolution does not fight alongside it for its own
> demands.[12]

The Peace Treaty of Brest-Litovsk

The question of the Treaty of Brest-Litovsk with Germany, which arose in February 1918, was to divide Bukharin and his left communist supporters from the rest of the Bolshevik Party. The issue of war or peace was the first major test of practical politics after the October insurrection. All agreed revolution must spread from Russia to Western Europe, if socialism was to survive. At the same time, the new government was in an extremely precarious position. It was threatened by German invasion and depended for defence on a largely peasant army in the process of disintegration. How was it possible to aid international revolution against imperialism and yet escape the wrath of German imperialism at the same time?

Initially there were two main positions, represented by Lenin on the one hand with Trotsky and Bukharin on the other. Lenin was for a rapid conclusion of peace:

> There is no doubt that it is a shameful peace which we are forced to
> conclude now, but if we embark on a war our government will be
> swept away and another government will make peace. Now we not
> only have the support of the proletariat but of the poor peasants, too,
> and that will leave us if we continue the war.[13]

Trotsky did not want war with German imperialism, but hoped also to avoid concluding a peace with it. This meant continuing the armistice as long as possible. Bukharin supported this tactic, although it would later become clear that his motivation and understanding of the situation differed from Trotsky's.

At first Trotsky's line of 'neither war nor peace' prevailed in the Central Committee, with Bukharin's support. Then, in February, the armistice came to an end when the Germans resumed their offensive. At the negotiations in Brest-Litovsk they insisted on a treaty which would give them 780,000 square kilometres of Russian land, including 56 million people, one third of the rail network, 73 per cent of iron ore and 89 per cent of coal output.[14] In the crucial Central Committee vote of 18 February Trotsky, though unhappy with Lenin's position, backed him and accepted the German terms, humiliating though they were. Bukharin, however, rejected this decision as capitulation to imperialism.

To clarify his attitude it is important to clear away a common misconception. Many histories of the Brest-Litovsk crisis assert that Bukharin argued in favour of revolutionary war while the majority was against revolutionary war. This is an incorrect description of both the left communist and the majority positions.

First, Bolsheviks as a whole accepted revolutionary war *in principle*. Lenin, for example, told the First Soviet Congress in June 1917: 'under certain circumstances we shall be unable to do without a revolutionary war. No revolutionary class can rule out revolutionary war, or it will doom itself to ridiculous pacifism. We are not Tolstoyans.'[15] In the same month Lenin wrote: 'Under no circumstances can ... socialists (and hence the Bolsheviks) agree to a separate peace treaty between the capitalists. The basis for the foreign policy of the politically-conscious proletariat is no separate peace treaty with the German capitalists.'[16] Lenin had not foreseen the critical circumstances of early 1918 and was flexible enough to eat his words. And a year *after* the Brest-Litovsk treaty, the new party programme stated that the revolutionary struggle against imperialism 'inevitably leads to the merging of the civil war within individual countries with the defensive wars of revolutionary countries.'[17]

Second, no-one voted with the motion 'for a revolutionary war' that was discussed by the Bolshevik Central Committee on 17 February. Bukharin led a grouping which said it 'refuses to vote on the question put in this way'.[18] In other words, in the conditions of early 1918 revolutionary war was rejected *in practice* by everyone in the Bolshevik Central Committee.

So why did Bukharin fall out with the majority? The common belief, that revolutionary war could not be excluded as a possibility and would have been impractical in the circumstances of early 1918, masks an important disagreement. Bukharin had backed Trotsky's 'no war, no peace' line on grounds of principle when Trotsky had posed it as a tactic. Trotsky gave this reason for rejecting Lenin's proposal for immediate peace: 'I maintained that before we proceeded to sign the peace it was absolutely imperative that we should prove to the workers of Europe, in a most striking manner, how great, how deadly, was our hatred for the rulers of Germany.'[19] By contrast, Bukharin ruled out a negotiated peace with German imperialism under any circumstances, both because he found compromise unacceptable and because he doubted that Brest-Litovsk would bring the 'breathing space' that Lenin promised.

The practical consequences of Bukharin's approach were highly dangerous. The Germans were on the offensive and if the Red Guards had not sought peace the outcome would have been war and swift annihilation. The Russian army was on its headlong fall from 11.4 million members in 1917 to disbandment in March and Bukharin's idea of partisan warfare was no substitute. The new Red Army would only reach 350,000 members in late 1918.[20] For these reasons, Lenin insisted that Bukharin's policy meant suicide. To make peace was one thing, to declare war with adequate forces was a different matter. But deliberately to fall into a war when the operational commander of your army declares 'We haven't any troops. None at all'[21] – was surely folly.

How had Bukharin reached the position he adopted? He began from the established principle that the prime duty of the Russian revolution was to assist international revolution. Arguing this put him politically head and shoulders above Stalin, who even then saw things in narrow national terms, believing that the point of the revolution was 'the deliverance of Russia from [imperialism's] clutches.'[22] While Lenin and Trotsky took account of both internal and external factors in reaching their conclusions, however, Bukharin stressed only the external issue.

For Bukharin the situation confirmed his vision of revolution which consisted of the 'world bourgeoisie confronting the world proletariat', a description of revolution which Lenin had already contested. In early 1918 Bukharin wrote: 'Europe must be considered as one single territory for the class struggle by the international proletariat, one of whose detachments – the Russian – overpowered a corresponding detachment of the international bourgeoisie.'[23] This presented the situation too simplistically. The class struggle must be seen as an international battle, but this did not mean that the Russian workers' state had to be needlessly sacrificed in a hopeless struggle. The crushing of Soviet power by

German imperialism would not have assisted world revolution but would have demoralised the working class everywhere.

In Bukharin's view, if any workers' contingent refused to fight imperialism there and then, this was breaking ranks along a common battlefront; this was strike-breaking. Lenin's reply to this charge was that the world revolution did not consist of a single simultaneous confrontation. 'Workers who lose a strike and sign terms for the resumption of work which are unfavourable to them and favourable to the capitalists, do not betray socialism'[24] – they live to fight another day when the balance of forces is more favourable.

Left communists like Bukharin disagreed. They wrote that whatever the chaos in Russia or German's military strength at that time, once the world revolution had been declared from the podium in Petrograd, 'the proletariat unavoidably confronts the task of developing civil war on an international scale, a task it must face *any* dangers to fulfil.'[25] This argument did not prevail and on 23 February 1918 Bukharin, three other Central Committee members and three candidate members resigned 'from all responsible Party and Soviet posts'.[26] However, in later years Bukharin came to recognise that Lenin had been right in the dispute over Brest-Litovsk.

The Theoretical Roots of Left Communism

The peace with Germany exposed the enormous gulf separating the socialist aspirations of the Bolsheviks and the means at their disposal. In trying to bridge that gulf they found themselves in a paradoxical position. As Marxists the Bolsheviks believed socialism could not simply be willed into existence by well-intentioned people. Marx and Engels cut their political teeth in polemic with utopian socialists on this very point. Exploitation could only be ended when socialism had a definite material basis and a social force to fight for its abolition. The historical development of the modern working class was the solution.

The very existence of the working class was proof that, compared to previous societies, production was highly developed and used cooperative, social methods. It was thus possible to end hunger and poverty, creating a situation of abundance for all. Moreover, not only was it in the interest of the working class to organise society in this way, the class also had the collective economic and social power to bring this about. The proletariat was the sign and the agent of social progress.

However, the Bolsheviks faced an acute dilemma when the 1917 revolution did not spread to other countries. Instead it remained isolated and within national borders. Workers had taken power in Russia, but every other condition for the establishment of socialism was lacking there. The high level of production needed for socialism required world cooperation and world division of labour, but the absence of revolutions elsewhere meant that these requirements were denied for the time being. Instead of the Russian working class being a detachment of a mighty world proletarian army, it constituted a tiny island of some 3.6 million industrial workers[27] (10 million including their families), in a vast sea of peasants numbering some 115 million – 80 per cent of the population.[28]

Where the material basis and the social goal are so mismatched, tactical decisions must be framed between two poles – between what should be and what is. One approach is to strive for the final goal and dismiss the lack of means – an ultra-left policy. An equally mistaken policy is to capitulate to the weak material basis and forego the higher aims. Bukharin's initial left communism involved the first strategy, as he tried to force the material world to conform to his socialist theory through sheer will-power. But in the mid-1920s he swung over to the opposite pole; theory would be adjusted to justify and rationalise what was, and what should be was almost forgotten. The connection between his two positions was his *economism*.

Originally the term 'economism' had been associated with right-wing socialists at the turn of the century. They held a passive attitude towards politics, reasoning that if economic change led automatically to political change, there was no need for hazardous political struggle. Bukharin certainly could not be accused of political passivity at this time, but his economism was real enough. His interventions at the Central Committee during 1918 included comments such as: 'This is the iron logic of events, things happen as they were bound to.'[29] In 1918 this economism led to voluntarism. The 'iron logic' of the theory of imperialism *dictated what must be done* irrespective of the capacity of human beings to carry it out.

There was an alternative which avoided the traps of passivity and voluntarism and which, despite their differences, both Lenin and Trotsky tried to employ. In both foreign and domestic affairs they sought, through giving concessions, to win a breathing space for the struggling workers' state. By these means they hoped to consolidate its position in order to go forward later. This policy needed great flexibility and to the outsider might seem both unprincipled and contradictory. It could be likened to sailing against the wind by tacking from one side to another.

The direction of the boat cannot be judged by single manoeuvres, but in combination they offer the only chance of moving forward.

Left Communism in Action

Bukharin's ultra-leftism was not an isolated phenomenon. Roused by the Brest-Litovsk treaty, a powerful current of left communism was developing. It had the support of Bolsheviks of the highest calibre, such as Radek and Preobrazhensky. 'Thus', says Cohen, 'for two months, at [the age of] twenty-nine, Bukharin headed the largest and most powerful Bolshevik opposition in the history of Soviet Russia.'[30] Left communism was strong among leading Bolsheviks of the most battle-hardened section of workers, in Petrograd, Moscow, the Urals and Kostroma.[31]

There may have been an element of truth in the title of Lenin's pamphlet of May 1918 on *'Left-wing' Childishness and the Petty-bourgeois Mentality*, but the left communists were an impressive group. They took their inspiration from the surge of self-confidence that swept the proletariat along in 1917. It had been manifested in the movement for workers' control, factory committees and the like.[32] It is important to remember this, given Bukharin's later evolution to right-wing Bolshevism. The two contrasting positions were founded on quite different social forces. In 1918, left communism reflected the confidence, indeed overconfidence, of a section of workers and party intellectuals. Bukharin's later rightward swing came from a loss of confidence within the working class and the degeneration of the revolution.

Left communism drew upon a recent mass revolutionary upheaval and direct experience of workers' potential to change the world. For this reason, even if Bukharin talked about socialism in an idealised form, his left communist writings such as *The ABC of Communism* and *The Programme of the Communists* still rank as classics of Marxism. Here Bukharin exercised consummate skill as a *populariser* of Marxism. This term is not meant pejoratively, as in capitalist society where the masses are despised and talked down to. On the contrary, as a superbly equipped theoretician he explained in a clear, accessible form, without diluting the most complicated ideas, the fundamental arguments of Marxism, a theory that guides action.

Left communist policies were based on the view that not only was Brest-Litovsk harmful internationally, it might be fatal at home. The decision was said to have been:

taken under the pressure of petty-bourgeois elements and petty-bourgeois attitudes [which] will inevitably result in the proletariat losing its guiding role inside Russia, too ... the result will be the ruin of the proletariat from internal demoralisation equivalent to suicide.[33]

This argument was outlined in the most comprehensive statement of left communism – a set of theses adopted on 4 April 1918. They were published under the names of the four editors of *Kommunist*, who included Bukharin.[34]

The 'Theses' stated that preserving Soviet Russia in isolation was pointless since socialism could not be built in isolation.[35] Furthermore, the working class would quickly be 'dissipated in the ranks of the semi-proletarian petty-bourgeois masses', whose influence would touch even 'the Communist Party and the Soviet power leading [to] petty-bourgeois politics of a new type'.[36] The consequence would be 'the political rule of the semi-proletarian petty-bourgeois masses, and prove to be only a transitional stage to the complete rule of finance capital'.[37] The ultimate end would be 'a system of state capitalism'.[38]

The 'Theses' were prophetic, in the light of the 1920s and 1930s which saw the physical and spiritual destruction of the revolutionary working class, the pressure of the peasantry on the Bolshevik Party and Soviet state and the eventual transition to state capitalism. However, as had been the case with *Imperialism and World Economy*, the method of abstract projection was a poor guide to practice. It was one thing to recognise the problem of the isolation of the Russian revolution, but quite another to propose strategies which would stave off the dire consequences that had been foretold. In the latter respect, the 'Theses' failed totally.

Their solution was to ignore Russia's problems and insist on the instant establishment of a full-blooded socialist system. The idea of an ' "organic construction" of socialism'[39] was thrown out. Capitalism must be abolished forthwith: 'the proletariat's attitude towards the bourgeoisie is total negation, its annihilation as a class.' This was to be achieved as follows:

> Nationalisation of the banks must be combined with socialisation of industrial production and complete removal of capitalist and feudal survivals in the relations of production which hinder its planned, broad organisation. Control of enterprises must be handed over to mixed bodies of workers and technical personnel, under the control and leadership of local economic councils. All economic life must be subjected to the organised influence of these councils.[40]

The answer for the isolated workers' state, which was pronounced incapable of achieving socialism without world revolution, was thus the immediate introduction of extreme socialist measures.

The State Capitalism Debate

Left communist policies were framed in sharp opposition to Lenin's, whose policy went by the title of 'state capitalism under the dictatorship of the proletariat'. Lenin's use of the term 'state capitalism' differed from Bukharin's, whose idea on this score he characterised as 'scholastic'.[41] The way Lenin conceived state capitalism must also be distinguished from the way the term is used today by organisations such as the Socialist Workers' Party (SWP). Lenin's understanding of state capitalism was drawn from wartime experience, where private ownership of the means of production had operated under state supervision. The SWP's use of the term was developed primarily to explain the system developed in Stalinist Russia, where there was direct state ownership of the means of production.

Following Marx, Lenin argued that the transition to socialism must contain elements from the past, but that these must be systematically subordinated to elements leading to a future socialist society. Under capitalism the development of the productive forces had taken place within a shell of exploitative social relations. For socialism to be a higher stage than capitalism, it must be able to use the productive forces which had developed under capitalism without recreating its social relations. It was this use of some of capitalism's productive and organisational methods by a workers' state that Lenin called state capitalism. Even before the October revolution he argued:

> For socialism is merely the next step forward from state-capitalist monopoly. Or, in other words socialism is merely state-capitalist monopoly *which is made to serve the interests of the whole people* and has to that extent *ceased* to be capitalist monopoly.[42]

State capitalism under the proletarian dictatorship was not easy to achieve. First of all workers had to learn to run production, which involved a period of economic collaboration with the old capitalist managers. At the same time this had to be combined with a struggle to dominate these same capitalist managers in order to bring forward the arrival of socialism. The need for a combination of collaboration and struggle even extended to portions of the old capitalist state. As Lenin wrote on 1 October 1917:

In addition to the chiefly 'oppressive' apparatus – the standing army, the police and the bureaucracy – the modern state possesses an apparatus which has extremely close connections with the banks and syndicates, an apparatus which performs an enormous amount of accounting and registration work, if it may be expressed this way. This apparatus must not, and should not, be smashed. It must be wrested from the control of the capitalists; the capitalists and the wires they pull must be *cut off, lopped off, chopped away* from this apparatus: it must be *subordinated* to the proletarian Soviets; it must be expanded, made more comprehensive.[43]

Lenin was not losing his commitment to socialism and the transformation of all social relations when he wrote this. He had nothing in common with modern Soviet marketeers, some of whom, such as Nikolai Shmelev, have pretended Lenin thought capitalist forms were neutral and could be taken over en bloc.[44] Lenin's 'state capitalism under the proletarian dictatorship' was a strictly transitional though necessary stage. The economic base inherited from tsarism would inevitably become socialist more slowly than state structures would. He deliberately chose the term 'state capitalism' to describe his policy because it provocatively exposed the contradictions of the situation. It was clear that what existed in Russia was not yet socialism, it was an attempt to prepare the *transition* to socialism.

The proof of this contention was everywhere. While workers had taken political power, in April 1918, before the civil war, one third of Petrograd factories were shut down.[45] The volume of Russian external trade stood at one fifth of its 1913 level,[46] and production as a whole was down by a quarter in value.[47] The number of broken-down railway locomotives, vital for the provisioning of the towns, tripled in the same period to 41 per cent of stock. The calorie intake of Russian workers dropped to 44 per cent of the 1913 level.[48] Indeed, in many ways, since 1917 change had often meant disintegration rather than development on socialist lines.

Bukharin opposed Lenin's policy of applying state capitalism under the dictatorship of the proletariat. He refused to see the complexity of the situation facing the Bolshevik government. There could be no elements of state capitalism in Russia because:

The essence of capitalist relations consists in the fact of capitalist ownership. That is the basis of capitalist relations. State capitalism exists when this class collectively rules over the means of production ... State capitalism as it exists in Western Europe is absolutely different from what we have, and the tasks that stand before the capitalist are not those that confront us; on the contrary, our task is totally different from theirs.[49]

To left communists like himself state capitalism meant a fusion of capitalism's economic base and political superstructure which made it impossible to separate one from the other. *Everything* to do with the old government and the capitalist economy had to be uprooted at one stroke. Unless the economic base became socialist forthwith, the political superstructure would automatically conform to it. It would first become petty bourgeois and then really state capitalist. The necessarily flexible strategy proposed by Lenin was ruled out in such an analysis.

Differences between Lenin and Bukharin were highlighted in the question of nationalisation. The left communist 'Theses' declared that the smashing of 'the old relations of production and the material class power of the bourgeoisie and its allies is almost completed'.[50] The reality was rather different. Early in 1918 there were 500 nationalised enterprises. But more than 70 per cent had only been taken over because the employers had tried either to shut them down or to resist workers' interference, rather than because the workers' state was ready or able to administer them.[51] In contrast to the left communists, Lenin argued that the aim should not be to nationalise all industry immediately, but that workers should exercise control over the old managements, since even at that early stage the state had nationalised 'more [enterprises] *than we have had time to count*.'[52]

These differing attitudes to state capitalism were to have a significance beyond 1918. When Lenin introduced the New Economic Policy (NEP) in 1921, he stated that it embodied his policy of 'state capitalism under the dictatorship of the proletariat'. This prevented him from giving the NEP a false idealistic gloss. Bukharin supported the NEP but denied its state capitalist nature. As a result there was no check on his enthusiasm for the NEP and he embraced it too uncritically. However, in the short term the civil war, which began in mid-1918, meant that the debate over state capitalism was rendered academic. A policy which looked to elements of continued private ownership, the preserving of commercial accounting and so on could not operate when the whole economy had to be geared to war production. Left communists and mainstream Bolsheviks quickly closed ranks and reconciled their differences. In the process Bukharin was forced to break with many of his previous ideas and move from left communism to war communism.

3 War Communism

While the 'breathing space' won by Brest-Litovsk was probably crucial for the revolution's survival, it was woefully short. In the summer of 1918 simmering military conflicts blew up into a full-scale civil war which lasted until the end of 1920. It created a world of extraordinary contrasts and contradictions, with its heroism and its tragedy, its struggle for the highest principles and its loss of hope, and finally its victory and, in that victory, degeneration and defeat.

The policy of the government from late 1918 until the spring of 1921 was known as war communism. Recent Russian writers have argued that it was the model that Stalin copied in 1928–9 to build his system. One describes war communism as 'the method of the "lefts", consecrated from above through administrative command ... They wanted – and considered it possible – to "introduce" communism immediately.'[1] Another writes that the process of forced industrialisation and collectivisation at the end of 1920s shows that: 'Stalin and his supporters had still kept to their previous [war communist] positions. They were dominated by the idea of a speedy socialist offensive on all fronts.'[2] Bukharin originated this interpretation in 1928, long after he had abandoned the ideas of war communism of which he had been a major proponent. It was he who warned the plenum of the Central Committee in July of that year that Stalin's series of 'extraordinary measures' amounted to a 'strengthened tendency to War Communism'.[3] However, this analysis of events was and is mistaken. There were similarities between the Stalinist period and war communism, but their *content* must be distinguished if any sense is to be made of either.

War communism grew out of an extraordinarily desperate struggle to save the 1917 revolution from being crushed by the White armies – an unholy alliance of anti-Bolshevik forces ranging from tsarists to capitalists and even reformist socialists. A study written just after the end of the war declared:

> The triumph of the Red Army in the civil war was not only a military but an economic and administrative technical victory. It was a triumph on the economic front. At the end of 1920 the army's

strength stood at 5½ million men. This army had to be clothed, fed and armed. It had to defend an enormous 16,000 mile front.[4]

Although victory against enormous odds was won, it exacted a terrible price. The working class alone could lead the fight to end human suffering, but the cream of that class was lost in the war. The 600,000 workers under arms comprised 15 per cent of the army, a far higher proportion, especially of its front-line units, than was contributed by any other section of the population. A quarter of the proletarian contingent were metalworkers, who formed the most radical section of the class.[5] Some 180,000 workers were killed.[6] Civil war, coming hard on the heels of three years of crippling imperialist war, was devastating for the economy. Socialism could banish poverty, but to save it the vast proportion of the state's meagre resources — such as 60 per cent of the country's fish, meat and sugar, and 90 per cent of all men's boots that were produced — had to be channelled to the front.[7] In 1921 the industrial workforce had fallen to 1.2 million from 2.6 million in 1913. The percentage of workers who were skilled, a vital economic as well as political resource, was down to 40 per cent of its prewar level.[8] There was a 180-fold decline in imports and 2,000-fold fall in exports.[9] Pig iron output in 1919 was a mere 1.5 per cent of the 1913 level.[10] Behind the lines, Petrograd's death rate quadrupled and its birth rate fell to one third of its prewar figure.[11] Kritsman, author of the classic account on civil war society, states: 'There is no example in the history of mankind of such a decrease in productive power suffered, not by a small community, but by a great hundred-million strong society.'[12]

War altered the balance of social forces. In 1917 the working class had been the leading element, with peasants in support, but by 1921 war had tilted the scales in favour of the peasants because the war effort was unequally shared. As Kritsman puts it:

> The destruction of industry, as we have seen, was much more considerable than the destruction of the agricultural economy. In this respect it was industry above all that bore the immediate burden of the war's cost, for which industry gave almost half the gross production of its most important branches, while the agricultural sector never contributed as much as a tenth.[13]

It was not just the size of the burden but the damage done to industry's complex and integrated productive system that led to the breakdown. By contrast, the small peasant farm was able to continue to function virtually in isolation. One result of this imbalance was a haemorrhage of urban dwellers to agricultural areas in search of food. By 1920, the calorie intake of those workers who stayed was only one third of the level it had been in 1913.[14] This contributed to the decline in Petrograd's population from 2,400,000 in 1916 to only 720,000 in 1920.[15]

While survival might have been easier in the countryside, it provided no haven from the demands of war. The government needed provisions for cities and soldiers, and it had next to nothing to sell to the peasants. There was no choice but to requisition grain without payment, leaving the peasants only enough to live on and to grow next year's crop. The peasants showed that they understood requisitioning was unavoidable by a grudging toleration of this system and a readiness to join the Red Army to fight the landowners. However, toleration had its limits and after a time requisitioning provoked a partial 'peasants' strike', a reduction in the sown area that went beyond the simple destruction caused by war. The peasants grew unwilling to supply what amounted to a third of prewar quantities of grain, while receiving only 12–15 per cent of prewar manufacture in return.[16] The 'strike' added to the existing wartime disruption, resulting in a decrease in sown area of 8 per cent, – greater than the 5 per cent fall due to the 1914–18 conflict. Harvests dropped by 30 per cent during the civil war, compared to a 12 per cent decline in the imperialist war.[17]

In both the towns and the countryside, the ultimate cost of the prolonged fighting was enormous. It has been projected that the population in 1921 was 30 million less than it would have been had peace prevailed.[18] Robert Conquest estimates that 2 million men were killed in the imperialist war and up to 1 million died in the civil war. On top of this came the 1921–2 famine, costing 5 million lives, and epidemics – dysentery, typhus, typhoid and cholera – which between 1918 and 1923 swept away 3 million more: 'The events of 1918–21 had produced a disruption of the social and economic order of a type only comparable to the effect of the Thirty Years War in Germany.'[19]

Costs of Survival – the Roots of the War Communist Illusion

Despite their arguments with the Bolshevik Central Committee majority over Brest-Litovsk, left communists such as Bukharin did not welcome the arrival of civil war. He wrote:

> No sensible person would argue that all armies, be they thrice red, are anything but forms of unproductive expenditure from an economic point of view ... Therefore it is absolutely clear that despite the

complete justification for an offensive communist war, for example, in support of the German Spartakists, the proletariat of Austria-Hungary etc., such war is unthinkable for us at present. We are far too weak economically for that.[20]

Nevertheless, Bukharin expected that the war would drive forward the political development of the working class. In the edition of *Pravda* for New Year's Day 1919, he wrote:

It might be said that the proletariat is in an increasingly bitter and violent struggle with its enemies and is therefore more in danger. But this struggle is not civil war in the literal sense that we are fighting within national boundaries. Now it is a question of a higher form of struggle with the old world, a question of revolutionary class war in which the proletarian state, the working class organised as state power, struggles with the organised state power of the bourgeoisie.[21]

Bukharin's description seemed to fit the situation, at least at first. Workers made an unprecedented effort to defend their revolution. Fully half of all trade unionists joined the Red Army. Mass enthusiasm was shown in other ways. The *subbotnik* movement – unpaid voluntary labour on Saturdays – began on the Moscow railways in May 1919 and spread throughout the republic. Linked to this was the voluntary lengthening of the working day, which lasted up to 10 or 12 hours in some sectors.[22] Right-wing historians scoff at the notion that the mass of the proletariat rallied to defend the revolution, but cannot escape the fact that the war was eventually won in spite of incredible material difficulties. This must have been due to the sort of popular enthusiasm expressed in *subbotniks*.[23]

The factory proletariat did not only work harder, it went on the offensive against individual capitalists. At the end of 1918 the process of nationalisation, which Lenin had already feared was too rapid for the government to cope with, became a spontaneous movement for 100 per cent state control. Nogin of the Council of National Economy complained in December 1918: 'Small businesses have been nationalised in their thousands; we have been made responsible for an enormous number of enterprises that are totally independent of us and not managed rationally.'[24] War communist ideas emerged because this wholesale takeover of the industrial economy put the organs of the working class – the party, the state and, above all, the trade unions – in what *appeared* to be an immensely powerful position. Aleksei Rykov stated in December 1918:

> The trade unions now play the dominant role in the economic life of Russia ... The Congresses of workers and employees of all branches of production or individual groups of enterprises were the main laboratory in which the apparatus for the organisation of the economic life of Russia had been and will be created, out of which we will draw the power for the socialisation and regulation of production.[25]

These early days confirmed Bukharin in his belief in the beneficial effects of direct struggle against capitalism. When the Brest-Litovsk treaty had been signed, he had warned it would demoralise the working class, causing it to 'lose its guiding role inside Russia.'[26] Now war had begun, was not the working class making great strides towards a new society? However, this claim only stands up if the purely formal organisational aspect is considered in isolation. A gap between formal appearances and reality had opened up, as illustrated by the bread ration. In early 1919 many lived on equal state rations, because bread cost 638 times more than it had in 1913.[27] It *seemed* that money was giving way to communistic direct distribution, but in reality there was only the equality of near starvation. Here was one source of war communist thinking.

Trotsky later described another reason for war communism's hypnotic spell:

> 'Illusions,' so far as this word has any application at all here, are rather what we may call those economic hopes which we bound up with the development of the world revolution. The common and inseparable conviction of the whole party at that time was that the victory of the proletariat in the West, beginning with Germany, would reveal vast technical and cultural possibilities, and thereby leave the ground free for a direct passage from military Communism to a Socialistic system of production.[28]

However, while hopes soared and workers conquered the old society at the levels of politics, the state and formal economic organisation, the new structures were being gnawed away from within, as quickly as they were being created. The working class was in a state of disintegration, in spite of its heroism. Many proletarians were at the front, others were absorbed into running the administrative machinery and so ceased to be 'workers at the bench'. Most serious of all, the actual number of proletarians decreased by two thirds between 1917 and the end of civil war while the peasantry expanded.[29] Those workers who remained bore little resemblance to the working class of October 1917. Kritsman writes:

The dying away of large industry and the steep and continuing decline of the proletariat's living standards led to a situation where the worker was frequently absent. He did not spend working time for production but used it for other purposes, above all to maintain his household (journeying in search of essentials). Work on the side increased constantly so that the worker was both in the factory and in the little workshops. But at the factory the worker was not toiling for the enterprise. The great social enterprises turned into numerous independent artisan workshops ... All these events showed the tendency towards the degeneration of the industrial proletarian as a social type. He was no longer involved in social production but declassed, becoming more like the independent petty bourgeois commodity producer.[30]

Under these circumstances it is no surprise that initiatives that had been taken in the early days of war communism became hollow caricatures of their original forms. For Lenin the *subbotniks* were of 'enormous historical significance precisely because they demonstrate the conscious and voluntary initiative of the workers.'[31] But what could be left of this initiative when the extra day's labour had to be made compulsory?[32]

In industry spontaneous nationalisation put factory committees in direct managerial control. Yet even before the civil war, such was the state of disorganisation and the pressing needs of production that central state bodies, like the Supreme Council of National Economy, had to step in. The factory committees were absorbed into the trade unions to impose a higher discipline upon them. Soon management was being undertaken on a 'collegiate' basis, comprising elements elected by the factory workers themselves and officials appointed centrally. In April 1918 Lenin took the argument one stage further by calling for one-man management. By October a draft decree placed nationalised enterprises under the control of state-nominated managers. 'The trade unions could indeed nominate candidates, but only the People's Commissariat for State Control was empowered to approve them or have them removed from their posts.'[33] By the end of 1920 one-man-management covered 86 per cent of large-scale industry.[34] Since the trade unions formed a majority in the Supreme Council of National Economy, it could be said that the workers were still in control. But the surface appearance was deceptive, because even the trade unions were becoming bureaucratised.

Centralisation of control could be represented as a sort of progress. The Bolsheviks were convinced socialist production would not be based on an anarchist or syndicalist break-up of industry. Modern production, as Bukharin had shown through his insistence on 'world economy', was 'methodically organised in large units' requiring centralisation. As he put it in 1922 during a polemic against the anarchists:

> The society of the future will not be conjured out of a void, nor will it be brought by a heavenly angel. It will arise out of the old society, out of the relations created by the gigantic apparatus of finance capital. Any new order is possible and useful only insofar as it leads to the further development of the productive forces of the order which is to disappear. Naturally, further development of the productive forces is only conceivable as the continuation of the tendency of the productive process to centralisation.[35]

However, for socialist centralisation to be able to take advantage of the legacy of capitalist centralisation, the controlling state must be genuinely that of the workers. This was becoming less and less the case. As the working class degenerated, so the soviets atrophied and the state upon which they were based changed its character. The increased formal power of the workers' organisations became a meaningless parody when, as was reported by provincial delegates to the Eighth Party Congress of 1919, a single individual was often the local party president, president of the soviet, of the Cheka (political police), of the revolutionary tribunal and of still other bodies.[36] Filling official positions, workers 'from the bench' became cut off from their social base. Even if they retained socialist politics, they were swamped by a tide of former tsarist officials who were brought in because their expertise was essential for the continued functioning of the state machinery. By the end of the civil war this bloated apparatus numbered 5,880,000 people – five times the number of industrial workers.[37]

No institution was immune from bureaucratisation. During the civil war the Bolshevik Party, like the working class as a whole, followed a pattern of early enthusiasm and an offensive against its old enemies (in this case the Mensheviks and Social Revolutionaries). By establishing a one-party state the Bolsheviks apparently cleared the way for the unhindered progress of revolutionary Marxist policies. However, nothing could have been further from the truth. Although every step made under the terrible compulsion of war and economic collapse somehow appeared to be a gain, all the time the party suffered still greater losses in terms of damage to the proletarian forces, internal degeneration and bureaucratisation.

This situation was extremely difficult to analyse, because it combined such a constellation of contradictory changes, both open and hidden, ideological and material. As part of the process itself, the Bolshevik leadership was carried away with enthusiasm for war communism. Some leaders did have the occasional doubt, however. Trotsky, for example, was for abandoning war communism in early 1920, while Lenin made statements showing a vague awareness of the contradiction between war communist ambitions for a direct transition to a higher society and the backwardness of the Russian situation. Nevertheless, even the most experienced leaders found it difficult to stand outside the events and regard the situation analytically. Only Bukharin tried to do this. His *The Economics of the Transition Period,* written in 1920, was both a triumph of revolutionary thinking and deeply flawed.

The Economics of the Transition Period

The Economics of the Transition Period was among Bukharin's most abstract works; as he himself said, it was written in 'algebraic formulae'.[38] In spite of this he saw it as a tool in the revolutionary struggle: 'The object of this work is to demolish common, vulgar and quasi-Marxist ideas about the nature of the Zusammenbruch [collapse] of capitalism.'[39]

Bukharin's book challenged the Second International concept of socialist transition as painless, smooth and gradual.[40] Kautsky, for instance, believed the ballot box would remove the need for strikes, insurrections or other self-activity. Attacking the *'Tartar socialism'* of the Bolsheviks, Kautsky compared Russia to Western Europe where, instead of revolution, 'Democracy offers far better prospects for socialism ... In such countries every advance and increase in the power of the proletariat must immediately bring an improvement in its living conditions and must work towards "higher forms of life".'[41] But *The Economics of the Transition Period* showed revolution was an unavoidable necessity, because under capitalism progress to 'higher forms of life' was inevitably interrupted by crisis. In the long-term the means of production could only grow if capitalism were overthrown and replaced by a more advanced society. However, the very act of opening the way to new possibilities – the smashing of the obsolete system through revolution – entailed an economic cost. Bukharin demonstrated that the cost of proletarian revolution was greater than for all previous social transformations. While earlier revolutions involved a transfer of power from one set of exploiters to another, in a workers' uprising the exploited producers ripped off their chains. In such a situation the economy could not escape unscathed:

> *proletarian* revolution is inevitably accompanied by an extremely profound decline in the productive forces, for no other revolution knows such a profound and far-reaching *breaking* of the old relations and their reconstruction on a new footing. Yet, nevertheless, with regard to the development of the productive forces, the proletarian revolution is an objective necessity.[42]

This argument is an important counter to those who bemoan the 'economic damage' caused by class struggle. It squares with Trotsky's assertion that 'to lay this [extra cost] at the door of the Soviet economic system is like accusing a new-born human being of the birth-pangs of the mother who brought him into the world.'[43]

Another reason given by Bukharin for the necessity of revolution was that this form of working-class conscious self-activity was essential not just to overthrow capitalism, but to establish a new order. In contrast to reformists who see socialism as being created *on behalf* of workers by 'leaders' in a Parliament, Bukharin wrote:

> the proletariat has to *actively build* socialism and at the same time re-educate itself in the process of this construction ... When the bourgeoisie was overthrowing the feudal lords and the capitalist mode of production – based in its early days on the private economic cell – was blazing a trail, the economic process took place almost completely spontaneously; for there was no organized collective, no class subject at work ... They did not build capitalism, but it was built. The proletariat, as an organized collective subject, is building socialism as an organized system. If the creation of capitalism was spontaneous, the building of communism is to a marked degree a conscious, i.e. organized, process.[44]

Bukharin's book predicted that capitalist economics, with its categories such as market, price and commodity, would disappear under communism. Market socialists cannot imagine a society without these capitalist paraphernalia. Cohen, for example, dismisses Bukharin's contention as 'a digression' which 'weakened and obscured' the argument.[45] On the contrary, it was essential. To suggest that capitalist economic categories do not disappear under a new society is to make capitalism supra-historical, necessary and eternal. Bukharin showed capitalist economics was the product of a specific type of society, with its own system of production. He saw its unique character as lying in the fact that 'all economic regularity expresses itself in conforming to *anarchic* laws, "blind" force.'[46]

If the capitalist system is abolished its laws lose their force. Blind economic forces are replaced by planning of production – '*a conscious social control mechanism is introduced, in the place of the anarchic element.*' Even the commodity, an article produced specifically for exchange, disappears with the end of capitalism. In a socialist society the 'commodity is *transformed into product* and loses its commodity character'.[47]

This is a necessary development. Under capitalism workers do not see their exploitation clearly. There is no time at which the boss announces that the workers' wages have been earned and the rest of the day is to be spent working for his/her profits. All is hidden behind money and the notion of 'a fair day's pay for a fair day's work', or what Marx called commodity fetishism. Only when this system is abolished can workers truly master their economic destiny. Socialist economic relations will not be hidden by the medium of exchange. They will be transparent and direct, in what Bukharin called a 'socio-natural system'.

Bukharin's spirited defence of the revolutionary road to socialism was recognised by Lenin. Written during the period of war communism, his notes on *The Economics of the Transition Period* were mainly favourable, declaring that it was an 'excellent book', a 'splendid work'. But it did have a 'small defect' or *'spoonful of tar in a barrel of honey'*.[48] Lenin underestimated the weaknesses of *The Economics of the Transition Period*, which, despite the work's great merits, added up to more than a spoonful of tar.

Making a Virtue of Necessity

The key problem was that Bukharin, while alluding to both theory and the actual situation in Russia, made no distinction between the two. He rightly showed that a society moving towards socialism will both suffer 'costs of revolution' and abolish capitalist economic 'laws'. Yet he failed to point out that although Russian workers had won state power, because of poverty, isolation and war they were in no position to move towards a socialist economy. This omission had serious consequences for political practice.

Hyperinflation meant that Soviet currency was not worth the paper it was written on, yet in works of the war communist period Bukharin portrayed this monetary crisis as a desirable method through which the state would supersede capitalism. 'First of all, money is expelled from the domain of product-exchange as far as the nationalised undertakings are concerned ... Money likewise disappears from the domain of account-keeping between the State and the workers.' He did not think that in the midst of civil war chaos the abolition of capitalist economic categories and the establishment of communist ones was a distant objective. On the contrary: Soviet Russia was 'in the process of abolishing monetary calculation ... *today*'.[49]

The problem of failing to distinguish between theory and reality was demonstrated by the way *The Economics of the Transition Period* presented the transition to socialism. This was described as taking place in a series of stages:

1. *The ideological revolution*. Economic conditions demolish the ideology of civil peace. The working class becomes aware of itself as the class which is bound to become master ...
2. *The political revolution*. The ideological revolution is converted into action, in civil war and the struggle for political power. Here the political apparatus of the bourgeoisie is destroyed, the whole huge organization of the state machine. It is replaced by a new system, that of the dictatorship of the proletariat.
3. *The economic revolution*. The dictatorship of the proletariat, which is the concentrated power of the working class organized as a state power, acts as a powerful lever of economic upheaval. The capitalist relations of production are smashed ... a new model of relations of production emerges. The foundations of socialist society are laid.
4. *The technical revolution* ... the revolution in technical methods, i.e. the growth of the productive forces, the alteration and speedy improvement of social, rationalized technology.[50]

If used with care as general concepts for understanding the transition to socialism, these headings could be very useful. However, Bukharin implied that this schema was the sequence of events occurring in Russia. Instead of the decisions of the government appearing in their true light, as pragmatic responses to an emergency situation, Bukharin thus made them appear as deliberate steps towards a socialist and even communist society.

In *The Economics of the Transition Period* it was impossible to tell where theory ended and apology for practice began. Take the issue of 'costs of revolution'. Bukharin was right to say that the proletarian economic revolution caused temporary damage to production. However, he set no limit to this damage: 'there can be no halt to the decline in the productive forces before a new social structure and a new socio-productive equilibrium are established.' This ignored the risk to the working class if industrial output fell too far. Bukharin went on to suggest the decline could be reversed 'only after the reconstruction of the human labour apparatus'.[51] By a wave of the theoretical wand the catastrophic collapse of industry and agriculture that took place in Russia during the civil war ceased to be a problem. It was 'historically inevitable and historically necessary'.[52] But what if there was no working class, no 'human labour apparatus' left to be reconstructed?

Bukharin's stress on self-activity was also distorted beyond recognition. It was correct to argue that a socialist society 'builds its own apparatus, whose foundations are the *workers' organizations*'[53] – the soviets, the Communist Party, trade unions, cooperatives and factory committees – but he mistakenly made the yardstick for measuring progress the degree to which these organisations were sucked into the state machinery:

> The smallest units of the workers' apparatus must be changed into the vehicles of a general organizational process, systematically directed and led by the collective intelligence of the working class, physically embodied in its highest and all-embracing organization: the state apparatus.[54]

Once again the problem of theory versus reality arose. In the abstract one could argue there was no contradiction between the workers' state and other workers' organisations. It might seem plausible to say the less sectional an organisation was, the more it represented the proletariat as a whole and its conscious class activity. But it was highly questionable to suggest that the best workers' state must be a better judge of workers' interests in each and every circumstance than were unions, factory committees and so on, and so it should subordinate all these organisations to itself. How could the state express the 'collective intelligence of the working class' if all organised forms of workers' expression were 'systematically directed and led' by the state?

If Bukharin's argument was doubtful in general, his assertion of the primacy of the state was definitely not justified in Russia at the time, because the Soviet government was a very imperfect institution. Lenin described its current position in these terms:

> Ours is a workers' state *with a bureaucratic twist to it*.
>
> We now have a state under which it is the business of the massively organized proletariat to protect itself, while we, for our part, must

use these workers' organisations to protect the workers from their state, and to get them to protect our state.[55]

This is not to deny the necessity of increased state power to win the civil war. However, it is one thing to see this as a tragic necessity, quite another to pretend that it was the ideal solution and without contradictions. It is important to be clear on this point. There was a current of opinion, in the Bolshevik Party and among critics abroad, which held that by 1920 the virtual disappearance of the proletariat under war communism had destroyed the Russian revolution and its workers' state. Bukharin answered this point with a blank denial. For him, not only was Russia a pure proletarian dictatorship, it was rapidly advancing: 'The communist revolution ... a process of gigantic economic improvements and grandiose changes is under way.'[56] Alas, if the critics were wrong, so too was he.

To gauge accurately whether all was lost, or if full-blown socialism was at hand, it is necessary to recognise the contradictory character of the situation. Regarding the fundamental question of the status of the working class, Cliff writes:

> Of course, to a vulgar materialist it sounds impossible to have a dictatorship of the proletariat without the proletariat, like the smile of the Cheshire cat without the cat itself. But one must remember that the ideological as well as the political superstructure never reflect the material base *directly and immediately*. Ideas have their own momentum.[57]

What did this mean in the civil war? Although the Russian working class was being atomised by economic collapse, the 'momentum' of socialist ideas, of the dictatorship of the proletariat, continued, if ever more weakly. It was embodied in the diminishing minority of class-conscious workers and revolutionary Bolsheviks. In practice war communism represented an effort to preserve the position of this narrow base. It was neither a bold advance nor a betrayal.

Such a viewpoint was alien to Bukharin. He saw no separation between the class base and the political superstructure. They were one and the same. As a left communist this had led him to say that the political superstructure was defined directly and immediately by conditions at the class base; if there was no international revolution the workers' state was instantly doomed. Now he reasoned that if the workers' state still existed then its will could overcome any effects of degeneration. Before war communism workers' self-activity was his sole criterion for judging policy. Now the power of the workers' state was the defining factor.

To excuse this revision, he denied any clash between rank-and-file self-activity and centralised administration. If the state was a workers' state *its activity must be equivalent to the activity of the class itself*. He told the Third Comintern Congress in 1921:

> If the dictatorship of the proletariat is accomplished – if that party is really Communist, i.e. expresses the interests of the working class, then its *dictatorship is the dictatorship of a class even if the proletariat in the mass has been declassed*, and the dictatorial Communist Party continued to hold power in its hands.[58]

Bukharin had previously argued that means and ends were inseparable. Compromise, such as the Treaty of Brest-Litovsk, would make the goal of socialism unattainable. Now, he claimed, means and ends were not linked at all:

> Any social class may find itself in a variety of circumstances to which the methods and forms of control must be adapted. These forms are determined by **the norms of technical expediency**, whereby *different* forms have the same class content, given certain relations of property and a certain class character of state power.[59]

Now, apparently, any 'technically expedient' policy could be pursued without compromising the socialist aim. Bukharin was wrong. Means and ends are neither inseparable, nor completely independent of each other. Though each is different, they are dialectically related.

Bukharin's flawed approach to the relationship of ends and means showed in practical areas. At the time of Brest-Litovsk, he wanted immediately to replace the conventional capitalist army with a decentralised partisan militia. This was to be run by elected bodies and do without the expertise of any former tsarist officers.[60] In *The Economics of the Transition Period* his earlier policy was described as appropriate only to the primitive early stages of the revolution:

> nobody will begin to contend that the [elected] regimental committees make the army efficient. But their objective task, after all, is not to maintain the fighting efficiency of the old army but is, on the contrary, to demoralize it and train the forces for a *different* apparatus.[61]

Now, said Bukharin, the destructive phase was over, and a new constructive phase had begun. Instead of democratic rule, there should be a strongly centralised structure in the army. Bukharin did not see this as a retreat from his original position, but as an advance: 'in the military sphere, development proceeds in leaps and bounds and the whole process is expressed in stronger, coarser, if you like, more revolutionary terms.'[62] Centralised authority was 'more revolutionary' than self-activity because it was more efficient. The form of the Red Army in the civil war was thus not a sad necessity but desirable in itself.

Bukharin's war communist idealisation of the Soviet state came into play in the debate over management of industry. Since 1918 Bolsheviks had been divided on this issue. People such as the trade union leader Mikhail Tomsky supported 'collegial' management comprising representatives from the unions, state administration and so on. Another group, including Lenin and Trotsky, wanted one-man management. Bukharin resolved this knotty problem by casuistry. He said the civil war posed an obvious need for efficiency and therefore one-man management. But 'the basic fabric of the economic apparatuses is *already* saturated with worker-administrators.' Therefore one-man management

> is neither a diminution of the rights of the class nor a diminution of the role of its organizations. It is a contracted, condensed *form* of workers' control of industry, a form adapted to the conditions of rapid work and a 'military' tempo.[63]

Indeed, Bukharin almost suggested that one-man management was an advance on workers' self-activity. It was a sign, as in the army, that the preliminary destructive phase was over. The proletariat, relieved of having to run industry through Red directors, could go off for training in management skills 'in special institutions, by special ways and means, and much more systematically than was possible in the previous phase'.[64]

Before he became a war communist Bukharin treated the working class as a single unit. *The Economics of the Transition Period* described the class as consisting of two almost separate elements – a vanguard and a rearguard. The vanguard was embodied in the state. The rearguard included groups 'completely corrupted by capitalism', for 'even comparatively broad sections of the working class bear the stamp of the capitalist commodity world'. Hence the state was justified in believing '*compulsory discipline* is absolutely inevitable' for keeping the working class in line. The centralised power made necessary by the war was not a cause for worry, but a sign of progress:

> It stands to reason that this element of compulsion, which is the self-coercion of the working class, increases from its crystallized centre towards the much more amorphous and scattered periphery. It is the *conscious cohesive force* of a fraction of the working class which for certain categories subjectively represents an external pressure but which, for

the whole of the working class, objectively represents its *accelerated self-organization*.⁶⁵

Such logic led Bukharin to support the militarisation of labour. This policy involved conscripting workers and placing them under full state control, using the sort of undemocratic and severe discipline normal in conventional armies. Those who supported the militarisation of labour justified it as essential to winning the civil war.

Several writers portray Trotsky as almost the sole protagonist of this extreme line, but it was backed by most leading Bolsheviks and was established policy for a time. For example, Lenin, in his capacity as president of the Council for Labour and Defence, signed militarisation orders covering vast areas of industry right up to 1 February 1921, just a week before proposing the New Economic Policy at the Politburo.⁶⁶ However, he had, by this time, concluded that militarisation of labour was a mistake.

Bukharin was an enthusiastic supporter of the policy. At the Ninth Party Congress in early 1920 he argued: 'we must proceed directly to a system of militarisation of labour and to a system of one-man-management in the lower levels of the administrative productive apparatus.'⁶⁷ When his former left communist ally, Ossinskii, argued against militarisation, Bukharin counterattacked with criticisms that had been used against himself during the Brest-Litovsk debate. Ossinskii's objection 'was', he said, 'in absolute terms and without limit'. Ossinskii had wrongly overlooked

> a fundamental idea, that we have a dictatorship of the proletariat; that our militarisation is nothing other than the self-organisation of the working class, and the organisation by the working class of other classes, that stand alongside the working class.⁶⁸

By 'other classes' Bukharin meant the peasantry. While labour was being militarised, coercion should be used against the peasants. This was technically expedient because, if the peasantry did not supply the towns with food, force became 'an absolute categorical imperative'. Bukharin did not stop there. However incredible it may seem, he argued that even the peasant who identified closely with workers should be coerced, because 'coercion represents *his unity and labour organization, his education and involvement* in the building of communism.'⁶⁹ It is a mark of the spell cast by war communism that Lenin should write at the end of this section on 'Non-Economic Coercion in the Transition Period', '*This is an excellent chapter.*'⁷⁰

If there was a difference between Bukharin and Trotsky on the militarisation of labour it was that Bukharin went further, justifying the unlimited use of 'extra-economic coercion' by a fraction of the working class, the 'crystallised centre' over the 'amorphous periphery': 'It must be said with absolute clarity and without trepidation that we should so construct our own party that it is the most militarised organisation that exists anywhere.'[71] Trotsky never argued for militarisation of the party. Bukharinists are therefore wrong in suggesting that 'during the Civil War period Bukharin was no more left-wing [i.e. war communist] ... than Trotsky or Lenin.'[72]

Many of the faults of Bukharin's *The Economics of the Transition Period* were shared by the rest of the Bolshevik Party. However, Cohen is wrong to say his mistake was to put war communist beliefs into print in this 'literary monument to the collective folly'.[73] The book suffered from Bukharin's individual tendency to one-sided abstraction and lack of dialectics. Although they did not always succeed, both Lenin and Trotsky proved more capable of recognising a necessary compromise or deviation for what it was. Thus it was Trotsky who first suggested replacing war communism with a form of New Economic Policy, in February 1920. Only when it was rejected by the Central Committee did Trotsky throw his energies back into extreme war communist methods as the sole alternative option. Lenin was one of the first to realise the faults of war communism and argue for an alternative approach.

Bukharin's method made him incapable of such flexibility. Change was *never* posed in pragmatic terms of strategy and tactics but *always* presented as fundamental theory. This made him the 'biggest theoretician', but imposed a political price. Only he would have wanted and dared to create such an elaborate and logically developed 'literary monument' to war communism.

The Trade Union Debate

The issue of 'statification' of trade unions blew up between November 1920 and March 1921. It was a logical extension of the campaign for militarisation of labour and was led by Trotsky, who argued that the collapse of production made further centralisation of power necessary.

Bukharin supported this position as early as January 1919, when he spoke at the Second Congress of Trade Unions. He said that while workers' unions were right to oppose absorption into the imperialist states during the First World War, under Russian conditions the correct direction must not be struggle, and not even competition, but close contact and, as far as possible, organisational unity ... Workers' organisations cannot be 'independent' in principle, because here 'independence' would mean *counter-posing* one organisational expression of the *self-same* class to another.[74]

At the Ninth Party Congress (1920) he proclaimed the rights of the state superior to all others: 'Soviet power is the broad, all-embracing form of workers' organization, if you like – the universal form ... this clearly means that it is impossible to counter-pose any other workers' organisation to the Soviet state.'[75]

In part both Bukharin and Trotsky were reflecting a process already in motion. Under war communism unions were being increasingly statified or 'coalesced'. As Lenin put it: 'there is not a single large gubernia [regional] economic council, no major department of the Supreme Economic Council, the People's Commissariat for Communications, etc. where something is not being coalesced *in practice*.'[76]

The situation changed when the civil war ended in the autumn of 1920. Many who had tolerated state centralisation because of the emergency now wished to see it loosened. However Trotsky advocated moving from an informal process of statification to a direct and open one. He believed that still stronger state direction was needed to pull the war-torn economy back from the brink of total disintegration. Trotsky ignored another danger – that the final elimination of any workers' democratic influence would drive them into direct opposition to the state and destroy its very basis.

Leaders of the trade unions, who had been resisting the advance of state centralisation in production, saw Trotsky's proposals as the final straw. They were supported by powerful voices on the Politburo, such as Lenin, Zinoviev and Stalin, who established the 'Platform of the Ten'. Their arguments boiled down to two propositions. The first was that voluntarist methods of conducting the economy could not go on. They pointed to the real danger of a complete break between the Communist Party and the masses:

> If the Party falls out with the trade unions, the fault lies with the Party, and this spells certain doom for the Soviet power. We have no other mainstay but the millions of proletarians ... If we cause a split, for which we are to blame, everything will collapse because the trade unions are not only an official institution, but also the source of all our power.[77]

Second, opponents of statifying the trade unions rejected the idea that there could be no conflict between the workers' state and other workers' organisations, particularly in Russia at that time. The truth was that the workers had to protect themselves from their bureaucratically deformed state.[78] The Platform's solution was to maintain a high degree of centralised direction of industry, but give the unions room to combat bureaucratic excesses. The hope was that this would preserve links between workers and the government while keeping a level of state control.

Another important group in the trade union debate was the workers' opposition, which demanded 'the concentration of industrial management in the hands of the Trade Unions'.[79] This faction wanted workers' democracy and the strengthening of unions at the expense of the state, which they mistrusted deeply. The workers' opposition was correct to say that proletarian democracy is indeed *absolutely necessary* for the achievement of socialism, as is the withering away of the state. Unfortunately, socialism was not on the agenda at that time. The issue was the survival of what remained of the workers' state. The workers' opposition policy of decentralisation would have led to the final disorganisation of industrial production and the collapse of the Soviet state. The tragic condition of the proletariat and the breaking up of large-scale production meant workers were in no position to run industry themselves.

As the debate developed, Bukharin separated from Trotsky to propose a 'Buffer Platform' between the warring camps. His motivation may have been to avoid an open party split. However, according to Lenin this step 'did the most harm and created the most confusion'.[80] The reason for Lenin's fury was the way the Buffer Platform constructed its argument. Bukharin's remarkable powers of abstraction and logical gamesmanship led him to a position which managed to support all sides of the argument at once – the 'Ten', Trotsky *and* the workers' opposition! The state did not need to take over the unions; the unions would be merged with the state, and yet the state would wither away. Point 9 of the 'Buffer' theses put the argument in this way:

> If the general progressive line of development is to combine the trade unions with the organisation of governmental power, that is to statify the unions, at the same time this process is the process of the 'withering away' of the state. Its logical and historically limited role will not be the absorption of the trade unions by the state, but the disappear-

ance of general categories such as the state and the unions too – and the creation of a third form, an organised communist society.[81]

Perhaps this is how, in ideal conditions, a socialist society would develop; but it was absurd to suggest that the contradictions could be transcended in Russia, in 1920, by an organised communist society.

Bukharin's viewpoint could be interpreted in many different ways. Lenin saw it as a stalking horse for the workers' opposition. The Buffer Platform seemed to him to be advocating the dismembering of the economy, because the trade unions would take over from a state in the process of withering away. Bukharin said Lenin had misunderstood him and that he was not for weakening central control. If so, his position was dishonest. Bukharin claimed he was fulfilling the 'sacred slogan of workers' democracy'.[82] Yet his explanation of what the Buffer Platform meant in practice showed that the real goal was centralised control disguised as something else. The following statement by Bukharin illustrates this:

> Although the trade unions more and more support government functions they must temporarily remain *formally* non-party ... Imagine a concrete example. Suppose the question at hand is the constitution of the management board of a state corporation. Who puts forward the compulsory candidate? The committee of the corresponding union. But this institution is controlled by Communists.[83]

In other words, pretend to have workers' democracy but really operate control through the party state.

It was in the middle of the trade union debate that Lenin remarked: 'We know how soft Comrade Bukharin is; it is one of the qualities which endears him to people, who cannot help liking him. We know that he has been ribbed for being as "soft as wax".'[84] Bukharin's Buffer Platform was eloquent proof of this. It bore the stamp of three different seals.

The Platform of the Ten was eventually to become party policy and bring the trade union debate formally to an end. However, Bukharin did not concede defeat immediately. On 25 January 1921 he still vigorously defended his position on the unions in *Pravda*. In fact the outcome was largely academic, as Bukharin admitted when, just three weeks later, he pronounced his verdict on the debate:

> For some months we have feverishly been discussing on 'high' and on 'low' and even in the 'middle' the question of the trade unions and workers' democracy ... We can live with bad resolutions on the trade unions, but we cannot live with the present fuel situation, or

the current level of efficiency. Now, it seems, it is crucial to understand that the main thing is not to write good resolutions about links with the worthy masses, but to *build this in practice*.[85]

In the end the pressure of reality was bound to triumph over the illusion of direct transition to communism.. The descent from the towers of abstraction to the hard ground below was the more painful the higher one had climbed; and no-one had climbed as high as Bukharin. However, Bukharin's war communism was yet to have its final fling. As *Pravda* filled with editorials bearing titles such as 'Organisation or Chaos' and 'Improve or Collapse', and with reports of the uprising of sailors at Kronstadt, he argued for a desperate gamble on the international front – the 'March Action' in Germany (see below, p. 55).

Red Imperialism

Bukharin's deep commitment to world revolution meant that he treated international work as equal in importance to the struggle on the home front. The urgent need for foreign assistance was underlined by the immense problems of civil war. With Zinoviev, Lenin and Trotsky, Bukharin was one of the key figures in the Communist International. He helped write the Platform of the International and proposed it to the Founding Congress in Moscow in March 1919.

Bukharin's approach to international affairs during war communism was a culmination of several of his specific theories. The first was his rejection of the slogan of 'national self-determination', although he did now recognise the colonial liberation movements in the East as a factor which '*hastens the collapse of imperialism*'.[86] However, Bukharin sharply distinguished between the East (where he thought the small numbers of workers ruled out socialist revolution) and the situation in the West. In regard to the latter, he explained to the Eighth Bolshevik Congress (1919):

> It is my deep conviction that the slogan 'right of nations to self-determination' is logically associated with the slogan of 'defence of the fatherland'. Recognising the right of the bourgeois fatherland to exist in our epoch means recognising the *right to foolishness*, nay, worse than that, it is positively harmful. I do not think we can or should recognise this 'right'.[87]

A second element in Bukharin's attitude towards foreign policy was his voluntarism. He did not see war communism as the pragmatic response of a half-starved country in the grip of civil war. It was a positive step forward. So why not spread it? This led to his 'theory of the offensive'.[88] In a 1921 article, Bukharin drew a parallel between Russia after 1917 and France after 1789, saying that 'the Napoleonic wars had a vast historical significance and liberating character' and that the Red Army could play the same role. In fact he overestimated the role of military force after 1789. Bonaparte's armies assisted the spread of bourgeois revolution where they were supported by a rising local bourgeoisie in the more advanced areas of Western Europe. Where such a force was absent, such as Spain and Russia, the French armies failed. Napoleon was eventually defeated because he made the mistake of fighting in these two countries.

Bukharin's article on the 'theory of the offensive' went on to assert:

> The *Communist Manifesto* says that the proletariat have a world to win. But how? Through the revolution, it follows in consequence, through the 'bayonet' ... If the proletariat of a country has gained sufficient power to go on to the offensive against bourgeois states, that will show that the revolution is powerful, well-organised, and that victory is very close to hand.[89]

He dismissed the idea that the forced 'importation' of revolution might be considered an inappropriate tactic by communists in countries facing Red Army invasion:

> Once the 'importation', in the case of external 'Sovietisation', has begun, so Communists are obliged to use their full energy in its support ... There can be cases which must be considered unripe. But then the duty of the [Communist] Parties is to make their basic position clear, to swim against the stream and not act as a channel for petty bourgeois chauvinism and bourgeois petty-mindedness.[90]

Bukharin's references to Marx's writings were rather selective on this issue. The opening words of the 'Provisional Rules' Marx wrote for the First International in 1864 were 'that the emancipation of the working classes must be conquered by the working classes themselves'.[91] By contrast, Bukharin, as a war communist, had gone as far as claiming that a 'fraction of the working class' organised as a militarised state, with militarised unions, a militarised party and militarised labour force, represented the 'self-emancipation' of the working class. So why not argue that international revolution was also a military process?

This tied in with Bukharin's theory of imperialism. While valuable in many respects, it tended to overemphasise the internal rational organisation of the 'state capitalist trusts' and so made the external contradiction – war – the prime source of revolution.

Bukharin's defence of Soviet expansionism was described by Menshevik critics as 'Red imperialism', a charge he did not deny.[92] At the Fourth Comintern Congress Bukharin took the argument one step further:

> It ought ... to be stated clearly in our programme that the proletarian state should and must be protected not only by the proletariat of this country, but also by the proletariat of all countries ... The second question is: should the proletarian states, for reasons of the strategy of the proletariat as a whole, conclude any military alliances with the bourgeois states? Here there is no difference in principle between a loan and a military alliance ... Under this form of national defence, i.e. the military alliance with the bourgeois states, it is the duty of the comrades in every country to aid this alliance to victory.[93]

These arguments, years before Stalin took control, amounted to a justification for using the Comintern and its constituent parties as tools of Russian foreign policy, even when this clashed with the interests of the workers' movements within individual countries. Bukharin denied such political complications even arose. Red imperialism was 'purely a matter of strategic-tactical expediency'.[94]

This abstract approach had three main weaknesses. First, it left no place for the *contradictions that existed in workers' heads*. In places such as the newly created state of Poland there was enthusiasm for socialism and the Soviet idea among many workers. Yet they also believed in national liberation. Second, Bukharin reduced the process of world revolution to a fight between armies, rather than portraying it as the highest form of class struggle. Workers' self-activity was written off. Finally, whereas over the Brest-Litovsk treaty he went too far by insisting that Soviet Russia's fate depended entirely on revolutionary movements in the West, now he suggested that revolutionary movements in the West depended totally on Soviet Russia.

The war against Poland brought into play all three elements of Bukharin's thinking. When the army of Pilsudski, the future Polish dictator, invaded Russia in April 1920 and was repulsed in June, the question arose as to whether the Red Army should counterattack in Poland itself. The background to this discussion was a deeply disappointing year for hopes of international revolution. In Germany there had been a serious setback with the abortive Spartakist uprising of January 1919 followed by the murder of the Germany revolutionaries Liebknecht and Luxemburg. The Bavarian and Hungarian Soviet states were then smashed in turn. Against the advice of Trotsky, both Lenin and Bukharin argued for an offensive war to break out of encirclement and drive the international revolution forward. Unparalleled internal collapse was another motive for action. In the midst of the debate on Poland, *Pravda's* editorial warned:

> Heavy blows are raining down on our effort towards economic construction. It can only be saved by the force of red bayonets, which appear in this particular way to be weapons of economic construction, the essential method of revolutionary economic development.[95]

Since Bukharin wrote off Polish self-determination as no more than the demand for 'defence of the bourgeoisie's fatherland', he had no qualms about a Russian offensive. In *Pravda* he told Polish workers to forget their heroic struggles for national unity and independence against the centuries-long oppression by Russia:

> During the war, when the struggle was only between bourgeois fatherlands, the proletariat of every country had to fight against their own bourgeoisie; but they did not have to assist the other side. But now the whole working class, if it actively understands its position, must *immediately* relate to this first proletarian fatherland in order to help it smash the capitalist fatherlands.
>
> Take an example. Polish workers must now directly help the Red Army and do everything possible to assist its victory.[96]

Bukharin had decided that the internationalist 'ripeness' of the Polish workers was irrelevant. But it was precisely the lack of this 'ripeness' which rapidly turned initial Red Army successes into a costly defeat.

By the beginning of March 1921 the situation in Russia was even more desperate than it had been in the summer of 1920. On 1 March 1921 Kronstadt exploded into open rebellion against the government. The next day Bela Kun, the leader of the unsuccessful Hungarian Soviet Republic, set off from Moscow to Berlin. He had been entrusted with a mission by those in charge of the Comintern's day-to-day policies – Zinoviev, Radek and Bukharin. Although the terms of this mission are not known, when the old Communist leader Klara Zetkin met Kun and heard his proposals she was so shocked she refused to see him again unless witnesses were present. Perhaps the nature of Kun's instructions can be gleaned from Bukharin's 10 March article announcing 'A Shift in Western Europe':

> an external shift must lead to an internal one: either the dictatorship of the Orgesch [paramilitary police force] or a proletarian offensive

against the Orgesch ... the main slogan of the German workers was the demand for *'union with Soviet Russia'*.[97]

The March Action which followed was not a purely Russian-inspired adventure, however. Kun tapped into a strong ultra-left current that already existed in Germany. In the mining area of Mansfeld, central Germany, clashes between militant workers and the police developed spontaneously in the spring of 1921. This was essentially a localised and defensive struggle. However, flushed by the recent influx of several hundred thousand Independent Socialists into their party, the leadership of the German Communist Party decided the events in Mansfeld should be expanded into a full-scale general strike. This was to begin on 17 March and was expected to lead to open revolution. The party leaders were helped towards this conclusion by the 'theory of the offensive' as propounded by the emissary of the Comintern. The situation had been badly misjudged and the hoped-for revolution did not materialise:

> there was no mounting revolutionary tide ... only resolutions from the top agreed by the Central Committee [of the German Communist Party]. To keep the fire burning the Party resorted to sabotage, bomb-throwing and outright provocation ... Unemployed workers were formed into storm brigades to force their way into factories and try to stop work.[98]

The results of the March Action were disastrous for the German Communist Party. Some 3,500 communists were arrested and 145 killed while party membership dropped from 350,000 to 180,000 in a matter of months.

War Communism: a Final Account

This chapter has been heavily critical of Bukharin on many counts. However, it is important to keep a sense of perspective. Modern Russian writers seek to dismiss this period in his life as demonstrating a youthful deviation which he outgrew.[99] Bukharin's later political position is said to be an improvement on the earlier one. This is wrong. The Bukharin who extolled the virtues of the New Economic Policy would *not* represent an advance on the war communist Bukharin. It is true that the rigours of the war period had wrought ideological confusion among all the Bolshevik leaders. The extreme circumstances did lead to a general tendency to make a virtue out of necessity. This distortion was parallel with, and formed an element of, the degeneration of the

Russian revolution as a whole, although it was minor in comparison with the physical destruction of people and production.

However, this degeneration did not stop with the coming of the New Economic Policy, even though that policy did seem to negate so much of what war communism had stood for. Awakening from the spell of war communism some Bolsheviks – Lenin, Trotsky, and from 1923, supporters of the left opposition – would rise above this continuing process of distortion and recognise its dangers. Bukharin was not among them. This does not mean he failed to change after war communism, but the change was for the worse.

As a war communist Bukharin could be criticised for his one-sided approach to internationalism, but at least he was an internationalist. If he made errors on the home front it was with the intention (if not the effect) of strengthening the fragile hold of the proletarian dictatorship. If he was too often keen to hurry events, at least this was with the aim of speeding the arrival of communism. Under the New Economic Policy Bukharin's internationalism would be replaced by 'socialism in one country'; emphasis on strengthening the proletarian dictatorship would give way to capitulation before rich peasants and traders; instead of voluntarism and conscious direction of events there would be a policy of a 'snail's pace' development based on the spontaneous workings of the market. Hopes of a new society were consigned to an indefinite future.

4 The Bridge of Philosophy and Culture

In the years 1917 to 1920 Bukharin was consistently on the extreme left wing, or, since that term may be inappropriate for war communism, on the extreme voluntarist wing of Bolshevism. From the end of 1923 Bukharin led the extreme right, anti-voluntarist section of the party. There appears to have been a complete revolution in his thought. How can this be explained?

One reason was the changing political environment. At the end of 1920 and in early 1921, war communism suffered shattering blows. Of all the Bolshevik leaders the failure of this policy was most shocking to Bukharin. He was then bewildered by the initiation of the New Economic Policy, as he was less prepared for it than Lenin or Trotsky were. Lenin saw the NEP as a return to the policy of state capitalism under proletarian dictatorship which he had advanced even before October 1917. Trotsky had argued for a form of the NEP back in 1920. Bukharin had a much greater mental adjustment to make. This was because the more he aspired to pure theory and abstracted himself from his immediate surroundings, the less he was able to adapt to changing circumstances.

A second reason lay in Bukharin's *method*. On this point Lenin made a telling observation in his so-called 'Testament' of 1922/3. Lenin recognised both Bukharin's talents and his key weakness:

> Bukharin is not only a most valuable and major theorist of the Party; he is also rightly considered the favourite of the whole Party, but his theoretical views can be classified as fully Marxist only with great reserve, for there is something scholastic about him (he has never made a study of dialectics, and, I think, never fully understood it).[1]

Historical Materialism – Mechanical Failure

At the end of 1920 and early in 1921 Bukharin felt the need to step back from the immediate political situation and sort out his fundamental ideas. The result was a book, *Historical Materialism*. This is an invaluable guide to his method. Its timing is also significant. Cohen believes that the writing of *Historical Materialism* 'coincided' with Bukharin's war communism phase. However, internal evidence suggests that at least a portion was written after *The Economics of the Transition* period and indeed shortly after the introduction of the New Economic Policy in March 1921.[2] *Historical Materialism* is the pivot around which we can follow both the constant elements in Bukharin's thought and his political turn.

The book was subtitled 'A Popular Manual of Marxist Sociology' and it ranked as one of Bukharin's most widely read works,[3] being translated into many languages. However it also had trenchant critics, which in Bukharin's lifetime included Antonio Gramsci, Karl Korsch and Georg Lukács. It began with the assertion that Marxism is a science, ranking alongside natural sciences like physics or geology. Its only peculiarity is its field of enquiry, which is society, making it a form of 'sociology'. Bukharin believed that just as it is possible to discover immutable natural laws such as gravity, it is possible to find and formulate 'an explanation of social phenomena ... a cause and effect relation, as their law. And for this reason there is no difference at all in this regard between the social sciences and the sciences concerned with nature.'[4] For both natural science and sociology, the world exists as an object external to the mind which can be fully understood through observation.

If society, like nature, obeys fixed laws, it follows that human action cannot ignore them or overcome them. All change is therefore determined: 'any law of cause and effect may be expressed by the following formula: *If certain phenomena are actually present, there must necessarily be also present certain other phenomena corresponding to them.*'[5] While proudly proclaiming this *'social determinism'*, Bukharin was concerned to differentiate it from *'fatalism'*, which he described as 'a belief in a blind, inevitable destiny, a 'fate' weighing down upon everything, and to which everything is subjected.' He wrote that fatalists believed: 'Man's will is nothing. Man is not a quantity to be considered among causes; he is simply a passive substance.'[6] The classic example of fatalism in the labour movement was Kautsky, who said of revolution: 'it is just as little in our power to create this revolution as it is in the power of our opponents to prevent it. It is not part of our work to instigate a revolution or to prepare a way for it.'[7]

Although Bukharin could certainly not have been accused of fatalism up till now, he only avoided his social determinism becoming a type of fatalism by some extremely mechanical reasoning. He declared that, unlike the laws of natural science, social laws are enforced *through* human action. Although events are determined, it is human beings who execute them. But no freedom of action was implied, because, as

Bukharin put it, each individual 'is filled with the influences of his environment as the skin of a sausage is filled with sausage-meat'.[8] Bukharin's alternative to Kautsky's fatalism was only a marginal improvement, as passages like this indicate: 'Socialism will come inevitably because it is inevitable that men, definite classes of men, will stand for its realization, and they will do so under circumstances that will make their victory certain'.[9] Where Marx says, 'Man makes history, but not in circumstances of his own choosing',[10] Bukharin in effect holds that 'circumstances decide what history is made but people are used to achieve it.'

Gramsci, writing in his *Prison Notebooks* (where he called *Historical Materialism* the '*Popular Manual*'), rejected Bukharin's approach. Gramsci maintained that: 'it is the concept itself of "science", as it emerges from the *Popular Manual*, which requires to be critically destroyed.'[11] He accepted the need for a scientific analysis of society but showed that human action could not be predetermined as a result. Human beings do not serve as a vehicle for changes formulated independently of them. Historical development is the product of the struggle of individuals and groups interacting with each other and the material world.

Gramsci's criticism of Bukharin mirrored Marx's criticism of Feuerbach, which was that:

> The chief defect of all hitherto existing materialism ... is that the thing, reality ... is conceived only in the form of the *object of contemplation*, but not as *sensuous human activity, practice*, not subjectively. Hence in contradistinction to materialism, the *active* side was developed abstractly by idealism.[12]

Bukharin, like Feuerbach, was a vulgar materialist rather than a Marxist. In other words, overemphasising the material influence on society, he underplayed the active role of humans in shaping their own fate. His book offered a clumsy imitation of Marxist philosophy without its inner drive. Korsch reinforced Gramsci's argument when he wrote that in *Historical Materialism*:

> the fluid methodology of Marx's materialist dialectic freezes into a number of theoretical formulations about the causal interconnections of historical phenomena in different areas of society – in other words it became something that could best be described as a general systematic sociology.[13]

These may seem abstract points, but Bukharin's argument had direct political consequences. Overconfidence that social change was determined led him on many occasions to talk of human beings as 'living machines'.[14]

Certain that he had the scientific tools to discover future developments through passive observation, Bukharin was led to 'scholasticism' – framing policies by reference to theory alone. As one writer has noted:

> Marx, Engels, Lenin and Gramsci always warned of the need to recognise the dimension of hypothesis, of testing out, of the ambiguity of immediate experience, and therefore of the need to modify, to be open to adapt one's conceptual apparatus in some way, to some degree, if not on every occasion. In Bukharin this was quite overlooked. For him concepts are fully true ... and based on premises of absolute certainty.[15]

One example of the practical implications of Bukharin's method was shown in the trade union debate. Lenin described Bukharin's approach as 'one of pure abstraction: he makes no attempt at concrete study [and] because no *concrete* study is made of *this particular* controversy, question approach, etc., the result is a dead and empty eclecticism.'[16]

This abstract approach to formulating policies was accompanied by Bukharin's lack of interest in carrying them out. During a Central Committee discussion it was said that 'organisational work does not suit comrade Bukharin',[17] while at the Tenth Party Congress Riazanov 'complained that "our nice comrade Bukharin", who was a pure theorist, had been called on to make the report on party organisation'.[18] Bukharin, the theoretician, journalist and public speaker, was never entrusted with major operational responsibilities. Even his most stalwart defender has recognised that 'The historical judgement upon Bukharin as a *political* leader is one that points to his deficiencies. In this respect Trotsky stands head and shoulders above Bukharin.'[19] The tendency to remain aloof from organisational activity was not only the result of Bukharin's method, it exaggerated his faults. Practical work is the furnace in which the subjective aim and objective reality are welded together. Not to have experience in this area is not to have experience of the dialectic as a day-to-day reality. It cannot help but encourage abstraction either of a voluntarist or determinist nature at the level of theory.

Bukharin's method was a constant characteristic, but it was also brittle. Under pressure his theoretical outlook was susceptible to dramatic ruptures and transformations. During the Brest-Litovsk debate the conviction that world revolution was determined made him ignore the consequences of German invasion. Bukharin insisted that *reality must conform to the conclusions of social science* regarding international revolution. When reality, in the shape of the Kronstadt rebellion against war communism, imposed itself in 1921, the same mode of thought would lead to an opposite result. If reality would not conform to social science, then *social science must conform to reality*. Internationalism would be replaced by 'socialism in one country'. Changes in theory occurred within a consistent but mistaken philosophical outlook.

Having settled to his satisfaction the starting point for Marxism in *Historical Materialism*, Bukharin then considered social change. He proposed a 'theory of equilibrium'. It is no surprise that equilibrium was at the heart of Bukharin's thinking in 1920 and early 1921. The precipitate end of tsarism in 1917, followed by appalling economic collapse during the civil war made him ask: how is society capable of surviving, what is the basis for a stable social system?

Bukharin was anxious to prove that his theory of equilibrium was identical to Marx's dialectical materialism. Bukharin, following Marx, stressed 'that changes are produced by constant internal contradictions, internal struggle'.[20] However, Bukharin's equilibrium theory was more concerned with the source of stability, while dialectical materialism stressed change. *Historical Materialism* stated:

> Whether we like it or not, society lives within nature: is therefore in one way or another in equilibrium with nature. And the various parts of society, if the latter is capable of surviving, are so adapted to each other as to enable them to exist side by side: capitalism, which included both capitalists and workers, had a very long existence!
>
> In all these examples it is clear that we are dealing with one phenomenon, that of *equilibrium*.[21]

This was not a picture of internal contradiction, but of one discrete entity (society) neatly coexisting with another (nature). It was lifeless because, as one writer puts it: 'inner contradictions were dependent on external development.'[22] This squared with Bukharin's view that revolution in the West had to be brought about from outside by revolutionary war.

Bukharin, the revolutionary, was aware of sudden change. He needed to incorporate this possibility into his theory of equilibrium. In *Historical Materialism* he wrote:

> It must be recalled that such equilibrium as we observe in nature and society is *not* an absolute, unchanging equilibrium, but an equilibrium *in flux,* which means that the equilibrium may be established and destroyed, may be re-established on a new basis, and again disturbed.[23]

This was not the same as Marxist dialectics, which holds that contradiction is inherent in all phenomena.[24] Bukharin's view of change plodded heavily from one fixed stage to the next:

> in the first place, the condition of equilibrium; in the second place a disturbance of this equilibrium; in the third place, the re-establishment of equilibrium on a *new* basis. And then the story begins all over again: the new equilibrium is the point of departure for a new disturbance, which in turn is followed by another state of equilibrium, etc. *ad infinitum*.[25]

He claimed that this is 'a process of motion based on the development of internal contradictions', in line with Marx and Hegel, who 'called the original condition of equilibrium the *thesis*, the disturbance of equilibrium the *antithesis*, the re-establishment of equilibrium on a new basis the *synthesis*'.[26] However, genuine dialectics implies constant contradiction and movement, the simultaneous interpenetration of forces making for equilibrium and forces making for disturbance. Marx did make use of the abstract concepts – thesis, antithesis, synthesis – but applied them far more fluidly than Bukharin did.

A clue to Bukharin's understanding of Marxism is to be found in his brief 'Autobiography', where he said it attracted him because of 'its exceptional logical harmony'.[27] But Marxism does not stress harmony. Where this occurs it is only because of a temporary balance of social contradictions. An analogy could be drawn between Bukharin's philosophy and the Ptolemaic system in astronomy. This insisted that heavenly bodies moved in perfect circles. Yet it was almost able to mimic the perceived motions of stars and planets by means of ever more complicated circles within circles.

The contrast between the two systems is demonstrated in the way Lenin and Bukharin viewed developments since the Russian revolution. Lenin's approach had been closer to Marxist dialectics because it stressed the interaction of elements of change and continuity – proletarian dictatorship existing alongside state capitalism, or the formation of the Communist International in parallel with a temporary truce with imperialism. By contrast, Bukharin posited a complete break between one state of equilibrium (capitalism) and a new equilibrium (socialism). Between the two stages equilibrium would be entirely absent and the transition from one to the other would have to be forcibly generated. From this perspective the almost complete disruption of economic relations during the civil war appeared inevitable and desirable to Bukharin. War communist coercion was the means to reaching the next stage. Yet when the New Economic Policy was introduced, he could argue that a new state of economic equilibrium had been achieved and should not be interfered with.

Equilibrium theory was attractive to Bukharin for another reason. He drew part of his inspiration for it from Marx's *Capital* Volume II, which describes the reproduction of capital. Here equilibrium – balance between different sectors – makes sense as a method of exposition, of explaining abstract concepts. Over time there must be a definite balance between, for instance, the output of tyres and the output of cars. On a grander scale Marx demonstrated a theoretical equilibrium between industries making means of production (what he called Department I) and those satisfying consumption (Department II). But a method of explaining theoretical concepts is no substitute for understanding reality, and Marx did not limit himself to describing abstract equilibrium. For *Capital* Volume II was just one part of a larger structure. It was sandwiched between Volume I, with its detailed and concrete historical studies, and Volume III, in which Marx showed the tension within the apparent harmony: capitalism's tendency towards a falling rate of profit. Bukharin's mistake was to extend the valid tool of abstract economic equilibrium models to the whole of social life.

Furthermore he made the economy – the point where human society and nature interact – the direct determinant of social development. The theme is hammered home repeatedly:

> the character of the equilibrium between society and nature determines the fundamental course of the motion of society.[28]

> the *social and political structure of society*, which is directly determined, as we shall see, by its economic structure.[29]

Here the *content* of the superstructure (politics, ideology, culture and so on) was presented as a faithful expression of the economic base. Just as the individual was filled like a sausage skin with the influence of the environment, so social life was filled by economic influence. Marx's famous treatment of the same subject was quite different. He said that the mode of production only '*conditions*' the social, political and intellectual life process'. Marx stressed the

> distinction [which] should always be made between the material transformation of the material conditions of production, which can be determined with the precision of natural science, and the legal, political, religious, aesthetic or philosophical – in short ideological –

forms in which men become conscious of the conflict and fight it out.[30]

Not only did Bukharin make the economic base determine the superstructure in an undialectical fashion, his understanding of the economic base – the mode of production – was dubious. *Historical Materialism* describes the mode of production in this way: 'society applies its human labor energy and obtains a certain quantity of energy from nature ... The *balance* between expenditure and receipts here is obviously the decisive element for the growth of society.'[31] For Bukharin, therefore, social growth came about through alteration in the balance between 'expenditure and receipts' of energy. In other words the fundamental factor for change is located in technological advance: 'The technology conditions the mode of production; the mode of production conditions the view of life; this chain uniting the material, human, and mental system creates a certain type of society.'[32]

Lukács criticised *Historical Materialism* for this obsession with technology: 'Technology is but a *part*, albeit a very important part of the productive force of society, but it is neither identical with it, nor ... the direct or final decisive element in the transformation of this force.'[33] Lukács's point was demonstrated in the transition from feudalism to capitalism. The arrival of modern machine technology with the industrial revolution was 'the *fruit* of a century-long process of social upheaval, the crowning and completion, but not the original cause of modern capitalism'.[34]

Historical Materialism, despite its honourable intention of defending Marxism from its critics, [35] was a failure. Although Bukharin's approach was original, in many respects it still bore marks of the political milieu in which he had grown up – Second International Marxism. While Kautsky was the target of his most vigorous and most successful assaults, the method employed was often a highly voluntarist application of Kautsky's vulgar Marxism. When Bukharin's will was broken by the hard realities of life in Russia, the result would be a reversion to a mode of thinking quite close to Kautsky's own. Determinism would lead to passivity, to a loss of faith in the power of the revolution to solve its problems. Emphasis on equilibrium would reinforce this tendency, suggesting that the choice was either stability or absolute chaos. Crudely relating the superstructure to the economy would lead Bukharin to insist that economic processes would automatically accomplish social transformation.

Thus Cohen is quite wrong to argue that it is 'especially misleading' to correlate Bukharin's philosophy with his politics, or that 'one does best to heed the 1909 lament of a party leader that no two Bolshevik philosophers could agree.'[36] Marxist philosophy was not mere squabbling without relation to political practice. The one-sidedness that led Bukharin to ignore immediate contradictions in fact helped him achieve profound insights into imperialism and the state. It could be remarkably fruitful as long as it was corrected by an active revolutionary party through which the working class and its leaders, such as Lenin, tested hypotheses in practice. In the early 1920s Alfred Rosmer, a French representative in the Comintern, described the situation well: 'Lenin, solid and stocky, advancing at an even pace, and the slight figure of Bukharin galloping off in front, but always needing to feel Lenin's presence.'[37] But what would happen when the personal presence of Lenin and links with a live proletarian movement were broken by Lenin's death and the degeneration of the party?

Culture and the Proletariat

Apart from *Historical Materialism*, Bukharin wrote little in the early 1920s. Even the flow of *Pravda* articles dried up, although he was still editor. It is therefore difficult to judge the transformation of his thinking on practical issues. There was, however, one area where this transition was expressed – the field of culture, in its broadest sense. This was an important issue for him, as he signalled in a speech of 1925: 'Of all the questions which I disputed with V.I. [Lenin] only two remained which were not resolved – the question of proletarian culture and of state capitalism.'[38]

That these particular issues should figure in Bukharin's dispute with Lenin was due to the influence of Alexander Bogdanov, who propounded an 'empirio-critical' or 'monist' philosophy. He had crossed swords with Lenin and left the Bolsheviks as a result. Bukharin freely admitted that around 1909 he had 'had a certain heretical deviation towards empirio-criticism'.[39] In his review of *The Economics of the Transition Period* Lenin was adamant that Bogdanovism was still a harmful influence. Indeed Bogdanov provides clues to sides of Bukharin's philosophy that are obscured by their Marxist admixture.

For example, Bogdanov's method was: 'Abstraction, which removes all complicating factors, reveals in pure form the fundamentals of a given phenomenon, that is its constant element, which is concealed under its complex exterior.'[40] Although this approach is a necessary part of theoretical work, Bogdanov explicitly rejected the notion of dialectics. Therefore the complicating factor of contradiction was not brought back in to complete the theoretical process. The result was the sort of one-sidedness that was typical in Bukharin's work.

The 'monism' of Bogdanov referred to the belief that a single factor explained everything in nature and society. For Bogdanov this factor was 'organisation', which in the case of society was expressed in technology: 'In technology we find the organisation of things to satisfy human ends.'[41] Technological change was the root of social change for Bogdanov: 'The development of the economy is determined by technology. Ideology is determined by technology and economy.'[42] How close this was to the phrase already quoted from Bukharin's *Historical Materialism* that 'technology conditions the mode of production' and so on.[43]

Bukharin found it politic to distance himself from Bogdanov in the 1920s, both to bolster his claim to Marxist orthodoxy and because Bogdanov remained deeply ultra-left when he himself had ceased to be so. Bukharin's defence of *Historical Materialism* led him to write an article showing his great philosophical difference from Bogdanov, but the result was unconvincing: 'For Bogdanov *technology* is not the important thing, so much as the *skill* of people working with the aid of particular instruments of labour, so to say the psychological clothing [not] *materialistic* production relations.'[44] The problem was not whether technology or skill were the all-determining factors but the concept of mechanical determination itself.[45]

There were indeed strategic disagreements between the two men. Bukharin specifically singled out Bogdanov's idea of the 'cultural-organisational ripening of the proletariat in the lap of capitalist relations [as] utterly wrong'.[46] But this did not mean he disagreed with Bogdanov over proletarian culture *after* a socialist revolution and it was here that the impact of Bogdanovism on Bukharin's philosophy was clearest. It provided the connection between Bukharin's distinct line on the question of state capitalism under the proletarian dictatorship and the issue of culture. If there is a 'chain uniting the material, human and mental system' (Bukharin), or if society is 'monist' in structure (Bogdanov), then both state policy and culture must be absolutely different for each society. There could be no such ambiguity as 'state capitalism under the proletarian dictatorship'. The same applied to culture. As Bukharin put it: 'I personally consider that to "conquer" bourgeois culture in its entirety, without destroying it, is as impossible as "conquering" the bourgeois state. What takes place in culture is what takes place in the state.'[47] Bogdanov had pioneered this view:

each class has a different world view, a different evaluation and different norms of human relationship to other classes ... And so different cultures exist, not simply alongside one another, each residing each in its own corner or class setting – no, they oppose each other as implacably hostile forces.[48]

Bukharin did accept that some elements of bourgeois culture could not be dispensed with before they could be replaced. Thus he claimed in 1918 to be 'to the right of Lenin'[49] in wanting to use the technical abilities of bourgeois technicians and specialists. Much of the *Economics of the Transition Period* was concerned with this problem. However, he ardently believed in the distinct character, in all spheres, of the culture of the proletariat and the culture of the bourgeoisie. *Historical Materialism* has a section headed '*Why is Proletarian Science Superior to Bourgeois Science?*'[50] By proletarian science Bukharin meant 'social science' or Marxism.

Lenin and Trotsky, however, argued that Marxism could not be treated as a form of proletarian culture. It was built on the highest bourgeois intellectual culture united with the sum of experience of the workers' movement and its struggles. This debt to bourgeois culture was not altered by the fact that it involved a critique of even the greatest achievements of the bourgeoisie. Trotsky wrote:

> Marx and Engels came out of the ranks of the petty bourgeois democracy and, of course, were brought up on its culture and not on the culture of the proletariat ... its theory was formed entirely on the basis of bourgeois culture.[51]

One area that underlined the practical differences resulting from the culture debate was military skill. Bukharin made his first alliance with Stalin to oppose Trotsky's use of ex-tsarist officers in the Red Army. Bukharin, then a left communist, believed in the viability of waging war through guerrilla bands, in contrast to conventional bourgeois armies. As editor of *Pravda* he gave full rein to Trotsky's critics.[52] But the defeat of the Whites vindicated Trotsky's contention that the officers' skills were essential. To have cast them aside would have been 'just the same as if we were to say that all the machines that hitherto serve to exploit the workers were now to be scrapped. That would be madness.'[53]

For Bukharin the vehicle for a new culture, at least in the artistic field, would be the Proletkult movement founded in 1917 by Bogdanov's supporters. Its first conference declared 'socialist overthrow of society must soon lay the basis for a new socialist culture.'[54] While Bukharin had differences with Proletkult he remained its staunchest Bolshevik supporter, writing in 1919: 'The art of our day must be revolutionary ... mass culture grows out of heroic struggle.'[55]

On its own the issue of proletarian culture was not central, but it became the focus of furious debate because of its wider political implications. Before assessing these, it must be stressed that there was agreement among Bolshevik leaders about developing new mass culture as a final goal. The October revolution was not just meant to end capitalism's scourges of exploitation, oppression and poverty. Socialism means more than satisfying material needs. It is aimed at enabling people to achieve their full potential in all spheres, including the cultural. As Marx put it, the new society of abundance 'makes it possible for me to do one thing today and another tomorrow, to hunt in the morning, fish in the afternoon, rear cattle in the evening, criticise after dinner'.[56] Cultural activites would take place in a different context and would reflect different human relations to those that obtained in all previous societies.

The dispute was about how and when this vision of the future would be reached. Bukharin said the new culture could be created straight away and would already be superior to bourgeois culture. In 1922 he wrote: 'bourgeois culture is in crisis ... with the bankruptcy of the bourgeois economy, we see the bankruptcy of the entire bourgeois intellect.'[57] The crisis of capitalism was certainly deep and was affecting all areas of social life, but this did not mean that Russia was in a position to replace it with a new culture. The ideas of Proletkult enraged the ailing Lenin, who had Iakovlev lead an assault on them in *Pravda*.[58] Lenin himself wrote:

> only a precise knowledge and transformation of the culture created by the entire development of mankind will enable us to create a proletarian culture. That latter is not clutched out of thin air; it is not an invention of those who call themselves experts in proletarian culture. That is all nonsense. Proletarian culture must be the logical development of the store of knowledge mankind has accumulated under the yoke of capitalist, landowner and bureaucratic society.[59]

But did not the new culture emerge from 'heroic struggle'? Trotsky strongly disagreed:

> At the present time we can only create fancies about [proletarian culture]. In a society which will have thrown off the pinching and

stultifying worry about one's daily bread ... the dynamic development of culture will be incomparable with anything that went on in the past. But all of this will come only after a climb, prolonged and difficult, which is still **ahead of us** ... We are, as before, merely soldiers in a campaign. We are bivouacking for a day.'[60]

The truth of Trotsky's statement was borne out by Proletkult itself. It was, according to Lenin's widow, Krupskaia, never able to reach the proletariat or shed its character as 'a haven for intellectuals needing a job – particularly, she claimed, socialist intellectuals with anti-Bolshevik leanings.'[61] Perhaps, as one sympathiser says: 'At best, Proletkult studios might be seen as oases of artistic diversion in an otherwise harsh industrialization process.'[62] But what chance had the impoverished millions of enjoying a new culture? How could the theatrical staff of the Commissariat of Education be freely creative during the civil war when they were paid in shoe polish to be bartered for food, or when they had to go foraging in the countryside?[63]

Culture and Leadership

The second element in Bukharin's view of culture developed in 1922, after the introduction of the New Economic Policy (NEP). It did not concern artistic creation so much as culture in the broad sense of skill in organisation, administration, politics and economics. This issue was brought to the fore by the rising state bureaucracy. Where did this new force come from? The 'declassing' or atomising of the proletariat had left the workers' state without a mass basis. Although the Bolsheviks were still determined to hold out for world revolution, the state and party could not remain unaffected. Most obvious was the influence of officialdom, often composed of former tsarist officials hostile to communist ideas. By 1920 one in four adults in Petrograd, the citadel of the 1917 revolution, was an official of some sort.[64]

When Bukharin wrote about bureaucracy in 1922, the physical existence of a group of administrators was not new, but its character had changed with the introduction of the NEP. To see this, it is important to distinguish between *bureaucratic methods* – that is, command methods, orders from above, rule by decree – which had been the dominant feature of war communism's struggle against counter-revolution, and a *bureaucracy* – a grouping with a distinct interest and policy of its own – which developed apace after the introduction of the NEP in 1921. Under war communism it was difficult for bureaucrats to feather their own nests. The interests of the entire population were rigidly subordinated to the needs of the war drive. Under the NEP the pressure was off. By 1922 Lenin could tell the Eleventh Bolshevik Congress: 'If we take Moscow with its 4,700 Communists in responsible positions, and if we take that huge bureaucratic machine, that gigantic heap, we must ask: who is directing whom? [The Communists] are not directing, they are being directed.' He blamed this situation on the weakness of the communists compared with the superior culture of the old tsarist officials:

> If the conquering nation is more cultured than the vanquished nation, the former imposes its culture upon the latter; but if the opposite is the case, the vanquished nation imposes its culture upon the conqueror. Has not something like this happened in the capital of the Russian Socialist Federation?[65]

There was a basis for believing that this was happening in Russia. A deep cultural gap separated the old privileged groups and the masses, and ran through the whole of society. A survey in the 1920s discovered that 82 per cent of non-party factory directors had received middle and higher education, while 83 per cent of Bolshevik directors had had only 'elementary or home education'. In the party itself just 13 per cent had received higher or middle education, 84 per cent had only elementary education and 3 per cent were illiterate.[66] Among the peasants, surveys found that 'literacy grows in direct relation to the size of the farm.'[67] In rural European Russia in 1920 60 per cent of men and 79 per cent of women were illiterate. But among those owning 25 dessiatins of land (1 dessiatin = 2.7 acres), only 11 per cent were illiterate.[68]

In the discussion of culture neither Lenin nor Bukharin denied that in the realm of state administration the ex-tsarist bureaucrats were needed. But, if they could not be dispensed with, how could the risk of cultural conquest be avoided? The culture of the masses themselves must be raised to help control and supervise the activities of these bourgeois specialists. Whether this involved imbibing something 'new' (as Bukharin would have it), or 'an assimilation of the old' (Lenin and Trotsky), mattered little given the urgency of the problem. That is why in later years Bukharin said: 'I disagreed with V.I. on the theoretical position, but fully shared his practical conclusions' on culture.[69]

Bukharin wrote two brilliant essays on bureaucracy and culture. These saw off the Western social democrats who said Russia's revolution was premature because the cultural level of the masses' was too low to enable them to rule effectively. In the first, 'Bourgeois Revolution and

Proletarian Revolution', written in 1922, Bukharin showed that to delay the seizure of power because the masses were 'uncultured' was to renounce revolution altogether. When capitalists overthrew feudalism they did indeed have superior culture – in the towns and the universities, having ideological hegemony and so on. However, bourgeois and proletarian revolutions were '*absolutely dissimilar* in respect of culture', because *'relations between the bourgeoisie and feudal landowners were not those of exploiter and exploited ... The non-exploited bourgeoisie was able to create in the bosom of feudalism a culture higher than its enemy which it was therefore able to overthrow.*'[70]

As an exploiting class itself, the bourgeoisie held means of production which it used to build its culture *in advance* of its political revolution.

Could workers do the same? In the second article, 'Proletarian Revolution and Culture', Bukharin wrote:

> Of course, such a thing is impossible, even in the most developed capitalist countries. Could anyone imagine a capitalist regime in which workers are found running the factories? ... It is impossible for the simple reason that the bourgeoisie is the ruling class, which economically, politically, and therefore culturally, holds the working class in a position of slavery. It would be absolutely ridiculous and complete nonsense to maintain that within the framework of capitalist society the working class might raise itself to the point where it stands at a higher cultural level than the bourgeoisie.[71]

If workers could not create a culture *before* the revolution, what effect would this have on a *post-revolutionary* society? Developing Lenin's argument, Bukharin had already showed that workers' power might be subverted by the bourgeoisie who, though defeated, remained a culturally superior class. This was because *'the bourgeoisie did not need leaders from its class enemy, but the working class draws its leaders from the bourgeois intelligentsia.*'[72] The very poverty and exploitation that make the working class revolutionary mean that it cannot fully equip from within its own ranks a rounded leadership, armed with the intellectuals tools adequate to analyse and organise the destruction of capitalism. As a result:

> Any workers' insurrection, in even the most favourable country, inevitably runs the risk, in its course of development, of inner degeneration of the revolution, of the proletarian state and of the party. Because, if the working class is culturally backward and yet possesses power, it inevitably must employ other forces, which are its social enemies, but which stand culturally higher than itself.[73]

This degeneration does not have to be via direct restoration of private ownership of the means of production. Capitalism can return through the corruption of the working-class leadership in the party and the state:

> Even with a proletarian background, the most horny-handed sons of toil with impeccable proletarian credentials are not guaranteed against turning into a new class. That is because a situation might conceivably arise where a gulf opens between the working masses and a specific group which has emerged from the working class. This may harden ... into a definite caste, which can itself become a new class. During the epoch of great revolutions, of gigantic transformations, classes cannot be seen as remaining as they were before the revolution. On the contrary, after the revolution, when the old world comes crashing down, earlier classes are pulverised, they are deformed, and thus they can be reshaped into new classes. Out of previous classes absolutely new, and opposite, classes can arise.[74]

Bukharin's analysis here went far beyond Lenin's. The latter saw bureaucratisation arising from the influence of remnants of the old regime. Lenin did not stress the tendencies within the *new* regime towards bureaucracy. Cohen rightly points out that 'Bukharin was among the first (if not the first) Bolshevik leaders to raise the question'[75] of the degeneration of party and state. His argument did indeed point to the Stalinist counter-revolution with its new class of state capitalists. Here we have perhaps the last flash of the prophetic genius that Bukharin had displayed in his *Imperialism and World Economy* and wartime writings on the state. However, it is one thing to recognise danger and another to know how to escape it.

This analysis of culture, the post-revolutionary situation and the relations between party leadership and the rank and file, was clearly valuable. It could add to the Marxist understanding of the vanguard party with its dynamic relationship between leaders and the base. However, Bukharin's theory was open to abuse if employed mechanically. It had to be part of a vision that did not split the leadership from the rank and file, with the active dictating to the passive, the cultured dominating the uncultured. Lenin expressed the correct relation with the concept of 'democratic centralism':

> We must centralize the leadership of the movement. We must also ... *decentralize responsibility to the party* on the part of its individual members, of every participant in its work, and of every circle belonging to or associated with the party. This decentralization is an

essential prerequisite of revolutionary centralization and an *essential corrective to it*.[76]

With democratic centralism, differences in consciousness, experience and culture are recognised as inevitable in the anti-capitalist struggle, but are not accepted passively. They form part of a larger process in which they are continually overcome through action and inner development. Lenin saw the Bolsheviks as having no rank and file but forming 'a party of leaders'. Gramsci expressed a similar idea:

> That all members of a political party should be regarded as intellectuals is an affirmation that can easily lend itself to mockery and caricature. But if one thinks about it nothing could be more exact. There are of course distinctions of level to be made. A party might have a greater or lesser proportion of members in the higher grades or in the lower, but this is not the point. What matters is the function, which is directive and organisational.[77]

Alas, Bukharin never understood the dialectical character of democratic centralism. As a left communist he was deeply suspicious of any differentiation between the government and the masses and of the notion that mass spontaneity should be guided and advised by considered leadership. For him any such action was equivalent to 'the most accursed bureaucratism, destruction and degeneration of Soviet power'.[78] The views he had held during the period of war communism changed – the leadership now represented the actual embodiment of the class. This attitude continued into the NEP period, in spite of his developing analysis of the bureaucracy. Rebuking Norwegian delegates at the Comintern in 1923 Bukharin argued:

> It is said: 'the emancipation of the working class must be the act of the working class itself.' ... [But] in order to win, the whole proletariat must know that there is a proletarian vanguard. Thus there are comrades who are suited for leadership and they have more weight than other comrades. That is the reality.[79]

In later years Bukharin would distinguish himself from the Stalinists by his recognition of the problems of bureaucracy and leadership – mass relations, but his solution to both was posed in passive cultural terms. He would not advocate the gap between the top and bottom being overcome through action, for fear of the disruptive consequences. Instead he proposed passive schooling to raise the masses' educational level.

Bukharin's analysis was also one-sided because it portrayed culture as the *exclusive* source of degeneration. This ignored the physical destruction wrought by war and international isolation. As such it had the effect of damning the working class for having been oppressed and exploited and so encouraging bureaucracy.

Was there a solution to the problem of culture? Of course the spread of revolution internationally would have helped, but Bukharin was right to argue that the cultural oppression of workers under capitalism would cause problems for post-revolutionary societies in general. Nevertheless there was a way out, and Russia itself had shown it. The year 1917 had seen workers advancing in a highly uneven fashion and seizing political power without an equivalent mastery of economic or cultural affairs. This unevenness was inevitable, but it could be overcome. Through the system of soviets the masses had established the basis for controlling their destiny (and therefore their domination over bureaucracy) by building upon their self-confidence and self-activity. This rather than the absolute level of culture had been the motor of change. And it was through self-activity, through active struggle, that a further advance towards higher culture would follow. The famous mass meetings of thousands who assembled to hear Lunacharsky speak on ancient Greece just after the revolution were evidence of this. Gramsci summed up the revolutionary approach to the development of culture in these terms:

> There is no place for 'objective study' nor 'disinterested culture' in our ranks, nothing therefore similar to what is considered the normal function of teaching in the humanistic, bourgeois concept of schooling. We are an organisation of struggle and in our ranks study takes place to refine the capacity to struggle.[80]

Bukharin's inability to reason dialectically meant that he swung from a left communist denial of leadership to a war communist denial of the rank and file. In *Historical Materialism* he set in theoretical concrete a view of party – class relations as a top-down process:

> We may *distinguish* between class and party, as we distinguish between the head and the entire body ... capitalist conditions of 'being' and the low cultural level not only of the working class, but of other classes also, produce a situation in which even the *vanguard* of the proletariat, i.e. its party, also lacks internal uniformity ... and this makes necessary the formation of more or less stable groups of individual 'leaders'. Good leaders are leaders because they express the proper tendencies of the party.[81]

As we have seen, in 1922 and 1923 Bukharin became painfully aware of the threat of bureaucracy inside the party. His solution was the production of 'good leaders'. His 'Proletarian Revolution and Culture' states:

> If we want a victorious end to the workers' revolution – and, I think we all want this – then what stands before us is the problem of the remoulding of people who to a great degree still find themselves under an ideological influence that is hostile to us. We must turn them into living machines who in administration, the factories or teaching in any school, will guide the formation of the new principles of proletarian ideology. If we have a sufficient quantity of such people there will be one result, if an insufficient quantity, there will be another result. That much is clear.[82]

The development of cadres as outlined above was important, but the raising of culture through education should not be seen as an alternative to workers' democracy in the economy and state, or as an alternative to democratic centralism in the party. Yet this is precisely how Bukharin viewed it. Culture, as something dished out to workers who were supposed to imbibe it passively, would become *a replacement for their own struggle*, the struggle to maintain collective power in the face of difficult circumstances. Whenever Bukharin returned to the theme of culture in the 1920s this would be his practical conclusion.

Finally, we come to the point where Bukharin's ultra-left support for proletarian culture flipped over to become its dialectical opposite. In the mid-1920s he attacked Trotsky for denying the viability of a new proletarian culture and declared that Bogdanov 'had said some quite good things' on this score. Bukharin's argument with Trotsky was that there was no need to wait for the world revolution before tackling cultural tasks. Russia could, and should, proceed to 'the accumulation of proletarian culture' immediately.[83] If, as he argued, the Russian working class could create its own culture – the highest expression of social life – then society must, in a sense, have arrived at its socialist destination. Whereas Trotsky saw the 1917 revolution as but a stage towards the world revolution, its Russian contingent simply 'bivouacking for a day', Bukharin talked of the creation of proletarian culture in one country. It was a short step from this to 'socialism in one country'.

Bukharin as Theorist

The strengths and weaknesses of Bukharin's approach are clearly apparent in his writings on philosophy and culture. He had some brilliant insights precisely because he was prepared fearlessly to pose and confront new questions, to generalise theoretically where others feared to go beyond surface manifestations. Even when he was wrong he forced others to sharpen their arguments. But these qualities were offset by a disastrous one-sidedness which led to the wrong strategic conclusions. Trotsky described the situation in this way:

> Bukharin's mode of thought is formally logical and abstractly analytical through and through. His best pages are in the domain of formally logical analysis. Wherever Bukharin's thought moves along the furrows already dug by the dialectical blade of Marx and Lenin, it can give valuable *partial* results, even if they are almost always accompanied by an aftertaste of scholasticism. But where Bukharin penetrates independently into a new sphere, where he is obliged to combine elements borrowed from different fields – economics and politics, sociology and ideology, or in general, the base and the superstructure – he manifests a completely irresponsible and untenable arbitrariness, pulling generalizations out of the clouds and juggling the ideas as if they were balls. If you took the pains to assemble and classify chronologically all the 'theories' that Bukharin has served up to the International since 1919, and especially since 1923, you would end up with a scene from some Walpurgis Night, with the wan shades of Marxism being whipped about wildly by the icy winds of scholasticism.[84]

Bukharin's level of abstraction made it appear that his theory was above and superior to reality. This was an illusion for two reasons. First his theories were often weakened because, as Clausewitz suggested:

> in the same way as many plants only bear fruit when they do not shoot too high, so in the practical arts the theoretical leaves and flowers must not be made to sprout too far, but kept near to experience, which is their proper place.[85]

Second, far from being above reality Bukharin's thinking was subject to the pressure of circumstances, which in the 1920s took the form of the weakening of the proletariat and the degeneration of the Bolshevik Party and the revolution.

5 The New Economic Policy

The Legal Framework

Two circumstances prompted the New Economic Policy in 1921. First, the peasants would no longer tolerate grain requisition now that victory in the civil war had banished the fear of landowners returning. Evidence of the peasant mood was demonstrated by peasant insurrections such as the Antonov rebellion in Tambov province, involving 40,000 fighters, and that in western Siberia, with between 55,000 and 60,000 taking part. In February of that year 118 risings were in progress.[1] Second, industrial production had almost ground to a halt. The result was that the very existence of a working class – people who earned their living by labour in factories, mines and the like – was threatened. The Bolsheviks called this process 'declassing'. Many of those who remained in productive employment had become hostile to the government. In the winter of 1920/1 more than three quarters of Moscow's medium and large enterprises were affected by strikes. A metalworkers' conference in February recorded 'a complete breach between the party and the masses'.[2]

The climax was the Kronstadt rebellion, a spectacular expression of mass discontent. Sailors at the naval base in the Gulf of Finland, near Petrograd, rose in protest against harsh conditions, Bolshevik rule and wartime restrictions on opposition parties. Some called for 'soviets without Bolsheviks'.[3] Although the revolt was crushed, at the Tenth Bolshevik Congress in March 1921, held in the shadow of the rising, no-one needed convincing that a change of course was essential. The state could not continue to requisition all but the minimum grain needed for the peasants' subsistence. Discussion on the reports of Lenin and Tsiurupa (an old Bolshevik in charge of supplies) proposing a moderate tax, to be paid in kind, to replace requisitioning was cut short because so few delegates felt moved to argue the issue.[4] On 15 March the NEP was inaugurated and the peasants were assured that they could

> approach the next sowing season with the certainty that the fruits of their heavy labour would not only assist the Worker – Peasant

Government, but their own position. After the tax has been paid the peasant has the chance to exchange the surplus remaining to obtain goods needed in the upkeep of the farm.[5]

On 28 March trading of peasant surpluses in local markets was permitted.[6] The same day the state's target for grain acquisition, 6,900 million kilos, was scaled down to 3,900 million kilos, to be raised by the new tax.[7]

Although an apparently simple change, the NEP had far-reaching consequences. It rapidly defused discontent in the countryside and restored the flow of food to the towns. Victor Serge observed:

> The New Economic Policy was, in the space of a few months, already giving marvellous results. From one week to the next, the famine and the speculation were diminishing perceptibly. Restaurants were opening again and, wonder of wonders, pastries which were actually edible were on sale at a rouble apiece. The public was beginning to recover its breath.[8]

This success encouraged further steps which made the NEP much broader than originally planned. In May trade was opened to non-peasants and small manufacturers. Private trade in non-municipalised buildings was allowed in August and private publishing houses in December.[9] On 9 August came the 'principles of precise economic accounting' for all state enterprises.[10] They now sank or swam financially by their own efforts in trade. The same applied to those once eligible for food from the state.[11] The year 1922 brought private trade in medicine and health care, the end to state monopoly of agricultural tools, freedom for traders to ship freight by railway, to buy horses, set up financial associations, own foreign currency and precious metals. Even private inheritance (up to 10,000 gold roubles) returned.[12]

Bukharin's Assessment of the NEP

Bukharin's first reaction to the NEP was still that of a war communist. He grumbled that peasants had forced a new line on the government: 'If we had had a German revolution at our disposal, we would have borrowed some proletarian elements from there to carry out a little surgical operation. Alas, we could only count on our own forces.' He added that the NEP had only been introduced because of duress: 'If we had not made some concession to the peasantry we would have suffered the fate of the Hungarian revolution'.[13] At this time *Pravda's* editorials accepted the NEP as unavoidable but firmly denounced the opportunities it provided for speculation:

> The replacement of requisition by a tax means at the same time the unleashing of free trade. Speculators are already exploiting this freedom and will do so on an increasing scale in the future ... Only organised exchange, only exchange through Soviet organs and through cooperatives, only exchange which directs the whole surplus that remains after the tax has been paid towards organised consumption can preserve us from an orgy of speculation and exploitation by the swindlers.[14]

However, by August Bukharin's cautious attitude was transformed into unqualified approval. In his *New Course of Economic Policy*, the NEP was no longer portrayed as a temporary deviation from the direct transition to communism compelled by national isolation and peasant pressure. It was war communism that had been at fault:

> In essence, our economic policy in the epoch of so-called 'War Communism' *could not* have been a policy directed towards the development of the productive forces ... Not 'production' but 'grabbing'; grabbing in order to supply the Red Army and munitions workers in as short a time as possible. This, and *only this* was the focus of attention.[15]

He was right about war communism's practice, but to say that '*only this*' had been the focus was inaccurate. With a stroke of the pen all the arguments of *The Economics of the Transition Period* were consigned to the dust as though they had never existed. War communism had not just been an emergency policy but had been mingled with efforts, premature though they were, to create a new society. Bukharin's one-sided version of the past risked losing this heroic if misguided vision. In *The Economics of the Transition Period* Bukharin had made an economic virtue out of a political necessity. Now the NEP's economic necessity was made a political virtue.

By contrast, Lenin spoke in deliberately contradictory terms about the NEP. It was a return to his preferred policy of 1918 – state capitalism under the proletarian dictatorship. A mark of the continuity in policy was that the tax in kind had in fact been passed once before, on 30 October 1918, but, as Lenin pointed out, 'never became operative' because of the civil war.[16]

As much as Bukharin's earlier rejection of state capitalism under proletarian dictatorship had been ultra-left, his refusal after 1921 to see state capitalist elements in the NEP was right-wing. He idealised the NEP. At the Eleventh Party Conference in December 1921, the economist Larin contended that when the Soviet government employed capitalist methods of trading, accounting and control this was state capitalism. Bukharin was indignant:

> It seems to me that this scandalously confuses our understanding. Capitalist relations generally are not encompassed by commodity relations in the market. The essence of capitalist relations is found in the fact of capitalist ownership. State capitalism only exists when capitalists collectively rule over the means of production.[17]

By identifying the social system so closely with forms of ownership, Bukharin was ignoring what he had written elsewhere – that the key determinant in society was not formal juridical relations but relations between people: 'the social relationships of class oppression and class economic exploitation'.[18] His view meant the term 'state capitalism' was ruled out in the Russian context. Overemphasis on property as opposed to social relationships led him increasingly to discount the possible regeneration of capitalism under a formal proletarian dictatorship.

Other mistakes followed. If property alone determined the character of an enterprise, then private concerns were capitalist, while those owned by the state were socialist. In his defence, Bukharin could point to how Lenin had said that the 1917 revolution had ushered in the building of a socialist order. But Lenin did not mean this in the sense that the day after the revolution capitalist social relations had been replaced by socialist ones. At his last party congress, in 1922, Lenin stated that 'no power on earth can erase the fact that the Soviet state has been created. This is a historic victory', but 'we are now confronted with the task of laying the foundation of socialist economy. Has this been done? No, it has not. We still lack the socialist foundation. Those Communists who imagine that we have it are greatly mistaken.'[19] Political control had passed to socialists, but many economic and social relations were not yet socialist. At the Eleventh Conference Bukharin expressed no such doubts, saying 'we have our own state socialist production.'[20] It followed that if in Russia 'socialist production' was growing, then *socialism* was growing *in one country*. This was an implication that Bukharin would take up later.

Bukharin also withdrew his warnings about the dangers of capitalist speculation introduced by the NEP.[21] By the Fourth Comintern

Congress in 1922 he affirmed that the NEP 'is not a strategic retreat'[22] and at the Fifth, in 1924, he went further:

> After the establishment of the new economic policy almost all Russian communists and also our foreign friends had the feeling that something had been done that was not quite orthodox, and that they had to justify themselves. This feeling led us to consider the new economic policy exclusively from the point of view of political expediency, as a concession to the petty bourgeoisie. We did not think that it was good in itself, nor rational, but only that it was demanded by certain political considerations. That was how we looked at things, but it seems to me now that just the contrary is the case. The only good economic policy of the proletariat, the policy which assures the growth of the productive forces, is what we call the new economic policy.[23]

Bukharin saw the NEP as a virtually self-regulating economic transmission belt to socialism. In place of voluntarism came the notion that it was necessary only to sit back and watch the economic mechanism generate socialism:

> I repeat, I insist, the demands of military policy inevitably led to a fall of production in the economic sphere, but once the political goal is reached, our power consolidated and the proletarian dictatorship set up — the hegemony of the proletariat is an established fact and it is only a matter of setting production moving to build it further.[24]

Lenin and the NEP

Lenin's view of the NEP was of exceptional importance both during his lifetime and after. In life he was its chief architect. In death he was worshipped, and political credibility on the issue of the NEP, as on all others, depended on being able to claim Leninist orthodoxy.

That Lenin did not consider the NEP an ideal recipe was illustrated early on. Six days after the introduction of the tax in kind, a decree signed by himself and almost all the leading members of the government, Stalin and Trotsky included, apologised for a situation where peasants would have to go to market, because this would allow middle-men and speculators to fleece them. Direct exchange without market intermediaries was preferable but not yet practical: 'Later on in the construction of the socialist economy we will attain the successful point where in return for every unit of peasant grain the Soviet state will give products needed in the countryside of equal value.'[25] For Lenin this was the only 'correct policy of the proletariat exercising its dictatorship in a small-peasant country'.[26]

However, great obstacles stood in the way of its realisation. The collapse of industry meant that few manufactures were available for exchange and the tax in kind fell 1,360 million kilos short of what was necessary to feed the non-grain-producing population. These shortfalls had to be made up somehow. Therefore, in his key pamphlet of May 1921, *The Tax in Kind*, Lenin proposed reinforcing the elements of state capitalism within the NEP:

> [We must] not try to prohibit or put the lock on the development of capitalism, but to channel it into *state capitalism* ... This is exactly what I argued in May 1918. I hoped I proved it then. I had also proved that state capitalism is a step forward compared with the small-proprietor (both small-patriarchal and petty-bourgeois) element. Those who compare state capitalism only with socialism commit a host of mistakes, for in the present political and economic circumstances it is essential to compare state capitalism also with petty-bourgeois production ...
>
> Concessions [agreements with native and foreign capitalists to set up business in Russia] are the simple example of how the Soviet government directs the development of capitalism into the channels of state capitalism and 'implants' state capitalism.[27]

So Lenin wished the main benefit of the the NEP to be a return to the policy of state capitalism under proletarian dictatorship. In so doing, domination by anarchic market forces prevalent in petty-bourgeois production could be avoided. Instead the state would employ the advanced organisational structures of modern capitalism.

When Bukharin became an enthusiastic supporter of NEP he did not see the policy in this light. One wonders if Lenin had Bukharin in mind when he filled the first four pages of *The Tax in Kind* with a verbatim extract from his 1918 diatribe against left communism – *The Chief Task of Our Day. 'Left-Wing' Childishness and the Petty-Bourgeois Mentality*. It included this phrase: 'we must expose the error of those who fail to see the petty-bourgeois economic conditions and the petty-bourgeois element as the *principal* enemy of socialism in our country.'[28]

Lenin did not simply repeat his words of 1918. After the peasant uprisings of early 1921 the relevance of state capitalism under the proletarian dictatorship was revealed even more clearly. This policy was not just a means of using the most advanced techniques of modern capitalist organisation; it was explicitly a means of bolstering the regime *against* pressures from the petty-bourgeoisie, including elements of the peasantry: 'What are [foreign] concessions under the Soviet system ...? They are an agreement, an alliance, a bloc between the Soviet, i.e. proletarian, state power and state capitalism *against the small-proprietor (patriarchal and petty-bourgeois) element.*'[29] Such a bloc required private capitalists to play ball, but few were prepared to do so. By the end of 1922 there had been 233 enquiries about arranging concession agreements, but only 13 had been concluded.[30]

This failure forced Lenin to readjust the NEP once more:

> In the spring we said that we would not be afraid to revert to state capitalism, and that our task was to organise commodity exchange ... It implied a more or less socialist exchange throughout the country of the products of industry for the products of agriculture ... [But] this system of commodity exchange has broken down; it has broken down in the sense that it has assumed the form of buying and selling ... Now we find ourselves in the position of having to *retreat even a little further*, not only to state capitalism, but to state regulation of trade and the money system ... we say, for example, the task that confronts us is to make the state a wholesale merchant, or that it must learn to carry on wholesale trade, that our task is commercial.[31]

Restoration of industry and pacification of the peasants had not been achieved through a combination of advanced state capitalism and direct, non-monetary relations. The government had been driven on to the far riskier terrain of trade, with its middle-men and speculators.

Contrary to Bukharin's claims, this did not mean Lenin was rethinking his basic views on transition to socialism. Although circumstances forced changes in the character of the NEP, Lenin's overall view was consistent. He saw the NEP as a strategic retreat, that is, a step backwards needed to prepare for advance later on. A speech six months after the introduction of the NEP included a section headed 'A Strategical Retreat', in which Lenin stated: 'there cannot be the slightest doubt ... we have sustained a very severe defeat on the economic front ... a more serious defeat on the economic front than any defeat inflicted upon us by Kolchak, Denikin or Pilsudski' in the civil war.[32] War communism had been misguided not because its final aims were simply wrong, but:

> we made the mistake of deciding to go over *directly* to communist production and distribution ... The New Economic Policy was

adopted because ... we could not continue with the tactics of direct assault, but had to undertake the very difficult, arduous and unpleasant task of a long siege accompanied by a number of retreats.[33]

From November 1921 until his death, Lenin called with increasing urgency for a halt to the retreat before capitalism. He wrote, for example: 'There are visible signs that the retreat is coming to an end; there are signs that we shall be able to stop this retreat in the not too distant future.'[34] In March 1922 he repeated: 'we can say with full conviction that *we can now stop the retreat we began, we are already stopping it. Enough!*'[35] The reason for his alarm was explained at the Eleventh Party Congress:

> the state is in our hands; but has it operated the New Economic Policy in the way we wanted in this past year? No ... The machine refused to obey the hand that guided it. It was like a car that was going not in the direction the driver desired, but in the direction someone else desired; as if it were being driven by some mysterious, lawless hand, God knows whose, perhaps of a profiteer, or of a private capitalist or of both.[36]

In the later 1920s Bukharin wrote that Lenin had actually held two views on the NEP, having dramatically altered his opinions at the end of his life. Bukharin believed that Lenin's final articles formed his 'Political Testament': 'these articles ... are not particular, separate items, but organic parts of a single complete whole, a *grand plan* of Leninist tactics and strategy.'[37] Writing today, a Bukharin supporter says:

> Bukharin was, very likely, the first to formulate the question about a change in the Leninist conception of NEP between 1921 and 1923 ... Bukharin came to the conclusion that there were 'two strategic plans' in the work of Lenin ... In his article 'On Cooperation' Bukharin saw 'a *different* setting out of the issue [as compared to *The Tax in Kind*].[38]

However, Bukharin's view was mistaken. One proof of this is that Lenin's widow, Krupskaia, specifically denied the existence of two separate plans in the way Bukharin described them.[39] Still more convincing is the evidence of Lenin's late articles themselves. They do indeed contain new formulations. The article 'On Co-operation', which Bukharin cited many times, emphasised the need to organise the peasantry into free associations of consumers so that they could obtain industrial goods in bulk:

In conclusion: a number of economic, financial and banking privileges must be granted to the co-operatives – this is the way our socialist state must promote the new principle on which the population must be organised ... And ***given social ownership of the means of production***, given the class victory of the proletariat over the bourgeoisie, ***the system of civilised co-operators is the system of socialism.***[40]

Bukharin would say this passage justified his view that the NEP was a straightforward *advance* towards socialism. This was a false reading. First, it is clear from the passage that Lenin considered 'civilised co-operation' to be 'the system of socialism' when there was 'social ownership of the means of production'. To achieve broad social ownership beyond the tiny base of industries run by soviets, the forces of private capitalism in the countryside, which the NEP had encouraged, had to be rolled back. Furthermore, in the same article Lenin wrote: 'We went too far when we introduced the NEP, but not because we attached too much importance to the principle of free enterprise and trade – we went too far because we lost sight of the co-operatives.'[41] He lamented the existence of markets and petty traders when a better alternative – organised direct exchange between state and cooperatives – had been available. Lenin's proposals meant halting the retreat and returning to a variation of state capitalism under proletarian dictatorship.

There is just one place in all Lenin's writings where the NEP was not treated solely as a strategic retreat. It too occurred in 'On Co-Operation':

Therefore our rule must be: as little philosophising and as few acrobatics as possible. In this respect the NEP is an advance, because it is adjustable to the level of the most ordinary peasant and does not demand anything higher of him.[42]

In other words, it was an advance only because war communist posturing had ended and because the state was adapting itself to peasant needs. This was clearly not a cause for self-congratulation, but a problem for a country aspiring to socialism.

The threat posed by the unbridled development of the market was borne out by Serge's eye-witness account of the NEP:

Retail trade ... passed into the hands of private enterprise, which has triumphed over the cooperative and State trading systems. Where does this capital, non-existent five years ago, all come from? From robbery, fraudulent speculation, and superbly skilful racketeering. Twisters start up a fake cooperative; they bribe officials to give them credits, raw materials, and orders. Yesterday they had nothing; the Socialist state has given them everything, on burdensome terms it is true, for contracts, agreements and orders are all fixed by corruption. Once launched they carry on, determined to become the universal middlemen between socialized industry and the consumer. They double the price of everything. Soviet trade, as a consequence of our industrial weakness, has become the hunting-ground for a flock of vultures in whom the shape of tomorrow's toughest and smartest capitalists can be clearly discerned. In this respect NEP is an unquestionable setback.[43]

Trotsky and the NEP

When Lenin died in 1924 he had been absent from active politics for more than a year. A battle then ensued between Trotsky and Bukharin about who was the true interpreter of Lenin's line on the NEP. Modern Russian writing takes Bukharin's side, accusing Trotsky of harbouring a secret hatred of the NEP, which 'objectively' put him in the same camp as Stalin who abolished it in 1929.[44] This is totally false.

In February 1920 Trotsky, who, as leader of the Red Army, had close contacts with peasants in uniform, argued that war communist policy towards agriculture 'threatens to completely disorganise the economic life of the country' and should be replaced by 'a sort of progressive tax on agricultural income'.[45] From 1921 Trotsky's view of the NEP as a strategic retreat coincided with Lenin's. In his speech to the Fourth Comintern Congress in November 1922 he declared that the NEP was necessary: 'we ourselves – for good and substantial reasons – call it a retreat', but, he added, 'how little this retreat resembles "capitulation".'[46]

There were differences in emphasis between Trotsky and Lenin. Trotsky was less favourably inclined to state capitalism under the proletarian dictatorship. He thought the policy was unnecessary, as 'actual development went along more favourable lines.'[47] He said this because of the NEP's assistance in the growth of state industry:

> the New Economic Policy does not flow solely from the inter-relations between the city and the village. This policy is a necessary stage in the growth of state-owned industry. In capitalism, under which the means of production are owned by private individuals and all economic relations are regulated by the market – I say, between capitalism and complete socialism, with its socially planned economy,

there are a number of transitional stages; and the NEP is essentially one of these stages.[48]

Trotsky went further than Lenin in emphasising the usefulness of market relations as a guide to economic accounting and policy, but at the same time he talked clearly of how the long-term advance towards socialism would negate the market.

At the heart of Trotsky's conception of the NEP, like Lenin's, was its contradictory character, which could only be resolved through *action*. This was summed up by the title of his pamphlet *Towards Capitalism or Socialism?* (1925), where he wrote: 'there is a struggle between capitalist and socialist tendencies in our economy (and the very essence of the NEP consists of both collaboration and competition between these tendencies).'[49] Implicit in this is the striving for victory and the possibility of defeat through 'opportunistic degeneration'[50] or a direct 'restoration of capitalism'.[51] The key to victory did not lie in the hands of the Russian communists alone: *'The NEP is calculated for certain definite conditions of time and space. It is a manoeuvre of the workers' state which exists in capitalist surroundings and definitely calculates on the revolutionary development of Europe.'*[52]

The NEP and the Class Balance

A key issue in the debate over the NEP was the possible consequences it might have on the balance of class forces in Russia. It was in operation from 1921 until 1928 and at first glance it seemed to bring a great improvement to the working class and its economic base in industry. Although by no means a smooth process, manufacturing began to recover from the low point of war communism (see Table 5.1).

Table 5.1: Industrial Output (thousand tonnes)

	1913	1921	1925	1928
Pig iron	4,216	117	1,309	3,282
Steel	4,231	220	1,868	4,251
Oil	9,234	3,781	7,061	11,625
Coal	29,117	9,531	16,520	35,510

Source: Adapted from R. Hutchings, *Soviet Economic Development*, New York 1982, page 42.

There was a corresponding recovery in the industrial workforce (an increase of 14.2 per cent in 1922–3)[53] and in the population of towns. In 1920 there were only nine cities with populations over 100,000; such had been the ravages of war. By 1923 there were 22.[54] Living standards for the employed also began to rise, although painfully slowly. (see Table 5.2).

Table 5.2: Average Earnings of Workers (in constant rubles)

	Monthly (roubles)	Hourly (kopecks)
1913	30.49	14.2
1920	10.15	5.4
1923	20.75	11.7
1925	28.76	16.6

Source: Adapted from A. Nove, *An Economic History of the USSR*, Harmondsworth 1969, page 114.

Bukharin took this as evidence that the NEP was pure gain for workers and for socialism. He wrote that 'the question of relative changes in numbers [of workers] appears the defining factor for their social force.'[55] But such quantitative factors are only one side of the coin. The United States has one of the world's largest working classes in terms of numbers, proportion of the total population and concentration. Yet this country has had one of the weakest socialist movements. It is also true that the qualitative factor – political consciousness – is not in itself sufficient to guarantee a powerful socialist movement. The Russian proletariat, with its tradition of revolutionary struggle and high degree of class-consciousness, was the most advanced in the world, but such had been the physical destruction of war that it was gravely weakened in the political sense. A revolutionary socialist view of the NEP therefore has to consider both its material and ideological impact.

Furthermore, overall figures for industrial recovery, numbers of workers or pay levels disguised severe fluctuations which were important in themselves. 'Economic accounting' meant industry fighting for survival in the marketplace. Shliapnikov, the old Bolshevik and former engineer, told the 1922 party congress of the consequences: 'The conjuncture of the market is beating us down ... we create such an anarchic competition, even on the market for metal products, that we have nothing to pay the wages with.'[56] Dobb estimates that as a result of the NEP real wages for those employed, which had risen a little in 1920 over 1919, were lower again as an average for 1921; and in the summer months ... real wages in Moscow [were] less than a half what they had been in December of the previous year.[57]

As Carr writes, the NEP 'meant a policy not only of concessions to the peasantry, but of concessions at the expense of the proletariat, or at any rate of concessions which left no room for corresponding favours to industry'.[59]

Eventually these problems were partly overcome, but the long-term damage done to the most class-conscious sections of workers was much harder to repair. The political capital won in three revolutions, that confidence in their power to remake the world, had already been substantially lost due to the appalling difficulties encountered during the civil war; now the NEP sapped the spirit of those who had survived this experience with their revolutionary politics intact. Industrial growth revived the working class physically and numerically, but it was not the same working class as had made the revolution. Growth was at the price of weakening its shopfloor strength:

> another whip lashed the industrial workers – the 'red managers.' Their power was massively increased by NEP. They came increasingly from traditional managerial sections and were increasingly integrated into the party hierarchy ... The managers acted in a more and more highhanded fashion towards the workers ... a reversion among the new managers to the traditional attitudes of employers to their workers.[59]

A speech by Maximov of the Ukrainian Council of People's Economy in 1924 confirms this. He denounced 'the abnormal manifestation of rough treatment of labourers by the administering organs. The people standing at the head of the enterprises must remember that they are only representatives of working men, the real masters of the country.'[60] In place of war communism's tough egalitarianism, the wage differential between unskilled and skilled workers increased from 4 per cent in 1920 to 65 per cent in 1922,[61] while a well-off shopkeeper could expect to earn 20 times more than workers.[62]

Equally damaging to morale was unemployment. It had been minimal during the civil war but remained high throughout the period of the NEP, despite economic expansion. In September 1922, one out of every 10 workers in the industrial centres was without work. By September 1923 the figure was one in five.[63] As a result of 'economic accounting', by 1922 some 300,000 had been sacked from the railways and 150,000 from water transport. Within four months of its introduction 54 per cent of postal workers had lost their jobs, and soon even doctors and teachers, hardly an abundant resource in disease-ridden, illiterate Russia, were finding themselves on the streets.[64]

Serge conveyed the contradictions of NEP society: 'money corrupts everything – even as it makes life blossom everywhere.'[65] Not surprisingly:

> the confusion among the Party rank-and-file was staggering. 'For what did we fight, spill so much blood, agree to so many sacrifices?' asked the Civil War veterans bitterly. Usually these men lacked all the necessities; clothes, decent homes, money; and now everything was turning back into market-value. They felt that money, the vanquished foe, would soon come into its kingdom once again.[66]

They had ample reason for such fears:

> The grocers have sumptuous displays, packed with Crimean fruits and Georgian wines, but [there are] hordes of beggars and abandoned children; hordes of prostitutes. We have three large gaming-houses in town where baccarat, roulette and chemin-de-fer are played, sinister dives with crime always hovering around the corner.[67]

The impact of the NEP on the emergent bureaucracy was rather different to its impact on workers. During the civil war, the bonds linking party leaders and the rank and file had been corroded by the process of declassing, but they did not break entirely. Despite the influence of ex-tsarist experts in the state machine, the core remained a band of dedicated revolutionary socialists bound to the workers' cause by a common ideological commitment. There was a universal, if spartan, equality. One example was the director of the State Library, a close relative of Zinoviev (the President of the Comintern), who died from malnutrition during the civil war.[68] While ordinary workers could exercise little control through their mass organisations – soviets, the party and unions – there was little in the way of material corruption to subvert the leaders' political aims. Indeed part of the problem with war communism was the overzealous idealism of the Bolshevik leaders and their impatience to reach a new society at a pace that the actual circumstances could not sustain.

Under the NEP this changed. Officials of the state and the party who had once been committed to workers' emancipation developed into a distinct bureaucracy not just in terms of the work they did, but also in terms of their attitudes and social position. There were two reasons for this. One was that under the NEP the working class was unable to keep an effective check on the bureaucracy through political pressure. The class-conscious core was not easily reconstituted after the ravages of the civil war. When workers with revolutionary experience returned to the newly reopened factories they were not welded into an effective force, but atomised by wage differentials and political demoralisation. Their influence was further diluted by the presence of many new, politically inexperienced ex-peasants in the ranks.

The second reason for the growth of a bureaucratic caste was the impact of the NEP on officialdom. The hothouse recovery of trade and private wealth not only demoralised rank-and-file Bolsheviks, it also had a corrupting effect on those running the various institutions in society. A gulf opened up between workers and officials in terms of incomes and social opportunities. The problem was compounded by the situation inside the Bolshevik Party itself. In March 1921, when the NEP was introduced, the party had been within an inch of destruction, facing Kronstadt and peasant insurrections and, moreover, massive internal arguments, epitomised by the bitterness of the trade union debate. Therefore, at the same congress where the NEP was adopted, Lenin declared: 'We want no more oppositions!' and a ban was placed on factions.[69] The curtailment of democratic centralism was, like the NEP, intended to be a strategic retreat, an extreme cure for a severe sickness, to be withdrawn when health returned. It was supported as such by all party leaders. But the ban was to suit the growing bureaucracy around Stalin and it was to remain in force indefinitely.

Today pro-marketeers see the NEP as an example of the benefits of 'pluralism':

> the distinctive feature of NEP ... was the existence of significant social pluralism within the authoritarian framework ... perhaps the truest reflection of the pluralism of NEP society was to be found in its cultural and intellectual life, always a barometer of genuine diversity and state toleration. For here the twenties were a decade of memorable variety and achievement.[70]

The NEP is portrayed as the victory of a new liberty over the tyranny of war communist fanaticism. In truth it revived the old tyranny of wealth (in the case of 'Nepmen' and rich peasants) and laid the basis for a new tyranny by a bureaucracy which, if it did not privately own wealth, ruled over it in the form of industry and the state. Although the NEP was unavoidable, its cost was the erection of barriers on the path towards creating a truly free society – which can only be achieved through the abolition, not the revival, of capitalism.

Bukharin attained his greatest influence in Russia as a result of his idealisation of the NEP. This was because his writings at this time appealed to a variety of social forces. His uncritical attitude reflected the outlook of many bureaucrats whose survival in a predominantly peasant country had been at risk before the NEP's introduction. These bureaucrats saw themselves as custodians of the national economy and approved of a strategy which argued for growth regardless of the social and political ramifications for the working class.

In his optimism regarding the NEP Bukharin deliberately overlooked its character as a strategic retreat. This approach was attractive to the considerable number of workers who had become exhausted by the constant struggle against foreign imperialism and domestic difficulties. Bukharin promised them a respite from trouble.

Finally, there were prominent Bolsheviks, from Rykov who headed the state apparatus, to Tomsky the union leader and Stalin, party general secretary, who needed the Marxist terminology of Bukharin's arguments to justify their opportunist policy of caving in to peasant pressure on all fronts.

Clearly there were major problems with Bukharin's attitude towards the NEP. He was becoming distanced from the needs of the working class and the spirit of the Bolshevik revolution. Despite this he cannot be put in the same camp as today's marketeers. Bukharin's view of the NEP was shaped by the political situation of a workers' revolution in *degeneration*, not by the *defeat* that from 1929 onwards would be the backdrop to the modern Russian ruling class. Although for him, the NEP represented a purely mechanical growth of the 'socialist economy', it was to be a transition to a society *different* from capitalism. There would be struggle of a sort, even if only economic, rather than class/political struggle. In 1922 Bukharin wrote:

> Over a number of years we will continue with this temporary co-existence of more than one (and in practice several) types of economic activity. We will, for a very long time, have not just state socialist enterprises, but mixed enterprises, the private capitalist economy and finally petty-bourgeois private undertakings ... Over this period the petty-bourgeoisie and big bourgeois economies will attempt on the basis of market relations to crush *our* socialist economy. By contrast our proletarian economy will try to squeeze them and strengthen socialism.[71]

A few months later he added:

> This economic rebirth [of NEP] goes along two paths: one leads to the strengthening of socialist economic forms, the other towards the growth of petty-bourgeois and bourgeois capitalist forms. The existence of these two alternatives may pose a special danger for us, that private capitalist forms swell up too quickly leading to the danger of inner degeneration.[72]

This element in Bukharin's view of the NEP is too often disregarded by friends and foes alike. In later years he would argue for the unfettered development of wealthy peasant farmers in his famous slogan 'Enrich yourselves'; his idea of the NEP as a straightforward advance did differ radically from both Lenin and Trotsky; but *at no point* did the NEP become an end in itself for him. Indeed by admitting the chance of failure, of a struggle between economic forms in which everything hinged on the relative economic expansion of capitalism versus 'socialism', he showed that these forms were distinct. It is true that for him the passage from capitalism to socialism had nothing of the revolutionary spirit in it. As his *New Course* put it:

> The more we ourselves expand ... the greater will be the *proletarian* share [of production], and if we increase still further we will, at the end of the day, swallow up the capitalist portion. That day will mark the final victory of communism.[73]

Nevertheless the crucial point is that he still saw the NEP as a method of fighting capitalism, not a means of capitulating to it. For him the final goal, however distant, was always the economic goal of 'squeezing', of 'swallowing up' capitalism to achieve the victory of communism.

When Bukharin embraced the idea of the workers' state relinquishing full control over the economy, he did this because 'Russia, being a backward country, found it impossible to socialise everything in the short-term.'[74] But in the long term it would be socialised. The super-centralisation of war communism had not been a viable policy and had to be replaced by the NEP 'to establish the correct proportions between that which can be taken by a centralised apparatus and that which cannot'. However, the aim remained 'to strengthen as much as possible the proletarian-state portion we have in our hands, raising it from one level to another'.[75]

Those who claim the mantle of Bukharin today do not wish to end 100 per cent state ownership in order to find the correct proportions between state and private ownership from which to relaunch the movement back to full collective control. They do not see the 'final victory' as the abolition of private property by workers' rule. Whatever his faults, Bukharin was very different from his admirers. Yet his arguments were extremely dangerous in their time. The cold blast of international imperialism and internal reaction exerted a tremendous backward pressure on the Russian revolution, a tiny ship in raging seas. If war communism represented a sharp tack to the left, the NEP swung the rudder rightwards. Both manoeuvres were necessary for the ship to keep afloat even if, at the end of the day, minimal progress or even a drift backwards occurred. To keep an overall sense of direction, the fact that these necessary manoeuvres did *not* lead directly to the final goal had to be understood. Bukharin's uncritical view of the NEP was therefore mistaken. Through it he not only reflected the degeneration of the Russian revolution and the rise of the bureaucracy, he also strengthened these processes by giving them a theoretical gloss.

Before the NEP was introduced, the thin layer of revolutionaries holding on to power in order to promote international socialism risked being swept away by peasant revolt and the obliteration of their working-class base. By helping to revive food production and industry the NEP offered a breathing space to regroup and recommence the socialist offensive. However, the policy was only useful if it was understood as a strategic retreat; if not, it risked turning a retreat into a rout. One source of danger was the development of capitalist tendencies among the peasantry, the vast bulk of the Russian population.

6 The Russian Peasantry

The first years after 1917 were dominated by the most fundamental question that can be put to any revolution: to be or not to be? Would October 1917 be the spark that ignited the flame of world revolution, or would it be snuffed out? By 1924 the question had been answered with a cruel paradox. Russia's revolution had survived and given a mighty impetus to international communism, but in no other country did the workers successfully hold power. At home victory in the civil war silenced the internal voices of reaction, but at a cost that profoundly affected the domestic balance of forces. Workers had been politically crippled *vis à vis* the rest of society. The strategic retreat of the NEP was the domestic reflection of the international deadlock, and so was rightly called 'the peasant Brest', a repeat of the Brest-Litovsk treaty where costly concessions were wrung out of a beleaguered workers' revolution, concessions needed to give that revolution a breathing space. In the absence of international help, the focus of attention switched to internal problems.

Although there were many social groups in NEP Russia apart from the working class – the bureaucracy, urban private sector, rural-urban traders and so on – it was the peasantry, forming the bulk of Russia's population, that now assumed exceptional importance. The peasantry had particular significance for Bukharin, who is credited with being the father of the 'comprehensive doctrine of Bolshevism' based on 'agrarian-cooperative socialism'.[1]

Marxism and the Peasantry

Peasants, as a social group, are a hangover from the prehistory of capitalist society. They pose a problem for Marxism, which focuses on capitalism and the struggle of the modern working class. How do the peasants fit into a world system dominated by the fundamental division between capital and labour? Marx's analysis of the social position of the peasantry was as follows:

> The independent peasant ... is cut up into two persons. As owner of the means of production he is capitalist; as labourer he is his own

wage-labourer. As capitalist he therefore pays himself his wages and draws his profit on his capital; that is to say, he exploits himself as wage-labourer, and pays himself, in the surplus-value, the tribute that labour owes to capital.[2]

According to this view the peasant was neither capitalist or proletarian, but was pulled in both directions. As market relations developed some peasants would grow wealthy while others became poorer. Over time this would lead to a gradual social differentiation, richer peasants tending towards capitalism, poorer peasants towards socialism.

In the last quarter of the nineteenth century Marx's ideas on the peasantry were questioned by the Narodniks in Russia. These revolutionary democrats had hoped to rouse the peasantry to overthrow tsarism, but were crushed by repression. The Narodniks denied the relevance of Marx's view that the peasant was half capitalist, half worker on the grounds that capitalism was barely established in Russia. They thought their country's evolution would be unique. Not only did the tens of millions of peasants easily outnumber all other sections in society, these small rural producers had only emerged from feudalism in 1861, when the institution of serfdom had been abolished. The Narodniks concluded that it was not inevitable that the peasantry would gradually divide into a rural capitalist class and a rural proletariat.

As proof of their contention the Narodniks held up the institution of the *mir*. The word *mir* is often translated as 'land commune'. However, this translation is rather misleading. It is true that the *mir* periodically redistributed land to peasant families, in the form of strips, on a more or less egalitarian basis (often according to the number of heads per family). In this sense the word 'commune' applied. However, once the land had been distributed it was farmed by individual families who kept the product as their own private property. Thus the process of production and distribution was not communal.

The Narodniks hoped that by using the *mir* Russia could pass directly to socialism without undergoing capitalist development. In 1882 they asked Marx and Engels whether they agreed and received this reply:

> The only possible answer to this question today is as follows: If the Russian revolution becomes the signal for the workers' revolution in the West, so that the one supplements the other, then the present form of land ownership in Russia may be the starting-point of an historical development.[3]

A decade later Russian capitalist development was undeniable. But, asked one Narodnik, what would happen if this embryonic capitalism were overthrown in Russia? Could not modern industry be

> grafted on the peasants' commune in a form which would, on the one hand, make the development of that [industry] possible, and on the other hand raise the primitive commune to the rank of a social institution superior to anything the world has yet seen?'

Engels's answer reiterated his previous position: 'the first condition required to bring this about, was the *impulse from without*, the change of economic system in the Occident of Europe, the destruction of the capitalist system in the countries where it had originated.'[4] If peasants had a material incentive (such as acquiring tractors or combine harvesters) to give up individual farming in favour of a more rewarding collective effort, then a direct transition from the *mir* to socialist forms could be completed. Such an incentive would only be offered if workers had taken over industry through revolution.

In the mid-1920s Bukharin would abandon the Marxist view and echo that of the Narodniks, arguing that although they might have been wrong before 1917,

> the 'non-capitalist evolution' that several writers have preached under *capitalism* ('cooperative-agrarian socialism') becomes *reality* under the *dictatorship of the proletariat* ... These cooperative organisations will not 'grow into' capitalism (and in fact, are already 'growing into' something else).[5]

This denied the conventional position that peasants were neither unequivocally the friend nor the foe of the working class. Instead Bukharin said: 'there are two *different* theories before us: according to one, the peasant is an ally; according to the other, the peasant is inevitably an enemy.'[6] Choosing the former, Bukharin concluded that the Russian peasantry was ready to pass over into socialism without any assistance or links with successful workers' revolutions in the West.

However, the productive forces which the peasants needed to establish socialism on their own were entirely lacking. Russian agriculture as a whole was primitive by European standards. The characteristic tool until 1917 was the wooden plough 'as least as old as the Pharaohs'. As late as 1928 it was still used by 5.5 million peasant holdings.[7] This, combined with backward techniques such as strip farming, meant that yields of grain were 'only slightly higher than in fourteenth-century English estates, lower than in fourteenth-century French estates'.[8] The human consequences were terrible. The *mir* may have contained elements of egalitarian land distribution, but the limited impact of such egalitarianism was demonstrated by the position of women in peasant society. Gorky wrote:

> women are nowhere beaten as mercilessly and terribly as in the Russian village; and probably in no other country do proverbs offer such advice. 'Hit your wife with the butt of the axe, get down and see whether she is breathing. If she is shamming, she wants more'. 'A wife is nice twice: when she is brought into the house and when she is carried to the grave.' 'There is no court for old women and cattle.' 'The more you beat the old woman, the tastier the soup will be'.[9]

Peasant life in general was brutalising:

> No doubt 'the vital gold of luxuriant cornfields' is fine in summer, but in the autumn the ragged, bare earth lies before the tiller once again, and again demands yet more hard labour. Then a severe six-month winter sets in, the land is covered in a blinding white shroud, the snowstorms howl fiercely and man gasps from idleness and boredom in his close, dirty hut. Of all that he does there remains on earth only straw and the straw-thatched hut ... The technically primitive labour in the countryside is unbelievably heavy.[10]

1917 and After

In the years before the First World War the tsarist authorities had deliberately accelerated differentiation among the peasantry in the hope of creating a conservative layer of wealthy peasants who would support the regime. By 1917 this process had led to three main strata appearing:

> the poor, living to a considerable extent by the sale of their labour-power, and forced to buy additional food for their requirements; the middle peasants, whose requirements were covered by the products of their farms, and who were able to a limited extent to sell their surplus; and the upper layer – i.e. the rich peasants, the vulture (kulak) class, who systematically bought labour power and sold their agricultural produce on a large scale.[11]

However, this neat categorisation was sometimes difficult to observe in practice, for, as Trotsky explained: 'It is quite unnecessary to point out that these groups are not distinguished by definite symptoms or by homogeneity throughout the country.' Even so differentiation was politically all-important:

> Still on the whole, and generally speaking, the poor peasants represented the natural and undeniable allies of the urban proletariat, while the vulture class represents its just as undeniable and irreconcilable enemies. The most hesitation was principally to be observed amongst the widest, the *middle* sections of the peasantry.[12]

On the eve of the revolution rich peasants numbered 17 million, comprising roughly 15 per cent of the peasantry. They held 37 per cent of peasant land and half the working animals – a vital factor in the pre-tractor age.[13] The rich peasant was known as 'kulak', or 'fist', because he showed 'the hard unflinching cruelty of a thoroughly uneducated man who ... has come to consider money-making, by whatever means, as the only pursuit. [He exhibits the] rapacious and plundering stage of economic development.'[14]

Despite the features common to peasant life in general, differentiation permeated every pore. It was not simply a matter of the size of farm or landownership. Differentiation had to be measured through relations to the means of production in general. Thus exploitation appeared when a rich peasant loaned seed-corn in the spring in return for a portion from the harvest later on, or when terms were set for the loan of a horse. In a situation where millions might lack seed-corn[15] or a horse, and this might mean starvation for a family, the possession of a little surplus grain or an extra animal gave the kulak immense power over his powerless neighbour. The relationship between Henry Ford and his exploited workers dotted around the world has nothing of the *personal* intensity and class bitterness that was engendered here, even though the gap between the kulak and the poor peasant might seem marginal to us.

During the revolution of 1917, the mass of peasants not only seized the nobles' estates, they also dispossessed the hated kulaks and shared their land out on an egalitarian basis. A levelling process occurred which turned the mass of the peasantry into middle peasants (see Table 6.1). Bukharin would see this as proof that the peasants were already moving towards socialism, and that their way back to capitalism was blocked.

However, there was another side to the land redistribution. It fragmented Russian agriculture to an even greater extent than before. The number of separate household farms rose from 14 million to 23 million.[16] But only the development of collective *cultivation*, as opposed to equal *land distribution*, could truly abolish the half-capitalist character of the peasantry. This tendency was actually obstructed by the results of the agrarian revolution. Luxemburg explained why:

> only the nationalisation of the large landed estates, as the technically most advanced and most concentrated means and methods of agrarian production, can serve as the point of departure for the socialist mode of production on the land. Of course, it is not necessary to take away from the small peasant his parcel of land, and we can with confidence leave him to be won over voluntarily by the superior advantages of social production and to be persuaded of the advantages first of union in cooperatives and then finally of industry in the general socialised economy, as a whole. Still, every socialist economic reform on the land must obviously begin with large and medium landownership ... immediate seizure and distribution of the land by the peasants, necessarily tended in the opposite direction. Not only is it not a socialist measure; it even cuts off the way to such measures; it piles up insurmountable obstacles to the socialist transformation of agrarian relations.[17]

Table 6.1: Land distribution in Russia 1917–1920

Size of farm	percentage in 1917	1920
Farms without seed	10.6	4.7
Farms up to 2 dessiatins	30.4	47.9
Farms with 2–4 dessiatins	30.1	31.6
Farms with 4–10 dessiatins	25.2	15.3
Farms with over 10 dessiatins	3.7	0.5

Note: 1 dessiatin = 2.7 acres.
Source: Adapted from L.N. Kritsman, *Die heroische Periode der grossen russischen Revolution*, Frankfurt 1971, page 110.

In truth the Bolsheviks had no choice about distributing the land. They could not have captured power in the towns without mass peasant support, or held power during the civil war. The peasants were taking the land anyway. But Luxemburg was right to point out that redistribution had generated great obstacles in the way of achieving socialist relations in the countryside. There was only one way out – the scenario depicted by Engels. Massive aid by socialist states in the West could help the egalitarian current in the peasantry make a direct transition to a society of abundance, to socialism.

Lenin and the Peasantry

Given the political orientation of the Bolsheviks, it is not surprising that the social compositon of this party was overwhelmingly working class at the time of the revolution. Nonetheless the Bolsheviks clearly had to connect with the mass of Russia's population, even if from the outside. It was Lenin who established the approach:

> the proletariat, after having defeated the bourgeoisie, must unswervingly conduct its policy towards the peasantry along the following fundamental lines. The proletariat must separate, demarcate the working peasants from the peasant owner, the peasant worker from the peasant huckster ...
>
> In this demarcation lies the *whole essence* of socialism ... The demarcation we here refer to is an extremely difficult one, because in real life all the features of the 'peasant', however diverse they may be, however contradictory they may be, are fused into one whole, nevertheless demarcation is possible; and not only is it possible, it inevitably follows from the conditions of peasant farming and peasant life ... Throughout the ages the working peasant has trained himself to hate and loathe these oppressors and exploiters, and this 'training' engendered by the conditions of life, *compels* the peasant to seek an alliance with the worker against the capitalists and against the profiteer and huckster. Yet at the same time, economic conditions, the conditions of commodity production, inevitably turn the peasant (not always, but in the vast majority of cases) into a huckster and profiteer.[18]

Lenin was arguing that even if both sides, exploiter and exploited, were sometimes fused within the same person, nevertheless political strategy had to be based on demarcation among the peasants. The kulak (where the capitalist side was most strongly present) must be fought. The poor peasant (who had most to fear from the return of exploitation) was the natural ally of the Bolsheviks. The middle peasants could be politically neutralised, that is, kept on the side of the socialist government, without forgetting that this stratum differed from that of the workers and could distort its policies.

One feature of Lenin's policy was a belief in the need for a worker-peasant alliance. Bukharin would later claim that this idea emerged at the end of Lenin's life and was proof of his grand new plan for the NEP. In fact, Lenin had always stressed the worker-peasant alliance, declaring in January 1918: 'in Russia only that power could last for any length of time that would be able to unite the working class and the majority of the peasants, all the working and exploited classes, in a single, inseparably interconnected force.'[19] Shortly afterwards he repeated that 'without this alliance it would be senseless to make any attempt to establish power.'[20] His very last article restated this: 'We must strive to build up a state in which the workers retain the leadership of the peasants.'[21]

The fact that Lenin called for a worker – peasant alliance after the Bolshevik revolution did not mean he had changed his views on the basic character of the peasantry. To avoid any misunderstandings on this score, Lenin frequently coupled his appeal for such an alliance with the warning that:

> We have one extremely dangerous secret enemy, more dangerous than many open counter-revolutionaries ... the anarchy of the petty proprietor ... How is it that they cannot see that it is the petty proprietor, small capital, that is our enemy? ... in the transition from capitalism to socialism our chief enemy is the petty-bourgeoisie, its habits and customs, its economic position.[22]

Why was Lenin so afraid of the petty-bourgeois instincts of the peasantry? First, because it would give birth to new capitalists:

> Yes, by overthrowing the landowners and the bourgeoisie we have cleared the way but we did not build the edifice of socialism. On the ground cleared of one bourgeois generation, new generations continually appear in history, as long as the ground gives rise to them, and it does give rise to any number of bourgeois.[23]

Second, as a 'petty-bourgeois peasant country' Russia's small-scale anarchic conditions of production were an obstacle to the collective control and wealth which provides the basis for socialism: 'socialism begins where larger-scale industry begins ... We have said: only these material conditions, the material conditions of large-scale machine industry serving tens of millions of people, only these are the basis of socialism.'[24]

Third, the large-scale capitalist, though still a class enemy, could be controlled and supervised by the centralised power of the workers. The rural petty bourgeoisie, in millions of atomised farms stretching over a 7,000 mile expanse, offered no such possibilities.

Lenin's fears of the peasantry did not disappear with the NEP, as Bukharin suggested. In 1922 Lenin told the Eleventh Party Congress:

> Permit me to say this to you without exaggeration, [we are fighting] 'the last and decisive battle' ... against Russian capitalism, against the capitalism that is growing out of the small-peasant economy, the

capitalism that is fostered by the latter, here we shall have a fight on our hands, in the immediate future, and the date of it cannot be fixed exactly, here the 'last and decisive battle' is impending; here there are no political or any other flanking movements that we can undertake.[25]

Was Lenin illogical when he talked simultaneously of alliance and 'decisive battle' with the peasants? No, the inner coherence of his view was shown on a number of occasions. During the civil war, victory against the Whites would have been impossible without peasant support; they formed 77.4 per cent of the Red Army.[26] But that army could not have been fed without abrogating the peasants' system of exchange and requisitioning their grain. Under the NEP, the need for a policy which took account of the peasantry's ambiguous class position and various levels of differentiation was even greater, because the peasantry became much more influential in society.

To sum up: Lenin's approach combined a consistent analysis of the peasantry's class structure with the political needs of the Bolshevik government. It was important that political expediency did not outweigh a Marxist understanding of the potential dangers that the peasantry posed. Thus, he specifically warned against his concept of the worker – peasant alliance being misinterpreted:

> Agreement between the working class and the peasantry may be taken to mean anything. Unless we assume that, from the working-class standpoint, an agreement is possible in principle, permissible and correct only if it supports the dictatorship of the working class and is one of the measures aimed at the abolition of classes, then, of course, it remains a formula on which all the enemies of the Soviet power, all the enemies of the dictatorship, operate.[27]

Bukharin and the Peasantry

Alas, the way Bukharin supported the worker – peasant alliance under the NEP would be one which allowed the enemies of soviet power to take advantage. His position before 1921 had been radically different. In *The Communist Programme* of 1919, he discussed the consequences of dividing the land among Russia's 23 million separate peasant holdings:

> Imagine what a Babel would ensue if these ... began acting independently! What chaos and anarchy we should have! Nor would it be surprising if such groups began, independently of each other, to

usurp the wealth of the rich, nothing but a sharing out would result. And sharing out leads, as we have seen above, to the reign of capital all over again, to violence and oppression of the labouring masses.[28]

What alternative did the *Programme* offer to redistribution?

> the plan of dividing or sharing the land offers us no way out of the dilemma. The only solution is in a communal national holding of land; in land being declared the common property of the labourers ... But that is not enough. We must aim at such an arrangement as would ensure the land being not only owned in common, but also being cultivated in common. If that is not done, then no matter what you proclaim or whatever laws you publish, the result will be most unsatisfactory ... Common cultivation of the soil – is what should be aimed at.[29]

Although common cultivation was an aim; it did *not* mean forced collectivisation. No Bolshevik, not even Stalin at that time, would have dreamt of such a monstrous proposition.

In *The Communist Programme* Bukharin's argument pointed to an ultraleft rejection of land redistribution and implied criticism of Lenin's aim of neutralising the middle peasants with an alliance:

> Our task therefore does not at all consist in making every peasant a manager of his own small allotment, but in making the poorer peasants join a common scheme of work on the largest possible scale ... by co-operative cultivation of what were formerly big estates ... But it is not enough to preserve the estates of former landowners and cultivate them on new principles. We must strive to organise large joint agricultural labour communes by uniting separate allotments.[30]

This was advocated as an immediate policy. Referring to the critical food situation in February 1919 he proposed:

> decisive steps in the direction of large-scale socialised production ... Already in the *Communist Manifesto* Marx included in his transitional measures a suggestion for the organisation of an agricultural army of workers for the socialised working of the land. Now when the working class goes hungry [and] is threatened with dispersal and dissolution into the petty-bourgeois mass, the organisation of collective state production on the land is ... more necessary than ever.[31]

Again it must be stressed that there was no idea of physically forcing peasants into collective farms as Stalin would later do.

Although Bukharin was ultra-left at this time, there was also an element of continuity with his later right-wing position. When the Bolsheviks debated the new party programme at the 1919 party congress, Bukharin argued that historical development had reached a point where there could be no revival of an earlier, more primitive stage of capitalism. The clock could not be turned back. A uniform system of imperialism dominated the world and so there was no possibility of an old-style market-based capitalism. The choice was between socialism or imperialism. In socialist Russia, therefore, the petty bourgeoisie and peasantry could not regenerate capitalism. In debate with Lenin he declared:

> To regard the peasant of today as a commodity producer, or as one who feeds off the soil of decomposing large-scale capitalism ... does not mean that he serves as a basis for the renewal of capitalism. To put things in such a way would suggest that the perspective of socialist revolution was unreal.
>
> It is a fact that these phenomena exist and are developing, but it is not true that they will lead towards the recreation of capitalist relations. We must see them not as the starting point for a new cycle of capitalist development, not as the embryo of an unavoidable rebirth of large-scale capitalism, but as a process showing the disintegration of the old capitalist forms, which will not lead to the re-establishment of new capitalist forms, but expresses the break-up of the old which must be taken forward to new forms of socialist organisation of communal economy.[32]

Lenin's reply to Bukharin was that it was a mistake to see capitalism as a single homogeneous entity which everywhere was moving through the same life-cycle from birth, through maturity, to old age and death. It developed unevenly from place to place. How else could one explain features of its birth (the rising petty bourgeoisie and differentiation among peasants) coexisting with elements of its imperialist decay (proletarian dictatorship)? How else could one explain 'such a category as a middle peasant in the era of pure imperialist capitalism ... this almost medieval phenomenon?' To the author of *The ABC of Communism* he pointed out, ironically:

> this is the ABC of capitalism of which we must speak, because we have not yet grown out of it. To brush this aside and say, 'Why should we study the ABC when we have studied finance capitalism?' would be highly frivolous.[33]

Bukharin stuck to his guns, and by the mid-1920s it was an article of faith for him that the peasants could not lead to the rebirth of capitalism. Any tendencies in that direction were simply proof of the decay of larger-scale operations. At worst the peasants would remain as simple commodity producers who exploited no-one; at best they would gravitate towards socialist forms of production over a protracted period. His reasoning was as follows:

> under a capitalist regime the whole mechanism of society drives towards the maximum tempo of differentiation among the peasants through decomposition of the middle peasants. But because we have nationalised the land the essence of the situation is that no such differentiation can take place.[34]

The legal formula of nationalisation, which prohibited the buying and selling of land, was taken to prove that all exploitative relations were excluded. This was a far cry from the *Communist Programme* of 1919, which declared that without common cultivation 'no laws from above would be of any use.'[35]

Moreover, Bukharin placed a Great Wall of China between simple commodity production and capitalist production:

> We must sharply distinguish the private economy in the country and the private-capitalist economy ... Not all private economic units are capitalist economic units. For example, the farms of the rural poor peasants and middle peasants, which do not employ paid labour, are part of the private economy, but not part of the capitalist economy.[36]

There was an element of truth in this distinction between simple commodity production and capitalist commodity production. For Marx, simple commodity production occurred when goods were exchanged not to make a profit, but to obtain other articles of consumption that the peasant family could not produce itself. Here exchange was not part of a process of exploitation. By contrast, under capitalist production there was exploitation. It took place through the labour process, during which surplus value was generated. Through exchange (selling the products) the capitalist realised this surplus value in the form of profits. Bukharin argued that, as peasants did not employ wage labour, capitalism and its accompanying exploitation were absent.

Nevertheless, Bukharin's arguments were insufficient to prove his case. While a theoretical distinction could be made between simple commodity production and capitalist production, it was not so sharply defined in practice. Bukharin implied that capitalism could only arise among

Russia's peasants if one group monopolised the means of production (through private ownership of land) and when there was wage labour. Experience in the West showed that capitalism could develop in diverse ways. In Britain, for example, capitalism only came to depend on a monopoly of the means of production and extensive wage labour when the factory system was established towards the end of the eighteenth century. This was a relatively late stage, coming after the bourgeois revolution of 1642, when capitalists gained political influence. The putting-out system, prevalent in British textile production before the factory system, was another example of how capitalism could grow up. Here the exploited domestic workers owned part of the means of production – spinning wheels, looms and so on. They were not paid wages as such, but paid for the finished articles they made. The trader only provided the raw materials and collected the final product for sale.

By the mid-1920s, then, Bukharin treated the peasantry as if it was a single mass out of which no threat could emerge to socialism. In 1920 his position had been less simplistic. In criticism of a Menshevik manifesto then he had written:

> They talk about compromise with the peasants. But which peasants do they suggest compromise with, and what sort of compromise? There is no concern here with the *poor* peasants, but with the *rich* who want to speculate with bread, to get rich from hunger, to strangle the urban workers and exploit their needs.[37]

So far only the theoretical bases for Bukharin's dramatic shift from left to right have been considered. It is now time to see how this was put into practice.

7 The Hammer of Trotskyism

Until recently historians, from both East and West, have seen the political background to the Five-Year Plans and forced collectivisation in terms of a fight between Trotsky's left opposition and the Stalin faction. Marketeers, however, require a fundamental reappraisal of this approach which gives them an honourable role in the party's internal struggles. This is where Bukharin comes in handy. His disagreement with Stalin in 1928–9 is used to dismiss the Trotsky – Stalin battle as shadow-boxing between two nearly identical groupings.

There was, according to the pro-market position, only one authentic anti-Stalin platform in the Bolshevik Party. This was 'the "Bukharinite alternative" which, both in terms of its premises and principle conclusions, has been justified by all the subsequent experience of social development'.[1] Bukharin is claimed to have provided the 'historical alternative to the arbitrary Stalinist system' because:

> The theoretical attitude of Bukharin can, without exaggeration, be characterised as consistent and uncompromising anti-bureaucratism. It must be stressed that both the political positions and theoretical views of Bukharin were orientated towards supporting and developing the creative initiative of the mass of labouring people in the country and the democratisation of society.[2]

This is nonsense, frankly. Stalin excepted, Bukharin was the individual who contributed most to the rise of the Stalinist system. He vied with the general secretary for the role of witchfinder-general, hunting down all internal opposition and defending the ruling bureaucracy from heresy. Bukharin's behaviour was not an accidental blemish on an otherwise pristine political physiognomy, but followed directly from his own political views. This is made clear in the following attempt at an apology for his actions:

> Stalin's faithful henchman' is correct as a description of Bukharin's role, but mainly insofar as he helped Stalin and was used by him to destroy the left-wing opposition. There are no laurels to be granted him for this performance, but it is important to emphasize that in the fields of theory and political strategy Bukharin was never Stalin's

mouthpiece. Insofar as thinking on internal and general policies were concerned, the theoretical basis for the strategies he defended were his own.[3]

In other words Bukharin was not duped; he assisted Stalin for his own motives and with his eyes wide open.

Making the Choice

The fight between Trotsky and Stalin began at the end of 1923 in the party's top institution, the Politburo. Bukharin was outside that body until Lenin's death created a vacancy in 1924. Which side would he take? His view of the NEP and the peasantry opened avenues towards the right; yet his warnings against bureaucracy in *Proletarian Revolution and Culture*, written at the same time, pointed left, as did his previous record.

In October 1922 Bukharin seemed to be moving rightwards. When Sokolnikov, the commissar of finance, proposed relaxing the state monopoly of foreign trade, Bukharin backed him, because, as Carr puts it: 'having sought to carry war communism to its logical conclusions and stood at that time on the extreme Left, [Bukharin] now applied the same thirst for logical consistency to NEP' and argued for free trade.[4] It was the incapacitated Lenin who sounded the alarm against this move, asking Trotsky to take up the cudgels on his behalf. Lenin's objection was that freeing foreign trade would lead to private capitalist growth quite outside government regulation and directly linked to international capital. This would be a social and political danger, as well as depriving the state of control over imports and exports, one of the few levers it had to assist the growth of industry. According to Lenin, Bukharin attached 'no importance to the fact that the peasants will enter into profitable transactions'; he concluded that:

> In practice, Bukharin is acting as an advocate of the profiteer, of the petty bourgeois and of the upper stratum of the peasantry in opposition to the industrial proletariat, which will be totally unable to build up its own industry and make Russia an industrial country unless it has the protection ... of the monopoly of foreign trade.[5]

The proposal to weaken the state's monopoly was eventually dropped.

Then, in April 1923, Bukharin took a leftwards direction. It was he, not Trotsky, who fired the first shots in the struggle against Stalin. The general secretary had been abusing his position by compelling the Georgians to fit in with his new constitutional structure for the USSR.

He called their resistance 'local chauvinism'. Stalin's policy amounted to restoring the old oppression by Russia over the smaller nationalities. Although Lenin was furious with Stalin, he was too ill to fight and appealed to Trotsky to speak for him. Trotsky was wary about beginning an open struggle at this point, so the task fell to Bukharin. At the Twelfth Party Congress Bukharin abandoned his old position on the national question and told the delegates:

> The essence of the Leninist attitude to the national question involves in the first place struggle against *the basic* chauvinism, which in our case is Great Russian chauvinism. Comrade Stalin has told us quite correctly that nine tenths of the problem consists of Great Russian chauvinism, but one tenth is local chauvinism. We must give a clear response to that, comrades. If we had not carried out an incorrect Great Russian chauvinist line, then as night follows day, we would not have had the expression of a whole number of local chauvinisms.[6]

In other words, it was Stalin, not the Georgians, who was the real threat to a socialist unity. Such unity had to be freely chosen if it was to be worth anything.

In late 1923 Trotsky began a campaign for inner-party democracy. At the plenum of the Central Committee and Central Control Commission, Trotsky revealed the existence of a 'troika', composed of Zinoviev, Kamenev and Stalin, which manipulated the party. Many expected Bukharin to back Trotsky. Indeed the latter felt obliged to deny that he had engaged with Bukharin in conspiratorial methods similar to those of the 'troika'.[7] It seems the first public statement of the Trotskyist left opposition, the 'Declaration of the 46', had a space left open for Bukharin to append his signature. His entire circle of past allies had already signed.[8]

Alas, those who looked to Bukharin as a champion of the left were soon disabused. The first sign of the path he would choose was revealed in the argument over 'Lenin's Testament'. Bukharin's supporters have stressed his close personal relationship with Lenin and the fact that they were together in his final hours.[9] This, it is said, made him the true apostolic successor to Lenin. Bukharin himself claimed this role with his article entitled 'Lenin's Testament' in 1929. Given the disgusting sycophancy that surrounded the name of Lenin after his death, this assertion was useful. The truth was different. As editor of *Pravda*, Bukharin held back publication of one of Lenin's last articles attacking bureaucracy and only published it under duress. Furthermore, at the joint meeting of the Politburo and Central Committee praesidium that discussed publicising Lenin's *real* testament (which demanded that Stalin be removed as general secretary because of his crude bureaucratic manner), Bukharin voted to suppress it. Only Trotsky opposed this move.[10]

When Trotsky went into print over party democracy with his 'New Course' articles in *Pravda* in December 1923, they were countered on the very same page by an anonymous series entitled 'Down with Factionalism'. No-one could have guessed from the content of this series that it was by Bukharin. He had, after all, been very insistent on the importance of workers' democracy. In 1918 he had warned:

> Once and for all, the bureaucratism that is already engulfing our soviet institutions must be destroyed; once and for all, in order to safeguard against the further growth of this bureaucratism, we must infuse soviet organs with the maximum influence of workers' organisations. If soviet power lies in one place, but workers' organisations somewhere else, it will be crippled by the most accursed bureaucratism and ultimately doomed.[11]

It was Bukharin who coined this immortal phrase: 'the history of humanity is divided into three periods: the matriarchate, the patriarchate, and the Secretariat.'[12] In June 1923 Bukharin appealed for local initiatives to take precedence over centralised commands on the grounds that 'We have cells developing from below' and they must be free from 'the dead hand of bureaucracy'.[13] As late as the Thirteenth Congress, in May 1924, Trotsky could quote a recent speech by Bukharin which was devastating in its criticism of the bureaucracy for having 'eliminated the internal life of the party'.[14]

'Down with Factionalism' presented a completely different attitude towards democracy. It radically revised Bolshevism's previous history. Now, Bukharin claimed that instead of democratic centralism, there had only ever been two choices before the party: either it was an absolute monolith or a loose and ineffectual federation. Bukharin had no doubt which approach he favoured: 'What was the *organisational principle* of the Bolshevik party? This party, our party, was always distinct because of its monolithic unity.'[15] In practice such monolithic unity could only be achieved by the top echelons dictating party decisions. Inner-party life would be reduced to the issuing of orders from above. Without saying this clearly, Bukharin drew the logical conclusion. He accepted that constructive criticisms of bureaucratic tendencies were useful, but insisted that:

Bolshevism has always and still does value highly the *party apparatus* ... because the party is *nothing* without the apparatus ... The *party leadership*, the central authorities of the party have always fulfilled an important role in inner-party matters. Bolsheviks have never played at formal, *hollow* democratism which always hides lack of principle. Lenin taught that we should value the authority of the basic cadres, those who had accumulated the greatest experience in struggle.[16]

Democracy was no longer Bukharin's 'sacred slogan'; it was a positive menace: 'the opposition only sees one danger – that of bureaucracy. Fearing the bureaucratic danger they are blind to the risks of political democracy. That is Menshevism.'[17]

Much of 'Down with Factionalism' was devoted to criticising Trotsky's past. He had 'deviated' from the correct line over Brest-Litovsk and the trade union debate. Max Eastman, who first brought news of the dispute to Western readers, pointed out that Bukharin needed the cloak of anonymity to raise such issues. At that stage it would hardly have been credible for the author of *The Economics of the Transition Period* and militarisation of the party to denounce ultra-leftism and war communist attitudes: 'For instead of a history of "the errors of Trotsky and other comrades" it would be a history of the errors of *Trotsky and I*', and 'it is obvious that such a history would not conclude with the rather pious statement that: "Our present divergences with Comrade Trotsky ... have always existed"!'[18]

How did Bukharin, even in anonymity, get away with this distortion of the party's past? Alas, the Bolshevik Party at the end of 1923 barely resembled that of 1917. Only 10 per cent of members were actually 'workers at the bench' and only 2 per cent had joined before 1917.[19] The 'Lenin levy' – mass recruitment in 1924 – was going to dilute further the influence of the revolutionary socialists with the enlistment of people who had dubious motives for joining the sole party of government. One Bolshevik wrote an article which explained why the party under the NEP was fundamentally different from the working-class party of 1917:

> It is extremely difficult to have real party unity [as opposed to monolithic unity] when there is only one legal party in the country but there are many different economic structures. On this latter point no-one would dispute that we have within our economy economic sectors where capitalist enterprises play an active role. In that situation, while the party may remain formally united, in practice

in its ranks there will be those who defend all the different interests in the country including those of capitalist enterprises.[20]

The Bolshevik Party, therefore, was now a battleground on which different class groupings fought for their positions.

'Down with Factionalism' was merely the opening salvo in Bukharin's political war. As Carr suggests, Bukharin

> threw himself *con amore* into the campaign ... But for the fact that these events were the prelude to Bukharin's own ruin, and made him the author of his own fearful punishment, it would be impossible to acquit him of an important share in any condemnation that may fall on Stalin's treatment of the opposition: for he was a self-proclaimed accomplice in everything that Stalin did at this time.[21]

Within a short time Bukharin and Stalin had formed an alliance based on a strict division of labour. The former possessed all the qualities of popularity, political brilliance and oratorical wit that Stalin, a cunning and manipulative administrator but clumsily inept in ideological matters, lacked. Serge's description of Bukharin highlights his talents:

> His mind was effervescent, always alert and active, but rigorously disciplined. The high forehead, slightly turned-up nose, chestnut-brown moustache and small beard – all made him look just like the average Russian, and his careless manner of dress completed the picture ... He was habitually surrounded by crowds of smiling young listeners, who drank in all his incisive observations.[22]

As Trotsky demonstrated, the different skills of Bukharin and Stalin were complementary to each other:

> It is not by chance that the thoroughly cynical empiricism of Stalin and the passion of Bukharin for playing with generalizations marched side by side for a relatively long period. Stalin acted under the influence of direct social collisions, Bukharin, with his little finger, set heaven and hell into motion in order to justify the new zig-zag. Stalin regarded Bukharin's generalisations as an unavoidable evil. In his heart, he believed as before that there was no reason to get excited over theoretical 'storms in a teacup'. But ideas in a certain sense live their own life. Interests become fastened to ideas. Basing themselves upon interests, ideas weld people together.[23]

Stalin readily showed his appreciation of Bukharin. Defending his ally at the Fourteenth Congress, Stalin said: 'You demand the blood of

Bukharin? We shall not give you that blood, be sure of that ... We stand, and shall stand for Bukharin'.[24] At the Fifteenth Congress Bukharin launched a scathing attack on the opposition in these terms: 'How dare you defame Soviet Russia! How dare you still persist in that reactionary course ... How dare you shout about us heading to Thermidor! How dare you cry out that we are causing degeneration!' Stalin interjected: 'Well done, Bukharin, well done. He does not speak, he slashes.'[25]

Bukharin may not have relished his role entirely. When Zinoviev began the first moves to expel Trotsky from the party, Bukharin voted against and was accused of being 'semi-Trotskyist'.[26] Answering Trotsky's gibe that he had 'acquired the taste' for repression, Bukharin wrote: 'You think that I have "acquired the taste", but this "taste" makes me tremble from head to foot.'[27] Trembling or not, he repeatedly stooped to the political gutter. In 1927 the unequal struggle approached its conclusion with the repression of the opposition and Trotsky's exile. At this point Bukharin's language became even more virulent:

> Comrades, our opposition group is headed by Comrade Trotsky, Trotsky, who denies he was a Menshevik from 1904, Trotsky whose view it is that Bolshevism armed itself only in 1917, Trotsky who nurses the deepest distrust of the alliance of the working class and peasantry. This group is fighting a struggle against the party ... we have, in reality, a group that will open the door to the greatest enemies of the proletarian dictatorship. Not only do you forget our party, not only do you trample our party underfoot, but at the same time you open the door to the anti-Soviet powers. Your growth would be the greatest misfortune and evil for us, the greatest disaster for our land ... I would say that never in the entire history of our party, has anyone opposed our party as Trotsky has.[28]

These charges bore an uncanny resemblance to those levelled against Bukharin himself in 1938. There are other parallels. At the Fifteenth Congress in December 1927, Christian Rakovsky, one of the last oppositionists still free to speak, warned that the party was under bitter 'ideological fire'. Bukharin broke in to shout: 'You are the one being shot at' and under a hail of abuse Rakovsky was silenced.[29] Rakovsky stood with Bukharin in the dock at the 1938 trial.

Four Theories of Revolution in Russia

To destroy a political tradition forged in the fire of revolution and war, Bukharin had to work carefully. He did not begin with a head-on confrontation on current policy, but with the past. An opportunity came with the publication of Trotsky's *Lessons of October* in 1924. Bukharin's first accusation was remarkable: Trotsky had the temerity to talk about the lessons of October! This, said Bukharin, proved that Trotsky was desperately trying to divert attention away from the time when he was close to the Mensheviks. In any case, a pamphlet on *The Lessons of October* was superfluous since 'this period has been brilliantly evaluated in the Collected Works of Lenin',[30] and no more need be said.

It would be a mistake to conclude from such arguments that Bukharin was always crude. His method was often surgical, logical and scholastic. He isolated Trotsky's theory of permanent revolution as his most vulnerable spot because it was a theory that Lenin had rejected. Developed around 1905, Trotsky's theory sought to map out the political tactics for socialists operating in the backward economic conditions of tsarist Russia. Permanent revolution broke with the 'vulgar Marxist' viewpoint that society develops in fixed and complete stages – slavery to feudalism, feudalism to capitalism and capitalism to socialism. He began with the fact that in Russia features of both feudalism and capitalism coexisted, because it had 'the most concentrated industry in Europe based on the most backward agriculture in Europe'.[31] Under these circumstances social revolution would not mean a smooth transition from semi-feudal tsarist Russia to an advanced capitalist society. Any revolution that occurred would constitute a challenge to both landowners and bourgeoisie at the same time. Therefore the bourgeoisie would not dare to initiate a major social transformation itself.

Although the capitalists would not attempt to smash the old feudal relations, the peasants had an interest in doing so. However, they lacked the social cohesion required to lead an independent movement. They would be led by the proletariat. Trotsky's theory did not deny the bourgeois character and tendencies of a peasant revolutionary movement, but he stressed the potential for working-class action at such a time:

> So far as its direct and indirect tasks are concerned, the Russian revolution is a 'bourgeois' revolution because it sets out to liberate bourgeois society from the chains and fetters of absolutism and feudal ownership. But the principal driving force of the Russian revolution is the proletariat, and that is why, so far as its method is concerned, it is a proletarian revolution.[32]

Permanent revolution cut across the Second International view that economic development – the overall level of the productive forces in the country – was the absolutely determining factor in political development. Trotsky showed that 'the day and the hour when power will pass into the hands of the working class depends directly not upon the level attained by the productive forces but upon relations in the class struggle.'[33] This did not mean that the economic backwardness (and consequently small working class alongside a massive peasantry), had no impact in the long run. The victorious proletariat would certainly 'come up against political obstacles [or] stumble over the technical backwardness of the country'. Trotsky concluded that:

> *Without the direct State support of the European proletariat the working class of Russia cannot remain in power and convert its temporary domination into a lasting socialistic dictatorship.* Of this there cannot for one moment be any doubt. But on the other hand there cannot be any doubt that a socialist revolution in the West will enable us directly to convert the temporary domination of the working class into a socialist dictatorship.[34]

International revolution was the key to solving otherwise insurmountable internal problems.

There were other socialist theories about Russian development. At the opposite end of the scale to Trotsky were the Mensheviks, who argued that history proceeds through rigidly separate stages. They contended that in Russia a capitalist stage must precede the socialist one, and the job of Marxists was to allow capitalism to grow as quickly as possible.

Between these two viewpoints lay Lenin's theory. Where Trotsky saw a merging of bourgeois and proletarian revolutions, and the Mensheviks saw sharply separate stages, Lenin, until 1917, argued a middle position. He believed the revolution would proceed by stages. However, the first stage would not be a capitalist regime but a 'democratic dictatorship of proletariat and peasantry'. Lenin took this view because, like Trotsky, he had contempt for the feebleness of the Russian bourgeoisie who would never dare to put a complete end to feudalism. For this to happen would require a revolution from below by the mass of people. But Lenin rejected the notion of permanent revolution. He wrote that the 'democratic revolution will not immediately overstep the bounds of bourgeois social and economic relationships'; it 'will not weaken but strengthen the domination of the bourgeoisie'.[35] Nevertheless, unlike the Mensheviks, Lenin did not expect the stages to be strictly separated in time:

from the democratic revolution we shall at once, and precisely in accordance with the measure of our strength, the strength of the class conscious and organised proletariat, begin to pass to the socialist revolution. We stand for the uninterrupted revolution. We shall not stop half way.[36]

It was the level of struggle that would decide how quickly one stage gave way to the next. Progress from the bourgeois to a proletarian regime would be helped by international revolution and by splitting the peasantry into two halves, with workers carrying the 'semi-proletarian' section with them.

Lenin spelt out his view of the relations between the democratic dictatorship and proletarian stages in these terms. First, 'The proletariat must carry out the democratic [bourgeois] revolution to completion, allying to itself the mass of the peasantry in order to crush the autocracy's resistance by force and to paralyse the bourgeoisie's instability.' Next, 'The proletariat must accomplish the socialist revolution allying to itself the mass of the semi-proletarian elements of the population so as to crush the bourgeoisie's resistance by force and paralyse the instability of the peasantry and petty bourgeoisie'.[37]

Bukharin's viewpoint changed when the factional debate broke out in 1924. During the First World War he had reached the conclusion that a revolution in Russia would be socialist.[38] On occasions he even used the term 'permanent revolution' to describe the process.[39] The existence of a world economy and imperialism rendered all previous social formations politically obsolete. This meant there would be no stages leading up to the socialist revolution and no possible merging of bourgeois and proletarian revolutions. The Russian revolution would be purely socialist. This version of permanent revolution had little in common with Trotsky's. As the latter wrote:

> Naturally, I never shared the Bukharinist version of the theory of the 'permanent' revolution, according to which no interruptions, periods of stagnation, retreats, transitional demands, or the like are at all conceivable in the revolutionary process. On the contrary, from the first days of October, I fought against this caricature of the permanent revolution.[40]

As 1917 unfolded, each of the four theories was put to the test. The Menshevik version failed first. It was not the bourgeoisie but the workers backed by 'peasants in uniform' who toppled the tsar. Next the theory of democratic dictatorship proved false. Lenin implicitly recognised this in his *April Theses*, when he wrote that since February 1917 the revolution had taken the form of struggle by workers' soviets against the Provisional Government. The choice was not for a democratic dictatorship of proletariat *and* peasantry, but between dictatorship by the proletariat (assisted by the peasants) or defeat of the entire revolution. When the Bolsheviks won power for the soviets in October 1917 and dissolved the bourgeois democratic Constituent Assembly, this confirmed that Trotsky's theory of permanent revolution was correct.

Trotsky's theory was vindicated again when the last alternative — that of Bukharin — had failed the test of events. If Bukharin had been right, and the Russian revolution had been a straightforward proletarian revolution, then the lack of immediate international revolution should have led to its rapid submersion in a sea of imperialist and petty-bourgeois hostility. This did not happen. Instead there had been a fusion of bourgeois and proletarian revolutions, as Trotsky had predicted. This was demonstrated in the civil war. The workers' state was able to survive because a major demand of the bourgeois revolution — land to the peasants — had been achieved under its leadership, and the peasants were ready to sacrifice much to protect this achievement from the Whites.

If Trotsky's theory was confirmed by history, it was never officially accepted within the Bolshevik Party itself. Lenin, for example, had come to accept permanent revolution in practice, but he never publicly repudiated the idea of 'democratic dictatorship'. This helped Bukharin, who, in December 1924, made a lengthy speech proclaiming that the 'democratic dictatorship of proletariat and peasantry' was the only authentic Bolshevik viewpoint. He contrasted it with permanent revolution, which 'misses out all the *intermediary stages* [between bourgeois and proletarian revolutions]; the separate steps in the revolution during which different classes fulfil their tasks and one replaces another requiring *specific* tactics from us which are adapted to each stage'.[41]

Bukharin's argument was double-edged. When he used it in the context of the 1925–7 Chinese revolution it meant turning the political clock back, not just to the pre-1917 Bolshevik position but to the Menshevik view that capitalism must be given full rein before the struggle for socialism could begin. In Russia Bukharin's argument was used in the opposite way and linked neatly with his old ultra-left stance. The USSR, Bukharin said, had completed its passage through *all* the necessary stages. The bourgeois revolution was over and quite finished. The new socialist stage had been reached and it alone determined developments in Russia. 'Trotsky', he said, 'had not noticed *the stage* at which our bourgeois revolution *grew over* into a socialist proletarian one.'[42]

This argument dovetailed with Bukharin's view of the peasants. To suggest, in an unambiguously socialist Russia, that some peasants might develop in a bourgeois direction was, to him, a gross insult. But it was precisely Trotsky's theory which best combined the ambivalent character of the peasants with the development of the Russian revolution. It showed why the October revolution possessed such overwhelming force in a predominantly peasant country. At the same time it explained all the contradictions that the revolution had faced from that moment onwards.

Although Bukharin attacked Trotsky in the name of defending Leninist orthodoxy, he was in fact introducing an entirely new way of thinking. Lenin had never argued that Russia was unambiguously socialist, that is to say, it did not have just a socialist political leadership but a socialist economy and society too. Bukharin's distorted use of the old 'democratic dictatorship of proletariat and peasantry' formula was used to suggest that if Russia had reached socialism irrespective of the level of the productive forces, and irrespective of the class composition of the majority of the population, then *socialism in one country* was possible irrespective of the world situation. This brought him into line with Stalin, who had the doubtful honour of creating this theory.

Socialism in One Country

The theory of socialism in one country was introduced by Stalin in a revision of his pamphlet on *The Foundations of Leninism*. The original, written in May 1924, read:

> Can we succeed and secure the definitive victory of Socialism in one country without the combined efforts of the proletarians of several advanced countries? Most certainly not. The efforts of a single country are enough to overthrow the bourgeoisie: this is what the history of our revolution proves. But for the definitive triumph of Socialism, the organisation of Socialist production, the efforts of one country alone are not enough, particularly of an essentially rural country like Russia; the efforts of the proletarians of several advanced countries are needed.'[43]

Seven months later Stalin changed this to state: 'Formerly, the victory of the revolution in one country was considered impossible ... Now this point of view no longer fits with the facts ... The history of the revolution in Russia is direct proof of this.'[44]

Stalin's theory both reflected and reinforced the feeling of resignation and loss of faith in international revolution produced by exhaustion and the failure of the 1923 German revolution. A conversation at the Dynamo factory in Moscow reported by Bukharin in 1926 summed up this mood:

> One comrade said: 'How can a country as poverty-stricken as ours possibly cope [on our own]?' but another answered: 'If we had known earlier that we would not be able to cope with our tasks, then why the devil did we make the October revolution in the first place? If we have coped for eight years already, why can't we manage in the ninth, the tenth or the fortieth for that matter?'

Bukharin's comment on this was: 'I think that this is an absolutely correct way of posing the issue.'[45]

Bukharin played a key role in ideologically preparing the way for the theory of socialism in one country and popularising it afterwards. As with his sudden turn against democratic centralism in 'Down with Factionalism', this must have come as a shock to those who had thought they knew his politics. His previous writings had pointed to exactly the opposite conclusions. The first two paragraphs of his well-known history of the Russian revolution, *From the Overthrow of Tsarism to the Fall of the Bourgeoisie*, have already been quoted in part. He had said: 'the final victory of the Russian revolution is inconceivable without the victory of international revolution ... A lasting victory of the Russian socialist proletariat is impossible without proletarian revolution in Europe.'[46] The last two paragraphs repeat: 'The great October revolution ... must immediately draw in the West European proletariat ... The Russian socialist revolution ... lives. It is spreading. And it is uniting directly with the great and victorious uprising of the world proletariat.'[47]

Yet from 1924 onwards Bukharin turned this argument on its head and he adopted the theory of socialism in one country. Henceforth this theory was incorporated into every argument that Bukharin put forward. For example, it shaped his understanding of the NEP: 'If you define NEP only as a retreat', he wrote, 'this is tied to the idea that socialism in one country is impossible ... The one and the other are closely linked.'[48] So defending the NEP meant accepting socialism in one country. When Bukharin said that property rights defined social relations, and that 'socialist' (that is, state) industry was expanding, then it followed that socialism was growing in one country. If the peasantry was united in a close alliance with the Bolsheviks, then why worry about assistance from an international revolution?

It was Bukharin's job to employ his scholastic skills to conceal the break with Marxism that the theory of socialism in one country involved. He did this in a pamphlet of 1925 called *The Present Period and the Basis of Our Policies*. This began by sowing confusion over the very word socialism:

> In the first place, what does the 'victory of socialism' mean? This would seem to be a simple question, but in fact it is not. One interpretation is that it should be understood as the act of conquering power by the working class. Once this is achieved we have socialism. A second interpretation might be that victory is to be found when a regime of proletarian dictatorship is more or less consolidated. Again, a third view might be that the final victory of socialism is found when absolutely no danger remains to threaten it, when socialism has become a fully developed form. In essence we know very little about what this fully developed socialism would be like. Marx and Engels wrote that we can only know the direction of march, but little of what the eventual goal will be.[49]

Bukharin's argument was inadequate. Socialism was not some beauty contest in which various stages lined up to win the coveted title of 'Socialism Class 1'. Socialism was not encompassed by the opening stage of the seizure of power, nor by the state structure it established, nor by the fact that this regime might become ultimately secure.

It is true that Marx and Engels rejected a rigid blueprint, but they clearly saw socialism as a general social system (rather than a type of government) and discerned tendencies within capitalism which suggested the lines it might take. They witnessed the possibilities opened up by the growth of the productive forces and the associated development of a collective class of exploited producers. They concluded that socialism would be based on the rule of workers over advanced industry which would abolish classes and exploitation. This was not the reality in Russia, with its backward peasant-dominated economy and bureaucratically deformed workers' state. Marx and Engels saw that the global scale of capitalist operations meant that socialism would come through international struggle and that its economy would depend on a worldwide division of labour. Proletarian internationalism, not autonomous national development, was essential for overthrowing capitalism and constructing a genuinely socialist society. Marx and Engels's most famous statement – 'Workers of the world, unite!' – was the outcome of this understanding. It ran directly counter to the theory of socialism in one country.

The Present Period and the Basis of Our Policies equated the attainment of socialism with issues of state or national security. The immediate tactics of the conquest and maintenance of power were thus divorced from the vision of socialist society (its 'fully developed form'). It has already been shown that means and ends are dialectically related. It is therefore impossible to discover the means without some sense of what the end goal should be. Bukharin denied this. In his *Economics of the Transition Period* the end had been everything and the means – whatever had been 'technically expedient'. Now Bukharin reversed the equation. In doing so he performed the same service for the Russian bureaucracy as Bernstein had done for the German social democrats before the First World War. The means became everything and the end – the abolition of poverty and exploitation – became irrelevant.

Bukharin concluded: 'The victory of socialism, in the sense of the conquest of power in one country is possible. The victory of socialism in the sense of the consolidation of this power in one country is possible.' However, questions still remained 'is the final victory of socialism, in the sense of its completion possible?' Two things might prevent it: 'intervention by the surrounding capitalism to strangle it ... or a lack of internal forces required to achieve complete socialist victory ... a lack of technical and economic resources.'[50] How likely was it that these dangers might prevent socialism in one country? Bukharin answered as follows:

> In regard to the question of guarantees against restoration [of capitalism] from abroad we reply: without international revolution we have no guarantee against restoration. On the second question, concerning whether or not we are doomed to defeat because of our technico-economic backwardness we answer: we will not be broken ... because daily, monthly, yearly we will overcome this technico-economic backwardness. Our economic growth represents this permanent process of overcoming technico-economic backwardness.[51]

By splitting internal development from the external situation, the theory of socialism in one country established an insurance policy against anyone who might recall Lenin's many post-1917 statements, such as:

> We are far from having completed even the transition period from capitalism to socialism. We have never cherished the hope that we

could finish it without the aid of the international proletariat. We never had any illusions on that score,

or his statement that 'The final victory of socialism in one country is of course impossible.'[52] Bukharin dismissed such statements by saying that Lenin was only referring to the problem of external security when he talked of socialism in one country being impossible.

To support his Leninist credentials, Bukharin fastened on quotes such as this, from Lenin's 'On Co-operation':

> We have to admit that there has been a radical modification in our whole outlook on socialism. The radical modification is this; formerly we placed, and had to place, the main emphasis on the political struggle, on revolution, on winning political power, etc. Now the emphasis is changing and shifting to peaceful, organisational, 'cultural' work.

However, Lenin had immediately added: 'I would say that emphasis is shifting to educational work, *were it not for our international relations*, were it not for the fact that *we have to fight for our position on a world scale*.'[53] In other words, in Lenin's perspective internal and external developments were not split. In Bukharin's they were.[54]

For Bukharin, socialism in one country was possible 'if we abstract from international factors'.[55] Trotsky found this method of reasoning hilarious: 'If we accomplish this "abstraction", then of course, the rest is easy. But we *cannot* ... It is possible to walk naked in the streets of Moscow in January, if we can abstract ourselves from the weather and the police.'[56]

The impact of the theory of socialism in one country at home and in the Comintern cannot be overestimated. It immeasurably strengthened the Stalinist bureaucracy, whose very existence was now identified with socialism. Any criticisms of the bureaucracy were therefore antisocialist.

Bukharin's theory of socialism in one country was perfected during battles with the left opposition which reduced Trotsky to temporary silence in 1925. Its full artillery was first deployed against the 'new opposition' which suddenly emerged during the Fourteenth Party Congress at the end of that year. Here Zinoviev and Kamenev broke away from Stalin. The latter promptly formed a 'duumvirate' with Bukharin to crush them.

Like Trotsky, the new opposition doubted the theory of socialism in one country. If Russian society was already socialist, they said, then what had happened to the state capitalist elements in the NEP? Safarov, a leading Petrograd Bolshevik, wrote: 'Although our industrial enterprises will eventually become of a socialist type, at the present time they include in their organisation a whole series of state capitalist elements inasmuch as they are *linked with the market* and suffer from *bureaucratic deformations*.'[57] Zinoviev added:

> Are there not already elements of state capitalism in today's state trusts, in their operations, in their system of work, in their environment, and also in our present system of co-operation? Are there not workers, peasants, people who sense this? How can workers not feel it is totally false if we present them with sugary phrases about this being socialism?[58]

Bukharin's answer to these criticisms showed the sheer violence he did to the concept of socialism:

> [The new opposition] says, literally: in terms of ownership our state enterprises are socialist, but in terms of relations between people they are not ... If you maintain that the means of production are in the hands of the proletariat, then this answers the question as to whether you are dealing with socialist relations.[59]

Here the formal ownership attained in 1917 was treated as the be-all and end-all of economic and social relations. Socialism became no more than economic growth under state ownership, an argument used by Stalinist regimes for decades afterwards.

Now compare Bukharin's assertion of socialist relations in Russia with an eye-witness report of industrial conditions at the end of 1925:

> The labour question is acquiring an ever increasing force, due to the following fundamental reason: *the process of differentiation of the strata of the labour mass into labour officials divorced from the factories and plants for Soviet work, and into working men at the workbench, is almost definitely concluded.*
>
> Two strata, entirely different as concerns character of work, manner of life, payment, and, what is of utmost importance, psychology [have appeared]. As a general rule, workingmen on quitting production, part company also with the labour milieu. In their private life they come already into touch with quite different strata of the population and form an independent Soviet class engaged in general and personal questions, but lacking the compactness of comradeship with the plant and factory proletariat. The latter, however, remain solitary, abandoned to its forces.[60]

Russia was neither state capitalist nor socialist in the mid-1920s. Its form of industrial ownership – nationalisation – could belong to either system. Everything depended on whom and what industry served. As long as the battle was joined between those who wished to see industry serve the workers and their needs, and those who opposed this, the class character of Russian society lay between the two poles of state capitalism and socialism. It was a degenerated workers' state.

The Critique of Bureaucratism

If Bukharin was a powerful supporter of Stalin's bureaucracy, how can his defenders proclaim him an example of 'uncompromising anti-bureaucratism'? Bukharin was certainly critical of bureaucracy, but this criticism took a peculiar form which avoided attacking the actual party bureaucrats, whom he called 'the iron cohorts of Leninism'.[61] His complaint was against the officials' style of operation, or 'bureaucratism', rather than their position in the political and social structures of the time. What did this approach mean in practice?

Bukharin appealed for mass involvement in party life, from his left communist period right through to the 1930s.[62] His appeals must be taken as genuine, unlike Stalin's call for the apparatus to subject itself to 'self-criticism', a cynical manoeuvre from someone directly involved in administrative repression. However, Bukharin's attitude was shaped by his line on culture. In 1927 he continued the theme first developed in his *Proletarian Revolution and Culture* of 1923:

> What is the *foundation* of bureaucracy, of the *certain* degree of separation of the 'apparatus' from the masses?
>
> The main reason, without doubt, is cultural backwardness. The masses are 'unripe', doomed as they were to backwardness under a capitalist regime.[63]

While this may have held a grain of truth, on its own it was an insufficient explanation of Russian developments in the mid-1920s. As Trotsky pointed out, if the problem of the bureaucracy had been due to a cultural gap:

> how could it happen that, despite the favourable change in economic circumstances and the cultural rise of the proletariat, the party regime has steadily shifted in the recent past in the direction of bureaucratisation? ... the uncultured character of the country is on the wane while party bureaucratism is on the rise.[64]

Since Bukharin located the origin of bureaucracy in the cultural backwardness of the masses, it followed that the solution was the imparting of culture to the population. The problem with this was that it left the masses passive. The active role was given to government institutions, which were the very places where bureaucracy held sway.

Another element in Bukharin's critique of bureaucracy, one which avoided an effective challenge to the Stalin faction, was his stress on the economic drain caused by ineffective administration. This contrasted with the emphasis of Trotsky and the left opposition on the political threat posed by the bureaucracy. As early as December 1921 Bukharin warned the Eleventh Party Conference of the dangers of:

> a universal apparatus which, without sufficient material premises, wanted to organise everything, and therefore imposed a heavy burden on the country. This was, from the economic point of view, a brake on the development of the productive forces ... Our apparatus, which should speed up the process, lengthens it. Through the market system ... production takes place in say 'X' amount of time. Through our apparatus it takes not 'X' but 10X or 20X time. The speed of circulation [of goods] is dramatically reduced.[65]

In 1927 this was still his theme. The apparatus should not be criticised for politically disabling the working class, but for inefficiency. His solution to this problem had remarkably Stalinist undertones, even if the intention was different: 'permanently "purging" and "modifying" the apparatus, struggling for good and honest state employees, permanently involving the masses, constantly "refreshing" and "reworking" the whole apparatus: this is the road *leading us to the "commune state."*'[66]

Moshe Lewin has correctly ascribed an 'anarchistic distrust of the state' to Bukharin.[67] The social origins of anarchism have often been located in the petty bourgeoisie, and it is true that Bukharin's critique of bureaucracy owed more to this social group than to the working class. Lenin showed that the petty bourgeoisie 'opposes *every kind* of state interference, accounting and control, whether it is state-capitalist or state-socialist'.[68] This is because the petty bourgeoisie wants minimal taxation and maximum freedom to develop through market conditions. It might be objected that to categorise Bukharin's approach as petty bourgeois or anarchistic contradicts his slavish defence of the monolithic party bureaucracy. Such a contradiction existed not just in Bukharin's head, but in the real world too, where the rising state bureaucracy coexisted with an influential petty bourgeoisie. This was not a mere accident of history. It has often been the case that while the petty bourgeoisie has individually desired freedom from the state, its social fragmentation has provided fertile soil for the most autocratic regimes. It was the preponderance of the peasantry in Russia that helped tsarism to survive for so long.

The petty bourgeoisie, however radical it might be, did not hold the key to overcoming bureaucracy. What was needed was collective control of power, through institutions such as the soviet. Socialism, by abolishing classes and class antagonism, could lead to the withering away of the state and its officials. Only this could end bureaucracy once and for all.

This conclusion does not suit bourgeois historians, of course. They picture the rise of the bureaucracy with Stalin at its head as an autonomous process, a form of totalitarian infection, which grew independently of political arguments or social relations. Bukharin's approach, which emphasised culture and cutting the economic cost of bureaucracy, was little better.

Only Trotsky and the left opposition provided an adequate explanation of bureaucracy and pointed the way to the solution. It was based on the following considerations: 'A party regime has no independent, self-sufficient meaning. In relation to party policy it is a derivative magnitude.'[69] So by what was the party regime conditioned?

> [It] is a function of policy, which in its turn carries through the interests and reflects the pressures of classes. The bureaucratisation of the Communist Party beginning in 1922, has paralleled the growth of the economic strength and political influence of the petty bourgeoisie, basing itself on NEP, and the stabilisation of the bourgeois regimes in Europe.[70]

This was an excellent description of the origins of the process. The weakness of the working class, and the counter-pressure exerted by the peasantry, had left the state and party balancing between these two key social forces. These were the conditions that encouraged a bureaucracy to develop and grow into an independent force.

Once in existence the bureaucracy not only reflected the social circumstances of its birth, it also shaped future events. Bukharin's role in the faction fight was evidence of this. As a leading Bolshevik he was not just an *effect* but a *cause* of change in his own right, for as Trotsky put it: 'the party regime is not merely a passive reflection of these deep-going processes. The party is a living force of history, particularly the ruling party in a revolutionary dictatorship.'[71] Trotsky judged the

Bukharin – Stalin regime in the party to be a more direct menace than the gradual social changes that were taking place:

> The second chapter of the October Revolution is not characterised simply by the development of the economic status of the petty bourgeoisie in the towns and in the countryside, but by an **infinitely sharper and more dangerous** process of theoretical and political disarmament of the proletariat.[72]

The policy that the left opposition put forward to combat this process involved an active struggle from below, to defend the right of free debate within the party, to have elections of officials and workers' democracy. This could not be isolated from the central task – the political campaign to uphold the principles of Marxism. But the left opposition was unsuccessful.

In this light, the enormous damage wrought by Bukharin becomes clear. In the chapter on war communism above it was noted that socialism in the USSR did not rest upon a socialist economic structure. The political apparatus created by the working class in 1917 – the soviets – had also disintegrated as a meaningful expression of class power. All that remained was a declining force of class conscious-workers and revolutionary Bolsheviks. The theory of socialism in one country served systematically to destroy this last vestige of the revolution's original spirit. So it was that in 1928 the bureaucracy, nurtured on a diet of Bukharinism, would turn on the hand that fed it. The ugly child of degeneration developed into a fully grown monster of a different sort – a counter-revolutionary force next to which its ideological parent, Bukharinism, appeared benign. In the mid-1920s Trotsky did not predict this final stage, yet the fact remains that it was he, and *not* Bukharin, who best understood and opposed the bureaucracy. Trotsky wrote: 'it is incontestable that of all the dangers, the most terrible one is the inner-party regime.'[73]

8 'Enrich Yourselves'

To understand the economic debates of the 1920s a tangled undergrowth of possible misconceptions must be cleared. First, in the 1920s official and opposition leaders often spoke in similar terms despite their different outlooks. For example, the *Platform of the Opposition* accused the 'Stalin-Bukharin group' of 'underestimation of the farmhands and poor peasants as the social base of the proletarian dictatorship in the countryside'.[1] Bukharin countered by claiming: 'the idea of supporting the poor peasants is the red thread running through my argument.'[2] He wrote that 'failure to understand the most fundamental problem of our constructive activity, the problem *of the worker – peasant bloc* ... is the basic shortcoming of all Trotskyism.'[3] Trotsky's riposte was: 'The task at home is to move forward as far as possible on the road of socialist construction by strengthening ourselves with a proper class policy, by proper relations between the working class and the peasantry'.[4] Even on the issue of Bukharin's famous, or infamous, slogan, 'enrich yourselves',[5] the verbal difference was not great. At the Twelfth Congress Trotsky welcomed agricultural expansion, hoping that the peasants would '*become more rich*'. 'What', asks Nove, 'is the difference between "become more rich" and "*enrich yourselves*"?'[6]

Second, modern discussions are influenced by the problems of Russia's economy today rather than interest in the past. Like the theory of socialism in one country, such analyses take as their starting point the isolated national economy. The various programmes are weighed up in exclusively economic terms and according to which strategy brings the greatest overall growth. This ignores their social and political implications.

So how are the economic debates of the mid-1920s to be evaluated? They cannot be judged by words alone, or abstracted from their historical context, with all its economic and political complexities formed from a background of socialist revolution and international isolation. Furthermore, economic policy does not just concern the relationship between people and the material world; it also includes relationships between people. During the 1920s economists discussed the economy in terms of urban and rural sectors, industry and agriculture, centralised planning and spontaneous market forces. However, behind these concepts were social and political interests – the collective proletariat, the fragmented peasantry and so on. Unlike bourgeois economists who play with pure economic systems, Marxism emphasises the way class relationships are affected by economic policies.

During the NEP period Bukharin played an important role in framing government policies. His first premise was that the needs of the 'national economy' took primacy over those of the working class and internationalism. He wrote:

> While the struggle for power is going on, the working class is *not concerned* with the national economy as a whole. On the contrary, its fundamental interest is to pull down, smash, and destroy capitalist society. But when the working class is the class in power, it becomes the leader of the whole society. The responsibility for growth of the national income becomes its own responsibility. Responsibility for developing the productive forces also becomes its own responsibility. And an interest in developing the national economy similarly becomes its own interest.[7]

This idea of 'national interest' transcending class interest fitted with the bureaucratic viewpoint which saw itself as above class conflict and representing the 'general interest'. Bukharin made this approach palatable for Bolsheviks by assuming economic growth was equivalent to socialism.

The reality was that Russia was not socialist but a degenerating workers' state in which there was a variety of different economic forms in growing competition. Bukharin was right to warn against narrow promotion of workers' immediate material interests, something that he called a 'shop-orientated' or 'trade unionist' approach. The overall expansion of productive forces was essential not only to abolish poverty, but to maintain the physical existence of the working class as well. Yet this was not the end of the matter. For the socialist goal to be achieved, economic growth could not be achieved primarily at the cost of workers, nor must it strengthen other classes whose interests diverge from the proletariat's. Secure in his faith in the socialist character of the existing regime, Bukharin failed to see that such possibilities could be harmful.

The Scissors Crisis

The scissors crisis, the first major economic dispute of the NEP period, was caused by an imbalance between the prices of industrial manufactures and agricultural goods. Victory in the civil war had come too late to avoid economic disruption and a horrific famine costing millions of lives. As a result in 1922 the purchasing power of the population was low. At this time the amount of grain available stood at just 40 per cent of its prewar level, while industrial output was 25 per cent of what it had been.[8] The people could survive without industrial goods, but they would die without food. What demand there was therefore was for food, and its price rocketed. By contrast, industrial prices collapsed, in spite of the limited supply of manufactures. This was because managers, forced to be self-financing under NEP arrangements, were desperately trying to sell their wares.

In 1923 the relative positions of agricultural and industrial prices were reversed. The harvest was good, climbing towards 70 per cent of the prewar level, while industrial production stood at 39 per cent.[9] Agriculture had revived rapidly because peasant farms operated as isolated units 'almost exclusively based upon the use of manual labour'.[10] Industry, with its complex web of connections – transport, fuel, machinery and distribution – took longer to recover. As food was more plentiful in 1923 than 1922 its price fell. There was now more demand for industrial goods, and as they were in short supply their prices rose. The trend was accentuated by managers who, behaving as rational marketeers in the NEP environment, now held back their wares until peasants had sold their harvest and had the cash to buy at high prices.

In September 1922 both sectors exchanged goods at prewar price ratios. But in February 1923 agricultural prices had fallen by 22 per cent, whereas industrial prices had risen by 31 per cent.[11] The consequence was that a single-horse plough, which had cost the equivalent of 200 kilos of grain before the war, cost 800 kilos in June 1923.[12] At the Twelfth Congress in 1923 Trotsky exhibited a graph showing the widening gap between industrial and agricultural prices – the scissors. The peasants naturally resented being able to buy few industrial goods in return for the fruits of their heavy labour. Some began consuming more of their own produce, and fattening their livestock. In some areas where bran and maize became cheaper than kerosene, these crops were burned as a substitute fuel.[13] Industry and agriculture risked splitting into self-contained economies, leading to a political rupture.

Such a breakdown was staved off by a government commission that restricted credit to industry and forced factory managers to sell at reduced prices. In four months industrial prices were cut by 55 per cent and agricultural prices raised by 87 per cent.[14] A semblance of equilibrium, which the spontaneous workings of the market had failed to achieve, returned. But the basic imbalance could not be abolished by decree. A gap between agricultural and industrial prices existed throughout the period of the NEP.

Table 8.1: Ratio of Agricultural to Industrial (Retail) Prices

1913	1923–4	1925–6	1927–8
100.0	33.7	71.8	79.0

Source: Adapted from C. Bettelheim, *Class Struggles in the USSR, Second Period 1923–1930*, Hassocks 1973, page 151.

Bukharin's response to the scissors crisis reflected the outlook of a bureaucracy under pressure from market-orientated peasants, traders and the urban private sector. These were the groups which had gained most from the NEP and who now had a new confidence. Bukharin ignored the underlying causes of the crisis – the imbalance between industrial and agricultural growth rates. He stressed only the surface issue of high industrial prices: 'The malady is ... *mainly in the sphere of circulation*', where high prices for manufactures led to 'the impossibility or extreme difficulty of *accumulation* in the peasant economy (the impossibility of *selling, buying*, or accumulating in monetary form)'.[15]

To say only this was short-sighted; it was the economics of the local village market. Bukharin wanted to lower factory gate prices without considering how the peasants' desire for more and cheaper industrial goods might be achieved *in the long term*. Pressure to cut industrial prices would not aid investment in new technology and expanded manufacturing. Only if industry invested and improved its production could it really satisfy the consumption needs of the peasants. By contrast, cutting the prices of industrial goods mainly helped those peasants and traders (Nepmen) who had sufficient cash to trade extensively. This problem was exacerbated by the fact that retail trade was largely in the hands of private middle-men who controlled 58 per cent after 1923/4.[16] Therefore, the cuts in state wholesale prices which Bukharin asked for would not reach consumers. The mark-up that private traders put on state wholesale prices was 47.7 per cent in 1925–6.[17]

The left opposition responded to the scissors crisis in a different way to Bukharin. Trotsky was the first to describe the scissors and warn of the risk of alienating the peasantry, but he rejected price cuts as a permanent solution. A healthy balance between industry and agriculture could not be left to anarchic market forces and then corrected by panic measures. Trotsky wrote that:

> The very creation of a commission for lowering prices is eloquent and devastating proof of how a policy that ignores the importance of planned and manipulative adjustment is driven by the force of its own inevitable consequences *into attempts to command price in the style of war communism*.[18]

Foresight and deliberate action were the answer. Trotsky realised the danger of sudden unexpected crises leading to arbitrary emergency measures years before Bukharin accused Stalin of the same things. Trotsky also pointed out how this could be avoided – through planning.

Circulation or Planning?

After the scissors crisis Bukharin elaborated further the idea that became the official economic programme. His key concern was to expand the circulation of goods in the marketplace. This would be assisted by depressing industrial prices still further:

> An acceleration in the *turnover*, an expansion of the *market*, an expansion of *production* on this basis, with the resulting possibility of a further reduction in prices, a further expansion of the market etc. – that is the route for *our* production. For us such a policy is *obligatory*.[19]

Once again Bukharin's policy showed a limited perspective. His faith in market circulation as a miracle cure for the backward Russian economy stemmed from the initial experience of the NEP. He stated: 'We simply unleashed commodity exchange and combined the different economic factors.'[20] The result was rapid industrial growth, amounting between 1922–3 and 1925–6 to 274 per cent.[21] This early phase was called the 'restoration period', because industry was being brought back to its prewar condition. But what would happen once all the existing reserves were mobilised; what would be the social consequences of merely restoring an economy in which the working class was a tiny minority of the population?

The answer from Bukharin was that circulation would continue to be self-expanding and solve future problems automatically:

> we have made it possible for the countryside to fertilize the city. In other words, the most profound meaning of the New Economic Policy

is that we created the possibility, for the first time, of mutual fertilization between economic forces and diverse economic factors.[22]

This was a perfectly correct argument if part of a wider programme. However, as usual, Bukharin emphasised only one side – circulation, at the expense of planning.

Bukharin's approach to planning was dictated by his belief that the concentration of resources in the hands of the state had led to 'monopolistic parasitism' in the economy:[23]

> All monopoly hides within itself a certain worm, the danger of going rotten, of complacently resting on one's laurels ... And when we have in our hands what amounts to the whole of large-scale industry we have a super-monopoly ... we have absolutely all the ingredients for monopolistic degeneration. The function performed by competition in capitalism is absent in our society (to all but a minimal degree). We must replace it with conscious pressure to meet the consumption needs of the masses: *better production, cheaper production, better supplies of goods, cheaper supplies of goods.*[24]

This argument sounds persuasive and even radical-sounding, because it implies criticism of bureaucratic state ownership and at the same time demands the satisfaction of mass consumption needs. Since Bukharin appeared to be a sort of Marxist Adam Smith, he has become very popular with marketeers. However, once again his views reflected the limitations of the petty bourgeois horizon.

Bukharin's notion that socialism must replace the whip of capitalist competition had a rationale. The satisfaction of human need has to be the driving force of a socialist economy. But his method – the unfettered market – could not express human need, since it was driven by the quest for profit. His warning that centralised production could create 'monopolistic parasitism' was another partial presentation of a genuine issue. Its weakness was the suggestion that centralisation was the crux of the problem. In fact, large-scale internally planned production is generally more productive than individual enterprise. The history of capitalism has demonstrated that large-scale organisations are able to swallow up smaller ones because of economies of scale, a more rational distribution of resources and similar factors. Recently East European economists have blamed their troubles on overcentralisation and overplanning. But in fact they lost out against capitalist competition chiefly because their economies were too small and less effectively planned than their giant multinational rivals in the West.

Even if centralised production is more effective than individual efforts, Bukharin was right to suggest that monopolies can create a high degree of alienation which saps the incentive of the producer to work efficiently. Large capitalist companies suffer tremendous waste because people in boring dead-end jobs lack motivation, especially when they know that any extra effort on their part will serve chiefly to jack up profits. However, the conclusion Bukharin drew from this argument was mistaken. He decided to prioritise motivating the isolated peasant farmer, seeing this as more important than giving an incentive to the industrial working class to achieve higher output. He subordinated the industrial sector to peasant production, saying: 'In our country the foundation of the entire economy is *agriculture*. Our *industry* is at a comparatively early stage, and its development depends upon agricultural growth.'[25]

Encouraging the peasant to greater efforts can perhaps produce a little more from the land. Yet the stimulation of industry can produce a relatively greater economic expansion because of its technological dynamism. Such a course would not only have brought benefits to the proletariat but, through tractors, fertilisers and so on, would also have enhanced the productivity of Russian agriculture. Monopolistic degeneration in industry could have been overcome if Russian workers had been shown evidence, through their democratic involvement and improvements in living standards, that the economy was really theirs. Though industrial growth would have remained limited until an international revolution took place, even without this event, growth here would also have been politically essential as a means to assisting the working class. By counterposing market circulation to collective planning, Bukharin necessarily promoted agriculture, which operated exclusively through the market, at the cost of industry, which needed internal planning in order to function.

Bukharin set the tempo of industry within the parameters of national isolation and priority for agriculture. This meant industrial growth would inevitably be slow: 'we will ride the scraggy peasant nag for a long time and *only that* will save our industry and supply a firm basis for the dictatorship of the proletariat.'[26] Elsewhere he talked about advancing at a 'snail's' or a 'tortoise's pace'.[27] Bukharin's confidence in agriculture was influenced by its strong recovery in the early NEP period. However, the long-term record was abysmal. From 1801 to 1914 the Russian grain harvest grew at less than 0.5 per cent a year, or 59 per cent in all,[28] while the population grew still more quickly.[29]

Trotsky gave the name 'tailism' to Bukharin's policy of subordinating industrial planning to agricultural circulation. However, Trotsky did not suppose that the potential of planning was unlimited:

> Peasant economy is not governed by a plan, it is conditioned by the market which develops spontaneously. The state can and should act upon it, push it forward, but it is still absolutely incapable of channelling it according to a single plan.[30]

Thus far Trotsky would seem to have agreed with Bukharin that the market was inescapable. But Trotsky looked beyond the peasant field. Industry, by its nature, could be far more 'dynamic, (driving, forward-thrusting)'[31] than agriculture. Its complex internal structure, even under capitalism, is not only more susceptible to more integrated and developed planning, it requires it. In Soviet Russia, given centralised state control, planning was feasible for industry where it was not for agriculture. One of the few economic gains of the revolution was that after it there were greater opportunities to develop planning than there had been before.

The scissors crisis showed that without the planning of industry the anarchic workings of the market would lead to crisis, hurting agriculture as much as industry. As Trotsky put it, the worker – peasant bloc depended on socialist planning:

> Although this [peasant] market develops spontaneously, it does not follow at all that state industry should adapt itself to it spontaneously. On the contrary, our success in economic organisation will depend in large part upon the degree to which we succeed, by means of an exact knowledge of market conditions and correct economic forecasts, in harmonizing state industry with agriculture according to a definite plan.[32]

Bukharin had argued the same policy before his conversion to right-wing policies: 'the uniform economic plan must be regarded not only from the point of view of industry, but also from the point of view of the whole national economy, from the point of view of the relationship between town and country.'[33]

Nevertheless, Bukharin's mid-1920s strictures against planning for threatening to bring bureaucratic degeneration were justified, in their one-sided way, because not all planning is socialist. Capitalists plan constantly. This is the function of management which intervenes to maximise exploitation. Its rule over the internal life of enterprises is used only to compete better in the anarchy of capitalist struggle outside. If the working class had lost all power in Russia, state planning would have gone the same way. However, socialist planning has a different character to capitalist planning. As Engels wrote, it is 'in accordance with the needs of the community and each individual ... The capitalist mode of appropriation, in which the product enslaves first the producer and then the appropriator as well will thus be replaced.'[34]

Even at his most right-wing Bukharin did not deny that ultimately rational planning would replace anarchic market conditions and that industry would outpace agriculture. In 1926 he wrote: 'in *what* is expressed the growth of rationality over irrationality? The reply is fairly uncontroversial: in the growth of planning.' And: 'What is the basis of planning? The answer is obvious: in the growth of the state-socialist elements of the economy, the growth of its influence and growth of its specific weight.'[35] But his immediate policy was to put the anarchic economy above the needs of the planned elements. In practice he led away from economic 'rationality'.

Which perspective, the right's or the left's, better fitted the 1920s? Clearly market circulation was indispensable when the majority of the population were autonomous petty producers; but the notion that policy should be primarily conditioned by this ignored the fact that three quarters of the production of large industry were actually consumed in the towns.[36] At the same time the peasants were consuming 86 per cent of their grain output.[37] Even though both spheres were connected, agricultural policy was not absolutely binding on industry, or *vice versa*.

There were other issues. Encouraging rural demand for manufactured goods would have benefited certain parts of industry, but, as Kagarlitsky puts it: 'If you have a wooden plough agricultural economy, then industry is only required to produce wooden ploughs, nothing else.'[38] Kagarlitsky goes on to show that Bukharin's model for growth was taken from nineteenth-century Britain, in which:

> industrialisation, above all of light industry, begins through commodity exchange between the town and the countryside. Out of a higher turnover there arises, naturally, the financial basis and resources for accumulation which are switched from light industry to become the basis for constructing heavy industry. The problem is that Russia in the 1920s was not Britain in the nineteenth century ... Above all Britain was then in a world monopoly position operating under exceptionally favourable circumstances. From no quarter was pressure exerted against it, but despite that it still took over one hundred years to industrialise.[39]

If Russia could have been abstracted from world competition, from external hostility and the threat posed by internal forces opposed to socialism, then Bukharin's 'snail's pace' plan might have worked; but as Trotsky showed, such abstraction was ridiculous.

Ironically, if Bukharin's programme failed the working class it also failed the peasants. The slow growth of industry had a crippling effect on the agricultural economy. Russian peasants were already among the poorest in Europe. Their technique remained primitive through sheer lack of agricultural implements, and yet the weakness of Russian industry meant that they paid the equivalent of twice as much for industrial goods as their Western counterparts did.[40]

Of course, forced industrialisation *at the expense* of the mass of peasants would have been disastrous. Bukharin accused Trotsky of advocating just this policy, taunting him with being a 'super-industrialiser'. The accusation was false. Trotsky wrote:

> The rate of industrial development, the acceleration of which is in the interest of both the city and the village, does not of course depend on our good will. There are objective limitations here: the level of peasant economy, the actual equipment of industry, the availability of working capital, the cultural level of the country and so forth. Any attempt to leap over these limitations would surely take its own bitter revenge, striking the proletariat at one end and the peasant at the other. **But no less danger would arise if industry lagged behind the economic upturn of the rest of the country** ...
> The dangers deriving from our whole development have a *two-sided* character. Industry cannot rush ahead too far ... But it is equally dangerous to lag behind.[41]

'Enrich Yourselves' – or 'Capitalism on the Instalment Plan'[42]

Bukharin's programme had implications for the key issue of accumulating funds for industrial investment. Discussing the popular view of the debate, Bukharin wrote:

> the policies were defined as if the opposition stood for high profit and a rapid rate of socialist accumulation whereas the Central Committee stood for minimal profit and a slow rate of socialist accumulation. These common formulations suffered from the flaw that they were both true and untrue: they were *crude*, because they did not convey the essence of the matter ... The Central Committee did not stand for minimal profit in general, but for minimal profit *per*

commodity unit. The Central Committee did not stand for a slow rate of accumulation, but rather for a policy that would *not cut us off* from the peasant economy and would, *in the final analysis,* yield a more rapid, indeed the most rapid possible, rate of accumulation.'[43]

So Bukharin was not against accumulation but claimed that his programme would yield growth based on a balance between agriculture and industry. This was reasonable, but it begged the question as to what the balance should be. Bukharin argued to continue policy on the current basis, which was both highly precarious and the result of the NEP's spontaneous market relations.

However, as we have established, industry was in greater immediate need of investment than agriculture was. Furthermore, the latter could only make serious progress on the basis of industrial technology. By tying industrial accumulation to circulation via the peasant market, Bukharin was limiting its pace and making it depend on the narrow group of wealthy peasants and Nepmen who had large stocks to trade. Poorer peasants and workers had nothing to gain from this. Such a policy had important social and political consequences. The physical development of the working class in terms of its numbers, material conditions and social weight vis à vis other classes was linked to the growth of industry and large industry in particular. Bukharin's policy forced it to wait for rising turnover in the peasant sector of the market. Given the weak position of the working class, the idea of *first* securing growth in agriculture was disastrous.

This can be demonstrated in a number of ways. Driven by failing small peasant farms, country people flooded the towns where, because of its retarded growth, industry was unable to reabsorb its own workers, let alone newcomers. The year 1925/6, a period of high output growth, illustrated the problem (see Table 8.2). These official registration figures, showing unemployment of between 698,300 and 777,300, excluded many people. The full figure for 1925/6 was closer to 1 million, rising two years later to 1.3 million: 17.3 per cent of all trade unionists.[44] Unemployment affected workers' self-confidence, as Carr and Davies show:

> In a period when labour was both inefficient and super-abundant, factory managers were prone to change it easily and often. The Moscow party leader Uglanov at the 15th Party Conference in October 1926 related a case in which a factory manager had recently discharged 300 workers and engaged 380 new ones.[45]

Table 8.2: Number of Officially Registered Employed and Unemployed 1925/6

Date	Industrial employment thousands	index	Unemployment thousands	index
1 Oct. 1925	2,034.5	100	698.3	100
1 Oct. 1926	2,279.2	112	777.3	123.9

Source: Adapted from 'Pod znameniia Lenina'. Democratic centralist document probably written by V.I. Smirnov, in *Arkhiv Trotskogo*, Vol. 2, Moscow 1990, page 155.

Workers' housing conditions were also affected by the retarded growth of the urban sector. As one metalworker put it in 1925:

> *The dwelling situation is catastrophic.* In a number of factory areas exist what are called 'coffin dwelling spaces' ... At the Makeev works the space available for one person is 4.4 sq arshins [10 square feet], which is even less than the 'coffin space'. At some factories beds are used in three shifts. Such dwelling conditions tend to increase the number of accidents, as the workmen have no opportunity of resting properly. According to the Central Committee [of the Metal Union] 30% to 40% of all accidents are caused by fatigue.[46]

Tomsky summed up the workers' plight in these words:

> Surely we can see that the workers live in crowded dreadful housing, that they lack the elementary everyday comforts, that there are nurseries sufficient only for an insignificant percentage of their children, that our canteens are disgusting and wages still low.[47]

In 'socialist Russia' economic backwardness meant extra sweat and effort for workers, as compared to their exploited comrades abroad (see Table 8.3). These problems could not be wished away overnight. The working-class self-abnegation that Bukharin wanted was worthwhile *if* the victory of 1917 inspired the emancipation of the whole world. But this sacrifice had to be minimised as far as possible if the workers' state were to survive at all. Bukharin's programme ignored this fact. With the bureaucrat's concern for appeasing the strongest pressure group (the wealthy peasants and Nepmen) he gave low priority to the material conditions which provided the basis for the workers' fighting spirit.

Table 8.3: Percentage of Energy (in Horse-power Hours) Provided by Different Sources (1927–8)

country	human power	animal power	mechanical power
USSR	9.3	58.0	32.7
Britain	2.3	3.2	94.5
US	1.1	9.1	69.8

Source: Adapted from E.H. Carr and R.W. Davies, *Foundations of a Planned Economy*, London 1969, Vol. 1, page 485.

By contrast, the opposition emphasised these material factors. *The Platform of the Opposition* did not set impossible aims – 'Economic difficulties do not allow us at present to chart a course towards a substantial rise in wages.' Yet it insisted that the 'present wage level is inadequate' and the state should at least 'not allow a decrease in real wages'.[48] Such a decrease did occur. Between October 1924 and October 1926, Bukharin's heyday, workers' output rose by 47.5 per cent while monthly income rose only 15 per cent and purchasing power still remained below prewar levels.[49]

The left's approach to accumulation recognised the limitations imposed by Russia's isolation and internal balance of forces. Its *Platform* drove in two potentially contradictory directions – towards speeding up industrialisation on the one hand; maintaining social stability, through the worker – peasant bloc, on the other. In the short term industrialisation would receive no outside aid and so funds, which would inevitably be restricted, had to come from the domestic economy. If the workers were not to bear the main burden, who should? The left believed that despite the urgent need for funds, the social basis of the government – the worker – peasant block – should not be disrupted. To keep poor peasant support and retain the benevolent neutrality of the middle peasants, accumulation from either source was ruled out. This left only those most able to bear the weight – kulaks and Nepmen. The proposals of the 1927 *Platform* clearly show that the intention was not physically to annihilate these groups, but to tax them. The scale of accumulation aimed at by the opposition can be judged from the fact that it called for a projected government investment of between 500 million and 1,000 million rubles in 1931, while Stalin's programme set a figure of 7,470 million rubles.[50]

The opposition's voice was not heeded. With Stalin and Bukharin at the helm of government the relative social importance of the workers continued to decline; that of the wealthy peasantry, traders and urban businesses continued to grow. The problem of industrial accumulation remained unsolved. The power of the wealthy peasantry and Nepmen could be seen in a number of areas. Exceptionally it was expressed in open rebellion as in Georgia in 1924. Mostly the influence was more insidious. Wealthy peasants exploited the dependence of the cities on food. The richest 3–5 per cent of peasant households controlled 20 per cent of the grain that was marketed.[51] This may not sound a great amount, but the kulaks were in a strategic position. Even in good years the total grain surplus was low. While most peasants had to sell grain as soon as it was harvested if they were to survive, the kulak stratum was in a position to withhold grain from the market until prices rose. This power of speculation gave them an influence out of proportion to their numbers. It was this sort of pressure, exerted through the marketplace, which had led to the scissors crisis and the price reductions imposed on industry.

The rich peasants and Nepmen also had a direct political influence. One route was via rural soviets. The state of affairs in late 1926 was described in *Pravda*:

> In Chernikhov Stanitsa the right to vote [in elections to soviets] was extended to rich owners of tobacco plantations ... What is the effect of such policy on the poor peasants? Obviously, the poor peasants are frightened; they don't even dare to vote in the districts where the rich tobacco planters live. This is understandable ... they are tied down by credit, advance payments, loans, all of which make them very careful not to offend the kulaks.[52]

The party was not immune either. Lewin describes the situation thus:

> *we have the economic advancement of the peasant who grows more comfortably off and turns into an enterpreneuer, a similar tendency in the case of the official who was still connected with a farm, the influences which each exerted upon the other by reason of the many contacts and interests which they had in common, and the solidarity, both at local and at raion [district] level, of officials and indeed entire administrations with the upper stratum of the rural population. Such was the process in which the members of the Party in the countryside found themselves involved.*[53]

The link between the kulaks, Nepmen and Bukharin's policies was obvious. Where the left opposition put the international interests of the working class first, and then elaborated the many compromises imposed by circumstances, Bukharin began by prioritising the expansion of the peasantry's purchasing power. This inevitably led him to favour those trading the largest surpluses from the most profitable farms, because, as he put it: 'It is patently clear that accumulation is absolutely confined to the framework of the more wealthy sections.'[54]

When Bukharin espoused the rich peasants' cause he undermined his earlier insistence that under Russian conditions the peasantry would remain a homogeneous mass of middle peasants. However, it was politically expedient to argue both things at the same time, even if they were contradictory. Indeed by the mid-1920s Bukharin staked his economic programme upon peasant differentiation. He claimed that 'the kulak, in the old sense of the word, is actually receding into the background, being doomed to destruction.' He was being replaced by a 'new type of kulak'[55], who had to be encouraged.

Bukharin had problems justifying this last twist to others. It caused a major shock when he said in a speech in Moscow in April 1925:

Consider the fact that the well-to-do upper stratum of the peasantry, along with the middle peasant, who is also striving to join the well-to-do, are both *afraid at present to accumulate*. A situation has been created in which the peasant is afraid to buy an iron roof and apprehensive that he will be declared a kulak; if he buys a machine, he makes certain that the conmunists are not watching. Advanced technology has become a conspiracy ... We must now proceed to remove a whole series of limitations both on well-to-do peasants and on farm labourers, who live by selling their labour power ...

In general and on the whole, we must say to the entire peasantry, to all its different strata: enrich yourselves, accumulate, develop your farms.[56]

Outcry greeted the phrase 'enrich yourselves', a quotation borrowed from the nineteenth-century French bourgeois politician Guizot. Krupskaia lent her weight to the campaign against Bukharin. Even the Stalin faction turned against him on this, forcing Bukharin to recant several times over. He did so grudgingly, saying: 'This formula was, without a doubt, a mistaken formulation of an absolutely correct position.'[57] In another article he admitted that his policy 'involved the so-called "wager on the kulak".' This was a reference to the policies of Stolypin, the prewar tsarist prime minister, who had promoted the kulaks as a rural bulwark of tsarism. Bukharin defended this on the grounds that 'From this "wager" we can only gain. It is this "wager" which gives us a chance of paying higher wages to the workers and gives the state greater means and greater resources.'⁵⁸ Bukharin anticipated that if the state gave the kulaks tax cuts and other concessions they would deposit their savings in state institutions. By this means rural accumulation would be ploughed back into industry. But this pious hope was never fulfilled.

In a sense, the grievance of Stalin's apparatus against Bukharin was that he had expressed too openly and clearly the tendencies of current policy. In fact, other prominent Bolsheviks made similar if less reported statements. For example, Kalinin, titular president of the Soviet Union and a former peasant, said:

> Differentiation in the countryside is a necessary consequence of its economic growth. And the Soviet state, which holds all available means to assist the economic growth of the country, indirectly assists differentiation. Whoever wants to seriously interfere with and brake differentiation inevitably stops the growth of agriculture.'⁵⁹

Larina, Bukharin's widow, recounts that the phrase 'enrich yourselves' only caused a furore in the establishment because he had used 'bourgeois terminology' by quoting Guizot.⁶⁰

Bukharin's indiscretion had betrayed a major shift in policy which the leadership hoped to slip by the Fourteenth Party Conference of April 1925. The change, the 'NEP's second wind', was prompted by the Georgian rising of autumn 1924. Stalin feared that 'what happened in Georgia may be repeated all over Russia if we do not radically change our very approach to the peasantry.'⁶¹ So while Bukharin's gaff was an embarrassment, it coincided with his greatest personal influence on domestic policy. This took the form of three measures.

The first was a reduction of the agricultural tax. Various exclusions were introduced to help richer peasants, so that in 1925–6 the average peasant tax level fell from 3 to 2.30 roubles per head. However, for the workers taxation rose from 1.95 to 2.70 roubles.⁶²

The second policy relaxed rules on the hiring of agricultural labourers. Bukharin justified this⁶³ on the grounds that 'the village poor, the victims of overpopulation ... grumble to us that we prevent them from hiring themselves out to [the] prosperous peasant.'⁶⁴ Of course, in the absence of industrial employment, and of tools and equipment to help poor peasants and encourage them to unite in modern productive farms, the choice was between submitting to the exploitation of their wage labour or starvation. The conditions of the NEP forced millions to choose the former course, with the number of agricultural labourers rising from 960,000 in 1920 to 2.4 million in 1924.[65] Bukharin pretended that this process was a great boon for the poor peasants and, still more grotesque, that it was part of 'growing into socialism'. This was reminiscent of the early British capitalists who claimed that by enclosing the land they were 'freeing' their population – freeing them, that is, for exploitation.

Three days after the new rules on hiring labour came permission for leasing land. This third measure was supposed to help those 'temporarily weakened in consequence of some natural disaster'.[66] In fact, it dealt a final blow to Bukharin's earlier claim that government land policy guaranteed a non-capitalist evolution. In the past he had said:

> Has the process of differentiation been delayed at all for the present? It has ... the land has been withdrawn from commercial exchange. If it had not been withdrawn from the process of purchase and sale there would have been a rapid transfer of land into the hands of the richest peasants. We do not have the buying and selling of land.[67.]

In practice the recent legal changes now recognised and encouraged a situation where those peasants who lacked the means of production to farm their land would be forced to sell its use if not its formal ownership to the rich.

What was happening on the land is brought out by two contrasting examples. Touring Georgia in the late 1920s, the Yugoslav communist Ciliga heard a woman saying she had just sold her vineyard:

> 'Sold? Does that mean that you can sell ground?'
> 'Certainly, you can sell anything,' she replied, and began to enumerate various cases of sales of fields, gardens and immovable property in general. My objections as to the abolition of private ownership in land did not seem to affect her in the slightest.[68]

From the other end of the class spectrum came this letter, written in September 1926 by a poor peasant from Skrylevshchina village to the Central Committee:

> As a poor peasant I fought willingly [in the civil war] for a bright future for those who labour, for brotherhood and equality ... [But now] my village is surrounded by a ring of kulak farms which weigh down on us from all sides and wish to strangle the poor peasants ... They control the vital local forests and decide who they will or will not sell wood to ... [One] says that if he catches peasants collecting

twigs in the forest without his permission he will shoot them ... The revolution means nothing to them.[69]

The reality of Bukharin's policy was shown by the value of private trade. In 1923/4 this was 18 per cent below its 1913 level, but as the direct result of government relaxation of restrictions in 1925/6 it was actually 16 per cent higher.[70] One historian writes of this 'NEP second wind':

> NEP's version of the Roaring Twenties went far beyond the reopening of expensive food stores, hotels and restaurants. Casinos and race tracks also operated legally, the private owned establishments being required to pay the state a portion of their receipts. Many nightclubs, gambling parlors and brothels operated semi-clandestinely ... and the trade in bootleg liquor flourished. Those in the know had little difficulty in acquiring heroin and cocaine.[71]

He also gives an account of the Praga gambling house in Moscow, which ran with stakes of up to US $30,000.

Was Bukharin's approach to the kulaks and Nepmen totally mistaken? The answer is not as simple as might appear. Even here his problem was one-sidedness. This is best shown by comparing Bukharin to Zinoviev and Kamenev on the one hand, and with Trotsky on the other. When the factional struggle began in October 1923, the 'troika' of Stalin, Zinoviev and Kamenev pushed a strongly pro-peasant line. Zinoviev told the Twelfth Party Congress:

> And when they say to me, 'You are guilty of a peasant deviation, you deviate towards the peasants,' I answer, 'Yes, we not only must deviate toward the peasants, but we must bow and, if necessary, kneel before the economic needs of the peasants, who will follow us and give us complete victory.'[72]

As president of the Comintern Zinoviev urged foreign communist parties to strive for 'worker – peasant' governments rather than socialist revolution. Communists at home were instructed to turn their 'face to the countryside!' Zinoviev was more overtly pro-peasant than Bukharin, who covered his position with a fog of radical-sounding phrases about 'socialism in one country'.

However, in 1925 Zinoviev and Kamenev became frightened by the depth of the concessions that had been made. In a fit of panic typical of the pair, they sounded the alarm. The kulak, they claimed, was responsible for all the ills afflicting the USSR. This simplistic analysis conveniently diverted attention away from the inner-party regime (for which Zinoviev, as the inventor of the doctrine of Bolshevik 'monolithism', was partly responsible). It exaggerated the direct danger represented by a group of peasants as opposed to the bureaucracy. Peasants, even rich ones, are too fragmented to act as an independent force. They have always depended on some outside agency – such as the rising bourgeoisie, the proletariat or a Bonaparte – to give them cohesion and leadership.

Trotsky's approach to the kulaks differed from Bukharin's but also from Zinoviev and Kamenev's. He did not take an ultra-left line and rule out all concessions:

> It goes without saying that in themselves the concessions to the bourgeois classes are not yet a violation of the dictatorship of the proletariat. In general, there are no historical examples of a chemically pure form of class rule ... The whole question is in knowing what are the limits to these concessions and what is the degree of consciousness with which they are made.[73]

And this is what he had to say about the measures Bukharin promoted to aid the rich peasants and kulaks: 'In the Spring of 1925 there came **the necessity** of executing a new retreat: granting to the rich classes of the village the right to exploit lower strata by hiring labour and renting land.' In its weakened state the socialist government could not afford the economic consequences of confronting or destroying the most productive farmers, and might on occasion make a tactical retreat before them. Trotsky continued:

> The new painful retreat in April 1925 was not called, as Lenin would have called it, a profound defeat and retreat; it was presented as a victorious step of the [worker – peasant alliance], as a mere link in the general mechanism of building socialism.

This was the real problem in Bukharin's method:

> the decisions of April 1925 legalised the developing differentiation in the village and opened the flood-gates to it ... Instead of recognising this terrible danger ... this process in its entirety was presented to the party conference, in the name of the party, as the 'building of socialism in one country' independent of world economy and world revolution.[74]

Like Zinoviev and Kamenev, Trotsky stressed the fact of differentiation between the kulak and other peasants, but he was not blind to the kulaks' connection with the peasantry: 'As a matter of fact, the kulak represents only one of the stages of the development of the middle peasant.'[75] Poorer peasants may have hated and despised kulak exploitation, but many aspired to be kulaks themselves. This meant that in its dealings with the kulaks the government also had to consider the impact these might have on the broader peasantry. Simple repression would not do. The link between kulaks and the mass of peasants meant that crude repression of the former would end up challenging the whole peasantry and destroying the worker – peasant alliance. Therefore Trotsky could have agreed with Bukharin when he said that:

> When the kulak danger is discussed, it is presented as if the only issue is the kulak's effort to advance his own farm and nothing more. But, comrades, that is not the issue. The kulak is a danger if he wins the middle peasant over to him; the danger is that he could use unfavourable circumstances to win a section of the middle peasantry from us.[76]

However, Trotsky parted company with Bukharin over the latter's policy of simply capitulating to the kulaks. In Trotsky's view the aim should have been to provide the mass of peasantry with an alternative that was better than becoming a kulak: 'What the peasant asks of us is not to repeat a correct historical formula of class relationships, but to supply him with cheaper nails, cloth and matches.'[77] For such an expansion of industry resources had to come from the kulaks and Nepmen, since there was no other source. Repression and unconditional concessions were both unwarranted. Each reduced the contribution of the rich to industrialisation and was politically damaging. Avoiding these extremes, the state had to syphon off a portion of the resources of kulaks and Nepmen in order to assist workers and poor peasants. Instead of this, what happened was that Bukharin's concessions weakened the already fragile basis for socialism in Russia. Not only was the development of industry held back but, as Trotsky wrote: 'The alliance with the kulak dilutes the alliance of the worker with the agricultural labourer, poor peasant and broad layers of middle peasantry.'[78]

A mass of recent literature in both East and West suggests that the re-emergence of the kulak under Bukharinist policies was a myth; that differentiation was exaggerated; that all was well under the NEP until Stalin abolished it. Danilov says the 1920s 'brought a marked decline in the number of exploitative peasant households'.[79] Lewin asks: 'Who was the kulak?' His answer, simply, is 'he who is declared to be such by the authorities'.[80]

Admittedly kulak numbers were small. Different definitions yield varying results, although most put the figure at well under 10 per cent of the peasantry. One study has suggested the breakdown in Table 8.4. This table implies that the process of polarisation (creating kulak farmers and agricultural labourers) was balanced by the expansion of the middle peasantry (poor peasants rising into the middle ranks). Such a view was propounded by the non-Marxist Chaianov and his influential Organisation and Production School of experts. Bukharin accepted their conclusions.

Table 8.4: Social Composition of the Soviet Village (percentages)

Able-bodied persons	1924/5	1926/7
Agricultural workers	9.7	11.3
Poor peasants	25.9	22.1
Middle peasants	61.1	62.7
Kulaks	3.3	3.9

Source: Adapted from R.F. Millar, 'Soviet Agricultural Policy in the Twenties: the Failure of Cooperation', in *Soviet Studies*, April 1975, page 229.[81]

However, Chaianov's approach was criticised by Kritsman's Agrarian Marxist School, which argued that judgements about the importance of particular peasant groups should not be based on sociological definitions of stratification, or on numerical proportions of the different groups. After all, in modern society capitalists form a tiny proportion of society and yet are dominant because the mass of the population must submit to exploitation by them in order to live. Therefore, while Chaianov looked at the size of landholdings, Kritsman looked at the peasants' relations to all the agricultural means of production. This gave a different picture. One study showed that households in the top group (comprising 3.2 per cent of the peasantry) owned 2.3 draught animals and 2.5 cows on average. For all households the figures were 1.0 and 1.1, respectively. At the bottom end of the scale, among the poorest quarter, 80 per cent had no draught animals and 57 per cent had no cows.[82] Since draught animals were essential for running a farm, these statistics demonstrate that the poor were dependent on the rich. All this had a direct impact on the political roles and confidence of the different sections of the peasantry. While commentators noted that rich peasants 'showed an immense interest in the [rural soviet] elections', the proportion of 'horseless peasants' in the soviets was 4 per cent and rural labourers comprised 2.9 per cent of members.[83] Kritsman concluded that:

> as a significant group of peasants farming independently by means of their own resources only, a 'middle peasantry' scarcely existed in Russia in the 1920s. What existed instead was what Kritsman described as 'a petty-bourgeois mass' all inextricably bound up in commodity relations ... almost all households experienced relations in which they were either exploited or exploiting and many experienced both together.[84]

This did not mean that a kulak-led counter-revolution was imminent, but neither was it a cause for complacency or a denial that capitalist trends were being reinforced.

Bukharin's policies of simultaneously discriminating against industrial growth and fostering rich groups of traders and peasants would prove disastrous and contribute powerfully to the crisis that occurred in the late 1920s and allowed Stalin to lead a counter-revolution.

Cooperation

As a mouthpiece for the bureaucracy of a degenerated workers' state, Bukharin did not consciously desire the return of capitalism, even if his policies unwittingly led in that direction. He did hope for a transition to socialism in the countryside. In a speech in 1926 he called for a policy 'which guarantees for each small peasant the possibility of participating objectively in the business of socialist construction'.[85]

Bukharin's view of how this might be achieved had changed over time. In 1919 he had favoured collective farms:

> We must aim at such an arrangement as would ensure the land being not only owned in common, but also being cultivated in common. If that is not done, then no matter what you proclaim or whatever laws you publish, the result will be most unsatisfactory. One man will fuss about on his allotment, another on his, and if they continue to live apart without mutual aid and common work, they will gradually come to look upon the land as their private property, and no laws from above would be of any use.[86]

This was the generally accepted policy of the Bolsheviks. It was hoped that the few modern large farms that existed prior to 1917 could be preserved and used as models to be followed by the peasants. Land redistribution had broken up many of these farms and the few that remained lacked the resources and expertise to set anyone an example. So what could be done?

In 1922 Lenin began promoting the idea of agricultural cooperatives as a meaning of bringing peasants together. Bukharin took up this idea, but in a way which counterposed cooperatives to the long-term aim of forming collectives. Having written off international revolution and technological assistance, he was left only with the limited social potential of the existing farms:

> it is not true when people assert that collective farms represent the *high road* for moving the mass of the peasantry along a socialist path. How must we draw the peasantry into our socialist organisation? The only answer is by using the peasantry's own economic *interest*. Cooperation must attract the peasant.[87]

Were cooperatives a viable alternative? The system of agricultural cooperation had existed before the revolution to buy and sell goods in bulk, that is, for collective consumption and distribution. But, as in Western Europe, these served the interests of those with the largest purchasing power and biggest surpluses to sell. They helped rural capitalism to develop. In theory they could work in the opposite direction, by demonstrating to the individualistic peasants the advantages of closer collaboration. Later this might be extended to encourage collective farming. If cooperation was to work in this way certain conditions had to be observed.

Cooperation had to avoid becoming a means by which peasants who had the greatest surplus benefited most, so confirming their belief in individual enterprise. Poor peasants, who had the least to gain by acting separately and the most to gain from collective action, should have been given preferential treatment in the form of whatever state aid was available. This aid needed to be plentiful. It was essential that those who collaborated should have had an advantage over those following the private method of production. All this would only have been possible with a high level of industrial development (tractors, fertilisers, and the like).

Bukharin liked to quote Lenin's late article 'On Co-operation' as justification for his cooperative policy, particularly the passage which ran: 'If the whole of the peasantry had been organised in co-operatives, we would by now have been standing with both feet on the soil of socialism.' He also cited Lenin's next point: 'But the organisation of the entire peasantry in co-operative societies presupposes a standard of culture among the peasants ... that cannot, in fact, be achieved without a cultural revolution.' He omitted the final link in the chain of Lenin's argument: 'to be cultured we must achieve a certain development of the material means of production, must have a certain material base.'[88] Cooperatives without this led back to capitalism. Cooperatives possessing a material base using collective labour led to socialism. This evolution was ruled out when Bukharin abandoned the international revolution and advocated a snail's pace industrial programme. In reality Bukharin's 'cooperative plan' owed more to the semi-Narodnik and non-Marxist theories of Chaianov than to Lenin.

The parallels between Bukharin's arguments and Chaianov's were great. The latter's Organisation and Production School looked at the countryside in isolation from wider social trends. The conceptual framework within which the school's members operated prevented a Marxist understanding. Studying individual peasant farms, they stressed the importance of a peasant economic cycle based on the family life-cycle. Their argument was that since labour was a key means of production in agriculture, families with many able-bodied members could quickly become wealthy. However, when the children broke away to establish their own farm households the large family became a small one once more. The arrival of young children reduced the surplus of the family still further and the bottom of the economic cycle was reached. An upswing recurred when the children begin to labour.

This was a good description of what happened to individual families considered in isolation. However, it abstracted them from the overall national and international context in which peasant production occurred. This was shaped by domestic poverty and a bitter struggle to survive, combined with the capitalist pressures of the NEP. Thus the Chaianov school underestimated the pressures towards social differentiation and its impact on social relations.

Snail's pace change of the sort Bukharin advocated made sense from Chaianov's perspective. Since capitalist development was ruled out there was nothing to fear from allowing the spontaneous process of economic growth on the land. Like Bukharin, Chaianov assigned a pivotal role to cooperation: 'When today we speak about the countryside of the future, our hopes are entrusted to cooperation.'[89] He too suggested very slow growth towards the new cooperative society: 'this prolonged stage of development of our rural economy, will, in all probability, only be reached through the persistent labour of several generations ... from fifty to one hundred years.'[90] The same criticism of Bukharin for drawing on non-Marxist ideas could be levelled at his macro-economic thinking. This drew partly on the bourgeois economist Kondratiev, who stressed economic growth cycles rather than the class character of the economic system.[91]

The idea of cooperation led to the most distinctive feature of Bukharinist doctrine, the theory of 'growing into socialism'.[92] Bukharin was convinced that:

> in the final analysis the peasant's own economic growth will move him along the road toward his personal conversion and the conversion of his farm into one particle of our state socialist system – just as he grows into a system of capitalist relations under a capitalist regime.[93]

Later Bukharin would be much attacked by Stalinists for such statements. His suggestion that as society moved closer to full socialism the elements of class antagonism between proletariat and peasantry would decrease was supposed to show that 'Comrade Bukharin has forgotten an elementary point of Marxism, that class struggle is an inevitable consequence of the existence of classes and class contradictions.'[94] This criticism was inaccurate.

In fact, Bukharin did not imagine that all peasants would 'grow into socialism'. He thought the kulak would remain under a cooperative system as 'an alien body similar, for example, to concession enterprises'.[95] Furthermore, the Stalinist suggestion of a fixed antagonism between proletariat and peasantry ignored the ambiguous nature of the peasants. While the immediate interests of the petty bourgeoisie were not the same as the proletariat's, they were not automatically antagonistic either. Capitalists could only lose by the establishment of socialism. The peasant, as half worker, half huckster, could in the right circumstances choose socialism. It was not inevitable that the peasantry would 'grow into capitalism' and had to be crushed.

Support for cooperation was not unique to Bukharin; it was shared by others, including Lenin and Trotsky. However, the latter two stipulated that the specific gravity of industry and the working class must be great enough, politically and industrially, to win over the mass of peasants to collaboration. The left opposition argued:

> Cooperative buying and selling will be a road to socialism only in the event that: 1) this process takes place under the immediate economic and political influence of the socialist elements, especially

of large-scale industry and the trade unions; and 2) this process of making the trade functions of agriculture cooperative gradually leads to the collectivisation of agriculture itself ... The task of the party is to see that agricultural cooperation constitutes a real union of the poor and middle groups of the peasants, and is a weapon in the struggle of those elements against the growing economic power of the kulak.[96]

Under Bukharin cooperation did not follow this path, but mainly helped the individualistic rich peasants. Carr gives examples of cooperatives where 'A poor peasant had to pay 30% down for a plough, and the remaining 70% after the first harvest; a middle peasant ... paid 15% down, and got credit for three years at half the rate charged to the poor peasant.'[97] Lewin reports:

> In 1929, the cooperative movement embraced only one third of the agricultural population ... There is agreement among reliable sources that the cooperative movement mainly served the interests of the better-off peasants ... It was the middle peasants and especially the better-off among them who were the most conscious of the advantages of cooperation. These strata were therefore the best organised, and inevitably they and the kulaks wielded greater influence and occupied a dominant position in the local cooperative associations. At this stage, therefore, the movement which, according to doctrine, was to be a major factor in leading the peasants to socialism ... helped the private farmer to improve his individual holding. *The only possible result of this was further to reinforce the general trend towards individual farming.*[98]

9 The Market and Transition to Socialism

Bukharin's economic policy raised wide theoretical issues. Prior to the NEP his views of the market were unequivocal. In an early article he attacked the German economist Oppenheimer, in ironical terms: 'do not be surprised, reader: he actually defends free competition, calling it *socialist!*'[1] In Bukharin's *Economics of the Transition Period* socialism is described as a system where 'the social economy is regulated not by the blind forces of the market and competition, but by a consciously followed plan.'[2] Under the NEP he spoke differently. Socialism was being built '*on the basis of market relations*';[3] and, 'the development of socialism is through market links, through market exchange of commodities between town and country.'[4]

His later stance involved a complete revision of Marxism and followed logically from the theory of socialism in one country: the USSR was building socialism; this was expressed by the rise of 'socialist industry'. If industry worked through market exchange, then – hey presto! – the market led to socialism.

In 1926 Bukharin was challenged by the publication of *The New Economics*, a book by Preobrazhensky, his former collaborator on *The ABC of Communism* and now a leading oppositionist. Preobrazhensky wrote that Russia was a battleground between two conflicting economic laws, 'the law of primitive socialist accumulation' and 'the law of value' operating in free market conditions. The former led to socialism, the latter back to capitalism. Preobrazhensky did not say that the law of value should be instantly discarded, a ridiculous idea in current conditions, but that it must be resisted.

Marx defined the law of value as follows:

> Two *commodities* exchange in proportion to the *labour materialised in them*. Equal quantities of materialised labour are exchanged for one another. Labour-time is their standard measure ... If the commodity A contains one working-day, then it will exchange against any quantity of commodities which likewise contains one working-day.'[5]

In the practical operation of capitalism prices diverge from the value embodied in them. Nevertheless, capitalist exchange is upon the basis of the labour time involved in the production of commodities.

Preobrazhensky summarised the effect of the law of value as:

> the law of spontaneous equilibrium of commodity-capitalist society. In a society without commanding centres of planned regulation, thanks to the operation of this law, direct or indirect, everything is achieved which is needed for the comparatively normal functioning of a whole productive system of the commodity-capitalist type.[6]

However, the law of value was not a neutral economic regulator, but a specific social relation which was part of capitalism and constantly regenerated its class structure:

> Under this economic system we have, if the expression may be used, congealed groups of people engaged in the process of production and distribution, as they are formed on the basis of the spontaneous self-regulation of the economy by the law of value ... these groups are constantly reproduced at each fresh state of capitalist development, forming definite types of relations of production and distribution.[7]

The workings of the law of value could clearly be seen in the NEP. It was restoring the economy using capitalist methods. If this was so, what remained of the struggle for a new socialist society? According to Preobrazhensky this was reflected in the 'law of primitive socialist accumulation' that worked alongside and against the law of value: *'By the law of primitive socialist accumulation we mean the entire sum of tendencies in the state economy which are directed towards the expansion and consolidation of the collective organisation of labour in Soviet economy.'* Preobrazhensky meant that whereas 'value' was the law of motion for capitalism, a different set of rules applied to the elements of socialist economy.

The law of primitive socialist accumulation would function in two areas:

> *(1) the determination of proportions in the distribution of productive forces, formed on the basis of struggle against the law of value inside and outside the country and having as their objective task the achievement of the optimum expanded socialist reproduction in the given conditions and of the maximum defensive capacity of the whole system in conflict with capitalist commodity production; (2) the determination of the proportions of accumulation of material resources for expanded reproduction, especially at the expense of private economy, in so far as the determined amounts of this accumulation are dictated*

compulsorily to the Soviet state under threat of economic disproportion, growth of private capital, weakening of the bond between the state economy and peasant production, derangement in years to come of the necessary proportions of expanded socialist reproduction and weakening of the whole system in its conflict with capitalist commodity production inside and outside the country.[8]

Instead of economic structure being shaped spontaneously through the capitalist law of value, Preobrazhensky believed there had to be a policy which would defend and extend the socialist tendencies from within and without. Preobrazhensky's law implied a struggle between two types of economy.

Bukharin rejected Preobrazhensky's law on various grounds. One was its immediate policy implications. Primitive socialist accumulation suggested interfering in price relations between industry and agriculture. The state should not lament its monopoly position, but use it consciously to alter prices in favour of industry. Preobrazhensky called his policy 'unequal exchange'. Prices should be deliberately set high to 'pump over' resources from the peasant economy into the industrial economy. Without such accumulation to strengthen itself, the revolutionary proletariat would be too weak to survive the pressure of capitalism. These ideas ran directly counter to all Bukharin had argued since the scissors crisis. Unlike Preobrazhensky, Bukharin had no fears for the internal economic development of an isolated Russia and saw industrial growth as guaranteed by agricultural expansion. He denounced Preobrazhensky's scheme for unequal exchange as a recipe for high prices and 'the *exploitation* of small producers'.[9]

However, Preobrazhensky was not advocating maximum industrial prices or seeking a return to the scissors crisis. He *did* want to end Bukharin's policy of pressing for the maximum possible reduction of industrial prices. Preobrazhensky thought the optimum position would be to regulate prices in favour of industry and simultaneously carry out 'a policy of reducing prices'.[10] How could industrial prices be both used to pump over value from agriculture and simultaneously lowered? Preobrazhensky's answer was that investment in new plant, particularly for heavy industry, would allow a fall in the costs of manufacturing. If only *part* of this fall were passed on to the peasant consumer through lower prices, an extra profit could be gained by industry, ensuring even more rapid progress (and lower prices) in the future.

Preobrazhensky was not offering an easy way out. The risk of provoking a new scissors crisis and reviving peasant discontent was great. His policy meant balancing on a razor's edge between promoting working-class interests and breaking the worker – peasant bloc, between accumulation for investment and mass consumption, between heavy industry (for rapid industrial growth) and light industry (for satisfying direct needs), between restricting circulation (through interfering with prices) and generating new goods for trade. This policy did not involve economics alone. It meant altering the government's treatment of the different classes in society. In particular it challenged Bukharin's assumptions about the need to give maximum and seemingly unlimited concessions to the rich peasantry.

As well as rejecting its policy implications, Bukharin denied the theoretical validity of the term 'primitive socialist accumulation'. It had first been used by V. M. Smirnov and then by Bukharin himself in his *Economics of the Transition Period*. Primitive socialist accumulation drew an analogy with the period of 'primitive *capitalist* accumulation' that Marx had identified.[11] During the rise of capitalism, plunder at home and abroad was used to gather resources for industrialisation. Through this the human and material resources for industrial capital to become self-generating were amassed. In Preobrazhensky's view Russia's backward economy needed a period of accumulation too, although in a different form to capitalism's.

Bukharin charged Preobrazhensky with wanting to re-enact the horror of primitive *capitalist* accumulation, treating the peasantry as its 'colony'. This accusation was easily made because the analogy with early capitalism invited critics to see parallels in Preobrazhensky's law. The first drafts of his book failed sufficiently to draw distinctions between the two processes. Yet Bukharin's attack was unfair. Bukharin might choose to ignore possible contradictions between the economic tendencies of proletarian industry on the one hand and peasant agriculture on the other, but this did not mean that these contradictions were not present, or that anyone who pointed them out was declaring war on the peasantry.

In fact, Preobrazhensky saw industry and agriculture as complementary as well as antagonistic, writing:

> In our economy there is, of course, a certain unity, a certain co-operation between the two sectors. But neither this unity nor this co-operation can be understood correctly if one does not take as the axis of one's study the struggle of the socialist sector against private economy, especially on the world scale ... And, secondly, we must not forget the forced character of our co-operation with private economy. There is co-operation in prison, too. Are we not in a sort

of concentration camp along with the capitalist elements of our economy? We are at one and the same time warders and prisoners. We are prisoners because we are separated by the prison-wall of time from the world socialist revolution ... We are warders because by the wall of our monopoly of foreign trade, our tariff system, our planned imports and the resulting forced internal price-level we have separated our private economy from world private economy.[12]

Preobrazhensky and the left opposition provided no instant solutions (for by definition there were none in national isolation), but they argued for an active policy to bolster the working-class position. By rejecting interference with the market mechanism Bukharin was defending a policy of socialist *laissez-faire* for capitalist economics. His opposition to primitive socialist accumulation left the working class passive in the face of internal and external forces.

It would, however, be an injustice to Bukharin to ignore his fear of new forms of exploitation. He reflected the degeneration of the revolution, not its death, as would Stalin. Therefore his opposition to forced industrialisation, his warnings against colonial-type exploitation, although a misreading of the left opposition's programme, had a rationale. Trotsky too was aware of the danger that Preobrazhensky's law would be misused:

> In the analysis of our economy from the point of view of its internal dynamics (struggle and co-operation) the laws of value and socialist accumulation are in principle fruitful in the highest degree. It is true to say that they alone are correct. The investigation necessarily must begin within the framework of a closed Soviet economy. But there now arises the danger that this methodological approach will be turned into the formalistic economic perspective of 'the development of socialism in one country'. It should be expected, for the danger is there, that the supporters of this philosophy ... will now attempt to transform Preobrazhensky's analysis, converting a methodological approach into a general quasi-autonomous process. Come what may it is necessary to avoid such plagiarism and such falsification. The internal dynamics of the law of value and socialist accumulation have to be posed in the context of the world economy.[13]

Indeed, remove the word 'socialist', subtract its internationalist class content and Preobrazhensky's law could become primitive *capitalist* accumulation. Alas, this was exactly what Preobrazhensky encouraged when he capitulated to Stalin. At the Seventeenth Party Congress in 1934

Preobrazhensky confessed to having missed something out in his *New Economics*: 'Collectivisation, that is the essential point. Did I foresee collectivisation? I did not ... What was needed was Stalin's remarkable far-sightedness, his great courage in facing the problems, the greatest hardness in applying policies'.[14] Nove adds: 'reading between the lines, what [Preobrazhensky] seemed to be saying was that primitive socialist accumulation had been ruthlessly imposed by collectivisation, not that his earlier doctrines had been proved false by events.'[15]

Forced collectivisation completely transformed the content of Preobrazhensky's theory. This policy had nothing socialist about it, but everything to do with primitive *state capitalist* accumulation, designed to help the USSR compete with the West. If the *New Economics* could be misused after 1929, this should not detract from its value in the different context of the mid-1920s. Exactly the same argument applies to Trotsky's programme, which market socialists allege led to Stalinism. The policies of Trotsky and Preobrazhensky were in fact the best means of avoiding or postponing the onset of Stalinist counter-revolution.

Bukharin's fight with Preobrazhensky went beyond questioning the law of primitive socialist accumulation to defending the law of value. He used this quotation from Marx for his purpose:

> Every child knows that a country which ceased to work, I will not say for a year, but for a few weeks, would die. Every child knows too that the mass of products corresponding to the different needs require different and quantitatively determined masses of the total labour of society. That this necessity of distributing social labour in definite proportions cannot be done away with by the *particular form* of social production, but can only change the *form it assumes* is self-evident. No natural laws can be done away with. What can change, in changing historical circumstances, is the *form* in which this proportional division of labour operates.[16]

Bukharin concluded that the law of value should not be combated, because it was, in his words, just one 'specific manifestation' of a 'law of proportional labour expenditure' which 'is a necessity for social development in *all and every social formation*'.[17]

Thus far his argument is broadly acceptable. An economy must operate according to certain principles and the distribution of labour time is the key regulator. However, while it is all very well to say that labour expenditure is one element of economic calculation and should inform policy decisions, this does not mean that it should *determine* those decisions. Neither is exchange in the marketplace the only or best way to ascertain labour expenditure.

By rejecting state interference with the market, Bukharin suggested that the economic mechanism inherited from before the socialist revolution should be left to develop autonomously. A socialist society required something different. As Marx put it: 'Communism differs from all previous movements in that it overturns the basis of all earlier relations of production and intercourse, and ... subjugates them to the power of the united individuals.'[18] How could the united individuals subjugate the economic forces if they continued to be ruled by an anarchic market system regulated by the law of value?

Bukharin was not so crude as to suggest that capitalism's basic law of motion would continue unchanged into socialism. He predicted that the transition from capitalism to socialism would witness *'the process of transforming the law of value into the law of labour expenditure, a process of defetishising the fundamental social regulator'*.[19] What he meant was that those features of the law of value that generated capitalism should disappear; but he did not explain adequately *how* this was to happen.

It is true that in the struggle for socialism no natural laws could be abrogated, nor could the technically necessary equilibrium between different elements of an economy be ignored for any length of time. It would be senseless, for example, to concentrate only on making bricks without using them for building houses, or to attempt to build houses without making bricks. But to say only this meant failing to show how a society could transform its economic structure from one type to another, from one state of equilibrium to another. Bukharin's own *Economics of the Transition Period* had shown why his later position was insufficient. The passage to socialism inevitably involved a disruption of economic relations during which the constituent elements were deconstructed and then reassembled in a new shape. The element which Bukharin did not grasp in his earlier phase was that disruption to the physical existence of the working class had to be minimised at the same time as the economic foundations for the new society were being laid down. Nevertheless, the basic premise in the *Economics of the Transition Period* had been sound. By now rejecting any disruption, Bukharin ruled out the new economic order that could have replaced the NEP's capitalist relations.

Bukharin's favourite analogy – the passage from feudalism to capitalism – is useful in considering who was right about the economic transition to socialism. To achieve their dominance the capitalists resorted to violent revolution on occasion. At other times capitalism coexisted with various forms of exploitation over a long period. This was possible because as long as the capitalists' right to exploitation was not challenged these other forms could be left to wither away. The working class cannot take a gradualist route of non-interference in the transition from capitalism to socialism. Capitalist exploitation cannot easily coexist alongside socialism, because capitalism presupposes the exploitation of workers. That was why, even if the capitalist law of value could not be overthrown instantly, as Preobrazhensky admitted, it had to be fought as much as circumstances allowed.

Conscious intervention was needed to alter the economic structure and move from one society to the next. This was not solely for material reasons. If the working class was fully to shed the ideology of capitalism it had to learn to rule, to control its fate consciously. In other words, the workers had to do battle with the law of value if they were to develop themselves as a ruling class.

This does not mean that Bukharin's emphasis on the existence of a 'law of labour expenditure' was erroneous. However, it was wrong to accuse Preobrazhensky of ignoring it. The latter's argument was not about imposing an *arbitrary* economic system. On the contrary, his policy of conscious intervention depended upon being aware of labour expenditure in different sectors of society. Interventions would occur in such a way that society was no longer left to the mercy of the chance operation of the market, with its in-built anarchy and tendency to give rise to exploitative class relations. This coincided with Marx's view of how a communist society would come about:

> On the basis of communal production, the determination of [labour] time remains, of course, essential. The less time the society requires to produce wheat, cattle etc., the more time it wins for other production, material or mental ... Economy of time, to this all economy ultimately reduces itself. Society likewise has to distribute its time in a purposeful way ... the planned distribution of labour time among the various branches of production remains the first economic law on the basis of communal production. ***It becomes law, there, to an even higher degree.***[20]

The transition from the law of value to the law of labour expenditure required a qualitative leap, to be achieved through the active intervention of the working class. Bukharin's policies obstructed this.

In the 1930s the Stalinists charged Bukharin with consciously advocating a return to capitalism. This charge was false. Bukharin did theorise about the transition from a capitalist to a socialist economy.

However, he failed to demonstrate successfully how to move from an economy ruled by the capitalist law of value to one where exchange of labour served to overcome exploitation and build socialism. Bukharin believed that a simple expansion of the state sector would accomplish this task, implying that there should be no interference with the law of value in the meantime. This approach overlooked the fact that economic growth, even under state ownership, does not equal socialism. The socialist character of state industry is not secured by the good intentions of a workers' state. That state and its workers must be free to use industry for socialist purposes – the abolition of poverty, of exploitation and ultimately of classes themselves. Without an international revolution, such freedom was beyond the reach of Russia in the 1920s. The size and significance of the peasantry at home and the need for defence from capitalism abroad imposed different priorities.

This is not to argue the ultra-left case that if Russian industry was not straightforwardly socialist then it must perforce have been capitalist, or that for socialism to be viable it must wipe out capitalism everywhere and all at once. But it is a recognition that socialism does not amount to abstract economic growth or certain forms of ownership. Stalinists and Western economists have described the difference between capitalism and socialism as the market versus planned economy. This is wrong. Both the market system and elements of planned production existed long before the rule of capitalism. Such forms on their own define nothing; *social relations* are the key. The reason that the market is inextricably tied up with capitalism today is that it operates in a context of autonomous economic units competing to survive. It is this economic struggle that imposes an imperative of exploitation upon all the participants. State ownership and planning can also be methods of capitalist exploitation if their context is competition between autonomous national units. In neither his early wish to abolish all capitalist economic categories instantaneously, nor his later acceptance of them, did Bukharin get to grips with these problems.

Bukharin's rejection of Preobrazhensky's law, and his prediction of monopolistic degeneration, followed the argument of a Western economist of the 1920s – von Mises. The latter predicted that communism must fail because without the market it was impossible to gauge the real costs of products or to realise higher levels of productivity. In fact, the solution to this problem is not difficult to find. A socialist society would set aside a portion of its social surplus for experimentation, just as capitalism does, although the portion would probably be higher and certainly not largely dedicated to arms, as is the case now. Using accounting techniques perfected in existing industry, the prototypes of such new inventions or methods could be tested and the quantity of labour time assessed, just as large-scale capitalist enterprises do today. The difference is that adoption on a mass scale would be decided by a balance between costs in labour time and *social advantage* rather than profitability. This opens up tremendous new choices, quite apart from abolishing the extraordinary suffering and waste inevitably linked to the competitive struggle and the boom/slump cycle.

Imagine, for example, that a new production process, say a new form of energy generation, allows for the lowering of labour time in the power sector. Under capitalism new techniques face an uphill battle to be applied because they challenge vested interests. If they are introduced their secrets are jealously guarded by patent so that the advantage is not shared generally. Those who have the most to gain from technical advance – the poor and exploited – are the very last to enjoy it, if at all. Very often technical progress brings only misery and unemployment to these people. Under capitalism technical advance *increases* the rate of exploitation (the time spent making profits for the boss as opposed to paying the workers' wages).

Under socialism the situation is different. Let us say investment in the new form of energy generation is deemed socially worthwhile. Now instead of profit dictating, the democratic choice is open as to whether the invention should help to shorten the working day in society as a whole, increase the social surplus available for future investment, lower consumption costs (that is, energy prices) or allow power to be included in the free distribution sector. It would be nonsensical to guard the new process from others, to resist its introduction, or to make anyone suffer through its application. New technology, which previously appeared as a threat or a means of greater exploitation in the hands of an alien class, now becomes an invaluable tool through social control and planning.

Such a socialist economy is not achieved by accident. It is won through struggling to take socialist relations forward (as Preobrazhensky described); production is organised on an increasingly rational basis to supplant the law of value, because that is made unnecessary.

Bukharin claimed that he provided a theory of transition to socialism. Rather, as Trotsky put it, his was a theory 'good only for paving the way to our "integration into capitalism"'.[21] The faults in Bukharin's position were illustrated in the speech he made to the Fifth Comintern Congress:

the experience, not only of Russia, but also of other countries, shows that one will only emerge from the anarchy of production through the market, through competition between the proletarian state economy, between the socialised enterprises and all the other economic forms. Externally the method is that of the capitalist economy. The great difference consists of the fact that in the capitalist economy the large and medium enterprises are found in the hands of private capital; but where the large enterprises are proletarian there is a competition taking place, a revolutionary struggle, a class struggle between proletariat and bourgeoisie ... Externally everything carries on more or less as under a capitalist regime ... We really do have capitalist forms: wage payment, monetary circulation instead of distribution of products; banks and stock exchanges, yes, even exchanges, these sanctuaries of the capitalist class. We have competition and even profit within our state enterprises ... but [their] social character is different, and this is what is important.[22]

Because Bukharin never thought dialectically, he did not consider that there might be a tension between capitalist forms and proletarian content, that one must influence the other. Timing and struggle are of the essence here. It is true that socialism does not exist the day after the revolution, and that there is a combination of both capitalist and socialist elements at work in the economy. But if the development of socialism is too slow, or the class too passive, then quantitative growth of capitalist relations turns into qualitative challenge and the political gains of the revolution can be overthrown. Bukharin's mistake in the mid-1920s was the converse of his earlier ultra-left errors. Previously form and content had been treated as identical. Capitalist forms meant capitalist content: peace with Germany meant total capitulation to imperialism; Lenin's state capitalism under proletarian dictatorship equalled counter-revolution; wage payment equalled wage slavery. That was ultra-left. Now as a right-winger Bukharin said that form had no bearing on content whatsoever. Capitalist forms of exploitation, such as sweated labour, could be used with impunity. This argument was later used by Stalinists to excuse the denial of workers' rights.

Bukharin's early policies were superior to his later ones because they delineated the basic line of development towards socialism. Problems chiefly arose when it came to the subsequent detailed steps of implementation. The right-wing Bukharin was inferior in that he suggested that the socialist goal had already been reached. With this approach it was impossible to advance further.

Marx had suggested an answer to the problem of the transition which avoided both ultra-left and right-wing traps. He described the immediate post-revolutionary situation in these terms. The new society would not have developed 'on its own foundations, but on the contrary, just as it *emerged* from capitalist society. In every respect, economically morally, intellectually, it is thus still stamped with the birth-marks of the old society from whose womb it has emerged.'[23] In these circumstances the transition to socialism involved a recognition of both the objective framework and the need to mobilise the subjective factor to transform social relations.

How can these two elements be combined? Although the socialist revolution will make workers the ruling class, they will still have to be a living productive force in society. Even after a successful revolution in an industrialised country, while workers will rule they will continue as producers, an object of production. Now, it is easy to declare that once workers have seized power and are managing the factories, then theoretically they cannot exploit themselves. This had been Bukharin's position during war communism and later followed from his certainty of 'socialism in one country'. But he confused the formal structure of power and management with its social content. Unless there is an impetus to advance, unless there is a struggle with the old world, workers' leaders may come to reflect the pressure of these old social forces and structures. The danger is especially great in unfavourable conditions, such as the presence of a large non-working-class sector or international isolation and imperialist pressure.

Under those circumstances the danger of capitalist restoration comes from two directions. First, any attempt to develop the productive forces voluntaristically over the heads of the masses will degenerate into elitist bureaucratic planning, accumulation *at the expense of the masses*. In that case the workers cease to be the ruling class and are treated solely as objects of exploitation. At the top of society now stands a bureaucracy which maintains itself by class oppression and competition with foreign ruling classes. This is a reversion, in the form of state capitalism, which Bukharin warned of in his dispute with Preobrazhensky.

On the other hand, if the working class renounces the attempt consciously to reshape the inherited economic structures, or if it does not strive to expand the productive forces (because this is regarded as too dangerous an exercise), then it fails to maintain the human or material basis for a different society. If the workers do not fight to master the means of production, they are mastered by them, just as under capitalism. It was this fear that was expressed in the *Left Communist Theses*. In this form, capitalism could reassert itself through its greater efficiency and might internally, externally or both. Such capitalism does not have to be private. It could come from a state bureaucracy shaped by the social pressures of production whose structure still included 'wage payment, monetary circulation instead of distribution of products; banks and stock exchanges'.

What happened in Russia was that both scenarios occurred. The NEP represented a necessary abandonment of the ultra-left attempt to transform relations of production through voluntarism. But under the NEP there was no attempt to alter those relations either. At the end of the 1920s Stalin led a new ruling class which had, thanks to this policy, become conscious of its self-interest, had become a 'class for itself'. In the Five-Year Plans Stalin turned to the voluntarist version of capitalist rule outlined above.

Trotsky and the Economic Debate Before the Stalin Counter-revolution

Hindsight gives a wonderful advantage to those who wish to be wise after the event. However, if used carelessly it can seriously distort our understanding of the past. Nowhere is this more true than with the economic debate. Today there are various explanations for the Stalinist counter-revolution. Pro-market historians in Russia have put forward a view that derives from Bukharin, according to which Trotsky and Preobrazhensky were the chief culprits.[24] Is this justified?

Trotsky's viewpoint was determined by an awareness of the contradictory position of the Russian revolution which contrasted with the bureaucratic complacency of the proponents of 'socialism in one country'. Trotsky may have proposed planning, for instance, but this was only one element of an overall approach which, he said, 'can only be a politics of manoeuvrability, one which requires the greatest attention to the soundings of the channel bottom, with special attention to possible shoals, and careful steering to avoid both banks, right and left'.[25] All the left opposition's proposals had to be understood in a context where 'No domestic policy can by itself deliver us from the economic, political, and military dangers of the capitalist encirclement.'[26]

In the years 1926–7, when the factional struggle reached its peak, Trotsky argued that under certain circumstances it might be possible to say: 'With Stalin against Bukharin? – Yes. With Bukharin against Stalin? – Never.'[27] Deutscher, his biographer, finds this 'an act of suicidal folly ... short-sightedness or blindness'.[28] Nove argues that 'it was evidently a tragedy for the party, and for the two men who would later be destroyed by Stalin, that its two most talented exponents had engaged so much of their energy attacking each other.'[29] Was Trotsky as misguided as Deutscher and Nove suggest? Would Bukharin have been a better ally than Stalin? To answer this we must go beyond the individuals to ask: what was the source of degeneration in the situation that was leading towards counter-revolution?

The key factor was the isolation of the world's only workers' state. As a result civil war had had a devastating effect. This caused the eruption of peasant discontent which led to the NEP, further altering the internal balance of forces against the working class. As a result pressure built up on the leading sectors in the party and state, distorting and eventually subverting their socialist aims.

Historians coming afterwards can point to all these elements. But one vital ingredient is missing – the subjective factor. All the others were the result of outside forces which the Bolsheviks had not created, did not want and could not do all that much about. A Marxist does not bemoan unfavourable objective conditions but tries to use analysis and knowledge of workers' past struggles to alter them. Here, I would argue, Trotsky was correct in ruling out an alliance with Bukharin, even if his position became wrong when Stalin changed course in 1928–9. The opposition had to grasp the one link in the chain of circumstances it could do something about. This was a political defence of the traditions of Marx, Lenin and the October revolution. Any hope of combating the rising bureaucracy, finding a correct relationship with the peasantry, helping to restore the working class and promoting international revolution, depended on winning and maintaining the revolutionary core of the Bolshevik Party. This was why Trotsky's target was rightly Bukharin, the chief ideological enemy of all these things.

But what of Stalin? Was Trotsky correct to see him as less dangerous than Bukharin? The distinction between Bukharin and Stalin at this time was an extremely fine one and rested more on a division of labour within the duumvirate than anything else. Yet Trotsky was right to see a difference (if only a marginal one) between the two men.

Bukharin was playing the key role in ideologically disarming the working class. Trotsky saw that it was his exceptional ability as a theoretician that led to:

> completely uncritical camouflaging of what exists in the USSR and of everything that is coming into being [which] blunts the vigilance and alertness of the party ... It nourishes a passive fatalistic optimism

beneath which bureaucratic indifference to the destinies of socialism and the international revolution is able to hide.[30]

Although he had originated the theory of 'socialism in one country' and shared many ideas with Bukharin, Stalin's strength lay in the party apparatus. Bukharin's base was more diverse, extending through the state to party and non-party intellectuals and a broad range of the bureaucracy. For this reason Trotsky evaluated Bukharin and Stalin differently. Discussing their respective supporters, Trotsky wrote:

> [The Bukharinists] are inclined to think that everything needed for human well-being has already been done, and to regard anyone who does not acknowledge this as an enemy. The attitude of these elements towards the Opposition is one of organic hatred ... This conservative layer, which constitutes Stalin's most powerful support in his struggle against the Opposition, is inclined to go much further to the right, in the direction of the new propertied elements, than Stalin himself, or the main nucleus of his faction.[31]

Trotsky should be criticised for underestimating Stalin's threat, but if we consider how matters stood at this time his mistake is comprehensible. As Bukharin's bureaucratic base was in the state, it was most accessible to the pressure of class forces outside the proletariat. In his call for the kulaks to 'enrich yourselves' Bukharin, with his characteristic zeal, was expressing the thoughts of the capitulationist wing of the bureaucracy. Stalin's wing on the other hand, closely identified with the party machine, was more distanced from petty-bourgeois pressures, more independent and less flexible. It was not about to capitulate to outside forces, but would fight for its corner. At that time it was an adminstrative threat to the revolution as it manoeuvred to crush opposition. However, its political capitulation did not seem to have gone as far as Bukharin's, as was shown by the criticism Bukharin received from the Stalinists for his slogan 'enrich yourselves'.

With hindsight it is clear Trotsky was wrong not to perceive that Stalin was at the heart of the bureaucracy, with control of the state and means of production, factors that would prove far more decisive than Bukharin and all his word-spinning. Moreover, if Trotsky did not see the whole picture he cannot be accused of suicidal folly over his distrust of Bukharin.

10 The Comintern and Disaster: World Bukharinism

When Zinoviev, president of the International, became an oppositionist in December 1925, Bukharin replaced him at the head of the organisation. This position was formalised when, in October 1926, Zinoviev was officially sacked from the presidency and his post abolished. Henceforth Bukharin would run the Comintern as general secretary of its executive committee.

His politics were now to be tested directly. With the exception of the summer of 1917, when Bukharin was on the Bolsheviks' Moscow Committee, his roles as theoretician and newspaper editor (even a paper as important as *Pravda*) had previously always kept him at one remove from active leadership. Apologists can therefore argue that Bukharinism never had a fair or practical test. No such excuses can be made with reference to the Comintern. Here he could pursue his vision on the grandest stage of all – the entire globe.

How strange, therefore, that today's Bukharinists seem so reticent, even coy, about his role in the two historic events of the mid-1920s – the British general strike and Chinese revolution. His Western biographer, Cohen, manages to cover these events in precisely three desultory pages out of some 400 pages of text. Gorelov, Cohen's Russian equivalent, ignores the general strike and Chinese revolution entirely. Perhaps this is because these absolute calamities demonstrate better than anything the morass into which Bukharin had fallen.

Bukharin's role in the Comintern was not just a supplement to his work but a core element, determining not only his personal fate but that of an entire period of world history too. Although the adherents of 'socialism in one country' could not see it, events in Russia had always and inextricably been linked to outside developments. The Brest-Litovsk treaty became an unavoidable necessity when Germany's mass strikes of January 1918 failed to break the German state. The failure of the Spartakist rising in January 1919 left the Bolsheviks facing civil war in desperate circumstances and with no choice but to pursue war communism. The German March Action of 1921 was a voluntarist attempt by elements in the international Communist movement to undo the noose that was compelling the adoption of the NEP at the very same moment. Its predictable defeat ensured that the NEP grew from piecemeal concessions to comprehensive retreat. The missed revolutionary opportunity in Germany during October 1923 immediately became a cause of, and a major issue in, the Russian factional struggle. The failure weakened the Trotskyists. This link between the internal and external worlds did not disappear when Bukharin adopted the theory of 'socialism in one country'.

Twin disasters in Britain and China would seal the fate of both the left opposition and of Bukharin himself. Although the crushing of the Chinese revolution in 1927 was the excuse for dismembering the Trotskyist movement, it left the bureaucracy feeling vulnerable internationally. This was compounded when mistakes committed in the 1926 general strike allowed the British ruling class to break off relations with the USSR and adopt an aggressive posture. Stalin used the ensuing war panic to impose his state capitalist policies, and in the process Bukharin and his 'right deviation' were destroyed.

Socialism in One Country as World Policy

The October revolution had been made under the banner of the *Communist Manifesto* – 'Workers of the World, Unite!' Bukharin's tenure at the Comintern saw this internationalism extinguished. The social roots of this process were to be found at the very base of society, as an eye-witness in Russia recounted in October 1926:

> As concerns questions of Communist international policy, there reigns complete indifference; no world-wide and universal revolution is being expected, and no personal welfare whatsoever is being expected from it. Resolutions in this respect are being passed as a political duty. In general the humdrum quiet of ordinary inhabitants predominates among these workmen.[1]

This broad sentiment was hardly surprising at a time when, as a Yugoslav communist visitor to Comintern headquarters observed:

> there was an abyss between the great speeches about 'the general staff of the World Revolution' and the reality. The importance of the Comintern was considerably less in Moscow than that of any of the People's Commissariats [government ministries]. It was nothing but

a foreign section attached to the Propaganda Service of the Central Committee.[2]

Bukharin had helped create this situation. With his customary ruthless but one-sided logic, he had applied to the Comintern exactly the same approach adopted at home. The result was the systematic dismantling, stone by stone, principle by principle, of the edifice of proletarian internationalism established in the early years.

In the summer of 1923 Bukharin hovered between the left and his future place on the right. Germany was then in the grip of hyper-inflation and a massive crisis that put international workers' revolution on the agenda once more. It is uncertain what role Bukharin played in the final decision to cancel the 'German October' and abandon the project of revolution in that country when it stood probably its best chance of succeeding.[3] However, the failure in 1923 had a profoundly demoralising effect on the USSR, where faith in international revolution was severely shaken.

The theory of 'socialism in one country' came forward as a rationalisation and justification for continued isolation. Few could have foreseen what an impact the theory would have when Bukharin took over the Comintern.

First, it destroyed the concept of 'world economy', that invaluable element of Bukharin's book on *Imperialism*. The concept was important because it meant that, although not developed evenly in each and every place, the forces of production had attained a point where socialism was on the global agenda for the first time. It explained the world crisis and internecine struggle among capitalists which made workers' revolution both a possibility and an urgent necessity. Finally, a world capitalist economy meant that proletarian revolution must be *international* if it was to match and defeat the old system economically and politically.

'Socialism in one country' denied world economy. Bukharin's report to the Seventh Plenum of the Executive Committee of the Communist International (ECCI) in 1927 stated: 'The contemporary world economy is a real unity only in a conditional sense of the word ... That is why any so-called "general conclusions" in regard to the whole world economy ... are still more conditional than they were before the war.'[4] The world, he said, was splintered into many different and arbitrary groupings. In 1927 he discerned no less than six of these, including American, Russian, British and Japanese blocs.[5]

Bukharin justified the throwing out of perhaps his greatest single insight by quoting an article Lenin wrote in 1915 about 'the law of uneven capitalist development'. This had stressed both the differences that existed between countries and their interconnection in the world economy. Bukharin's initial conclusion from this was valid:

> the Bolsheviks do not start out with the assertion that ... at every point of the globe the degree of concentration and centralisation of capitalism and the centralisation of the working class etc. was the same and equally adequate for the transition to socialism.[6]

However, until 'socialism in one country', this incontrovertible argument had driven the Bolsheviks to see October 1917 as part of a larger process, a single piece in the jigsaw of international proletarian revolution. Russia had been regarded as too poor, its working class too small, to create socialism without outside assistance. Now, by contrast, individual revolutions were treated as isolated self-sufficient entities, discrete national events separated from other revolutions by great stretches of time. World revolution was

> rather a prolonged process. It is a whole epoch. Of course, I hope that this epoch will be considerably shorter than the epoch of the bourgeois revolutions, but it must be borne in mind that the revolution in England took place in the seventeenth century, the Great French Revolution took place at the end of the eighteenth century. A number of bourgeois revolutions took place later.[7]

Bukharin 'hoped' the process would not take centuries.

Trotsky demolished these arguments in his critique of Bukharin's Draft Comintern Programme of 1928:

> That the international revolution of the proletariat cannot be a simultaneous act, of this there can of course be no dispute among grown-up people after the experience of the October Revolution, achieved by the proletariat of a backward country under pressure of historical necessity, without waiting in the least for the proletariat of the advanced countries to 'even out the front'. Within these limits the reference to the law of uneven development is absolutely correct and quite in place. [But Bukharin] seeks to deduce from the law of uneven development something which the law does not and cannot imply. Uneven or sporadic development of various countries acts constantly to *upset* but in no case to *eliminate* the growing economic bonds and interdependence between those countries which the very

next day, after four years of hellish slaughter, were compelled to exchange coal, bread, oil, powder and suspenders with each other.[8]

Bukharin's new outlook was that socialist states could develop independently of the capitalist world and of each other. As early as 1922 he told the Fourth Comintern Congress that even after the spread of international revolution: 'for a long time there will lie before us different national types of socialist forms of production.'[9] Although such arguments undermined the very basis of internationalism, at least in Russia damage was limited by the resistance of the opposition, basing itself on the mighty, if crumbling earthworks of a successful workers' revolution. The young international communist movement lacked such a basis and was more easily crippled.

The sort of havoc that Bukharin's persuasive tongue could inflict was shown at the Fifth Comintern Congress, where he told delegates:

> the proletarian revolution is not the whole world revolution, for there exist other processes of decomposition which have a great revolutionary impact, such as national crises. These are not in any way proletarian revolutions if one considers them in isolation. In the same way, the ever more frequent colonial uprisings are above all movements of the petty bourgeoisie and nationalist elements of the bourgeoisie. Looked at separately these secondary processes are not part of the proletarian revolution. In most cases, they are not directed by the proletariat. But they must not be isolated. In the history of the world they have a revolutionary impact.[10]

This correct argument was twisted to justify the Russian bureaucracy allying itself with 'nationalist elements of the bourgeoisie', not in order to strengthen the overall thrust of international proletarian revolution but to discriminate in their favour against the interests of workers' movements. Communist parties in colonial countries (such as that in China) were consistently subordinated to bourgeois nationalist politicians.

The path to unprincipled alliances was smoothed by Bukharin's misuse of the united front tactic. This policy was designed to show the mass of workers in the West, the majority of whom still supported reformist parties, that revolutionary politics were superior. This could be achieved by communists undertaking joint activities with reformists in temporary and limited alliances. Through the experience of common action the weakness of reformist leaders and their politics would be demonstrated to the rank and file. When the united front was adopted by the Comintern in 1921 Bukharin was still ultra-left. To him this tactic smacked of compromise and he opposed it. However, at the fifth Comintern Congress he announced his conversion:

> Radek has said that some comrades, whom he does not name, have hesitated more than once over the question of the united front. I was among them. My simplistic view was wrong ... [Now] we are fighting only a certain interpretation of this tactic.[11]

Alas, he now fought the correct interpretation of the united front in order to impose his own distorted version. Before, all compromises had been rejected; now, any unprincipled alliance was permitted. Originally the tactic was to unite the reformist and revolutionary wings of the working class in certain forms of joint action, with the communist aim to lead through this towards the overthrow of capitalism. Under Bukharin, however, alliances were forged with non-working class groups, and they were at leadership level only. These alliances were, crucially, *not* based on a commitment to action. In the mid-1920s Bukharin argued:

> The problem of the united front is the problem of allying with the petty bourgeois section of the working class and with the petty bourgeoisie although this does not mean that the section which leads the united front manoeuvre must be the petty bourgeoisie.[12]

By the mid-1920s Bukharin also moved from saying that the national question was '*the right to foolishness*'[13] to uncritical support of nationalist movements. He cited Lenin as his authority. Lenin *had* criticised those who declared national liberation movements irrelevant. But he had *never* suggested that proletarian movements should be held back and smothered so as to assist Russia or not to offend bourgeois nationalists. Yet this was the monstrous position which Bukharin would in practice adopt towards China.

There was a contradiction in Bukharin's position. He said that the international revolution might take centuries. In the same breath he suggested that bourgeois nationalist movements such as the Chinese proved international revolution 'is already a fact. It is on the march, it is a fact which simply cannot be denied.'[14] In his attitude to the proletarian movement his policies were right-wing in practice, but he sounded radical because he put a revolutionary gloss on petty-bourgeois nationalist movements. This was one example of what the left opposition called 'double book-keeping' – revisionist in practice but radical in appearance.

There was another form of double book-keeping that grew out of 'socialism in one country'. On the one hand, Bukharin claimed that there were 'national types of socialism'. Therefore, Russia was absolved from following the established Marxist traditions of class struggle, internationalism and so on. Its state was free to do as it pleased and still call itself socialist. On the other hand, even though Bukharin denied the right for anyone to criticise Russia, it was the only place 'actually building socialism' and so was the model all others *must* follow.

So it was that as early as 1922 Bukharin accorded the NEP universal status as a guide to policy:

> The NEP is indeed a specifically Russian phenomenon on the one hand, but on the other it is a general phenomenon ... When we have taken over the most developed industrial lands do you think that this problem [of the peasantry] will not arise immediately? It will. Could we, for example, organise the American farmer from the start? Do you believe the victorious German proletariat can organise on communist lines all the peasant units, particularly in Bavaria? Of course not.[15]

By 1925 anti-Trotskyism and placing peasants in the centre of politics were both obligatory policies, even where there were practically no Trotskyists or peasants:

> We [in Russia] are putting into practice the correct tactic on the peasant question. Here is the chief reason for our struggle against Trotskyism. Other parties will have to follow our example as soon as they declare themselves against Trotskyism. Their first problem will be to articulate the correct point of view on the peasant question.[16]

Lenin warned the Fourth Comintern Congress that the International had become 'too Russian'. Russian experience had been transposed directly without helping the foreign comrades to understand it or to develop themselves.[17] Undaunted, Bukharin pushed this process to the extreme. Even the historical peculiarities of Russia – a single country which contained both a large sector emerging from feudalism and the most concentrated capitalism with the most advanced proletariat – dissolved away. The USSR became the model for all to follow:

> If in Russia the problem [of the peasantry] stands at the centre of theoretical discussion and practical action, then with certain qualifications, ***exactly the same can be said of the capitalist countries and the semifeudal countries***. This is not accidental. There appears to be a strict

historical law at work ... in the relationship between town and country, the industrial metropolises and agrarian colonies.[18]

Making Russia the model for all countries, Bukharin went on to assert that the key factor for revolutionaries worldwide was not so much the working class as the peasantry:

> Actual concrete capitalism, which it falls to 'us' to overthrow and to 'them' to defend, is not the abstract capitalism of pure theory. It is a capitalism where the overwhelming majority of the population still consists of independent peasant cultivators, of whom only an insignificant portion have become an exploitative force, and who in their fundamental mass are, in various ways, an object of capitalist exploitation.[19]

Bukharin presented figures for the years 1923–4 to prove his point. The population of industrialised Europe, America and Australia came to 684 million; that of peasant Asia and Africa was 1,036 million. But was not the working class a majority in places like Britain, and here, at least, the key political factor? Not at all: 'the epoch of major world capitalism finds the proletariat but a minority of the population. It only *appears* to be the majority in exceptionally developed countries when the existence of their "colonial supplements" is ignored.'[20] So which was now the revolutionary class? – 'the mass force of the fragmented small producers may be – indeed it is becoming – the great liberating force of our time.' Bukharin grudgingly conceded that the peasantry must come 'under the leadership of the proletariat'.[21]

Bukharin was right to point out the importance of the peasantry and its relationship with the proletariat. Trotsky's theory of permanent revolution stressed the same issue. However, Trotsky had insisted on the primacy of proletarian politics, of the struggle for workers' power, as the key to carrying forward the struggle for liberation of both the peasant and the working class. The link between peasants and workers had been one of active proletarian leadership through revolutionary struggle. This was the case notwithstanding the numerical superiority of the peasants. Bukharin's argument led in the opposite direction. He wished to argue that socialist politics should be compromised in order to appeal to the petty-bourgeois leaders of the peasantry.

Trotsky found Bukharin's formulation astounding, adding that it:

> deserves being included in all the textbooks on the dialectic, as a classic example of scholastic thinking.

In the first place, it is quite probable that the correlation of forces between the proletariat and the peasantry on the world scale is not very much different from the correlation within the USSR. But the world revolution is not at all accomplished in accordance with the method of the arithmetical mean, and, incidentally, neither is the national revolution. Thus the October Revolution occurred and entrenched itself first of all in the proletarian Petrograd ... only as a result of this process, called revolution, was there established within the boundaries of the USSR the present correlation between the proletariat and the peasantry. The revolution does not occur in accordance with the method of the arithmetical mean. [22]

Indeed Bukharin's method would have proved that snow was an impossibility because the average world temperature is above freezing point!

Bukharin used other ammunition to obliterate the proletarian tradition in the Comintern. One was the concept of 'capitalist stabilisation', used to describe the ebbing of the world revolutionary tide since the heady days following the First World War. While stabilisation was an undeniable fact, Bukharin's mechanical formulation was an obstacle to understanding. The ebb and flow of class struggle is an extremely complex process, combining objective factors (such as the state of the economy) with politics and mass psychology. Bukharin viewed it more simply. He explained that capitalism had stabilised economically and so revolution was off the agenda in Western Europe. This reversed his 1919 view that 'Old Europe has no future. They cannot restore their economies.'[23] Up to the spring of 1921 he still saw 'in this massive heaving sea of wreckage which is the capitalist structure' only a 'permanent lowering and fall of productive force in all countries'.[24] His 'theory of the offensive' had been the result at that time. Though ultra-left, at least this theory welcomed opportunities for workers' revolution (even if they were sometimes a mirage). The converse position he adopted later on was far more politically dangerous. According to Bukharin, capitalist economic recovery meant that the working class must lapse into a complacent passivity. Nothing could be done about it. At the end of the 1920s, when the Western economies began to look less stable, Bukharin would again lurch towards an ultra-left position.[25]

Trotsky was the first Russian leader to point out the phenomenon of capitalist stabilisation. However, he saw stabilisation as conditional and crucially dependent on the subjective consciousness of the proletariat:

It is not the so-called stabilisation, arriving from nowhere, that checked the development of the revolutionary situation ... but on the contrary, the unutilised revolutionary situation was transformed into its opposite and thus guaranteed to the bourgeoisie the opportunity to fight with relative success for stabilisation.

Therefore, stabilisation was not a fixed phase determined by the economic fortunes of capitalism alone:

> the struggle for the further existence and development of capitalism prepares at each new stage the prerequisites for new international and class upheavals, that is, for new revolutionary situations, the development of which depends entirely upon the proletarian party.[26]

Bukharin did not aid the development of such 'new revolutionary situations'. Indeed he reinforced his view of Western workers' passivity with a 'labour aristocracy theory'. There is not yet a fully developed Marxist analysis of this concept, which Marx and Engels used to explain the roots of reformism. Whatever its validity, in Bukharin's hands it became another means of dismissing the proletariat, proving that anti-colonial movements must have precedence. Bukharin's Draft Programme for the Sixth Comintern Congress[27] stated that through colonial exploitation, Western capitalism extracted super-profits which it shared with its workers. As a result:

> Imperialism splits off the better placed section of the working class from the main and more oppressed section of the masses ... They have an interest in the Imperialist plunder of the colonies. They are loyal to their 'own' bourgeoisie and their 'own' Imperialist State.[28]

For Bukharin the boundaries of this labour aristocracy proved conveniently flexible. In 1928, when he began playing with the ultra-left notion of a 'Third Period', the labour aristocracy would be defined as a narrow group of social democratic politicians, dubbed 'social fascists', who were supposed to be confronting a seething revolutionary working class. Before then, however, the labour aristocracy was supposed to embrace most Western workers. Super-profits created a 'relative "community of interest" between the bourgeoisie and proletariat'.[29] This fitted neatly into the Comintern's current orientation, leaving a unified reactionary 'metropolis' facing the revolutionary colonial 'periphery':

> the contradiction in the world economy is none other than the contradiction between the world city, metaphorically speaking, and the world village, that is the colonial periphery of this centre. Conse-

quently we see the importance of the colonial question and that it is the key question of policy. Even the problem of overcoming social democratic opportunism is tied to the question of super-profits in the colonies ... [30]

Bukharin implied that national liberation movements would have to cut off the super-profits of imperialism before Western workers would revolt.

'Socialism in one country' had a final sting in its tail. Once more it involved a complete reversal of an earlier position. At the beginning of the 1920s Bukharin's opposition to Brest-Litovsk had crudely articulated a fundamentally correct idea – that the mission of the Russian state was to assist the world revolution and any sacrifice to achieve it was legitimate. Starting with his speech to the Fourth Comintern Congress, which made defence of the USSR the priority of the Comintern, Bukharin had come to an opposite conclusion. The Draft Programme announced:

> the USSR is inevitably becoming the base of the world movement of all oppressed classes, the centre of the international revolution, the greatest factor in world history ... It is a living example of the ability of the working class not only to destroy capitalism but to build up socialism ... As the USSR is the only fatherland of the international proletariat, the principal bulwark of their achievements and the most important factor in the cause of international emancipation, the international proletariat must facilitate the success of the work of socialist construction in the USSR and by all means in their power defend it against the attacks of the capitalist powers.[31]

By 1928 the mission of the world revolution was to assist the Russian state and any sacrifice to achieve it was legitimate.

Dry Run – the British General Strike

The British general strike set Bukharin his first major practical test as leader of the Comintern. It grew out of a national strike of miners against the imposition of cuts in pay and longer hours. The Trades Union Congress (TUC) was pledged to support the miners and on 4 May 1926 it began calling out other sections in solidarity. At its height the strike involved 3.5 million workers who enthusiastically supported the miners. The very scale of the conflict gave it a political dimension which ordinary disputes over economic issues lacked. This was confirmed by the actions of the British government, which declared from the very first that it saw the general strike as a direct threat to the constitution and which threw all efforts into breaking it.

If the British ruling class saw the general strike as a clear challenge to its power, the same could not be said of the Communist Party of Great Britain (CPGB). Its policy had been laid down by Zinoviev in the years before Bukharin replaced him at the Comintern. He had responded to the same bureaucratic and class pressures that Bukharin later experienced. First, Russian national interest (or rather Soviet bureaucratic interest) was put before the needs of the workers' movement. This led to the establishment of the Anglo-Russian Trade Union Council (ARTUC), an alliance of Russian union officials and members of the British TUC General Council. This supposed united front lacked the key criterion of that tactic – mass involvement of revolutionaries and reformists in joint action. Formed over the heads of rank-and-file British trade unionists, the Russian bureaucracy hoped to neutralise a key imperialist power by winning friends in important places. In this it failed, for in effect the ARTUC did nothing except lend certain 'left' members of the TUC a radical aura with which to shroud their treacherous practice.

The second policy followed from the first. Workers' revolution was no longer the priority, and therefore neither was the building of the CPGB. Zinoviev told the Fifth Comintern Congress: 'We do not know whether the Communist Mass Party of England will come ... only through the [CPGB]. And it is entirely possible, comrades, that the Communist Mass Party may still appear through still another door.[32] Bukharin would later explain that this 'other door' was the trade union movement, whose leadership must be captured through such devices as the ARTUC.[33]

When the general strike began, the CPGB, with just 5,000 members, was clearly not in a position immediately to win the leadership of such a movement. Nevertheless its activities made a significant contribution to forming councils of action which, in areas like the north east, posed a real challenge to the state. However, its revolutionary *political* contribution was nil, because its line was to insist that the union officials' authority should not be questioned.

The error of this policy was cruelly exposed on 12 May when the TUC General Council, members from the left and right together, called off the strike. This was despite the fact that the action was solid, and was indeed finding increasing support in the working class. The

General Council's decision crippled the labour movement and caused a collapse in confidence that lasted for years.

Trotsky had predicted just this outcome in January 1926, before the strike. He warned the Comintern leadership that even the most left-wing TUC leaders could not be trusted:

> to think that the leading figures ... might become the leaders of a revolutionary overthrow of power would be to lull oneself with illusions ... It must be clearly understood: this sort of leftism remains only as long as it does not impose any practical obligations. As soon as a question of action arises the lefts respectfully surrender ... [34]

Criticising the idea that there were easy alternative routes to socialism, he went on to say that the task of the Comintern and its constituent parties was to lead the movement forward to socialist revolution. The building of the CPGB as an independent force was the only way this could be achieved:

> the role of the British proletariat in production and in society will guarantee its victory — on condition that there is a correct and resolute revolutionary leadership. The Communist Party must develop and come to power as the party of proletarian dictatorship. There are no ways round this. Whoever believes there are, and propounds them, can only deceive British workers.[35]

Small though it was, the CPGB's development, and with it the political progress of the class, depended on its 'perpetual, systematic, inflexible, untiring and irreconcilable unmasking of the quasi-left leaders of every hue'. [36]

But by 1926 Trotsky was not listened to. Instead the Comintern led the CPGB to subordinate itself to the TUC leftists. During the strike the CPGB gave no hint of any doubts about the weakness of the TUC leadership. On the contrary, it called for 'All Power to the General Council', a grim parody of the Bolsheviks' 1917 slogan of 'All Power to the Soviets'. The CPGB leadership capitulated to the TUC left wing, who in turn gave in to the TUC right. The latter then surrendered. It was not that the British Communists shared the same politics as the likes of Purcell, Swales and Hicks on the left wing of the General Council. Equally Purcell and Co were to the left of Pugh and right-wing union leaders. The problem was that the Comintern line led to the absence of an independent, principled line and the political disarmament of the best fighters in the class. Having ignored Trotsky's warnings, the Comintern was taken completely by surprise when the TUC betrayed the general strike.

In the summer of 1926 it fell to Bukharin to explain away the Comintern's disastrous line during the strike. His first concern was to prove that no mistakes had been made and, above all, that the ARTUC should continue. After all, the TUC traitors had not yet turned against Russia, only their own members, and Russia's interests came first. Bukharin claimed accusations that Russian leaders had failed to take a principled line and had only supported the Anglo-Russian Trade Union Committee 'out of national-State considerations have been smashed to atoms by actual facts'. [37]

Whatever the past may have been, one question remained: why stay in the ARTUC now that the TUC leftists had behaved so treacherously? According to Bukharin, the USSR's unions were in the ARTUC 'for the sake of connections with the masses'.[38] In truth the ARTUC was a bureaucratic body that gave no access to the masses, while the TUC leftists had gained credibility which helped them disarm the strike.

To the charge that the Comintern had been taken in by the rhetoric of the TUC leftists, Bukharin replied that we 'have not had such illusions for a single moment'. [39] If so, why did the CPGB call for 'All Power to the General Council' if they knew all along this body would stab the movement in the back? Bukharin's sophistry in answering this knew no bounds:

> 'All Power to the General Council' – this slogan emerged, as was shown, at the beginning as a demand for centralisation of the movement. 'Power' means here the leadership of all organised proletarians. But to the degree that this movement developed and transformed itself into a political struggle this demand gained a new content. It more and more became analogous to the slogan 'All Power to the Soviets.'[40]

Bukharin absolved the Comintern's guilt by pretending its timid opportunism had been the opposite:

> To the degree that events overflowed lines of economic struggle, to the degree that the trade union movement in the course of the strike grew over into the political struggle of the whole working class against the ruling apparatus of the bourgeoisie, this slogan also grew over *objectively* into a demand analogous to 'all power to the Soviets' ... the General Council was forced against its will to grow beyond its organisations and organise insitutions similar to soviets at a moment when they would lead directly to the struggle for power. [41]

Struggles can develop and grow more ambitious, but it was dangerous nonsense to suggest that avowed enemies of revolution would lead the fight for workers' power. Still worse was the notion that communists should not tell the truth to the working class about reformist bureaucrats (in whom, we are told, they had no illusions 'for a single moment'). Bukharin was either naive or disingenuous when he suggested that without communist leadership the masses would spontaneously become revolutionary and force their traitorous leaders to launch an insurrection.

Finally, the fundamental achievement of Leninism, an understanding of the central need for a revolutionary party, was dispensed with, on the grounds of 'national types' of socialism:

> Because of its history, because of the extreme importance of its trade union organisation, because of its historical traditions, when the English proletariat goes towards posing the question of power the *trade unions will not take power, but it will be taken through the trade unions* ... the question of workers' power in England goes through the unions.[42]

Marxism provides no insurance against mistakes and no guarantees of victory, but the essence of its method is to learn from the class struggle, its victories and defeats, and so take the movement forward for the next battle. Bukharin ensured this did not happen. The General Council was given an alibi through the ARTUC, and its revolutionary opponents at home were ideologically disarmed rather than politically matured. Bukharin wrote: 'The Executive Committee of the Communist International was quite right when it unanimously approved the position taken up by the Communist Party of Great Britain [during the general strike]. The latter foretold the struggle and prepared for it'.[43]

These lies would politically undermine the CPGB and corrode the political development of the Communist International as a whole. If Bukharin's policy towards developed countries was distorted by his general orientation towards the peasants and petty bourgeoisie, would he fare any better in a backward country where such groups were numerically preponderant? The Chinese revolution would be the test.

Blood Run – the Chinese Disaster

After the 1911 Chinese revolution overthrew the Manchu dynasty the Chinese state fragmented. The country was divided between rival warlords, various imperialist spheres of influence and a newly formed nationalist party, the Kuomintang (KMT). Its leader, Sun Yat-sen, put forward a hazy programme of the 'Three People's Principles' – Nationalism, Democracy and People's Livelihood. In 1919 a second revolution began with the May 4 Movement. On that day students demonstrated against Japanese attempts to take advantage of China's weakness and impose humiliating terms upon the country. Unlike the first revolution, industrial workers, whose numbers had doubled from 1 million to 2 million during the war, became involved.

Out of this the Chinese Communist Party (CCP) was born. Its membership was small at first (57 in 1921, 423 two years later) and so it sought an alliance with the KMT. This was turned down. Then Maring, a Comintern representative, persuaded the communists to join the KMT as individuals.[44] This was a very different proposition to the alliance sought earlier. Maring's merger of the CCP into the bourgeois nationalist KMT ran against Comintern policy as set down at its Second Congress:

> A determined fight is necessary against the attempt to put a communist cloak around revolutionary liberation movements that are not really communist in the backward countries. The Communist International has the duty to support the revolutionary movement in the colonies only for the purpose of gathering the components of the future proletarian parties – communist in fact and not just in name – in all the backward countries and training them to be conscious of their special tasks, the special tasks, that is to say, of fighting against the bourgeois democratic tendencies within their own nation. The Communist International should accompany the revolutionary movement in the colonies and the backward countries for part of the way, should even make an alliance with it; it may not however, fuse with it, but must unconditionally maintain the independent character of the proletarian movement, be it only in embryo.[45]

Individual entry by Chinese communists into the KMT broke the cohesion that would have been given by affiliating as a body and made criticism and independent thought difficult. What they were entering was a heterogeneous body, including militarists, bourgeois, urban petty bourgeois, peasants and workers, in which overall the bourgeoisie was dominant. Although Maring feared a small party like the CCP might waste away in sectarian isolation, his cure proved worse than the disease. Affiliation to the KMT immediately stymied the political growth of the CCP, an inexperienced party as yet without a strong identity. For example, right up to 1927 it did not publish its own newspaper.

CCP leaders such as Ch'en Tu-hsiu opposed Maring's proposals for entry into the KMT. But at the Second Comintern Congress in 1920 the full authority of Radek and Zinoviev was thrown into the scales in favour of this policy and it was eventually accepted.

As if the CCP was not harmed enough, in January 1923 Adolf Joffe, a senior Soviet diplomat, made a further compromise with the KMT. This was a joint statement with Sun Yat-sen conceding important ground to the KMT's bourgeois nationalism:

> because of the non-existence of conditions favorable to their successful application in China, it is not possible to carry out either Communism or even the Soviet system ... Mr Joffe agrees with this view; he is further of the opinion that China's most important and pressing problems are the completion of national unification and the attainment of full national independence.[46]

If, as a representative of a workers' state surrounded by hostile forces, Joffe had sought foreign allies on the limited but common basis of resistance to imperialism, this would have been acceptable. However the Sun–Joffe agreement had gone much further. Harold Isaacs writes that as a result of this agreement, 'it was automatically assumed that the Chinese Communists would henceforth devote themselves solely to the job of helping to make the Kuomintang a worthy ally.'[47] The USSR did its best to make this a reality. The KMT was given military aid, advisers such as Michael Borodin, and training in Moscow for army commanders like Chiang Kai-shek. Neutralised as a political force, the CCP:

> confined itself religiously to building the Kuomintang and propagating its programme. Its members were the most indefatigable party members, but they never appeared as Communists nor presented any programme of their own. The Communist Party became in fact and in essence, in its work and in the manner in which it educated its own members, the Left-Wing appendage of the Kuomintang.[48]

These political problems were masked by spectacular growth in CCP membership, from 950 in January 1924 to 10,000 a year later, climbing to a peak of 58,000 in April 1927.[49] This reflected a new upsurge of revolutionary activity after a demonstration on 30 May 1925, when 10 Shanghai workers were killed by police. The May 30 Movement grew into a general strike involving 130,000. Some 50,000 workers in Hong Kong then came out for their own demands and fought on for 15 months. At the same time huge numbers of peasants rose up against high rents, landowners and usurers. Although the bourgeois leaders of the KMT regarded these movements with disdain, they did not make this too public. With no other organised political groupings in competition with it, the KMT gained massively in prestige.

The revolutionary upswing could have revived the CCP's political fortunes. It should have signalled to the Comintern that tailing the bourgeois KMT would squander the opportunity for working-class politics to play a dominant role in the revolution. Bukharin's Comintern leadership was aware of the significance of the workers' movement. The Sixth Plenum of the ECCI in March 1926 declared:

> The wave of strikes in the course of 1924 and 1925 and the consequent powerful political offensive of the industrial proletariat in Shanghai, Canton and Hong Kong makes the Chinese proletariat the most decisive and consistent fighter for full independence within the national liberation movement. [50]

Knowing this, it was all the more criminal that the Russian Communist Party consciously downplayed the CCP and turned instead to the bourgeois-dominated KMT with these words: 'To our party has fallen the proud and historic role of leading the first victorious proletarian revolution of the world ... We are convinced that the Kuomintang will succeed in playing the same role in the East.'[51] But why, seeing the strength of the workers' movement, did the Comintern leaders still support the bourgeoisie, whom they were rightly proud of having overthrown at home?

There were two reasons for this. One was Bukharin's readiness to sacrifice long-term international working-class interests for the short-term gain of Russia's bureaucracy. Alliance with the KMT was prioritised because it was the expression of 'a perfectly obvious inclination, which is deeply rooted in the nature of things, towards the formation of an *anti-imperialist bloc*: the Soviet Union and the Chinese Revolution'. This was needed as a 'counter-weight to ... a tendency on the part of the Capitalist States to form a bloc against us'.[52] Reacting to Trotskyist criticisms, Bukharin presented this unprincipled alliance with the KMT as '*real internationalism*. Real internationalism does not consist in sounding "super-international" phrases, but in supporting ... everything which consolidates an organising centre of the world revolution such as the Soviet Union seems to us to be.'[53]

The second reason Bukharin supported the KMT was that it fitted into his view of revolution developing by stages, in contrast to permanent revolution. According to the former, in backward countries the bourgeois and socialist revolutions could overlap and a workers' state be established even if workers were in a minority. Bukharin said revolution proceeded *by stages* – first bourgeois and only later socialist. He traced this development in China: 'at the present stage of development, the Chinese revolution is a bourgeois revolution, although, of course, this does not mean that the decisive motive force of this revolution is the bourgeoisie.'[54] So for Bukharin the tasks of the revolution were confined to 'bourgeois democracy', 'national liberation' and 'anti-imperialism'.[55]

Bukharin was mistaken when he claimed to be following Lenin's pre-1917 theory of 'the democratic dictatorship of the proletariat and peasantry'. Lenin was not a Menshevik who believed in bourgeois pre-eminence in the revolutions of backward countries. He had only contempt for the Russian bourgeoisie. Before 1917 he insisted that the democratic revolution could only be achieved by workers and peasants. Furthermore, Lenin's theory had proved to be a step towards advocating direct socialist revolution. It worked in this way on three counts. First, the 'democratic dictatorship' theory made no concessions to the bourgeoisie. Second, it was carried by a strong and independent proletarian party which could quickly change course towards workers' power. Finally, it recognised that the peasantry's revolutionary potential depended on leadership from the workers.

Bukharin's 'democratic dictatorship' formula was a step in the opposite direction, on all of these points. To win influential friends in China, all manner of concessions were made to the Chinese bourgeoisie, including arming them. The CCP, instead of being independent, was shackled to the KMT. Surely on the issue of the peasants' revolutionary potential Bukharin should score well? At the spring 1925 ECCI plenum he staked everything on this: 'The Chinese question is the question of the possible resistance of the Chinese peasants against foreign finance capital'.[56]

Yet it was precisely Bukharin who failed to understand how to galvanise that revolutionary potential. Mighty though it was, the peasant struggle had to be led by another class if it was to succeed. Due to their geographical and social fragmentation peasants have never had a successful autonomous movement of their own. In 1917 Russia proved this. The majority of the mass peasant party – the Social Revolutionaries (SRs) – quickly fell under the spell of the bourgeois Provisional Government. A minority allied with the Bolsheviks. The peasants only retained the land they seized because leadership of the rural revolution was wrested from the SRs by the proletarian Bolsheviks. It was not enough to extol the virtues of peasant revolution. A working-class leadership was necessary and in China Bukharin denied it this.

His slogan of 'democratic dictatorship' slid into Menshevism by directly supporting the bourgeoisie. This could be seen in the resolution of the Seventh ECCI Plenum in December 1926, which despite the dominance of the bourgeoisie stated that: '[The KMT Government] fundamentally and *objectively* contains within it the germ of the revolutionary petty bourgeois state – the revolutionary democratic dictatorship bloc of proletariat, peasantry and urban petty bourgeoisie'.[57] So chalk is objectively cheese. To add insult to the injury inflicted on the CCP, the Russian Politburo decided to make the KMT a 'sympathising section of the Comintern'. Only Trotsky voted against.[58]

The Comintern repeated, again and again, that the KMT was a 'bloc of four classes' – bourgeoisie, proletariat, peasantry and petty bourgeoisie. This idea was introduced to the Comintern by the ex-Menshevik Martynov. Bukharin too was sure that 'the Kuomintang [is] a party with a quite peculiar construction, a party which combines various classes into one political bloc', and that it was on this that 'the present power of the revolutionary fight is based.'[59] Accepting, for the sake of argument, that China was heading for a 'democratic dictatorship of workers and peasants' rather than 'permanent revolution', how could it be achieved through the KMT? The Comintern's theses tell us:

> The apparatus of the [KMT] national revolutionary government provides a very effective way to reach the peasantry. The Communist Party must use this way ... to penetrate into the apparatus of the new government to give practical expression to the agrarian programme of the national revolution ... The Communist Party must strive to develop the Kuomintang into a real party of the people – a solid revolutionary bloc of the proletariat, peasants, urban petty bourgeoisie and other oppressed and exploited classes.[60]

As had been the case with the Anglo-Russian Trade Union Committee, the reality did not match Bukharin's theory. Far from the KMT being a channel for the influence of the CCP, the opposite was true. As Radek said, the KMT leaders 'see democracy as an instrument to tie down the masses'.[61] For Trotsky, Bukharin's 'bloc' was a misnomer: 'Taken politically, a bloc is the expression of an alliance of sides "with equal right", who come to an understanding on a certain joint action. Only, this was not the case in China.'[62] On the idea of using the KMT apparatus Trotsky added:

To consider the Kuomintang not as a *bourgeois party, but as a neutral arena of struggle for the masses*, to play with words ... in order to mask the question as to who is the real master, meant to add to the strength and power of the summit, to assist the latter to convert ever broader masses into 'cattle' ... Stalin and Bukharin imagined that the Communists, together with the 'Lefts' would secure a majority in the Kuomintang and thereby power in the country ... In other words they imagined that *by means of ordinary elections at Kuomintang congresses power would pass from the hands of the bourgeoisie to the proletariat.* Can one conceive of a more touching and idealistic idolization of 'party democracy' ... in a bourgeois party?[63]

Unfortunately, Bukharin's approach was more than a 'touching and idealistic' view of the KMT. If he had harboured illusions he might have had some excuse for what happened later. No. His leadership of the Comintern was more cynical than deluded, for as this ECCI resolution shows, workers were invited to put the noose of the Kuomintang around their necks, even though its politics were known to be a trap:

> Come what may, in spite of all the conflicts that will inevitably arise at different points of the common struggle, the task of the Communist Party must be to maintain the fighting union of the CCP and KMT. As before, Communists must enter the structure and leading organs of the KMT. They must help the KMT in its political and organisational work, pursuing a flexible tactic and not allowing obstruction. At the same time the Communist Party must explain to the masses of Chinese workers and peasants the petty bourgeois character of the KMT programme, *the impossibility* on the basis of its programme and tactics for the KMT to achieve full social liberation of the labouring classes, and the necessity for an independent class party of the proletariat.[64]

So 'come what may' the communists must help the KMT. Yet as far as the masses were concerned it was 'impossible' that this would solve their problems. This was another example of double book-keeping; capitulation in practice, radical in appearance.

Signs of what this capitulation to the KMT would mean emerged on 20 March 1926. Chiang Kai-shek staged a 'coup' in Canton, demanding CCP membership lists and banning communist members from various leading positions. Soon local strikes were being broken and union organisations smashed up. This culminated in six days of street fighting in which more than 50 workers died.[65] The year long Canton-

Hong Kong strike was then brought to an end, defeated. At this time the Comintern stayed silent while the relations of the Russian adviser, Borodin, with Chiang 'became more cordial than ever'. He even advised this dictator-in-the-making to become commander-in-chief of KMT forces.[66] Borodin's view was that 'The present period is one in which the Communists should do coolie service for the Kuomintang.'[67] Given the Comintern's premises, Borodin's actions were as logically irrefutable as they were disastrous. The more threatening Chiang became, the more craven must be the attitude of Moscow to avoid a break. And the more powerful Chiang became the better, because a China under the KMT would be a more effective component of the 'anti-imperialist bloc' that Moscow was trying to sustain. If the CCP had to be sacrificed along the way, so be it.

The same thinking dictated that the CCP should hold back insurgent peasants for fear of disturbing the KMT. This was despite the fact that the March 1926 coup had been a signal for landowners to begin repressing peasants in Kwantung and elsewhere.[68] A secret telegram urging the Chinese communists to keep them quiet was sent by Moscow in October 1926. When Stalin was confronted with it he had to admit it was 'a mistake'.[69]

Things were going too far even for Bukharin. He was worried about exposing himself to opposition criticism. During the Seventh ECCI Plenum at the end of 1926 he began talking left:

> The outcome of the Chinese revolution will not necessarily be the creation of political and social conditions conducive to the capitalist development of the country ... The Chinese Communist Party must exert all its efforts to realise this revolutionary perspective of *transition to lines of non-capitalist development*.[70]

This was just the left face of a double book-keeping exercise. Bukharin's article on 'Perspectives of the Chinese Revolution' went on to say that in spite of the above:

> *in China we cannot make such a proletarian dictatorship* [as we created in Russia] *our task*. That is the originality of the situation in China. Our party must at present steer a course towards establishing a particular dictatorship, *a block between the working class, peasantry and petty bourgeoisie*. Our efforts must be bent in this direction. The key task and the key problem of the Chinese revolution today is *victory over the imperialist enemy. That is the key task*.[71]

Which was it to be – non-capitalist development or cross-class unity, socialism or capitalism? The stages theory solved the dilemma scholastically.

> [Stage 1:] At the beginning of the development of the Chinese revolution the advanced *bourgeoisie* ... plays a dominant, almost exclusive role ... [Stage 2] of the national anti-imperialist revolution will be characterised by the leadership falling to *a block of varied forces* – bourgeoisie, working class, petty bourgeoisie and working class ... [Stage 3:] *the leading role more and more passes to the working class.*[72]

Such neat formulae worked on Kremlin notepaper, but they made the position of the CCP impossible. In 1917 the Bolshevik Party had fought to complete the bourgeois revolution (chiefly 'land to the peasants') by means of proletarian revolution ('All Power to the Soviets'), fusing both in one strategic sweep. In contrast, the Chinese communists were being asked to efface themselves and support their class enemies in the KMT leadership. Somehow they were to emerge from this all the stronger and capable of leading a 'non-capitalist evolution'. However, this talk was only a smokescreen for the real thrust of policy – Russia's 'anti-imperialist bloc' with the KMT.

On 9 July 1926 Chiang set out with his army on the Northern Expedition, an operation to expand the area under KMT control at the expense of hostile warlords. Revolutionary enthusiasm spread through the country ahead of the advancing troops:

> ordinary people rose in a veritable tidal wave that swept the expeditionary armies to the banks of the Yangtze. The spontaneous rising of the people gave the KMT armies little more to do, often, than occupy territory that had already been secured for them. The bands of political workers which went out in advance of the troops were able, with the slightest touch, to unleash forces which levelled all opposition.[73]

Although the expedition had unleashed revolutionary forces, it was no intention of the army commanders that these should take over. As the expedition advanced, it consolidated control by smashing workers' and peasants' organisations.[74] The ambiguity of this situation was not reflected in the Comintern's comments.

Instead, Bukharin was truly ecstatic about the Northern Expedition. According to him the revolution was virtually won – not because of mass actions independent of the KMT, but because of Chiang's army:

The present stage of the Chinese revolution is characterised by the fact that the forces of the revolution are *already* organised as a *State power*, with an attribute, such as the regular, disciplined army which fills the imperialist enemy with fear. The advance of this army, its brilliant victories, the systematic dislodgement of foreign imperialism by the Canton troops and by the troops of their allies is *a special form of the revolutionary process*.[75]

All news of the smashing of worker and peasant organisations in areas falling under Chiang's control was suppressed in the communist media.

Just in case things turned out wrong for the Comintern, Bukharin inserted escape clauses in the fine print of the above article:

> Within this bloc, the commercial and industrial bourgeoisie still plays a fairly important part. This bourgeoisie will, however, inevitably secede from the revolution, the more the deeper strata of the Chinese people, the petty bourgeoisie and the Chinese working class, enter the great arena of the revolution.[76]

Later on Bukharin and Stalin were to claim that such passages as these constituted a warning which the CCP failed to heed. However, as Isaacs puts it, they

> omitted to say which bourgeoisie, what persons, what events, what places, names, dates were involved ... Where, when, how? To these natural questions the document provided no answer ... said nothing of Chiang Kai-shek's March coup, of the repression of the workers in Canton, the killing of peasants and party workers in Kwangtung and Kiangsi in the wake of Chiang's advancing army.[77]

By 20 March 1927 the KMT army had reached the outskirts of Shanghai. The next day the workers there staged a massive general strike. Up to 800,000 were involved. A carefully planned insurrection followed, putting Shanghai in the hands of the workers. On 26 March they welcomed Chiang's forces into the city.

Bukharin made his speech on 'Perspectives for the Chinese Revolution', quoted above, in January 1927. Unfortunately for him it appeared on 5 April 1927 in the Comintern's German publication. It said:

> The Chinese Communist Party and class conscious Chinese workers *dare not in any way pursue a tactic of disorganising the revolutionary army* ... Before the bloc of forces of the workers, peasants and petty bourgeoisie stands the task of showing *foresight and wisdom in following the*

> *correct tactic: the strengthening of its influence in all organisations, in the army, government and Kuomintang.*

The usual vague hints, that 'differentiation in the Kuomintang is inevitable' were the only qualifications, but any immediate fears were dispelled by this amazing injunction: 'As the further advance of the revolutionary troops takes place, it must be arranged that they are not only joyously welcomed, but sent on their way with tokens of gratitude.'[78]

Trotsky had a different prognosis in an article submitted to Bukharin's newspaper on 3 April 1927, but rejected:

> If the Polish Pilsudski [ex-socialist who became a fascist dictator] required three decades for his evolution, the Chinese Pilsudski will require a much shorter period for the transition from national revolution to national fascism ... The policy of a shackled CP serving as a recruiting agent to bring the workers into the KMT is preparation for the successful establishment of a Fascist dictatorship in China ...[79]

Trotsky was not claiming guaranteed success for permanent revolution. He wrote later:

> It would be pedantry to contend that the Chinese Communist Party, had it pursued a Bolshevik policy in the revolution of 1925–1927, would *certainly* have come to power. But it is pitiful philistinism to contend that this possibility was entirely out of the question ... Had the Comintern pursued a more or less correct policy ... the Chinese proletariat would have supported the Communists, while the peasants' war would have supported the revolutionary proletariat.[80]

The verdict of history on the two alternative positions could hardly have been clearer, or more tragic. On 12 April Chiang's 'machine guns broke loose in a steady roll'[81] as he moved to suppress the workers bloodily. Many thousands were butchered in this one episode alone.

Was it possible that Bukharin, head of the all-knowing Comintern, had been caught unawares? Would that that were true. The reality was worse. Bukharin knew the character and methods of Chiang very well, but he did not forewarn and specifically did not fore*arm* the Chinese workers. As a CCP leader reported: 'The International telegraphed us to hide or bury all weapons of the workers to avoid military conflict between the workers and Chiang Kai-shek.'[82] The Comintern's *International Press Correspondence* carried an article on 16 April which stated that 'The bourgeois Right wing in the Kuomintang and its leadership had been defeated'. On 20 April another affirmed that rumours of 'a compromise of the Right wing with the militarists ... are lies and have no chance of succeeding'.[83] These ideas came from the highest authority – from Bukharin himself. He later justified his decision to give Chiang's army a free hand: 'rather than engage Chiang Kai-shek's executioners in open struggle, it was better to hide the weapons, to draw the workers' army out of battle for a time, to concentrate all the force of the mass of workers, soldiers and peasants'.[84] Even if the remarkable calculation was made that the cream of the Chinese proletariat, its vanguard in Shanghai, should allow its citadel to be occupied by a hostile army, the workers should at least have been warned of what to expect.

Bukharin claimed weakly that this had been done:

> As soon as it became evident that the Chinese bourgeoisie, in view of the revolutionary enthusiasm, was certain to go over to the enemy before long, we were bound to set at work at once to build new bridges, to unmask the traitors. This was done, but unfortunately we wrote less about our efforts in the Russian papers at the time than we were actually carrying out.[85]

This journalistic oversight appears rather strange, given that Bukharin was not just leader of the Comintern but an editor of *Pravda* and the theoretical journal *Bol'shevik*. In any case, the claim was rubbish. *Pravda* had not said 'less' than it should in order to 'unmask the traitors'. It had lauded them. On 22 March its editorial declared: 'Shanghai is taken! ... The red and blue flag of the Kuomintang, the flag of revolution, flutters over the streets.' The headline the next day was 'Revolutionary Shanghai welcomes the National Revolutionary Army!' Not a word of criticism was heard until 15 April, which brought news of 'contradictions within the Kuomintang' having led to *'bloody violence'* against the workers.

This sorry tale did not stop with the Shanghai massacre. Today Bukharin's admirers say that 'Bukharin counterposed the propaganda of humanistic ideals' to Stalinism.[86] This hardly squares with his behaviour in regard to China, which was frankly disgusting. Rather than helping the CCP understand what had happened (and so recover politically), or rallying the disoriented forces of revolution, Bukharin clung on to the hope of influencing the KMT through a new alliance. This time it was with the KMT 'lefts' under Wang Ching-wei, whose government in Wuhan was a rival to Chiang's government based in Nanking. Two communists became ministers in the Wuhan government. The communist minister of agriculture was called upon to curb peasant disturbances; the communist minister of labour was expected to stop strikes. By July it was clear that Wuhan was more intent on re-establishing friendship with Chiang than with communism. CCP members were attacked and executed and the Wuhan government began to mimic Chiang's brutal suppression of workers.[87] By now the Comintern's paroxysms of self-justification were almost unbelievable:

> The support given to the campaign to the North [Chiang's Northern Expedition] was perfectly correct *so long* as it aroused a revolutionary mass movement. And the support given to Wuhan was equally correct *so long* as it acted as the opponent of Chiang Kai-shek's Nanking [government]. But this same bloc tactic becomes fundamentally wrong in the moment at which the Wuhan government capitulates to the enemies of revolution. What was *correct during* the previous stage of the revolution is *now* absolutely unsuitable.[88]

Instead of admitting his own mistakes, Bukharin spewed forth a torrent of calumny against the unfortunate CCP:

> the leadership of the Communist Party of China has in recent times obstinately *sabotaged* the decisions of the Comintern ... The following are the facts: The Comintern has systematically given directions regarding the independence of the Communist Party of China, the necessity of letting loose the agrarian revolution, the arming of the workers and peasants, settling accounts with the counter-revolutionary generals and democratising the Kuomintang. The Comintern has day after day urged the C.P. of China along the way of further developing the revolution.[89]

Finally, when the CCP and mass movement was well and truly crippled, Stalin and Bukharin decided to attempt to salvage their political credibility through an insane move. They announced yet a further 'stage' in the revolution had been reached. The CCP must now, immediately, establish soviets. And, since the working class was totally confused and unable to respond to this unprepared turn, these soviets must be set up over their heads and without their mass involvement. A soviet was therefore *appointed* in Canton. The 'Canton Commune' lasted for three days in December 1927. When it was massacred 5,700 more were added to the death toll, making a total of 38,000 for that year, with the figure rising to 140,000 by 1930.[90] This was carried out by the army that Bukharin had said should be showered with tokens of gratitude.

If, as Lenin said, 'politics is concentrated economics', then Bukharin's international politics merely expressed in stark form the trend of his economic policies at home. In its turn the dashing of revolutionary hopes in China had a profound effect on domestic events. Though they had been the very ones who had warned against it, the left opposition was blamed for the fiasco and the level of repression against its members intensified. In China Bukharin had helped destroy a revolution by allowing it to be butchered from without by a former ally – Chiang Kai-shek. In Russia his schemes would also help destroy the revolution, but the butcher would come from within the Communist Party's own ranks in the shape of Bukharin's former ally – Joseph Stalin. Seeing Russia condemned to prolonged isolation and surrounded by hostile forces, the bureaucracy decided upon a crash programme to refashion Russian society into a state capitalist industrial power capable of competing militarily with the West.

11 The NEP in Crisis

Bukharin has been described here as reflecting the demoralisation of the working class and the growing influence of the bureaucracy, rich peasants and Nepmen. This position was expressed in the programme he developed in 1924 and 1925. But even before the finishing touches were applied to this programme, it had ceased to be viable. It had been based on the fact that both the bureaucracy and petty bourgeoisie were united in their rejection of calls for international revolution, inner-party democracy and the strengthening of the working class. However, once the opposition was crushed these demands lost their force, and in place of an alliance of the petty bourgeoisie and bureaucracy came a growing class rivalry between them.

There were other influences at work. One by one the warnings of the defeated opposition were coming true and the seeds of future division sown in the Bukharin-Stalin duumvirate. There was no way permanently to reconcile Bukharin's fantasy of smoothly 'growing into socialism', of a peaceful and harmonious internal life in poverty-stricken and isolated Russia, with Stalin's *Realpolitik*.

Industry at the Crossroads

It was in industry, which Bukharin had consigned to trailing behind agriculture 'at a snail's pace', that problems first appeared. Pressures for a change of industrial policy were both internal and external. Trotsky and Preobrazhensky had warned that abandoning planning and throwing industry to the tender mercies of the peasant market would be insufficient to maintain the growth of industry. By the mid-1920s this truth was obvious. The 'restoration period', during which industries paralysed during the civil war spontaneously revived, had produced some remarkable growth statistics, but this process was reaching its limits.

The evidence for the failure of unregulated market circulation to solve industry's problems was irrefutable. In 1925 the USSR's capital stock was still estimated to be 12 per cent lower than its 1913 level and 23 per cent below its 1917 peak.[1] Industrial investment for the year 1924-5 did little more than cover the cost of depreciation.² What this meant was illustrated by the fact that at the end of 1924 it took 3.2 working days to produce one unit of cotton goods, compared to 2.14 days before the war.

Bukharin, like the rest of the leadership, could not remain untouched by this situation. After the Fourteenth Party Congress of December 1925, when a course was officially set for industrialisation, he wrote:

> At the present time a series of cardinal, fundamental questions concerning our revolution are being posed ... we are in a transitional period passing from the so-called restoration process to the reconstruction process ... [There must now be] above all an effort to discover and apply capital resources, the means leading to the broadening of the productive base.³

Bukharin was trying to adjust to the bureaucracy's need for industrialisation without abandoning his pro-peasant orientation. However, his approach was still minimalist. As late as September 1927, in the run-up to the Fifteenth Party Congress, the *Platform of the Opposition* pointed out that according to official plans:

> *Capital investments in industry* will hardly grow at all from year to year ... And in proportion to the total sum invested in the national economy they will fall ... *The individual consumption of industrial goods*, beggarly at the present time, is to grow by only 12% in all during the five-year period ... To propose such a parsimonious, thoroughly pessimistic plan on the tenth anniversary of the October Revolution really means to work against socialism.⁴

Bukharin evidently hoped that a slight adjustment to his 'snail's pace' approach would suffice. In the late 1920s this was judged inadequate even by the bureaucracy he had once spoken for. Much industrial equipment was old and due for total replacement. Half the steam boilers and one third of the other sources of mechanical power had exceeded their normal service life of 20–25 years.⁵

Not only was much industrial equipment worn out, it was often of the wrong type. The industry of tsarist Russia was functioning once more, but formerly it had been a subsidiary part of a much larger economic whole – the world economy. Russian machinery had been largely imported and paid for by foreign investment. To pursue a policy of economic independence as implied by 'socialism in one country' demanded that Russia be self-sufficient in most spheres and, above all, that it should generate its own means of production. This required input from the metallurgical industries. So it was particularly worrying that by late 1924, when the value of the output of large-scale industry was at 42 per cent of its pre war level, the metalworking sector had only reached 20 per cent. Progress had been concentrated in light industries such as food processing (76 per cent of its prewar level) and paper (54 per cent).[6] While trying to protect the peasant and the market system, even Bukharin now grudgingly admitted 'we must not fail to emphasise that production of the means of production is the central focus'.[7]

The internal situation may have made complacency more difficult, but the external factor was crucial in forcing a change of course, despite Bukharin's talk about 'abstracting from the international situation'. As a *Pravda* editorial put it:

> It is an indisputable fact that we are on our own as far as economic construction is concerned ... We *ourselves* without any sort of external help have raised our economy, we *ourselves* will now push it forward. The 'assistance' of foreign capital, foreign loans or credit could be used only in an infinitesimal degree ... we are left to our own devices.[8]

In the late 1920s industrialisation became a matter of life and death for the bureaucracy for three reasons. One reason was military. 'Stabilisation' strengthened the West's fighting capacity and freed it from the fear of revolutionary overthrow. This security was enhanced when the Comintern abandoned internationalism. Although little of the spirit of 1917 remained, its memory still haunted Western capitalists and they resented the Soviet bureaucracy's exclusive rights to one sixth of the world's surface. A chance to invade the USSR would be welcomed.

Second, the bureaucracy had to defend itself economically. Its only safeguard against submersion under a flood of cheaper and better Western imports was the state's monopoly of foreign trade. This could not indefinitely survive increased pressure from outside (the expanding 'stabilised' Western industries) or peasant protest from within, caused by discontent with the high prices, poor quality and limited quantities of Soviet manufactures. The Central Committee was gradually forced to the conclusion:

> We must hold a course for 'economic independence', for the *industrialisation* of the socialist state, always promoting the development of production of the means of production and creating our own technical basis for broad development of socialist industry. We must

not take the 'line of least resistance' and give in to our inherited historical backwardness, allowing ourselves to become merely a socialist supplement to the surrounding world capitalist economy.[9]

Unless it developed a viable industrial base, the USSR would remain part of the 'agrarian periphery' for the metropolitan industrial core.

Third, failure to industrialise held particular terrors for the Soviet bureaucracy. It could not hope for even the client relationship with Western capital that occurred in colonies. There foreign industrial capitalism collaborated with native landowning classes and exchanged manufactures for raw materials and rewarded them for subservience. The bureaucracy's existence rested exclusively on control of state *industry*, which foreign capitalists would regard as a competitor. The same problem has since faced other ruling classes in backward economies which have sought to stand on their own two feet. On all three fronts, the USSR in 1925/6 was in a desperate state, despite the recovery initiated by the NEP.

Today marketeers describe the NEP as:

> without exaggeration one of the most brilliant pages in the history of our fatherland, indeed in world history, a period of stunning development of a new society ... By any historical measurement the 1920s were and remain until today the period of the greatest all-round economic development. Never, either before or after, had the Soviet economy expanded so successfully as during NEP.[10]

The growth statistics were impressive if considered in isolation. Between 1921 and 1928 total national income grew annually by 18 per cent, industry by 23 per cent and agriculture by 11 per cent.[11] This even outstripped the period of Stalin's Five-Year Plans in the 1930s. But these statistics were largely irrelevant. The USSR could not base its economic and military strength on approaching the prewar levels of output[12] in food processing and paper production. If survival depended on military competition with the West (rather than on workers' revolution), then what was important was not rates of growth but the absolute size of the rival industrial–military complexes. To take one illustration of the USSR's position *after* its 'greatest all-round economic development', in 1924 just 10 motorised vehicles were manufactured; by 1926 'stunning development' led to an output of 336. Compare this to production in the US at this time – 3.6 million vehicles annually![13] In 1927 the USSR, with 12,000 vehicles on the road, lagged behind India, which had 100,000.[14] A year later, when the period of the NEP was drawing to a close, the performance of heavy industry, which was strategic for both military and industrial growth in the vast and populous USSR, was lagging far behind that in the US, France and Britain (see Table 11.1).

Table 11.1: Production of Key Industries in 1928 (million tons)

	USSR	USA	France	Britain
Steel	4.3	52.4	9.5	8.7
Cast iron	3.3	38.3	10.0	6.7
Coal	35.5	522.6	51.4	241.3

Source: Adapted from F.M. Vaganov, *Pravyi uklon v VKP(b) i ego razgrom (1928–1930)*, Moscow 1970, pages 88–9.

As the industrial needs of the bureaucracy grew, Bukharin found it harder to hold the line on a slow tempo. He wrote: 'The *main* thing now is to obtain the appropriate *tempo of development, guaranteeing the fastest possible pace of growth of the economy*'.[15] He dutifully echoed the watchword of the party about the need 'to catch up and overtake the capitalist countries'.[16] Bukharin wanted to satisfy the rich peasants, but he also had an ear to the needs of the bureaucracy:

> We must go forward more quickly than our capitalist enemies and competitors in all spheres – in technology, in machinery, in labour power ... in order to give a sufficiently decisive rebuff if they encroach on the borders of our socialist fatherland.[17]

If the pace was no longer set by the agricultural sector but by the need to stand up to international capital, more state intervention was essential. In 1927 Bukharin wrote:

> thanks to the planned economy we can more effectively develop our national productive forces; thanks to the planned economy we direct more resources into our industry, into our socialist industry; thanks to all this we have achieved an unprecedented hegemony through the concentration of our whole national economy. This is formed into an exceptionally powerful economic fist – and *this is the growth of socialism.*[18]

While retaining reservations about planning, Bukharin thus accepted the need for some intervention, hoping all the while to minimise disruption to the existing NEP set-up. Once the opposition was dealt with, however, Bukharin's ideological wizardry became less necessary. Free to operate, the bureaucracy now followed its own agenda. When a sudden and catastrophic crisis struck at the end of 1927, Stalin's apparatus would lack Bukharin's scruples on the proper relations between town and country.

Neither Bukharin's minimalist planning nor Stalin's later voluntarist planning had anything in common with the opposition's programme. If the latter had been implemented, early, planned industrialisation could have limited the amount of capital tied up in new projects. This would have avoided stripping the marketplace bare of consumer goods. Once the new projects had come on stream and more consumer goods had become available, further controlled amounts of capital could have been withdrawn for investment, and so on. As Trotsky put it:

> There is not, and of course cannot be, a policy which would permit us to solve all our difficulties at one stroke, or leap over a prolonged period of systematic elevation of our economic and cultural level. But our very cultural and economic backwardness requires a rational and timely mobilisation of all our accumulated reserves, the correct utilisation of all our resources for the fastest possible industrialisation of the country.[19]

Neither voluntarism nor capitulation was Trotsky's watchword. The bureaucracy behaved differently. Its initial delay meant that when, from 1928 onwards, it was forced to invest in industry, massive capital resources had to be injected in one lump. Thus the proportion of overall investment tied up in new industrial construction shot from 12 per cent in 1925/6 to 23 per cent in 1927/8[20], rocketing thereafter. This was less planning than a headlong charge designed to 'catch up and overtake the West' in record time. The result would be the worst of both worlds, the consequences of having been too slow in the past overlapping with the problems of now running too fast.

Agriculture at an Impasse

Just as Bukharin's policies of the mid-1920s led to problems in industry, so difficulties in agriculture were inevitable. Those who glorify the market forget that the NEP was racked with problems from birth to its early death. The competitive market system can be dynamic, but it is also inevitably accompanied by crisis. Individual enterprises are smashed on the rocks of competition; the whole system oscillates between boom and slump. The scissors crisis was not the last conflict between industry and the peasants. It was but the first of a series, because in 1923 the underlying causes were simply concealed beneath the sticking plaster of government-imposed price cuts. As Davies puts it: 'Only two of the nine harvests of the 1920s – those of 1922 and 1926 – proceeded without a major crisis in economic policy'.[21] And 1922 itself was arguably a troubled year, since industrial prices plunged to rock bottom, while agricultural prices soared. A brief summary will show that the fundamental problems revealed in 1923 persisted till the end of the NEP.

In the year 1924/5 drought resulted in a poor grain harvest, 14.8 per cent below the previous year's. By August 1924 limited supply meant the price of grain was double that of the year before. To feed the towns and army the government halted grain exports. It tried to impose maximum prices at which it would buy grain, but the only result was to drive peasants to sell to private Nepmen. They in turn sat on the grain, waiting for the price to rise still higher. By the end of the year the state had only collected one third of its target. It was even forced to authorise grain imports, a disastrous position for an agricultural country. The crisis was only overcome when the government doubled its official buying price for grain.[22] This drove Zinoviev, at that time the most prominent communist in the leadership, to issue his slogan 'face to the countryside'. That was the effect of a bad harvest. Would a better one improve things? Bukharin, with his stress on accumulation in agriculture, believed so. Trotsky predicted it would lead to crisis.

The grain harvest of 1925/6 was 42 per cent higher than the year before. A larger supply should have lowered grain prices and given a higher state collection rate. This occurred initially, but thereafter the price rose and collection dropped sharply. Peasants had grain to sell but would not part with it cheaply. For example, in one bazaar there was 10 times more grain available than buyers wishing to purchase it, yet still the price stayed up.[23] Why? A combination of factors had caused this phenomenon. To encourage agriculture the tax burden on peasants had been cut, leaving the countryside awash with paper currency. 'Snail's pace' industrial growth and the forcing down of industrial prices meant that there was an affordable but very limited supply of commodities on which to spend this cash. This created the so-called 'goods famine'. When the manufactures dried up, the peasants stopped selling grain to the government. Those with large surpluses, and the financial means to wait till the price was right, felt no pressure to exchange grain for worthless money. The lack of goods was deepened by the initial stages of a too-late programme of industrialisation, in which investment was tilted towards heavy industry and away from production of consumer goods.

Catastrophe was only averted when the government directed a flow of manufactures into the country to win grain in exchange. Already vital foreign earnings from grain sales had been lost, the value of exports achieving only 63 per cent of the target. Machinery imports and investment plans were reduced sharply. This was the result of a good harvest! These events now convinced the volatile Zinoviev that capitulation to the peasants was fatal and that there had been a 'kulak grain strike' which had held the country to ransom. There was an element of truth in this, although the withholding of grain was part of a more complex process involving broader sections of the peasantry, and was less coordinated than the term 'strike' would suggest.[24]

The trouble-free agricultural year of 1926/7 was merely the calm before the storm. In 1927/8 the harvest fell short of the previous year's by several million tons. Between October and December 1927 state collection agencies only acquired half the volume of grain it had collected for the same period in the previous year. Reiman writes that:

> The difficulties with grain deliveries had an immediate and powerful effect on the entire unhealthy mechanism that was the Soviet economy ... Grain exports fell off dramatically, and at the same time the Soviet balance of trade became increasingly unfavourable ... the government hastily reduced imports. The supply of many goods urgently needed in production was thus cut off, greatly aggravating the shortage of raw materials, especially in light industry ... Finances, too, were thrown into disorder ... The supply of goods to the market was in a disastrous state. In the course of a month – from December 1927 to January 1928 – it decreased by 15.5 per cent Severe shortages arose, involving an entire range of basic necessities. In a number of provincial cities, supplies fell so low that the needs of the population could be met for only a few days. By the end of January 1928 it was evident that rationing would have to be introduced.[25]

There were various reasons for this new crisis. In the summer of 1927 Chiang Kai-shek massacred the Chinese revolution and the USSR lost its 'anti-imperialist bloc'; the Tories in Britain severed diplomatic relations; finally, Voikov, the ambassador to Poland, was assassinated. At Voikov's funeral Bukharin warned of the 'capitalist world turning to more desperate measures against us'.[26] As Reiman states:

The new international situation produced abrupt changes in the political conjuncture. Prior to the defeat in China and the break with Britain, the Soviet leadership had not given much consideration to the possibility of war in the near future. The new events shook that confidence ... the statements of the political leaders were permeated with the conviction that ... the period of the 'peaceful breathing spell' was ending, and that war was inevitable in the near future. It was expected, if not in 1928, then soon after.[27]

War panic led to a run on the shops. This added to the already existing goods famine. Food shortages were exacerbated by the government's pricing policy, which encouraged peasants to grow crops for use as raw materials in industry (such as flax and cotton) rather than grain. In 1925 industrial crops were worth 5 per cent more than grain. Industrial demand encouraged the former to expand, so that by 1927 the gap was 39 per cent.[28]

These were the short-term causes of the problem. There were, however, also structural difficulties which could not be overcome easily and which made the 1927 crisis more serious than preceding ones. The historic backwardness of Soviet agriculture was one factor. Grain production per head of total population was half that of the US, even though a vastly higher proportion of the Soviet workforce was employed in agriculture.[29] This was at a time when the state was desperate to finance the purchase of foreign machinery through grain exports. The population was growing by 2 – 3 per cent annually, while grain production showed signs of declining.

Even if enough grain had been grown, the proportion of output that the peasants were willing to sell would still have been too low to meet the needs. As one writer comments: 'It had once been possible for Imperial ministers to decree, "We may go hungry, but we will export"; now it was possible for the peasants to decide, "We will eat", and eat they did.'[30] Lower taxation and the absence of industrial goods reduced still further the peasants' incentive to obtain cash and meant that the proportion of output they brought to market was barely half the pre-war level – 13 per cent instead of 26 per cent.[31] Furthermore, the main suppliers of grain were a fairly narrow group, and if they refused to sell the state was vulnerable. Davies writes: 'A mere 10–11% of all households in the European USSR supplied 56% of all net sales of grain ... in 1927/28.'[32]

This final point demonstrates that the economic problems were compounded by a political mistake. Bukharinist policies had stimulated the petty-capitalist side of the peasants' character, which Lenin had described when he called them 'half huckster'. The half-worker side had been demoralised. Great numbers of middle and poorer peasants had been forced into various forms of dependence on the rich. If grain collection difficulties could not be blamed entirely on a clear group of kulaks and Nepmen (as Stalin now declared), it was nevertheless true that a petty-capitalist market mentality reigned supreme, and Bukharin more than anyone had helped create it.

Words Turned Upside Down

The split between Stalin and Bukharin in 1928 occurred when the former broke with previous policies and rushed towards forced industrialisation, collectivisation and centralised planning. Until this time the universal touchstone of political debate had been industrialisation. This was not because industrialisation equalled socialism (after all, the most industrialised countries in the world today are capitalist), but because until 1928 it symbolised one's attitude towards the two main social forces: the working class and the peasantry.

When the opposition called for industrialisation it was for this reason:

> The basic condition for our socialist development at the present preliminary stage and in the present historical situation – capitalist encirclement and a delay in the world revolution – is a rate of industrialisation sufficiently rapid to ensure that, in the near future, at least the following problems would be solved:
> The material positions of the proletariat within the country must be strengthened both absolutely and relatively ... Industry, transport and power plants must increase operations in order at least to keep pace with the growing demands of the country as a whole and not to lag behind ... It must be made possible for agriculture to attain a higher technical level ... etc.[33]

When Stalin called for industrialisation after 1928 it would amount to the creation of a new state capitalist system, ending what remained of workers' rule.

Stalin's turn to planning was not automatically socialist either. As Marx had written, internal planning (as distinct from relations between economic units) was a fundamental element of capitalism from the very start:

> as soon as the capitalist mode of production stands on its own feet [there develops] on an ever-extending scale, the co-operative form

of the labour-process, the conscious technical application of science ... the economising of all means of production by their use as the means of production of combined, socialised labour.[34]

Planning would only have been socialist if it had become a tool in the hands of workers enabling them freely to determine their future. This had been the aim of the opposition. Stalin's bureaucracy planned not in order to free workers from slavery to the means of production, but to subordinate workers to the means of production still more in the competition to survive.

The same argument applied to collectivisation. The opposition believed that, given time plus the right technical basis and inducements, collectivisation could bring the benefits of socialism to the peasant population of the USSR. However, in the hands of Stalin, it would become a brutal form of exploitation.

What was Bukharin's attitude to the crisis developing at this juncture? It is very difficult to know exactly what he was thinking throughout the period of 1927 until his break with Stalin in mid-1928. In some pronouncements he appears to have been trying to neutralise opposition criticisms by verbally adopting some of their policies. He may have been trying to maintain his influence over the leading ranks of the party by adopting some of Stalin's policies. Given the scale of the crisis, it is even possible that he was prepared to abandon some old positions to take new ones. In the end, circumstances would force him to choose more clearly. But this is running ahead. For the moment he tried to caution against too hectic a pace of change but was dragged along reluctantly by the Stalinist machine.

In 1926 and 1927 Bukharin came to applaud an increased industrial tempo and planning. He even called for a 'forced offensive on the kulak'. But these statements did not represent moves towards the Opposition. Take the issue of capital accumulation. Bukharin now said that the situation demanded an increased pace of investment, but his formulation of the problem contrasted with that of the left opposition. He said:

> We are often reproached for wanting to get the capital we lack at the expense of the people. But in fact there is nowhere else to get it ... the chief, it could be said the decisive source of wealth is the labour of the people ... Only our own resources, the labour of the people, the labour of the workers and peasants can provide us with our capital.[35]

Contrast this with the *Platform of the Opposition*, written about the same time. Here the concentration was on those who could most afford to contribute:

> It is necessary: a) to tax all kinds of excess profits from private enterprises to the extent of not less than 150 to 200m rubles, instead of 5m as at present, b) in order to strengthen our export, to assure a collection from the well-to-do kulak strata, constituting approximately 10% of all peasant households, of not less than 150m poods of grain. This should be collected in the form of a loan from those stores of grain which in 1926–27 amounted to 800 to 900m poods, and which are concentrated, for the most part, in the hands of the upper strata of the peasantry.[36]

Bukharin's argument, in distinction to the opposition's, was conceived entirely in terms of 'socialism in one country' and Russian state interest. Under capitalism, he wrote, workers resisted increased capital accumulation at their expense, but Russian industry 'was socialist' and so:

> It is quite obvious that the proletariat has an absolutely different attitude to large-scale industry as it is the common 'master' of it. Therefore it follows that one cannot adopt the point of view of taking the maximum share of profits: because part of it must contribute towards the 'accumulation fund.'[37]

This abstract truth entirely ignored the bureaucratisation of the state since 1917, which meant that, in reality, workers were less and less masters of industry and their contribution to accumulation was being exploited by others.

Bukharin's new line was still compatible with a pro-rich peasant position. As a *Pravda* editorial put it in April 1926: 'all the party decisions, now as before, reject the theory and proposals of all the "super-industrialisers".'[38] What this meant was that the first steps towards industrialisation did not burden Nepmen and rich peasants but began with the extension of that typical capitalist method of sweating labour – the piece-rate system. By 1927/8 this covered almost two thirds of workers.[39] Then followed 'the regime of economy' which *Pravda* launched in the editorial quoted above. The 'regime of economy' meant finding savings in many areas, but it is clear where the bureaucracy lay the emphasis:

> The state and economic apparatus costs us dear; overhead expenses in industry and trade continue to remain high [but] in the final

analysis, and as far as concerns our general position, one of our most important tasks must continue to be *the raising of the productivity of labour* ... the further growth of industry, the process of industrialisation and raising of living standards for the working class is dependent, as before, on *growth of the productivity of labour*.[40]

It was kind of *Pravda* to mention raising workers' living standards. However, for Bukharin it was a case of jam tomorrow but nothing today, because: 'we are caught in a vicious circle. We cannot at present quickly raise wages and yet we must develop the slogan of the regime of economy.' This had meant 'some discontent among portions of the working class'.[41]

This was hardly surprising. When Bukharin made his statement in the spring of 1926 the value of real wages had fallen by 10-15 per cent since the start of the year.[42] One young worker responded:

[we] drudge for all we are worth for eight hours, and we cannot relax. If you relax you'll earn little. Yet all sorts of campaigns are going on here: 'Raise productivity!' 'The Regime of Economy', and whatnot. [It] means squeeze the last drop out of the workers.[43]

Another expression of discontent was so-called 'indiscipline'. As the pressure mounted indiscipline became a mass phenomenon. By 1929, out of 200,000 coalminers in the Donets (eastern Ukraine) the annual rate of 'violation of labour discipline' was 476,000. There were 340,000 cases of 'failure to report', 63,000 of 'failure to execute orders' and 51,000 of 'property damage'.[44] Even union officials, normally placid supporters of the government line, added their voices to the rising discontent with the regime of economy and its consequences.[45]

The Stalinist bureaucracy did not blame itself for intolerable working conditions creating indiscipline. It blamed the workers:

It is simply sheer laziness, their non-desiring to work and the large number of days they lay off. We see the same thing, in a slightly lesser degree, in the metal industries ... In order to increase output it is necessary to take exemplary measures of a demonstrative character.[46]

Articles that appeared in *Pravda* included one from Ostrovskii which implied that workers should show the same discipline as the army.[47] However, in the same issue Bukharin struck a different note. Rather than the stick, he wanted persuasion. It was, he said, a matter of 'involving the masses' in the campaign.[48] Neither threats nor exhortation proved adequate. So stern measures were taken, such as legally limiting the number of workers' 'non-appearances without convincing reasons' to a maximum of three per month in order to 'make full use of workers' time and strengthen discipline'.[49]

The opposition was not against raising productivity. Socialism requires high levels of material wealth. What was at issue was whether productivity would rise either by squeezing workers or by using more productive machinery and, failing this, by compensating them for harder work with higher living standards. During the summer of 1926 Trotsky argued at the Central Committee that if the regime of economy were to be justified, wage increases must match productivity gains. Industrialisation must not be at the expense of the workers:

> The decisive factor in appraising the progress of our country along the road of socialist reconstruction must be the growth of our productive forces and the dominance of the socialist elements over the capitalist – *together with improvement in all the living conditions of the working class*. This improvement ought to be evident in the material sphere (number of workers employed in industry, level of real wages, the kind of budget appropriations for the workers' needs, housing conditions, medical services, etc.); in the political sphere (party, trade unions, soviets, the Communist youth organisation); and finally in the cultural sphere.[50]

The government was as yet unsure of its ground and in August the retreat was sounded. Officials were rapped over the knuckles for: 'the distortion of the regime of economy in its practical application. This has been expressed in absolutely impermissible measures by particular economic organs, severely harming the living standards of the workers, and worsening their material position.' The examples cited were:

> measures ignoring the legally established rights of youths, cutting provision of overalls, stopping provision of water and hot beverages, cutting off lighting to workers' clubs, cuts in factory schools, a mechanical approach to reducing employment, attempting to alter without negotiation with trade unions the correct internal working arrangements, hastily disregarding and even ignoring collective bargaining, surreptitiously cutting wages etc.[51]

However, the bureaucracy could permit no prolonged delay. In early 1927 a new campaign was launched – 'rationalisation'. In *Pravda* Bukharin wrote: 'We need rationalisation – to bring down cost prices, cheapen trading organisations and government ... We have to improve production. We are compelled to lower prices and must create a corresponding psychology.'[52] Bukharin promised workers that 'it is not their needs that are subordinate to our economic apparatus, but our economic apparatus serves to satisfy needs. It is such needs that our Bolshevik party serves, the needs of the labouring masses of our country.'[53] Very laudable sentiments. But when the opposition suggested that reducing the proportion of national income going to wages was 'anti-socialist' Bukharin replied:

> *That is rubbish – utter nonsense*, because any fool knows, that when we get better equipment, when we have electricity ... and heavy machinery, when high technology finds its full expression, then among other things, the portion of living labour in each unit of production *falls*.[54]

This was true, but the problem was that the country did *not* have good equipment or electricity at that time. Although Bukharin eventually baulked at the idea, the logical consequence of his 'socialism in one country' theory was that new technology would *first* have to be won by massively exploiting the workers. Indeed, as Bukharin himself admitted: *'Rationalisation will be accompanied by an increased intensity of labour.*[55]

The *Platform of the Opposition* viewed things differently:

> The attempt to push the vital interests of the worker into the background and, under the contemptuous epithet of 'narrow craft professionalism,' to counterpose them to the general historical interests of the working class, is theoretically wrong and politically dangerous. The appropriation of surplus value by a workers' state is not, of course, exploitation. But in the first place, we have a workers' state with bureaucratic distortions. The swollen and privileged administrative apparatus devours a very considerable part of the surplus value. In the second place, the growing bourgeoisie, through trade and by taking advantage of the price scissors [buying cheap wholesale goods from the state and selling them at high retail prices] appropriate part of the surplus value created by state industry.[56]

In the end, neither the dangling carrot of 'socialism in one country' nor the sticks of the 'regime of economy' and 'rationalisation' led to any great improvement in productivity. This was hardly surprising, given that workers were expected somehow to produce more despite the parlous state of machinery and their low living standards.

In October 1927 Bukharin tried a new tack. On behalf of the Politburo, he proposed a shorter working day of seven hours. This was supposed to be a demonstration of the rewards of socialism 10 years on from 1917. In reality it was designed to increase the intensity of labour and bring in continuous production on a three-shift system. In the textile industries it led to a 36 per cent rise in accidents.[57] In large-scale industry productivity rose 12 per cent and nominal wages[58] only 10 per cent. For the metal trades the corresponding figures were 14 per cent and 7 per cent; in electrics 25 per cent and 7 per cent. Other industries experienced similar rises.[59]

During the Bukharin – Stalin duumvirate the bureaucracy had evolved from its origins in the proletarian movement. The more it capitulated to Nepman and kulak influence the weaker working-class influence became; and the weaker the workers, the more room the bureaucracy had to develop its own separate interests. However, there would be a point when further independence for the bureaucracy could only be gained at the expense not only of the workers, but of Nepmen and kulaks and eventually the entire peasantry too. It was then that Bukharin and Stalin split. Until that time Bukharin went along with Stalin because the immediate costs of industrialisation were borne principally by the working class.

The recurrent crises of the NEP were forcing Russia's leaders to make difficult choices. Despite Bukharin's efforts, the bureaucracy found it impossible to reconcile the interests of agriculture and industry. The clash between them was not evidence of a fight between the different social systems of capitalism and socialism, as Stalin suggested. It was between forms of capital (in this case private versus state) for a division of spoils. History affords many examples of such struggles.[60]

Bukharin did not relish the re-emergence of social conflict in the late 1920s. Nevertheless the crisis in agriculture in late 1927 and pressure from the Stalinists forced him to question the holy of holies – his attitude to the kulaks. He evasively admitted that differentiation, that trend which should have been absent in a society 'growing into socialism', was present after all:

> We have a specific type of differentiation – I say this very conditionally and do not pretend to any precise definition ... In general terms, among our peasant masses, it seems to me that the characteristic figure can roughly be described as the middle peasant. But there is a numerical increase in agricultural labourers and an undoubted growth of the

kulak, a growth of their economic significance, because the kulak represents a group with stronger farms.[61]

Once the kulak threat had been admitted it became the scapegoat for past mistakes. It is likely that Bukharin was hoping to head off bolder moves from Stalin by taking the first step in the anti-kulak campaign himself.[62] It was he who first called for *'going over to a forced offensive against capitalist elements, and in the first place the kulaks'*, in a speech celebrating the tenth anniversary of the October revolution.[63] At this stage he did not envisage that in the 1930s Stalin would 'liquidate the kulaks as a class' and kill millions of peasants, many of them not kulaks at all. Bukharin was proposing only a temporary manoeuvre designed to get the government off the hook.

At the end of 1927 the economic situation was still desperate. In the words of the head of the Council for National Economy, Kuibyshev, between October and November:

Raw materials production declined by as much as 9.2% ... while *production in heavy and light industry*, taken together, was 21.5% below the expected amount. These are terrible figures ... our aim is reconstruction, but from month to month we are going backwards. So what we have is not reconstruction, but – to put it harshly – *a slow death*.[64]

The grain collection campaign was netting only a fraction of what was needed. So on 6 January Stalin threatened local officials with dire consequences if they did not improve the situation. Some 30,000 party activists were despatched to key regions, emergency committees were set up and a system of 'extraordinary measures' was instituted. Article 107 of the penal code was used to prosecute and seize the grain of those refusing to sell at state prices. Kulaks were supposed to be the sole target of this campaign, yet others fell into the trap too. Compulsory 'loans' were created, tax collected in advance, markets pressured or even closed down and road blocks mounted to stop the movement of private grain. By the April plenum of the Central Committee these methods had raised more grain than had been collected in the equivalent period of the previous year's abundant harvest. They also provoked a near civil war situation. Although the extraordinary measures were now suspended, the slide towards forced collectivisation had begun. Bukharin's attempt to head off Stalin's anti-kulak offensive by taking the first step had proved tactically inept.

Reiman rightly points out that: 'It is doubtful that Stalin consciously intended to create the social and state system so inseparably associated with his name' and that his war on the peasants began as 'A pragmatic response to particular social situations'.[65] Nevertheless, kulak and Nepman influence, once a force to be appeased, was now intolerable to him. It was a rival ruling class in the making; it was in direct competition with the bureaucracy for control of national resources; and insofar as it defended the market system (which, as petty producers, the rest of the peasantry also used) it was an obstacle to achieving full subordination to state capitalist accumulation.

By early 1928 Bukharin was struggling to maintain his political credibility. In a speech to the Young Communist League in May he referred cautiously to the need for collectivisation or, as he called it, 'cooperation on a production basis'. This was described as serving: 'the main, fundamental, decisive line of class struggle with the kulaks'; it constituted an '*offensive* by the working class against its economic (i.e. its *class*) enemies.'[66] Bukharin described Stalin's extraordinary measures as 'absolutely necessary because of intensified struggle against the working class dictatorship by kulak elements and discontented top layers of the middle peasantry'.[67] Two tasks now stood before the party: '*rationalisation of industry and collectivisation of agriculture*', although the latter (and only the latter) could not be achieved 'all at once'.[68]

Did Bukharin's fulminations against the kulak amount to an abandonment of positions he had held since the introduction of the NEP, or to an acceptance of the opposition's ideas? No. He only spoke of attacking the kulaks when the crisis had reached major proportions and he was forced to choose between the Nepmen and kulaks and the bureaucracy. All his speeches contained qualifications which showed he hoped the breach between these former allies would be temporary.

By 1928 the Soviet bureaucracy was ready to stand on its own two feet as an independent class force. Under Bukharin's ideological guidance, and Stalin's administrative fist, degeneration had reached the point where quantity turned into quality. The bureaucracy had begun by reacting to events, by a process of improvisation. Now it wanted to establish its own counter-revolutionary programme based on state capitalist accumulation. To do this it would have to go beyond Bukharin's programme and he would have to be annihilated politically.

12 Was Bukharin the Alternative to Stalin?

In this chapter, dealing with the period from spring 1928 to April 1929, we reach the heart of the argument regarding Bukharin, the Russian revolution and socialist politics today. October 1917 was the first and, as yet, only example of a successful workers' revolution, of an attempt to create a society that could abolish the horrors of capitalism, where fantastic wealth coexists with mass starvation, where millions suffer the poverty and degradation of unemployment and homelessness while a privileged elite live lives of luxury. The issues raised by the revolution are still dominant in today's socialist movements. Current debates can be traced to the revolution and its aftermath, via the three leading rivals – Stalin, Bukharin and Trotsky.

In this context Bukharin is sometimes presented as the real alternative, the mentor of a 'humanistic' and 'democratic socialist' alternative. His programme is portrayed as the only realistic choice at the crucial moment, in 1928 – 9, when the ultimate fate of the Russian revolution was decided. The argument has taken various forms.

One recent version that has been popular in Russia contends that the battle lines were drawn between, on the one hand, Stalin and Trotsky, both bearing virtually identical programmes, and Bukharin on the other. At the Thirteenth Round Table discussion of historians in 1988 one affirmed that:

> In 1926 Kamenev, Zinoviev and Trotsky were removed from the Politburo and in the following year excluded from the party. Experience, however, proved that the destruction of the 'left' was not the result of a disagreement with Stalin over their anti-NEP programme.'[1]

Another added: 'Neither in practice nor on the theoretical plane was Stalin really an antagonist of Trotsky and his supporters.'[2] Of Bukharin it has been written: 'the final programme of Bukharin, with its opposition to "extremism" in principle, was the actual alternative to Stalin. This is absolutely clear.'[3]

Western Bukharinists put it differently, although their hero stays the same. Cohen does not ignore the six-year struggle of Trotsky and the left opposition, culminating in exile, jail and judicial murder in the 1930s, but feels this was minor compared with Bukharin's confrontation with Stalin, which was 'the most momentous struggle in the party since 1917-1918 ...'[4] In Western versions the antagonism is not seen as Bukharin versus a Trotsky – Stalin bloc. It is a case of Trotsky and Bukharin sharing a similar approach and both opposing Stalin. Lewin writes:

> Neither the Left militants nor their leader realized at that time [1929] that the programme elaborated by Bukharin during his fight against Stalin was to become their own. The rightist dangers against which they were fighting were phantoms; Bukharin, paraxodical as this may sound, expressed at this stage better than anybody else the prospective common opinion of both Left and the Right. But the quarrels of the past made both sides unaware of this basic convergence, and they continued to fight each other fiercely at a time when the right-wing programme of 1928–1929 was the only counterprogramme and alternative to Stalin's which represented both wings inside the party.[5]

Finally, there is Trotsky's view of the events of 1928–9. Unlike the others, Trotsky distinguished not two but three separate groups. Continuing his line of 'with Stalin against Bukharin – yes; with Bukharin against Stalin – never', Trotsky believed that behind Bukharin stood the spectre of 'Thermidor'. (During the month of that name in 1794, the French revolutionary Jacobins were overthrown by a reactionary coup.) Trotsky thought that Bukharin would bring about capitalist restoration through the kulaks and Nepmen. He saw Bukharin as the opposite pole to his left opposition tendency, which stood for proletarian power and socialism. According to this view, the Stalinists formed a 'centrist' grouping which vacillated helplessly between the left and right poles. Trotsky saw Bukharin as a greater threat than the Stalinists, writing: 'The very reason we attack centrism is that by its whole policy of unprincipled zigzags it feeds and strengthens the Right tendencies.'[6]

To judge the accuracy of these three interpretations it is necessary to look at Bukharin's so-called 'new programme'. This emerged in the spring of 1928 when he became aware of just what Stalin's policies were leading to.

The New Programme

Although Stalin and Bukharin formed a 'duumvirate' in the mid-1920s, astute observers detected subtle distinctions between the two men even before 1928. These had been momentarily exposed in the row over Bukharin's call to the peasants to 'enrich yourselves'. It was after this that Trotsky set down his different attitudes to the two leaders. Nevertheless the common front uniting Stalin and Bukharin outweighed any divergences.

This still remained true at the Fifteenth Party Congress in December 1927. If there was any sign of the future conflict it was in the speeches of Rykov, chair of the Council of People's Commissars, rather than in Bukharin's. Presenting the first moderate draft of the Five-Year Plan, Rykov accepted, at least temporarily, the principle of 'pumping over' resources from the peasants. But he warned that this must be 'naturally within certain limitations' and 'only at the present stage in the country's economic development, and until such time as industry has achieved an adequate level of growth.' If not, there might be 'immediate and localized economic disorders' and even a 'general crisis'.[7]

While Rykov hinted at disquiet, Frumkin, a minor Moscow official, expressed alarm. In a letter to the Central Committee in the summer of 1928 he urged that relations with the peasants be restored by returning to the more temperate aims and tone of the Fourteenth Congress of December 1925.[8] Ignoring the Politburo decision to draft a collective reply, Stalin wrote individually to Frumkin, arguing that 'the more we advance the greater will be the resistance of the capitalist elements and the sharper the class struggle.'[9] The harvest crisis was therefore a sign of progress, not something to worry about. At the Politburo, uproar ensued. Bukharin accused Stalin of treating that body as 'a consultative organ under the general secretary'. Stalin tried to calm Bukharin telling him: 'You and I are the Himalayas; the others are nobodies.' But, as Cohen tells us: 'No longer on speaking terms, the personal breach between the former duumvirs was total.'[10]

Bukharin marked out his own position at the Central Committee plenum which met on 4 July 1928, and it attracted influential supporters like Rykov and Tomsky. Bukharin's first target was the Stalinist, Kaganovich, who said that although: 'It would be impossible to turn the extraordinary measures [against the peasants] into a system', they would be freely used in the future.[11] Bukharin's counter argument was familiar:

> If we evaluate the situation so as to consider that the reconstruction period inevitably entails such political disturbance that the [worker–peasant] alliance is threatened, then we inevitably arrive at the theory which Trotsky formulated; namely, that without state aid from

workers abroad our progress will lead to an inevitable conflict between workers and the peasantry culminating in the defeat of the proletarian dictatorship.[12]

In other words, faced with crisis Bukharin saw no alternative but to capitulate to peasant pressure once more. Anything else (whether Stalin's measures or the very different opposition programme) was to be damned as a Trotskyist deviation.

The tenor of debates at the plenum was shown by this exchange:

BUKHARIN: The situation is that when the poor peasants held demonstrations [on 1st May] in the towns, it was not as supporters of Soviet power ... We had speeches by old partisans – revolutionaries, who came to the Soviet power, to the military committee and said: 'how are we going to get bread?'...
KAGANOVICH: There were such speeches, but do you need to quote them?
BUKHARIN: ... Vladimir Il'ich would never have tolerated keeping quiet about facts. Facts must be foreseen, and such things must be taken care of.
VOROSHILOV: Who's denying them, who are you trying to convince?
BUKHARIN: I don't know who denies them, but I only knew about all this yesterday ... after two days spent at the GPU [secret police].[13]

Although the last sentence was evidence of Bukharin's distance from daily events, his concerns were well founded. The harvest of 1928/9 was lower than that of the previous year, which itself had been one of crisis, and the proportion of grain collected was even smaller. Bukharin concluded with these words:

our economy makes my hair stand on end, when there are horses eating only grain but in some places people eat chaff, when peasants have to buy bread in neighbouring towns, when an agrarian country imports grain but exports the products of industry. This alarming economic state will lead to crisis and arguments. It has to be sorted out.[14]

What was his solution? The first thing was to avoid further 'extraordinary measures'. Bukharin did not object to moves against the kulak, but to the fact that the extraordinary measures were an abandonment of 'revolutionary legality' which struck indiscriminately at *all* peasants.[15] He had dark forebodings about Stalin's methods turning into a form of civil war against the peasants, although it is unlikely that even he foresaw the mass murder, horrendous famine and even cannibalism which the counter-revolution would produce. Bukharin urged an alteration to the current system of 'economic leadership', where 'there is only one type of initiative, which comes from the state and exclusively from above'. He wanted local initiatives to counter the 'hypercentralised bureaucratic apparatus'.[16] Here Bukharin was referring principally to free initiatives by peasants and lower bureaucrats. This was indicated by his continued emphasis on appeasing the individual peasant farmer and further cheapening industrial goods. Since, according to the theory of socialism in one country, workers' power was secure, the rights of rank-and-file proletarians did not enter the equation. Thus, at the Moscow plenum where the Bukharinists' concerns were first publicly expressed, Uglanov, first secretary of the Moscow party and the right's most determined advocate, declared: 'the director has to become the director ... It is the director who is responsible [for production]. That is the essence. This has to be understood.'[17]

Bukharin was not simply reiterating his old pro-peasant policies. Like Rykov, he accepted some 'pumping over' of resources for industry as inevitable.[18] On the question of letting up on the offensive against the kulaks or granting concessions to them, Bukharin replied: 'Absolutely not.' The kulak could be kept in check, and 'we can shoot him with rifles' as long as the middle and poor peasants did not follow him.[19] Later he would say that kulak reprisals against communists

> must be fought with the utmost ruthlessness; to the use of the gun we must reply with the language of lead because it is impossible to respond in any other way than this to our impudent enemies. Such a reply is completely direct, completely precise and absolutely necessary.[20]

Responding to those who accused him of fathering the notion that kulaks would 'grow into socialism', Bukharin rightly denied ever having argued this (although he had come close at times) and reminded his listeners that he was the first to call for 'a forced offensive against the kulak'.[21]

Bukharin's new programme tried to adapt old policies to the current crisis conditions in order to save the NEP. It was still balanced between the peasants and the bureaucracy. So, on the one hand, Bukharin wished to satisfy the bureaucracy's desire to 'catch up and overtake' the West, and to do this he was ready to sacrifice the worker and now the kulak. On the other hand, he still hoped to salvage the goodwill of the bulk of the peasants who resented the panic measures, forced collectivisation and ill-thought-out and over hasty industrialisation programme. For this he was dubbed the leader of the 'right'. Up to this time the term 'right' was correct, but after that it was an inadequate designation. However, it has been so extensively used in the literature that we must continue to employ it to denote Bukharin's group from 1928 onwards.

The first clear statement of the new programme was the publication in the 30 September 1928 edition of *Pravda* of 'Notes of an Economist'. These 'Notes' were highly peculiar. They were framed as an attack on Trotsky. Bukharin castigated the 'Trotskyist ventriloquists', who 'failed to comprehend', who 'do not understand', who issued 'a document that is without precedent for its slander and hysterics' and so on.[22] There was not a single mention of Stalin, or even criticism of the party's current policy, a point that is somehow overlooked by its admirers. Yet this was neither accidental nor simply an early example of the Aesopian language which dissidents used from the 1930s onwards to avoid being gagged. It marked out a method that Bukharin would employ from the start of his campaign (at the July 1928 Central Committee) to the very end. His last free statement implied that the Stalin group was presenting 'a *Trotskyist platform*'.[23] Nevertheless, the 'Notes of an Economist' do attack Stalin, if not in person. One supporter explains how:

> the further you read, the stranger the tone becomes ... And suddenly you grasp it ... For the author of the article 'Trotskyism' is only a psuedonym. His opponent is Stalin. It is true that Trotskyists have said these things ... But the Trotskyists said it before. Stalin says it now.[24]

The 'Notes' concentrated on economic theory rather than political policy, returning to the idea of equilibrium that was contained in Bukharin's *Historical Materialism*. The USSR was witnessing '*moments of a crisis character*, which *disrupt the course of reproduction* ... They can originate only in *disruption* of the conditions for economic equilibrium, i.e. they can result only from *an incorrect combination of the elements of reproduction*.'[25] The answer was to return to a '*moving economic equilibrium*'[26] or balanced growth. On the grain campaign, Bukharin challenged the 'fairy tale' notion that kulaks were sitting on hoarded mountains of grain. The problems of agriculture were linked, he said, to the dispersed character of farming, the inadequate taxation of kulaks which had allowed them to increase in influence, poor pricing policies and the lack of industrial consumer goods, caused by too much stress on heavy industry. The scale of investment in 1928/9 in large-scale industry was already twice that of 1925/26 and rising. The solution to problems in both areas lay in properly coordinating industry and agriculture, but with emphasis on agricultural growth coming first and industrial growth occurring as its consequence:

> The highest rate can be *sustained* only by such coordination as allows industry to develop on the basis of a *rapidly growing agriculture*. It is precisely then that industry yields its *record* figures of development. But this pattern presupposes the possibility of rapid and real accumulation in agriculture, and consequently involves anything but the policy of Trotskyism.[27]

Balanced growth had a direct bearing on the pace of industrialisation. If growth in industry was too rapid, then:

> *in its own development, industry encounters the limits of its development.* That is the conclusion superindustrializer Trotsky evades or slurs over ... The fact that industry 'runs into' its own limits means that we have obviously not adopted a sufficiently correct relationship among the various branches.[28]

This led to the most quoted phrase from the 'Notes': it is ridiculous to suggest that '"today's" factories could be built with "bricks of the future".'[29]

The other side of Bukharin's new programme was a critique of bureaucracy, against which he had spoken out with increasing stridency since July 1928. In the 'Notes' he reminded his readers of Lenin's view that as socialism approached, the apparatus of power would wither away to be replaced by a 'Commune State'. Bukharin's most detailed presentation of this argument occurred in his last uncensored speech, made on the anniversary of Lenin's death, 21 January, 1929. It was published as 'Lenin's Political Testament', a title with special meaning for those party members who knew of Lenin's final letter to the Politburo. The speech was a powerful indictment of Stalin's theory that class struggle would become increasingly bitter in the approach to socialism: 'Lenin did not deny class struggle, but saw "peaceful organisational" and "cultural work" as a *specific form* of class struggle.'[30] The implication was that Stalin's confrontational style of operation had nothing to do with Leninism and was endangering the very stability of society. However, Bukharin's comments on bureaucracy did not go far beyond his previous critique of bureaucratism and its chief exponent remained unnamed.

Things were different in private. In July 1928 Bukharin told Kamenev that Stalin was a 'Genghis Khan', an 'unprincipled intriguer who subordinates everything to the preservation of his own power. He changes his theories depending on whom he wants to get rid of at the moment.'[31] There was doubtless truth in this personal characterisation. It became the accepted Soviet view of Stalin after Krushchev's denunciation of him. But even here Bukharin fell far short of a Marxist understanding of what was happening.

He believed that reasoned argument and economic rationality could win over the party leadership, but he misjudged his opponent. Stalin's apparent individual wilfulness and economic irrationality had a political purpose. As one writer has said, Stalin regarded problems 'not so much in economic as political terms', for 'political gain ... overrode all other concerns'.[32] Stalin was not just expressing a personal position but the needs of a class which was making its own sort of (counter-) revolution to establish state capitalism. It was Bukharin who, in *The Economics of the Transition Period*, explained so well that every revolution has its economic costs. In the case of Stalin the costs of counter-revolution would be enormous. Because Bukharin still dared not analyse the party apparatus in the 'land of the proletarian dictatorship' in class terms, he could not use insights from *The Economics*.

For the same reason Bukharin's concept of state capitalism was not dusted off to explain the phenomenon of Stalinism. In the summer of 1929 he did draw parallels between the organisational methods being used in the USSR and Western state capitalism. In a pair of articles he talked of the state capitalist West suffering from monopolistic degeneration and facing a future collapse like that of ancient Egypt.[33] Although Bukharin implied criticism of Stalin's bureaucratic command economy, there was no sign he had changed his view that the very fact of the 1917 revolution ruled out state capitalism in the USSR.

Which Interpretation of Bukharinism is Correct?

The Soviet Bukharinists' Approach: Bukharin Facing a Trotsky–Stalin Bloc
Does the existence of Bukharin's new programme, and his assertion that Trotsky and Stalin were identical, prove he *was* the real alternative to a common Trotsky–Stalin threat? Not at all. He had misunderstood Trotsky's position.

Trotsky was fundamentally opposed to Stalin, as this summary of his position in October 1929 shows:

> The practical concern now is not at all to 'outstrip' the entire world economy – a fantasy – but to consolidate the industrial foundations of the proletarian dictatorship and improve the situation of the

workers, strengthening the dictatorship's political precondition, i.e. the union of the proletariat with the nonexploiting peasantry.

This was based on the fact that 'even the most correct and farsighted leadership could not lead the USSR to the construction of socialism within its national borders.'[34] Therefore the programme of the opposition was not the same as Stalin's:

> Our estimation of the possibilities of industrialization was immeasurably broader and bolder than that of the bureaucrats up until 1928. But we never regarded the resources for industrialization as inexhaustible ... We have always advanced, as a basic condition for industrialization, the necessity for systematic improvement in the conditions of the working class.[35]

Finally, Trotsky's commitment to fighting the Stalinist bureaucracy cannot be doubted, as the bitter struggle of the opposition had shown since 1923.

The division between Stalin and Trotsky was between a platform founded upon the needs of a new state capitalist ruling class and a platform founded upon the needs of the working class. That Bukharin could confuse the two was a typical example of his unlimited capacity for 'abstraction', in this case from the entire purpose and context of the opposition programme. If you ignore everything except the word 'industrialization', then of course Trotsky and Stalin sound similar.

The Western Bukharinists' Approach: Bukharin with Trotsky versus Stalin
Could it perhaps follow that Bukharin's programme was a real alternative to Stalin because it summed up both his *and* Trotsky's positions?

Both Trotsky and Bukharin explicitly rejected that notion. When, in April 1929, Bukharin was accused of linking up with the Trotskyists he replied:

> all this talk of a bloc ... is aimed at *covering up evidence of another* 'bloc' which is presently being concluded between some members of the Politburo and certain former Trotskyists ... I have never united with Trotsky because for me there would be no political basis – *no* political basis for unity *in any shape or form*.[36]

The sentiment was reciprocated by Trotsky: 'we have nothing in common with the Right' and 'there cannot even be talk of a bloc ... This requires no commentary.'[37] The only possible common ground might have been a shared opposition to Stalin's dictatorial methods.

Trotsky considered an alliance, writing: 'if we limited our task only to the bare formula of party democracy, it might be possible to enter a bloc with the Right in the struggle with the bureaucratic centre.' He immediately added that he had no intention of limiting the fight in such a way: 'This danger threatens not us.'[38]

If it is wrong to equate Trotsky with Stalin because they both used the word 'industrialization', it would be equally mistaken to tie Trotsky to Bukharin just because both mentioned the word 'equilibrium'.

It is true that Trotsky and Bukharin shared a common belief in simple economic rationality, against the sort of voluntarism expressed in this speech by Stalin's foremost economist, Strumilin: 'Our task is not to study economics, but to change it. We are bound by no laws. There are no fortresses which Bolsheviks cannot storm. The question of tempo is subject to decision by human beings.'[39]

Bukharin's call for equilibrium in economic development brought him up against Stalin's policies in many respects. In November 1928, at the Conference of Worker/Peasant Correspondents, he reiterated his argument in its clearest form:

> It is impossible to alter the rural economy without developing the metal industry and all heavy industry, without supplying the bases for electrification; on the other hand it is impossible to build great new factories if there is an insufficient quantity of bread ... One cannot say: 'Give me metal, but I don't care about bread.'[40]

This challenged Stalin's over emphasis on heavy industry, which he claimed would forge a new 'metal link' with the peasants.

For his part, Trotsky also used the concept of equilibrium, writing in 1929: 'In my opinion we are heading for a disturbance of the total economic equilibrium and consequently of the social equilibrium.'[41] He added that 'Economics cannot be cheated'[42] and would doubtless have agreed with Bukharin that 'if any branch of production regularly fails to recover its production costs plus a certain increment ... then that branch of production either stands still or *regresses*.'[43]

So Trotsky and Bukharin accepted the existence of objective conditions of production, of the need for proportionality between economic sectors. Yet whether the positions of both men could be equated depended upon the use to which this understanding was put. Here the contrast was great. Trotsky's starting point was the international working class, with the Russian proletariat as a contingent of a larger army. Bukharin remained within a fundamental framework which he shared with Stalin and in opposition to Trotsky. This was the framework of isolated national development, in competition with Western capitalism and at the expense of the working class. At the Conference of Worker/Peasant Correspondents Bukharin said: 'Of course the immediate constructive tasks lie within our Union [of Socialist Republics]. On our banner there is the slogan *Catch up and overtake the capitalist countries of Europe and the United States of America*'. Although growth should be balanced, world revolution was not part of the equation: 'In the final account the source [of accumulation for industry] is the labour of the people ... Where else, if we cannot get new surplus value from abroad, can we get this surplus value except from within our country?'[44] Bukharin's approach meant continuing the 'regime of economy', 'rationalisation' which converted the working class into an object of production.

If Bukharin shared key concepts with Stalin he did so with an important qualification that put him in conflict with the general secretary. He still represented the degeneration of the revolution, rather than its final defeat. He had not become an organic part of the bureaucratic counter-revolution. This difference between Bukharin and Stalin was apparent in various ways.

It was one thing to believe in isolated national economic development, but quite another to aim at breakneck speeds or use force against the mass of the population to achieve development. Bukharin warned that the Western countries have 'an extremely high technical level, tremendous wealth, superb equipment and indeed culture',[45] and that the gap separating them from Russia could not be rapidly closed through sheer will-power without imposing tremendous and unacceptable suffering. For Stalinists like Kuibyshev this argument was irrelevant. The USSR was in 1928 only just overtaking the level of means of production achieved under tsarism,[46] and 'the most serious disproportion ... is the one between the output of the means of production and the requirements of the country.'[47] When Stalinists referred to 'the country' they meant the bureaucracy; nothing would be allowed to stand in the way of the party meeting its 'requirements'.

Trotsky's Version – Stalin's Centrism Covering Bukharin's Right-wing Policies
Since 1923 Trotsky had brilliantly analysed the problems of the Russian revolution and accurately predicted the course of events. He was able to do this because he had a class analysis of society which explained and foresaw the behaviour of the three key groups in society – workers, peasants and bureaucrats. As early as the autumn of 1926 Trotsky had foreseen first the emergence of a Stalinist group as soon as the left was

smashed, and then its fight against the right. He even named names, placing Bukharin, Rykov and Tomsky in a right-wing group struggling with a Stalin faction that included Molotov, Kaganovich, Mikoyan and Kirov.[48] From 1928/9 onwards, however, his predictions proved wrong almost without exception.

For example, Trotsky believed Stalin's turn against the right was made under 'the whip of the opposition'[49] and:

> There can be no doubt (only a blockhead could doubt this now) that if all our previous work had not existed – our analyses, predictions, criticism, exposés, and ever newer predictions – a sharp turn to the right would have occurred under the pressure of the grain collections crisis.[50]

He would attribute Bukharin's defeat to workers' influence within the party rather than evidence that the last vestiges of workers' influence were disappearing: 'The rights are silent; they yield and retreat without a fight. They understand that within the framework of the party the proletarian core, even in its present condition, could crush them to bits in two seconds'.[51] Finally, on 25 February 1929, just weeks before Stalin finally consolidated his dictatorial power over all wings of the party, Trotsky wrote: 'Thus Stalin's half-hearted policies have developed in a series of zigzags, with the consequence that the two wings of the party, left and right, have grown stronger – at the expense of the centre faction.'[52]

With hindsight it is clear that Trotsky's mistake lay not in his characterisation of the right's politics, or in the proletarian revolutionary politics of the opposition, but in an underestimation of the third element – the Stalinist bureaucracy. While he correctly gauged the class tendencies of the first two, he did not think that the 'centrists' could be a class:

> A right-wing policy is possible, leading to obvious and relatively quick 'gains' – for capitalism. A left policy is equally possible, a systematic policy of proletarian dictatorship, socialist construction and international revolution. What is not possible as a durable ... policy [is] centrist 'combinationism', while keeping the party suppressed and continuing to smash away at its left wing. This kind of left-centrist zigzag, unless the party forces it to 'grow over' into a genuine left course, will inevitably collapse.[53]

Why did Trotsky's predictions turn out so faulty? In the early 1920s he was right to suggest the bureaucracy was a caste, separated by its function from the proletariat. Bukharin had shared this belief in his writings on bureaucracy in 1922 and 1923. However, while Bukharin never went beyond this starting point, Trotsky saw in the mid-1920s that under the NEP the bureaucracy was influenced by distinct social pressures and came to balance between workers on the one hand and kulaks and Nepmen on the other. Trotsky's mistake was in not further developing his analysis when, in 1928, the bureaucracy took a wholly unexpected direction. There were reasons why he did not do so. As Reiman shows, Stalin's actions did not follow a preconceived plan but were a pragmatic response to the crisis in the NEP. It is therefore no surprise that Trotsky should be unsure of their significance when Stalin himself did not realise it.

The result of the counter-revolution was a form of government unprecedented in history. Moreover, the Stalinist regime was no ordinary bureaucracy. In the West the labour bureaucracy mediates between the ruling class (those in possession of the means of production) and the workers (those lacking the means of production). It cannot become a class itself because it lacks that which defines classes – a relationship to the means of production – controlling at most only offices, a few staff and newspapers. So it does follow a zigzagging or 'centrist' path. However, the Soviet bureaucracy was in direct control of considerable means of production and now, in 1928–9, sections of it were able and ready to act independently not only of the workers but of the peasants too.

Unlike Bukharin, Trotsky attempted to give a class explanation of what was happening, even though he ultimately failed. Despite flaws in his analysis, his political instinct was irreconcilable opposition to the Stalinist bureaucracy. Unfortunately, this was not always enough to safeguard his supporters. In July 1929, following the smashing of the right, the prominent oppositionists Radek and Preobrazhensky capitulated to Stalin. Others followed. Although state repression may have played a role in this, it was not the real explanation. These individuals had already proved their revolutionary steadfastness under the tsarist knout. Now, alas, they lacked the political guidance required to maintain this. One reason was that if, as Trotsky suggested, the problem with the 'centrists' was their inconsistent opposition to the right, then the annihilation of the right and its politics meant that Stalin was now trustworthy. Preobrazhensky demonstrated tragic confusion when he wrote:

In practice Stalin is following a left course, although in a different way to that expected by the Opposition which had looked to industrialisation and collectivisation through workers' democracy. But Stalin is fulfilling the demands of the Opposition ... At this time our duty is to approach closer to the party, to go back to it, in order to restrain the discontent which may be called forth in a peasant country when a policy of socialist accumulation and struggle against agrarian capitalism is pursued.[54]

The fact that Stalin disguised his counter-revolutionary industrialisation programme under left-wing rhetoric was another factor which reinforced this confusion.

The Solution to the Riddle

If all three explanations of 1928–9 are inadequate, what then is the answer? After 1928 Bukharin must be placed not to the right of Stalin, but between Stalin and Trotsky. Terms that roughly fitted in the mid-1920s – proletarian 'left' (for Trotsky), 'centre' (for Stalin) and opportunist 'right' (for Bukharin) were false after 1928. Neither Trotsky nor Bukharin had fundamentally changed their positions. What happened was that Stalin's policies had undergone a qualitative transformation which in class terms now put him to the right of both the others.

In the new correlation of forces Trotsky and Stalin were fully counterposed because they represented objectively hostile classes. Between the two social forces Bukharin still attempted to play the role of mediator. His identification with the bureaucracy and 'socialism in one country' brought him close to Stalin. His call for balanced, crisis-free growth was a plea against Stalin's ruthless methods of class exploitation.

This position contained elements of continuity and of change. In the mid-1920s Bukharin's pro-NEP, pro-peasant policies had meant weakening the working class economically and socially, and strengthening the influence of the kulak 'half-huckster' side of the peasant character. But defending the NEP's market mechanism in 1928 meant retaining a system where relations between economic sectors, particularly peasants and industry, were not entirely subject to the ruling-class drive towards accumulation for the sake of accumulation. Most peasants were still neither capitalists nor workers but petty producers whose only means of economic intercourse was trade. In this sense Bukharin was justified in claiming that he was not defending 'the capitalist market'[55] (unlike his followers today). It was the Stalinists who were establishing an unbridled capitalism by destroying the NEP. This lay behind the comment of Kuibyshev that 'the will of the state has smashed the market.'[56] The new state capitalism used direct state-organised exploitation to annihilate its rivals and accumulate resources.

When Bukharin upheld the rights of the peasantry against Stalin in 1928 it had a quite different significance to that which it had had before. In spite of differentiation since 1921, the bulk of the peasantry still had its 'half-worker' side. Defending the petty-bougeois peasantry against counter-revolution did not now mean weakening the workers. If the vast mass of the population was utterly subordinated to the iron heel of Stalinist exploitation, this could only strengthen the chief enemy of the working class and weaken the position of the proletariat further.

No doubt this was why Tomsky became Bukharin's most reliable ally. Although Tomsky was a bureaucrat who had helped impose the needs of that group during the mid-1920s, he was also subject to working-class pressure in his role as leader of the trade unions. For him, therefore, Bukharin's resistance to Stalin was a last chance to preserve something of the workers' revolutionary gains. The link between workers' and peasants' interests was shown when Tomsky, Rykov and Bukharin were publicly denounced for pro-peasant policies in April 1929. The Central Committee's resolution also declared that the unions would henceforth dedicate themselves to 'raising the productivity of labour and labour discipline'. 'Face to production', the new slogan, meant 'a decisive struggle against elements of trade unionism [that is, defence of workers' economic interests] and opportunism in the trade union movement'.[57]

Was Bukharin's 'New Programme' a Viable Policy?

The merits of Bukharin's platform must be judged on whether it met the economic needs and how effective it was in combating bureaucracy. Although it demonstrated his characteristic logical harmony, the economic proposals were still based on the old idea of reconciling the conflicting interests of the various players – the bureaucracy, peasants and workers. However, in 1928 national and international conditions were extremely unfavourable for this.

Any attempt to put into practice Bukharin's economic balancing act would have been tremendously unstable. In the last chapter we saw how social forces were tearing the NEP system apart even before 1928–9. Lack of foreign assistance, the pressure on the bureaucracy to guarantee its own survival, and the inevitable resistance of the peasantry, could not be conjured away by appeals to Lenin's testament, to reason or civilised behaviour. As Ehrlich puts it, if the government had carried out Bukharin's programme its grip on the situation:

> would be exceedingly tenuous and exposed to rude jolts – the crisis of grain collections proved this beyond the possibility of a doubt ... The well-to-do peasants, with the days of War Communism still fresh in their memory, could be relied upon to resist. [58]

Even if Bukharin's rifles had ensured that kulaks delivered grain, goods famines, climatic disaster, population growth and all the other problems would probably have wrecked his plan to satisfy both the state bureaucracy and the mass of the population.

Ehrlich believes there was only one way out of the almost inevitable crisis: 'it might not have been possible to avoid exploring a new line of approach and attempting to earn the goodwill of the upper strata of the peasantry by opening up for them avenues of political influence.'[59] In other words, whatever his personal preferences, if neither workers nor the bureaucracy resolved the crisis on their own terms the kulak and Nepmen would. Under the influence of international capitalism this could open the way to full-blooded private capitalism in the USSR.

Trotsky was convinced that this was the Bukharinist scenario: 'The driving force of the right-wing is the new evolving proprietor who seeks a link with world capitalism.' It was true that 'our right-wingers ... do not yet dare to straddle this war-horse openly',[60] but the logical consequence of Bukharin's position was counter-revolution:

> The Thermidorian tendency in the country, in the broadest sense of the term, is the private-property tendency, as opposed to proletarian socialism ... The petty bourgeoisie is its driving force, but which petty bourgeoisie? That which is most addicted to exploitation ... The central figure in this Thermidorian army is the kulak.[61]

Other factors lend weight to this argument. Bukharin's disastrous international policies meant that, had he survived in power, the Comintern would have continued to fail the world workers' movement, allowing a strengthening of international imperialism, with all the consequences that might have had. The idea of discovering, in the fourth decade of the twentieth century, some line of peaceful growth resting on peasant development using wooden ploughs and 'abstracted from the international factor' was utopian in the extreme. Far more likely was the fate that has attended those parts of the Third World which lack an industrial base and live at the mercy of international capital and the bony hand of famine.

If Stalin's counter-revolution had not taken place, at best Bukharin's method would have led to continuing degeneration of the Russian revolution. At some point, and contrary to Bukharin's intentions, the accummulating quantitative changes would have become a qualitative change and Thermidor would have triumphed. Trotsky's mistake was to see this longer-term threat as more serious than the immediate and direct counter-revolution of Stalin. This begs the question of whether a bloc with Bukharin, which Trotsky considered and then rejected, might have been a useful tactic. Alas, it is a question which must be left unanswered. There are simply too many unknowns to make a reliable judgement.

While Bukharin's economic programme failed to offer a viable solution to the crisis, did it at least present a serious alternative to the bureaucracy? Certainly, as the split with Stalin deepened Bukharin's criticism of bureaucratism became more insistent. In November 1928 came his most daring public attack:

> For us to achieve a better, wiser, less expensive and more successful resolution of the tasks of class struggle we have to turn our attention, not twenty but a million times more intensely to the struggle with bureaucratism, that great brake on our progress.[62]

He even uttered these dreadful words: 'A certain bureaucratic ossification is not only occurring in the state institutions [but] *party officials* are turning into narrow-minded bureaucrats of the Soviet state.'[63] However, there he stopped, carefully avoiding naming individuals. As if to reassure Stalin's spies, who were no doubt hanging on every word, he told his audience: 'I have not touched on questions of great significance such as the question of party leadership. This does not fall into my remit.'[64]

Bukharin's opposition to the bureaucracy was still largely shaped by peasant pressures. He worried about providing them with cheaper goods, but failed to address the political need for workers' free collective expression. This was the only means through which the proletariat could reassert its rule or ultimately assist the peasants. To achieve this Stalin's party regime had to be challenged head on. Bukharin patently refused to do this. Instead he offered a peasant critique of bureaucracy which centred on minimising the cost of the state to the taxpayer. In the speech on 'Lenin's Political Testament' he turned once more to the problem of accumulation needed for industrialising 'in one country': 'The source is, above all, *maximum curtailing of all non-productive expenditure*' by cutting the cost of the bureaucracy and '*raising the productivity of labour*' – which in current conditions meant sweating the workers.[65] Labour productivity was mentioned no less than three more times in his speech.[66] Thus bureaucrats and workers were lumped together as an unnecessary drain, while the whole issue of real workers' power and democracy as the antidote to bureaucratism was ignored.

One element in Bukharin's criticism of bureaucracy was to repeat warnings about monopolistic degeneration. This he did in June 1929 in a review of a German book on 'Organized Economic Disorder': 'a *bureaucratically centralized* organisation is necessarily distinguished by its separation from life ... Thus, they become readily susceptible to ossification and are very much inclined to develop bureaucratism'.[67] Here Bukharin was not returning to his near-total rejection of planning of 1925. He had come to accept a degree of planning because it alone could overcome the problems of a spontaneous market economy. In Bukharin's view planning should be used to meet the masses' needs rather than the demands of the Stalinist apparatus:

> Socialism continues the organizational trend at a rapid rate [and] infects all economic activity with the powerful impulse of a *growth in mass consumption*. The whole economy begins to adopt a new orientation. The stimulus coming from the masses, who want and must be able to live better; systematic pressure on the part of the masses; total elimination of the capitalist's 'accursed lack of demand': these forces more than compensate for the knout of capitalist competition.[68]

This argument was absolutely correct. The consumption needs of the masses, not the blind competition of the market or the accumulation needs of a state bureaucracy, will be the driving force of economic growth under socialism. This exposes the nonsense talked by market socialists about the absolute necessity for capitalist forms of competition to encourage economic growth under socialism. However, Bukharin's argument never moved from the realm of the abstract. There were no proposals to help the masses impose their consumption needs on the economy, apart from an appeal to preserve the market, which was no solution for the mass of ordinary people.

Bukharin also failed his first practical test in the fight against Stalin's counter-revolutionary actions. This was the Shakhty affair which, with its state-sponsored hysteria and frame-ups, was a precursor to Stalin's show trials of the 1930s. The Shakhty case concerned engineers and technicians in the Donbass coal industry who were accused of sabotage and wrecking. The allegations were made in March 1928 and convictions were upheld against 53 people in May.[69] It is certain that many of the charges were trumped up. Nevertheless Bukharin devoted a substantial part of a lengthy pamphlet to denouncing the engineers.[70] He told Kamenev: 'it was [Stalin] who proposed that no-one be shot in the Shakhty affair (we voted against).'[71] Bukharin was even more severe than Stalin in the Shakhty case because he was not so much opposed to bureaucratic repression by the state apparatus as determined that industrial managements should be cheap and efficient in carrying out their tasks.

Bukharin's criticisms of the bureaucracy were partial and limited to slating its policy towards the peasantry and its high cost. He said nothing about the relation of the party bureaucracy to the working class. Yet it was here that the solution was to be found. The internal party apparatus was where Stalin's strength was concentrated. It was bent on destroying the power of the one force that could effectively challenge it – working-class politics. In 1917 it had been demonstrated that workers' could generate effective democratic institutions such as the soviets. It had also been demonstrated that the peasantry, lacking a collective class character, could only challenge the bureaucracy when led by an active proletariat. Seeking to revive the spirit of proletarian democracy was no part of Bukharin's fight against Stalin. To have supported workers' or the opposition specifically against the *party* apparatus would have been to attack the very heart of the bureaucracy, and Bukharin still strongly identified with it, despite all his discontent with its policies.

'I Have Not Fought, I Will Not Fight'

The mettle of Bukharin's alternative to Stalin cannot be tested just at the level of political argument. To what extent was he an alternative to Stalin in the *practice of political struggle*? Even his apologists admit that Bukharin was

> a man of different and lesser calibre than [Lenin or Trotsky]. They theorised, acted in a vast arena and displayed a variety of intellectual, political and administrative talents ... In general he was not an infighter, political strategy was not his forte.[72]

Yet such personal characteristics are an insufficient explanation in themselves. Despite his failings Bukharin, not Trotsky, led the most powerful faction in the post-revolutionary period – the left communists in 1918/19.

Furthermore, in 1928 Bukharin was in an incomparably stronger position than the left opposition had been in 1923. All sources, from the Moscow correspondent of the Menshevik paper to Trotsky's informants, attest to the potential power of the right.[73] At Bukharin's disposal were the party daily, *Pravda*, the theoretical organ, *Bol'shevik*, and influential propagandists including Astrov, Slepkov and Maretskii groomed at the Bukharinist think-tank, the School of Red Professors. His close ally Rykov was head of the state apparatus, while Tomsky led the 10-million strong trade union movement. The pugnacious Uglanov controlled Moscow, a city which housed one fifth of the USSR's industry and 15 per cent of the Communist Party's membership.[74] To this list, Avtorkhanov, an eye-witness Red Professor adds:

> the sympathy and support, in some cases open, in some potential, of strong groups in the Central Committee and Central Control Commission, the sympathy and support of the entire apparatus of the Central Trade Union Council, Bukharin's good standing in the Red Army, the activity and support of prominent Party theorists and propagandists, and, finally, the sympathy and potential support of the peasantry, i.e., of the bulk of the population.[75]

Bukharin himself reckoned: 'Our potential forces are enormous', while Trotsky saw them as 'colossal'.[76]

A sign of this strength was that, as Bukharin claimed, the resolutions of the key party meetings of 1928 – April, July and November – were either 'written personally' or 'based on memoranda' he himself had drafted.[77] Stalin was driven to tortuous manoeuvres, tentative offensives, rapid retreats at the first sign of resistance, and then renewed offensives to unseat his opponent. A head-on confrontation with the right in the winter of 1928 had to be abandoned until extra forces were found. The nine-man Politburo was a battleground in which the trio of Bukharin, Rykov and Tomsky could sometimes call upon the support of Kalinin and Voroshilov, leaving Stalin in a minority.[78] As the Moscow correspondent of the *Berliner Tageblatt* saw it in 1929: 'One factor which was ignored abroad was the fragile quality of Stalin's "iron monolith" ... his control of the Party, and – surprisingly – of the OGPU [political police] itself, was not nearly as secure as supposed.'[79]

Yet with all this behind him Bukharin's struggle lasted little over a year and left almost all these forces completely uninvolved. Daniels' witty comment is accurate: 'The history of the Right Opposition offers the singular spectacle of a political group's being defeated first and attacked afterwards.'[80] The first public revelation that a fight had taken place only came in August 1929, when Bukharin was denounced by name, months after it was all over.[81]

Private letters from Bukharin to Stalin were the first sign of impending disagreement. In the first, dated 17 May 1928, Bukharin said that he was 'frightened to death' about rushing towards collectivisation and industrialisation with inadequate resources.[82] The second, of 1–2 June 1928, was addressed to 'Koba' (Stalin's nickname). Bukharin announced his surrender as early as this letter: 'I tell you, *that I do not want a fight, nor will I fight*. I know perfectly well what a fight would mean in the already difficult circumstances that the whole of our country and Party find themselves in.' He asked for 'only one thing' – to be allowed to conduct the Sixth Congress of the Comintern in peace. '*At the end of the Congress I will be ready to depart wherever it is convenient, without any argument, without any fuss and without any struggle*'.[83] Bukharin's surrender was not accepted. Stalin needed an atmosphere of conspiracy and threats from internal foes to build up the new class dictatorship.

To cover their shift to counter-revolution, Stalin and his followers found it necessary to demonstrate that it was the right who was abandoning the 'general line' and plotting a change of course. In 1970 Vaganov published an official Stalinist history of the clash. His book is called *The Right Deviation in the Soviet Communist Party and Its Defeat*. The choice of the title 'deviation' as opposed to 'opposition' is not fortuitous. Even Vaganov admits that Bukharin's group was no more than a deviation which:

> signifies an inner-party tendency in which some members allow a certain political vacillation, unsteadiness, departure from generally agreed party policy. A deviation differs from an oppositional factional group above all because of its relative absence of a clear-cut programmatic political expression, or organisational links between its supporters.[84]

Vaganov has a hard time stirring up his readers' indignation, having to conjure up a full-scale conspiracy out of spectacularly daredevil actions such as these: 'In the first period the Right limited themselves to arguing within the Politburo, now [in July 1928] all the issues where principles diverged were taken into a broader arena – the Plenum of the Central Committee of the Party.'[85] This hardly qualifies as mass agitation.

Vaganov's case looks superficially convincing when he reports the right 'attempting to enter into negotiations with Trotskyists to organise an anti-party bloc'.[86] Was there common ground between left and right after all? In fact, this bloc is a Stalinist myth. Bukharin's widow says: 'I definitely recall the words of N.I., that not even a hint of an organised bloc ... was discussed in the talks with Kamenev.'[87] It is true that on 11 July Bukharin contacted Kamenev and held frank discussions with him. Bukharin even said that he would prefer Zinoviev and Kamenev to Stalin in the Politburo, because at that time he had far fewer differences with them. But Zinoviev and Kamenev are not to be confused with Trotsky, despite their brief alliance in the 'united opposition' (1926-7). They had already capitulated to the party machine and been readmitted to membership in June 1928. Furthermore, Bukharin's interview with Kamenev was not to establish unity with his supporters, but to prevent their use as pawns in Stalin's game against the right:

> Things have gone so far in the Central Committee and in the party that you (and probably the Trotskyists too) will inevitably be drawn in and play an important role in deciding the outcome ... I know (or assume) that the Stalinists will approach you also ... and I want you to know what the struggle is about.[88]

A few days after this Stalin began a whispering campaign against Bukharin at the Sixth Comintern Congress (17 July to 1 September). Bukharin might have been expected to use this forum to build an international base for himself, but he specifically declined to do so, ignoring his dedicated supporters in the Lovestone group of the US Communist Party and in the German Communist Party.[89] Instead Bukharin joined Stalin and Rykov in a joint statement: 'The undersigned members of the Politburo of the Central Committee of the All-Union Communist Party ... protest in the most decisive manner against the spreading of any sorts of rumours about disagreements among the members of the Politburo'.[90] This was in spite of the barely veiled efforts by Stalinist delegates to discredit Bukharin by openly ridiculing his Comintern programme.

Nevertheless, until the summer of 1928 Bukharin did lead the Comintern. If there was to be a sign of the much-vaunted alternative it should have surfaced here. Today's Bukharinists blame foreign policy disasters such as the rise of Hitler exclusively on Stalin and his ultra-left course – the so-called 'Third Period' policy. This tactic involved splitting revolutionaries from reformist trade unions and denouncing all reformists as 'social fascists'. The Bukharinists suggest that if their hero had won, the Popular Front tactic, which they consider superior, might have been tried years earlier. In reality the insane voluntarism of the Third Period began to appear not after Bukharin's disgrace but during his ascendancy in the Comintern. It is impossible to be certain to what extent this line was initiated by Bukharin to cover up the disaster in China, or whether he was pushed into it by Stalin. The evidence is contradictory.

It was Bukharin who 'had coined the term "third period" – the end of the relative stabilisation of capitalism and the emergence of a new revolutionary wave – as early as 1926'.[91] On 30 November 1927 a circular letter to communist parties called for a shift to the 'united front *from below*'. This rejected the basic premise of the united front tactic – common action above and below to demonstrate the reformist leaders' practical weakness before the rank and file. The circular letter showed that the Comintern leadership was becoming ultra-left.

A study of the French Communist Party finds Bukharin intervening personally to push through a new left direction in September 1927, when, by contrast, Stalin appeared more concerned with maintaining the status quo.[92] At the Sixth Comintern Congress, despite his qualifications that 'social democracy could not be put under the same heading as fascism', Bukharin did insist that 'without any doubt, social democracy is a particular *social fascist tendency*'.[93] Cohen's claim that Bukharin opposed using this term is therefore questionable.[94] We have Bukharin's testimony to Kamenev: 'in foreign policy, Stalin is following a right-wing line ... Tomsky formulated it this way: I (Tomsky) am 30 kilometres to the right of you (Bukharin) in international questions, but I (Tomsky) am 100 kilometres to the left of Stalin.'[95] In January 1929 Bukharin told Angelo Tasca, the Italian communist, that Stalin's policy was 'right-wing' compared to his.[96] Whatever his private thoughts, Bukharin told a meeting in Moscow that the congress 'imposed upon all members of the Communist International the obligation to struggle with the Right Opposition, and at the same time to overcome resolutely those tendencies within the Communist parties which underestimate the danger'.[97]

Against all this we have the testimony of the Comintern representative, Humbert-Droz, whom Bukharin contacted to have him argue the case for communists to ally with social democrats against fascism. However, Bukharin explained he dare not say this publicly.[98]

After avoiding battle in the Comintern, Bukharin at last made a public declaration of his new programme in September's 'Notes of an Economist'. However, the coded manner of its criticism (through attacking Trotsky) meant that Stalin easily passed it off in this way: 'Bukharin in his article raised the abstract, theoretical question of the possibility or danger of retrogression. In the abstract, such a formulation of the question is quite possible and legitimate.'[99] Bukharin's further publications – the speech to worker/peasant correspondents, an article on 'Lenin and the Tasks of Science' of 20 January 1929 and one on 'Lenin's Political Testament' the next day – could all be ignored on the same grounds.

So throughout 1928 and into 1929 Stalin talked of the deviation of the right as 'a tendency, an inclination that has not yet taken shape.' While there were signs of it in the lower levels of the party and even up to Central Committee level: 'In the Politburo there are neither "Right" nor "Left" deviations nor conciliators towards these deviations. This must be said quite categorically'.[100] He was even assisted in this silent disarming of the right by Bukharin. Meeting with Kamenev in 1929 Bukharin was asked: 'who wrote the resolution on the struggle against the Right deviation?' Kamenev must have been astonished when Bukharin replied: 'Of course, I did. I had to show the party that I was not a right-winger.'[101] Only at the very end of January 1929 did Stalin report to a meeting of the Politburo and praesidium of the Central Control Commission that 'a separate Bukharin group has been formed.' He could even plausibly pretend that: 'The Party knew nothing of the existence of this group before – the Bukharinites carefully concealed its existence from the Party.'[102] The only reason that the existence of the right faction came out into the open was that on 20 January 1929 the Bukharin–Kamenev conversations were published by Trotskyists in a leaflet.[103]

The only real resistance to Stalin from anyone on the right came from Uglanov in Moscow. It was a battle that Bukharin never wanted. He told Kamenev that Uglanov was 'told to keep quiet so as not to give Stalin any excuse for interference in the Moscow Organisation. Uglanov couldn't stand it.'[104]

The right's criticisms of Stalin were articulated at the July Moscow party's plenum. The Stalinists soon counter attacked and on 2 November it was all over. Uglanov confessed to 'past mistakes' and was sacked three weeks later. Even in Moscow the great 'alternative' did not reach the masses. Rank-and-file party members bombarded the Moscow organisation with questions: 'tell us what disagreements there are in the Politburo'; 'how serious is the row between Stalin and Bukharin?'; 'tell us please, what is the Right danger?'[105] No information was forthcoming.

Local reports show the consequences of this silence for ordinary workers and party members: 'The top level is jumpy, but the rank and file know nothing' (Kolbas factory). 'We rank and file members of the

Moscow organisation only knew about the struggle in the Moscow organisation in October. Our comrades in the Moscow Committee, Moscow Control Commission and Raion Committee want to do without anyone – on their own without the masses' (Sokstroi). 'The administration does not consider the cells capable of resolving questions themselves. Where is the party?' (Base militia, Khamov raion).[106] The rights did organise small secret meetings,[107] but they never went outside the top echelons of the party. The fight had been conducted on Stalin's terrain – the internal party organisation – and so its result was a foregone conclusion.

Elsewhere Stalin dislodged Bukharin's supporters without trouble. In May 1928 Stalin turned his attention to taking over the organisation of the Red Professors.[108] *Pravda* and *Bol'shevik* succumbed between the July and August.[109] The Eighth Trade Union Congress in December 1928 might have been a rallying point for the right. Tomsky warned of simmering discontent and unofficial strikes, and that the unions had become 'detached from the masses'. He called for unions to be independent of 'the economic administrator ... when it comes to carrying out the collective agreement', but weakened the impact of his argument by saying 'both sides must fulfil their commitments.'[110] However, even as he uttered these words he was losing control of the unions to Kaganovich, who supported Stalin. Tomsky would be formally sacked on 2 June 1929.

To defend himself Bukharin ventured beyond resolution-mongering in top party bodies on one occasion alone. This was in November 1928, when he threatened to resign from his positions. Stalin did not accept his offer, demonstrating Bukharin's continuing importance and Stalin's lack of confidence. Alas, neither advantage was exploited. The threat of resignation was withdrawn and somehow Stalin persuaded Bukharin to draft yet another resolution denouncing the right. That the executioner allowed the condemned man to volunteer his head for the noose was no surprise. That the condemned man should accept this 'honour' is difficult to fathom, unless we remember how limited was Bukharin's real resistance.

Bukharin finally made an open factional declaration on January 30 1929, open that is to the party's Central Committee. On 9 February Tomsky, followed hesitantly by Rykov, joined him. One phrase of Bukharin's that caused particular outrage in the Stalin camp was the charge of 'military-feudal exploitation of the peasantry'.[111] This meant that the peasant was 'not a citizen from the point of view of the state, but a slave'.[112] At last the Rights clearly denounced the 'effective annihilation of *collective leadership in the Central Committee*' and 'bureaucratisation of the party'.[113] They called for Stalin's removal.

However, 'socialism in one country' and, by implication, accumulation at the expense of the working class, were still not challenged in any way. The basic assumptions remained as before:

> We must carry forward the industrialisation of the country, and I would add, at perhaps an even faster tempo – on one condition; that we raise the agricultural economy ... That is the fundamental point. If we do not raise it, then all our plans risk crashing down. We can hammer home enormous resources into industrialisation, but one fine day we will discover that we have to cut back, reduce and close down.[114]

The feebleness of the right had nothing to do with lack of organisational talent. It grew from two sources. First, despite the numerical size of the peasantry, it lacked the ability on its own to play a significant role in shaping events. In 1917 the enormous Social Revolutionary Party with its mass peasant support had been described as 'the great zero'. In 1928/9 the peasantry was no more capable of self-mobilisation on the political plane than before. Second, even if the Bukharinists had been able to rouse masses of peasantry, or their own supporters in the various state and union institutions, there was no desire to do this. They feared division inside the party would lead to a repeat of the Kronstadt scenario. Therefore, unlike Trotsky, Bukharin refused to confront Stalin publicly.

This makes for a startling contrast between the right 'deviation' and the left opposition. Over six years any number of public declarations were made by opposition leaders such as Trotsky, Radek and Preobrazhensky, and later Zinoviev and Kamenev. They fought in the Politburo, in the Comintern, the Central Committee, conferences, congresses. They organised local meetings, factory debates and mass demonstrations. Programmes, theses, books, pamphlets and leaflets were produced on legal and illegal presses. On the ground, bands of Trotskyists argued, struggled, fought and canvassed for support. When administrative measures were taken against them, when they were sacked, exiled, jailed and murdered, still the battle continued. A correspondence network was established and when this too was smashed, Trotsky continued a fight from abroad, producing a regular journal, constructing organisation after organisation, in one country after another, often in unbelievably harsh conditions. Even when the opposition was formally obliterated at the end of 1927:

the party organisations continued to be flooded – especially in the large urban centres and the two capitals – with opposition literature and leaflets. Reports of heightened opposition activity came one after another from various cities and from entire provinces – Leningrad, the Ukraine, Transcaucasia, Siberia, the Urals, and of course Moscow ... There was a steadily growing number of illegal and semilegal meetings attended by industrial workers and young people. The influence of the opposition in a number of large party units became quite substantial. It hampered the former free functioning of the Stalinist party apparatus. The army was also strongly affected by opposition activity. Reports on a significant rise in the authority of the opposition came from the Leningrad military district and the garrison in Leningrad, from Kronstadt, and from troop units in the Ukraine and Byelorussia.[115]

Although by no means a statistical proof, Ciliga's journey through the political prisons of the early 1930s revealed a network of Trotskyists. They argued. They split into a whole variety of sections – right Trotskyists, centrist and left Trotskyists. They continued to produce platforms, theories and policies.

Compare this activity with the Bukarinists, for whom I have found just one reference to attempts at mass organisation: 'some leaflets scattered in support of Bukharin' in Moscow in late 1929.[116] In prison Ciliga records only one case of a right oppositionist before 1932, a certain Koslov, who with friends in the Leningrad area set up a 'Union of Workers and Peasants'. But 'after the leaders of the Right-wing Opposition had, in 1928–29 given up all active struggle against Stalin, the group seceded from the Right-wing Opposition to follow its own lines.'[117] It was only in 1932, long after Bukharin had given in, that right-wingers were arrested in any numbers.

The difference in approach between left and right was explained in Bukharin's unpublished speech at the April 1929 plenum of the Central Committee and Central Control Commission. He had just been sacked from his post at *Pravda*. Here, with nothing to lose and free from fear of causing disturbances among the masses, Bukharin was conscious of this being his final opportunity to justify his position. This is what he said:

> Comrades, I ask you to listen to my speech with the greatest possible attention, because I speak *as a member of the Politburo* expressing myself for the last time. Above all, I must say that we three members of the Politburo [Bukharin, Rykov and Tomsky] find ourselves in a position

which no other member of the party, still less any other group, has witnessed until this time in the leading circles of the party.[118]

He then detailed the vicious campaign of lies and slanders conducted against them.

> But we *kept silent*. We kept silent because if we had appeared before any conference meeting or cell etc. then discussion would have begun independently of our will and we, of course, would immediately have been blamed for initiating discussion. We were in the position of people who are persecuted for *not* explaining themselves, for *not* justifying themselves and who are condemned *still the more* for not having *tried* to explain themselves or *tried* to justify themselves.
>
> I repeat: the past months have shown that on our side there has been shown the maximum, the *very greatest* restraint that, generally speaking, could have been demanded of any party member ... May I assure you, comrades, of this central point ... You have *not got* a new opposition. You *will not* have one in future! And not a single one of us *will* place ourselves at the head of any 'new' or 'novel' opposition. I have insisted on this point of view with full conviction and in conversations with whole groups of comrades whom I have had occasion to meet with. Because it is my deepest conviction that 'opposition' is fruitless ... the old methods of overcoming inner-party disagreement by means of factional struggle are now *impermissible* and at the present time they are for our party objectively *impossible* ... We do *not* want to use this method. We *will* not do it. We *cannot* do it. The whole inner-party situation prevents it. The whole situation of our country prevents it. The correlation of classes prevents it. And the correlation of objective forces on the greater *international* scale prevents it.[119]

And this is supposed to be the 'alternative'!

Death and Transfiguration

Bukharin was sacked from the Comintern in the summer of 1929 and from the Politburo in November. On 26 November *Pravda* and *Izvestiia* carried the joint capitulation of Bukharin, Rykov and Tomsky:

> In the course of the last one-and-a-half years there have been differences of opinion between ourselves and the majority of the Central Committee ... We consider it our duty to declare that the Party and its Central Committee turned out to be right in this dispute ... we

shall henceforth use all our endeavours to wage an energetic struggle, jointly with the entire Party, against all deviations from the Party's general policy line, and first of all against the right-wing deviation.[120]

In the 1930s Mussolini possessed and broke the body of the incarcerated Gramsci, but he never had dominion over his fertile mind. How pleasing it would be to be able to say the same of the relation of Stalin to Bukharin, who was also one of the best brains the revolutionary movement has produced. Alas, with the exception of his trial in 1938, this cannot be done.

Admirers have minutely screened Bukharin's late articles, teasing out hidden messages, double-meanings, construing arguments to mean the opposite of what was said. Appeal is made to discussions in Paris in 1936 (where Bukharin was sent to acquire the German social democratic archive) for evidence of resistance to Stalin.[121] Perhaps these accounts are accurate. He may have told the Menshevik, F. Dan, that Stalin was 'an accursed small man, no, not a man, but a devil'.[122] It may be that Bukharin's choice of subject matter for his late articles – science, poetry, Goethe and Heine – was a symbolic appeal to reason and humanism, against Stalin. But the veteran dissident, Roy Medvedev, an expert in the erudite arts of 'Aesopian language' has this to say: 'if there were any allusions and allegorical references they were **so heavily disguised as to pass unnoticed by even those of his political adversaries who had an extremely keen interest in that kind of thing**.[123]

Furthermore, as Bukharin wrote in March 1933, unlike the 'world religions', Marxism 'is very far from the *vita contemplativa* [contemplative life]. It is the banner bearer of the *vita activa,* of stormy and practical life'.[124] So the question for Marxists is not about Bukharin's inner convictions or secret confidences, but his effect on political life around him.

Unlike those Trotskyists who stuck to their beliefs and suffered repression, Bukharin remained prominent in public life almost to the very end. In 1929 he took a post in the Scientific-Technical Direction of the Supreme Council of National Economy. In 1930 he returned to the party Central Committee and a year later to the Central Executive Committee of the USSR. He had a book of articles published in 1932.[125] From 1934 to 16 January 1937, as editor of the Soviet daily, *Izvestiia,* Bukharin held a journalistic position second only to his old one at *Pravda.* In 1936 he collaborated in drafting the new Soviet constitution.

Yet it was during this time that Bukharin's worst fears were coming true. In May 1929 the most ambitious variant of the Five-Year Plan was formally adopted. It had the fanciful target of a 236 per cent increase in industrial output and the more sinister aim of a 110 per cent increase in labour productivity – sinister because while the final output figure was lower than projected, what growth there was occurred chiefly because of increased labour intensity.[126] At the same time collectivisation was ruthlessly pressed forward. The proportion of households covered increased five-fold between October 1929 and the end of January 1930. By 10 March 58 per cent were collectivised.[127]

Bukharin was an important official at a time when his supporters were being purged *en masse*. Between May 1929 and May 1930 some 170,000 people, 11 per cent of the party's membership, were expelled. Of these 10 per cent were explicitly excluded for factional activities, although not all of them were right-wingers.[128] The purge was most thorough in Tomsky's trade unions. Two thirds of the All-Union Trade Union Central Council were sacked;[129] in the former right stronghold of Moscow region, the Trade Union Council lost 93 per cent, while in Leningrad there was a clean sweep – 100 per cent went.[130]

From exile Trotsky could not help bitterly contrasting the fate of the rights to that of the lefts. In 'Lessons of the Capitulations. Obituary Reflections' of February 1930 he wrote of what had happened to prominent Trotskyists, contrasting this to the fate of leading Stalinists and Bukharinists:

> What is important politically is that at the peak of the 'ultra-left' [that is Stalinist] course the bloc between the centrists and the right was renewed, while repression against the left was not relaxed but intensified. Rykov, despite everything, is still the president of the council of People's Commissars, but Rakovsky cures his ailing heart in below-freezing weather at Barnaul. Tomsky and Rykov are on the Politburo, Bukharin is on the Central Committee, but Sosnovsky, B. Mdivani, Kavtaradze are in jail; Uglanov is the commissar of labour, but Blumkin is shot.[131]

According to Cohen, in 1930 Bukharin 'adopted an "intermediate position" between avowed resistance and the effusive glorification of Stalin's leadership and abject recantation that were becoming political norms. He maintained this posture for two years'.[132] Bukharin could have done much more. At this time the Stalinist system had yet to acquire a firm basis and was at its most vulnerable. Yet Bukharin repudiated all attempts to unseat Stalin. He did nothing when successive opposition groupings, such as those organised by Syrtsov-Lominadze, Eysmont-Tolmachev and V P Smirnov's circle, emerged and were snuffed out.

The most important opposition to Stalin during this period was the Riutin Platform of June 1932. Riutin was associated with the Moscow right wing in 1929. The aim of his 'Union of Marxists–Leninists' was:

> the systematic extension of industrialisation of the country on the basis of the actual improvement of the material situation of the proletariat and all who labour. But at the present time it poses its primary task as irreconcilable struggle against Stalin's methods and tempo of industrialisation which are causing unprecedented ruin, impoverishment and hunger for the whole country ... The Union of Marxists–Leninists accepts the need for every kind of assistance to voluntary collectivisation coupled with systematic help for poor and middle peasant farms.

The Platform ended: 'From comrade to comrade, from group to group, from town to town, our fundamental slogan must be passed on: down with the dictatorship of Stalin and his clique.'[133]

If not for the final injunction to action, this could easily have been written by the Bukharin of 1928/9. Yet in his posthumous message 'To a Future Generation of Party Leaders', composed outside of Stalinist control, Bukharin denied any connection with Riutin or his organisation and insisted he 'started nothing against Stalin'.[134] His widow explains:

> From the point of view of Nikolai Ivanovich, conspiring against Stalin could not, alas, benefit the country in any way. It could only bring repression. The open offensive against Stalin's policies by Bukharin, Rykov and Tomsky in 1928/1929 – three influential Politburo members with more authority and popularity in the country than Riutin – was not crowned with success. Nikolai Ivanovich considered that further struggle should stop.[135]

As the first Five-Year Plan gave way to the second in January 1933, there was a partial thaw in Stalinism. A sign of this was Stalin's comment that, as with the NEP, the 'productive alliance' with farming should be realised through exchange of commodities. His supporter Molotov suggested that 'insofar as there are commodities and money, NEP continues to exist'.[136] Under these circumstances Bukharin enjoyed a partial political rehabilitation, with the Stalinist Voroshilov declaring that he trusted Bukharin 'one hundred times more than Rykov and one thousand times more than Tomsky', because he was 'sincere and honest'.[137] No doubt Bukharin's 1930 article describing collectivisation as 'the socialist reconstruction of agriculture [which] was the only way out', convinced Voroshilov of this sincerity.[138]

Was it perhaps the case that Bukharin's tactic of lying low was paying off, that in 1933 he was, as one writer puts it, 'unique among the front rank Soviet leaders to analyse "the enormous quantity of problems in the development of socialist society" and offer a solution"[139] Alas, no. Those who noted his silence during the Riutin controversy or endured his post-collectivisation articles with titles such as 'The Great Reconstruction', 'Years of Victory', 'People and the Century: a Heroic Symphony', 'Why Are We Winning?', 'Let Us Overturn the Norms', did not witness a rejuvenated Bukharin after 1933.

At the seventeenth Congress, in January–February 1934, the so-called 'Congress of Victors', Bukharin gave a most excruciating yet indicative performance. His speech ended with these words:

> We – the only country which embodies the progressive forces of history, like our Party and Comrade Stalin in person – are the heralds of not just economic, but *technical* and *scientific* progress for the whole planet. We are going into battle for the fate of *humanity*. For this battle we must rally together, unite and unite again. Down with all disorganisers. Hail our party, its great fighting comradeship, the comradeship of tempered soldiers, hard like steel, revolutionaries with fortitude who win all victories under the leadership of the glorious field-marshall of the proletarian forces, the cream of the cream – comrade Stalin.[140]

This extract shows Bukharin's position, and indeed that of a whole generation of old Bolsheviks who succumbed to Stalin. It was not a question of a lack of moral fibre, or proof that Leninism is 'institutionalised mendacity',[141] as Cold War warriors argued. Under the hammer blows of Hitler's accession to power and the final extinction of the Russian revolution, the Marxism of many old Bolsheviks simply shattered. Their dedication to the cause remained, but their ability to recognise what that cause was, to be able to distinguish real socialism from its cruel Stalinist parody, to recognise a proletarian party from a ruling-class machine, had withered on the vine. People like Bukharin swallowed and even expounded the monstrous teachings of Stalin because they believed them an unavoidable evil, necessary to counter Nazism and to maintain socialism and its guardian, the Communist Party. This misguided belief did not make them heroes, but neither were they villains.

If there had been any lingering doubts as to whether Bukharin was a practical alternative to Stalin, the Seventeenth Congress speech should have dispelled them. It was Trotsky, not Bukharin, who kept alive the revolutionary tradition, even if those who look to him today may differ on some important elements of his legacy. By contrast, Bukharin left no movement behind him – no groupings at home or abroad, no published platforms- nothing.

A yawning gap of half a century separates Bukharin from those who profess to expound his principles today. But theirs is an entirely different context to his. The tragedy of Bukharin was that he began as part of the greatest workers' revolution the world has seen, yet one which, through no fault of its own but rather because of the lack of outside assistance, was placed in an impossible position. As the revolution became distorted, Bukharin, who had excellently expressed some of the finest traditions of that revolution, continued to be a mouthpiece, this time for its degeneration. He became an active factor in rationalising and furthering that process, both in the USSR itself and through the Comintern. But, unlike Stalin, he stopped short of the final step of betraying and destroying the revolution, and for this he paid the ultimate penalty.

Those who use Bukharin's name to justify the market today have not been revolutionaries. They have not suffered for the workers' cause. They are not driven by circumstances of unbelievable poverty and suffering, of international isolation, to mistakes of judgement. They live the lives of comfortable academics, politicians and economists, paid by the ruling class to perpetuate the ideas of capitalism. In the East they are striving amidst the ruins of Stalinism to reconstruct a system in which they can continue to rule. In the West they seek to hide the bankruptcy of reformism during late capitalism with new clothes. There is no degeneration of a fine tradition here, only a sordid travesty.

Just as a guttering candle has one last burst of flame, so too did Bukharin at his show trial in 1938. The omens had not been auspicious. Bukharin had been quite uncritical of secret police methods when used on others. Recently published letters show that in 1924, when the fight against the opposition began, he stressed that he was not opposed to extending the GPU's powers.[142] In December 1934, when Zinoviev and Kamenev were arrested on the phoney charge of murdering Kirov, then the leader of Moscow's party organisation, Bukharin wrote in an article entitled 'Severe Words':

> Any 'opposition' and any deviation ('left', 'right', 'rightist-ultraleft', 'nationalist'), when it insists on pursuing its mistaken ways and continuing to fight, inevitably leads to a break in the Party, a break

with Soviet legality, and to a counterrevolutionary function for the groups and people concerned. This is confirmed by the allegedly Fascist rebirth of such people as Trotsky and Zinoviev and their supporters who refuse to lay down their arms.[143]

In private his nerve appears to have failed. In 1933, as he felt the apparatus of repression drawing closer, Bukharin pleaded in a letter with Ordzhonikidze, who was close to Stalin, to intercede on his behalf:

> I am already 45 years old. I must define for myself what further road I must take in order to be useful to the cause. Help me, Sergo. I am certain that if Koba had not turned to hounding me, he might have seen things in a better light. I well understand it is difficult for him, and he doesn't want to complicate the position in my regard, all the more that the general tasks are immensely complicated and becoming even more so. But perhaps for the cause I could be given the chance to work for the time being, without impediments being put in my way and with a final end to the affair of five years ago.[144]

But the GPU rolled on relentlessly. The first of the Moscow trials, centring on Zinoviev and Kamenev, took place in August 1936. Piatakov, his old compatriot in the Baugy Group during the First World War, followed in January 1937. In March that year Bukharin was arrested. On 12 March 1938 his trial began. Twenty others were named in the indictment, including Rykov and Rakovsky. Bukharin's predicament after 12 months at the mercy of the GPU was horrific. His wife and young child were threatened if he did not testify exactly as the prosecutor, an ex-Menshevik, A. Vyshinsky, wished. In the forced confessions of others he had been roundly denounced, most notably by Radek, and now by his co-defendants. Bukharin could expect only death and had only his wits to fight with. Yet he managed to set an example of dignity and intelligence that showed why, so long ago, he had rightly been 'the favourite of the party'.

He was accused of the preposterous charge of:

> having on the instructions of the intelligence services of foreign states hostile to the Soviet Union formed a conspiratorial group named the 'bloc of Rights and Trotskyites' with the object of espionage ... wrecking, diversionist and terrorist activities, undermining the military power of the USSR, provoking a military attack ... dismembering the USSR ... restoring the power of the bourgeoisie.[145]

He dared not endanger his family, but still exposed the nonsense of the extracted confession by claiming: 'I plead guilty to ... the sum total of crimes committed by this counter-revolutionary organisation, irrespective of whether or not I knew of, whether or not I took a direct part, in any particular act.'[146] It was for 'the public opinion of our country, like the public opinion of other countries, as far as progressive mankind is concerned, to judge how people sank to such depths, how we all became rabid counter-revolutionaries [and] embarked on treachery, crime and treason.'[147]

When Vyshinsky tried to prove that Bukharin had had contacts with foreign police, the accused took him on a verbal jaunt around the world, showing how, as a revolutionary, he had indeed had contact with Russian, Austrian and Swedish police: they had been hospitable enough to put him in their cells for extended periods. In spite of the complete disproportion of forces, Bukharin played games with his omnipotent adversary. Vyshinsky exploded with fury:

> I will be compelled to cut the interrogation short because you apparently are following definite tactics ... hiding behind a flood of words, pettifogging, making digressions in the sphere of politics, of philosophy, theory and so forth – which you might as well forget about once and for all, because ... you are obviously a spy of an intelligence service.[148]

To the end Bukharin could not be compelled to confess to plotting to murder Lenin.

The outcome of the trial was, of course, never in doubt. Bukharin was convicted on 13 March and shot two days later. His best epitaph, and one which should stick in the gullet of today's Bukharinists, is the letter he recited to his wife, Anna Larina, a few days before arrest. He feared to burden her with incriminating written evidence, so she memorised it. It remained in her mind, through years in the labour camps, until March 1961, when she wrote it down to appeal to the Central Committee for Bukharin's political rehabilitation and readmission to the party. This was granted on 21 June 1988. But her appeal was misaddressed. Bukharin will be tried in the practical test of international working-class struggle, which can both use his great strengths and learn from his terrible mistakes. It is here that judgement must finally be made. But let the last word be Bukharin's:

> I have been in the Party since I was eighteen, and the purpose of my life has always been to fight for the interests of the working class, for

the victory of socialism ... If, more than once, I was mistaken about the methods of building socialism, let posterity judge me no more harshly than Vladimir Il'ich did. We were moving toward a single goal for the first time, on a still unblazed trail. Other times, other customs. *Pravda* carried a discussion page, everyone argued, searched for ways and means, quarrelled and made up and moved on together. Know, comrades, that on that banner which you will be carrying in the victorious march to communism, is also my drop of blood.[149]

Notes and References

Introduction
1. The key texts are S. Cohen, *Bukharin and the Bolshevik Revolution*, Oxford 1971, and M. Lewin, *Political Undercurrents in Soviet Economic Debates*, Princeton, NJ, 1974.
2. L. Trotsky, 'Behind the Moscow Trials', in L. Trotsky, *Writings, 1937–1938*, New York 1976, page 199.

Chapter 1: World Economy and Imperialism
1. R. Luxemburg, 'The Junius Pamphlet: the Crisis in German Social Democracy' [1915], in M.A. Waters (ed.), *Rosa Luxemburg Speaks*, New York 1970, page 262.
2. For his treatment of racial theories etc., see N. Bukharin, *Imperialism and World Economy* [1915], London 1987, pages 110–13.
3. Bukharin was greatly influenced by Hilferding's excellent book, *Finance Capital* [1910] (English edn, London 1981), although he had no hesitation in breaking with Hilferding when he became a chauvinist.
4. *Karl Kautsky: Selected Political Writings*, ed. P. Goode, London 1983, pages 90–1.
5. *Kautsky: Selected Political Writings*, page 86.
6. See M. Haynes, *Nikolai Bukharin and the Transition from Capitalism to Socialism*, Beckenham, Kent, 1985, pages 10–11 for details.
7. Bukharin, *Imperialism and World Economy*, pages 17–18.
8. Bukharin, *Imperialism and World Economy*, page 53.
9. Bukharin, *Imperialism and World Economy*, page 85.
10. Bukharin, *Imperialism and World Economy*, page 70.
11. Bukharin, *Imperialism and World Economy*, pages 73–4.
12. M.W. Herold, 'World Economy as Manifestation of Internationalization and Nationalization: the Contribution of Nikolai Bukharin', in N.N. Kozlov and E.D. Weitz (eds), *Nikolai Ivanovich Bukharin. A Centenary Appraisal*, New York 1990, page 16.
13. Bukharin, *Imperialism and World Economy*, page 118.
14. Bukharin, *Imperialism and World Economy*, page 155.
15. According to V. Stanovchich, 'Some Notes on Bukarin's Marxist Theory', in S. Bertolissi (ed.), *Bucharin: Tra rivoluzione e riforme*, Rome 1982, page 108.
16. Bukharin, *Imperialism and World Economy*, page 158.

17. Bukharin, *Imperialism and World Economy*, pages 108–9.
18. Bukharin, *Imperialism and World Economy*, page 138.
19. Bukharin, *Imperialism and World Economy*, page 21.
20. Bukharin, *Imperialism and World Economy*, page 27.
21. Bukharin, *Imperialism and World Economy*, page 108.
22. S. Cohen, *Bukharin and the Bolshevik Revolution*, Oxford 1971, pages 30–1.
23. N. Bukharin, 'Towards a Theory of the Imperialist State' [1925], *N.I. Bukharin: Selected Writings on the State and the Transition to Socialism*, ed. R.B. Day, Nottingham 1982, page 27.
24. Lenin's 'popular introduction' to imperialism has flaws of its own and ceases to be dialectical in parts. Like Bukharin, Lenin drew on Hilferding, but he also incorporated barely digested chunks of Hobson's work on imperialism. As a Liberal British economist, Hobson concluded that the outstanding feature of imperialism was the role of colonies. Lenin at points repeats this argument. These are precisely the points taken up in the 'orthodox' neo-Stalinist interpretation of Leninism that is still influential in the Third World left. V.I. Lenin, 'Imperialism the Highest Stage of Capitalism', *Collected Works*, Vol. 32, Moscow, n.d. See also the discussion in Richard Day's introduction to Bukharin, *N.I. Bukharin: Selected Writings*, page xxxvii and A.G. Löwy, *Die Weltgeschichte ist das Weltgericht*, Vienna 1969, page 54.
25. *N.I. Bukharin: Selected Writings*, pages 17–18.
26. V.I. Lenin, *Collected Works*, present author's translated from the 4th Russian edn. Vol. 22, Moscow, n.d., pages 208 and 266.
27. Quoted in N. Bukharin, *The Politics and Economics of the Transition Period* [1920], Henley-on-Thames 1979, page 31.
28. See V.I. Lenin, 'Notes on Bukharin's Article' in *Bol'shevik*, 1932, No. 22.
29. Published in *Bol'shevik* 1932, No. 22.
30. Cohen, page 42.
31. K. Kautsky, *The Road to Power*, Chicago 1909, page 100.
32. *N.I. Bukharin: Selected Writings*, page 80.
33. *N.I. Bukharin: Selected Writings*, page 13.
34. Luxemburg, page 78.
35. *N.I. Bukharin: Selected Writings*, page 16.
36. *N.I. Bukharin: Selected Writings*, pages 17–18.
37. *N.I. Bukharin: Selected Writings*, page 26.
38. *N.I. Bukharin: Selected Writings*, page 27.
39. A whole school of thought entitled 'bureaucratic collectivism' did indeed appear, making this very argument about the USSR under Stalinism.
40. Cohen, page 31.
41. Cohen, page 32.
42. Cohen, page 32.

43. *N.I. Bukharin: Selected Writings*, page 27.
44. *N.I. Bukharin: Selected Writings*, page 31.
45. *N.I. Bukharin: Selected Writings*, page 27.
46. Bukharin, *Imperialism and World Economy*, page 63.
47. Bukharin, *Imperialism and World Economy*, page 83.
48. K. Marx, *Contribution to the Critique of Political Economy* [1859], page 20, Moscow 1970, page 20.
49. K. Marx, *Contribution to the Critique of Political Economy*, page 21.
50. *N.I. Bukharin: Selected Writings*, page 31.
51. *N.I. Bukharin: Selected Writings*, page 26.
52. *N.I. Bukharin: Selected Writings*, page 32.
53. N. Bukharin and E. Preobrazhensky, *The ABC of Communism*, [1919], Harmondsworth 1969, page 87.
54. Bukharin, *Imperialism and World Economy*, page 160.
55. Bukharin, *Imperialism and World Economy*, pages 167 and 170.
56. O.H. Gankin and H.H. Fisher, *The Bolsheviks and the World War: the Origin of the Third International*, Stanford, Calif., 1940, page 221. The Baugy Group included Bukharin, Bosh and Piatakov and was named after the place where its supporters were staying at the time of its formation.
57. Gankin and Fisher, page 219.
58. T. Cliff, *Lenin*, Vol. 2, London 1976, page 52.
59. Gankin and Fisher, page 220.
60. Lenin, *Collected Works*, Vol. 22, page 346.
61. Lenin, *Collected Works*, Vol. 22, page 355.
62. Gankin and Fisher, page 188.
63. Lenin, 'Notes on Bukharin's Article', page 22.
64. Lenin, *Collected Works*, Vol. 23, pages 24–5.

Chapter 2: Left Communism
1. A.G. Löwy, *Die Weltgeschichte ist das Weltgericht*, Vienna 1969, page 69.
2. It should be noted, however, that Bukharin, in common with the entire Central Committee, did join in a rejection of Lenin's letter which made the first call for an insurrection on the basis that it was premature: 'Perhaps that was the sole case in the history of our party when the Central Committee unanimously decided to burn a letter of Lenin.' Quoted in L. Trotsky, *History of the Russian Revolution* [1932], London 1977, page 984.
3. N. Bukharin, *Parliaments or Soviets*, London 1920.
4. N. Bukharin, 'Speech to the Constituent Assembly', in *Na podstupakh k oktiabru*, Moscow 1926, page 184.
5. N. Bukharin, *Vom Sturz des Zarismus bis zum Sturze der Bourgeoisie*, Berlin 1919, page 7.

6. M. Haynes, *Nikolai Bukharin and the Transition from Capitalism to Socialism*, Beckenham, Kent, 1985, page 52.
7. G.J. Gill, *Peasants and Government in the Russian Revolution*, London 1979, pages 145 and 147.
8. Bukharin, 'Speech to the Constituent Assembly', pages 21–2.
9. N. Bukharin, *Programme of the Communists (Bolsheviks)*, Moscow 1919, page 6.
10. Bukharin, 'Speech to the Constituent Assembly', page 49.
11. *VI S'ezd RSDLP(b)*, [August 1917], Moscow 1958, page 138.
12. *VI S'ezd RSDLP(b)*, page 143.
13. *The Bolsheviks and the October Revolution. Minutes of the Central Committee of the Russian Social-Democratic Labour Party (Bolsheviks) August 1917–February 1918*, London 1974, page 174.
14. R.K. Debo, *Revolution and Survival: the foreign Policy of Soviet Russia*, Liverpool 1979, page 158.
15. V.I. Lenin, *Collected Works*, Moscow, n.d., Vol. 25, page 39.
16. Lenin, *Collected Works*, Vol. 25, page 86.
17. *Resolutions and Decisions of the Communist Party of the Soviet Union*, Vol. 2, ed. R. Gregor, Toronto 1974, page 57.
18. *The Bolsheviks and the October Revolution*, page 202.
19. Quoted in T. Cliff, *Trotsky: the Sword of the Revolution*, London 1990, page 39.
20. L.N. Kritsman, *Die heroische Periode der grossen russischen Revolution*, Frankfurt 1971, page 268.
21. M.D. Bonch-Bruevich quoted in Debo, page 133.
22. J.V. Stalin, *Works*, Vol. 4, Moscow 1953, page 137.
23. 'Theses of the Petersburg Committee of the RSDLP(b) on the Current Situation and the War' [1918], written by Bukharin and published in *The Bolsheviks and the October Revolution*, page 192.
24. Lenin, *Collected Works*, Vol. 26, page 444.
25. 'Statement to the CC from a Group of its Members and People's Commissars' [1918], in *The Bolsheviks and the October Revolution*, page 216.
26. See *The Bolsheviks and the October Revolution*, page 224.
27. M. McCauley, *The Russian Revolution and the Soviet State, 1917–1921. Documents*, Basingstoke 1975, page 3.
28. The latter figures are for 1914 and based on the area of the USSR as it was in 1939. They are from V.P. Danilov, *Rural Russia under the New Regime*, London 1988, page 39.
29. *The Bolsheviks and the October Revolution*, page 209.
30. S. Cohen, *Bukharin and the Bolshevik Revolution*, Oxford 1971, page 63.
31. N.N. Smirnov, *Tretii Vserossiiskii S'ezd Sovetov*, Leningrad 1988, page 97.

32. See C. Bettelheim, *Les Luttes de classes en URSS. Première periode*, no place of publication given, 1974, page 336.
33. *The Bolsheviks and the October Revolution*, page 216.
34. The authorship is uncertain. Most sources suggest Osinskii, but Löwy discerns the hand of Bukharin. Löwy, page 99.
35. 'Theses of the Left Communists (1918)' in *Critique* Pamphlet Series, No. 1, Glasgow 1977, page 9.
36. 'Theses of the Left Communists (1918)', page 14.
37. 'Theses of the Left Communists (1918)', page 15.
38. 'Theses of the Left Communists (1918)', page 14.
39. 'Theses of the Left Communists (1918)', page 17.
40. 'Theses of the Left Communists (1918)', page 18.
41. See his notes for a speech which were published in *Bol'shevik*, No. 4, 20 February 1922.
42. Lenin, *Collected Works*, Vol. 25, page 358.
43. Lenin, *Collected Works*, Vol. 26, page 103.
44. Shmelev writes: 'Lenin proceeded from the view that capitalism had already created for socialism all the necessary economic forms, and it was only required to fill them with a new socialist content.' N. Shmelev, 'Advances and Debts', in *Novy Mir*, No.6, 1986, page 143.
45. D. Atkinson, *The End of the Russian Land Commune, 1905–1930*, Stanford, Calif., 1983, page 190.
46. Kritsman, page 80.
47. Iu.P. Bokarev, *Sotsialisticheskaia promyshlennost' i melkoe krest'ianskoe khoziaistvo v SSSR v 20-e gody*, Moscow 1989, page 135.
48. Kritsman, pages 80, 283 and 295.
49. *XI Vserossiiskaia Konferentsiia RKP(b)*, December 1921, page 50.
50. 'Theses of the Left Communists (1918)', page 14.
51. Kritsman, page 66.
52. Lenin, *Collected Works*, Vol. 26, page 334.

Chapter 3: War Communism

1. O. Latsis, *Vyiti iz kvadrata*, Moscow 1989, pages 60 and 65.
2. V.C. Lel'chuk (ed.), *Istoriki sporiat: Trinadtsat' besed*, Moscow 1989, page 170.
3. Trotsky Archive, deposited at Harvard University, Document T 1901.
4. L.N. Kritsman, *Die Heroische Periode der grossen russischen Revolution*, Frankfurt 1971, page 344.
5. S. Malle, *The Economic Organization of War Communism, 1918–1921*, Cambridge 1985, page 481.
6. M. Lewin, *The Making of the Soviet System*, London 1985, page 212.
7. Kritsman, page 265.
8. *Izmeneniia sotsial'noi struktury Sovetskogo obshchestva*, Moscow 1979, pages 23–4.

9. Kritsman, page 80.
10. Kritsman, editor's introduction, page xxiv.
11. Figures from S.S. Maslov, *Russia after Four Years of Revolution*, Paris 1922, quoted in *Records of the [U.S] Department of State Relating to the Internal Affairs of the Soviet Union, 1910–1929*, Reel 110, Despatch 612.
12. Kritsman, page 257.
13. Kritsman, page 278.
14. Kritsman, page 295.
15. *Ekonomicheskaia Zhizn*, 17 June 1923.
16. M. Dobb, *Soviet Economic Development since 1917*, New York 1966, page 117.
17. Kritsman, pages 241 and 242.
18. Lewin, *The Making of the Soviet System*, page 210.
19. R. Conquest, *The Harvest of Sorrow*, London 1986, pages 53–4.
20. *Pravda*, 19 February 1919.
21. *Pravda*, 1 January 1919.
22. See Kritsman, page 143.
23. For examples of this support, see Kritsman, page 146.
24. Quoted in U. Brügmann, *Die russischen Gewerkschaften in Revolution und Burgerkrieg, 1917–1919*, Frankfurt am Main, 1972, page 247.
25. Quoted in Brügmann, page 249.
26. *The Bolsheviks and the October Revolution. Minutes of the Central Committee of the Russian Social-Democratic Labour Party (Bolsheviks) August 1917–February 1918*, London 1974, page 216.
27. Iu.P. Bokarev, *Sotsialisticheskaia promyshlennost' i melkoe krest'ianskoe khoziaistvo v SSSR v 20-e gody*, Moscow 1989, page 144.
28. L. Trotsky, 1935 introduction to *Terrorism and Communism*, Ann Arbor, Michigan 1972, page xlii.
29. T. Cliff, *Lenin*, Vol. 3, London 1978, page 113.
30. Kritsman, pages 334–5.
31. V.I. Lenin, *Collected Works*, Moscow, n.d., Vol. 29, page 423.
32. See C. Bettelheim, *Les Luttes de classes en URSS. Première periode*, no place of publication given, 1974, page 180.
33. Brügmann, page 254.
34. Malle, pages 314–15.
35. N. Bukharin, 'Anarchism and Scientific Communism', in *The Poverty of Statism*, Minneapolis 1981, page 3.
36. Bettelheim, page 261.
37. Cliff, *Lenin*, Vol. 3, page 158.
38. N. Bukharin, *The Politics and Economics of the Transition Period* [1920], London 1979, page 56.
39. Bukharin, *The Politics and Economics of the Transition Period*, page 55.

40. See also Bukharin's reply to Kautsky in *Pravda*, 15 January 1919, where he argued from the Finnish experience that other revolutions might be more bloody than the Russian overturn.
41. *Karl Kautsky: Selected Political Writings*, ed. P. Goode, London 1983, page 149.
42. Bukharin, *The Politics and Economics of the Transition Period*, pages 125–6.
43. Trotsky, *Terrorism and Communism*, page 7.
44. Bukharin, *The Politics and Economics of the Transition Period*, pages 98 and 99.
45. S. Cohen, *Bukharin and the Bolshevik Revolution*, Oxford 1971, page 93.
46. Bukharin, *The Politics and Economics of the Transition Period*, page 152.
47. Bukharin, *The Politics and Economics of the Transition Period*, page 155.
48. Bukharin, *The Economics of the Transition Period*, New York 1971, pages 223 and 224.
49. N. Bukharin and E. Preobrazhensky, *The ABC of Communism*, [1919], Harmondsworth 1969, pages 391–2.
50. Bukharin, *The Politics and Economics of the Transition Period*, page 100.
51. Bukharin, *The Politics and Economics of the Transition Period*, page 128.
52. Bukharin, *The Politics and Economics of the Transition Period*, page 90.
53. Bukharin, *The Politics and Economics of the Transition Period*, page 105.
54. Bukharin, *The Politics and Economics of the Transition Period*, page 106.
55. Lenin, *Collected Works*, Vol. 32, page 25.
56. Bukharin, *The Politics and Economics of the Transition Period*, page 147.
57. Cliff, *Lenin*, Vol. 3, page 128.
58. *Third Congress of the Communist International. Report of Meetings*, London 1921, page 111.
59. Bukharin, *The Politics and Economics of the Transition Period*, page 138.
60. See T. Cliff, *Trotsky: Sword of the Revolution*, London 1990, and Cohen, page 68.
61. Bukharin, *The Politics and Economics of the Transition Period*, page 143.
62. Bukharin, *The Politics and Economics of the Transition Period*, page 142.
63. Bukharin, *The Politics and Economics of the Transition Period*, page 143.
64. Bukharin, *The Politics and Economics of the Transition Period*, page 144.
65. Bukharin, *The Politics and Economics of the Transition Period*, page 163.
66. See for example the order prolonging militarisation in a vast range of industries until 1 June 1921, in *Dekrety Sovetskoi Vlasti*, Vol. 13, Moscow 1989, pages 4–8.
67. *IX S'ezd RKP(b)*, 29 March–5 April 1920, Moscow 1960, page 211, and *Pravda*, 2 April 1920.
68. *IX S'ezd RKP(b)*, page 137, and *Pravda* 1 April 1920.
69. Bukharin, *The Politics and Economics of the Transition Period*, page 165.
70. Bukharin, *The Economics of the Transition Period*, New York 1971, page 221.

71. *IX S'ezd RKP(b)*, page 225.
72. M. Lewin, *Political Undercurrents in Soviet Economic Debates*, Princeton, NJ, 1974, page 9.
73. Cohen, page 87.
74. *Pravda*, 16 January 1919.
75. *Pravda*, 2 April 1920.
76. Lenin, *Collected Works*, Vol. 32, page 29.
77. Lenin, *Collected Works*, Vol. 32, page 58.
78. Lenin, *Collected Works*, Vol. 32, page 50.
79. Quoted in I. Deutscher, *Soviet Trade Unions*, London 1950, page 46. See also *X S'ezd RKP(b)*, pages 361–2.
80. Lenin, *Collected Works*, Vol. 32, page 34.
81. *Pravda*, 16 January 1921.
82. Quoted in Lenin, *Collected Works*, Vol. 32, page 56.
83. *Pravda*, 16 and 25 January 1921.
84. Lenin, *Collected Works*, Vol. 32, page 51.
85. *Pravda*, 15 February 1921.
86. *Founding the Communist International, Proceedings and Documents of the First Congress: March 1919*, New York 1987, page 308.
87. *VIII S'ezd RKP(b)*, March 1919, page 111.
88. He later tried to palm this off as the exclusive property of the German Communist Thalheimer. See N. Bukharin, 'On the German Question', *Kommunistische Internationale*, March 1926.
89. N. Bukharin, 'On the Offensive Tactic', *Kommunistische Internationale*, No. 15, 1921, pages 69–70.
90. Bukharin, 'On the Offensive Tactic', page 71.
91. K. Marx, 'Provisional Rules' in *The First International and After* [1864], Harmondsworth 1974, page 82.
92. See *Pravda*, 19 Febuary 1919.
93. *Bulletin of the IV Congress of the Communist International*, Moscow 1922, Nos 14–15.
94. *Bericht über den IV Kongress der Kommunistischen Internationale, Petrograd-Moskau vom 5 November bis 5 Dezember 1922*, Hamburg 1923, page 104, and *Materialen zur Frage des Programmes*, Hamburg 1924, page 94.
95. *Pravda*, 24 June 1920.
96. *Pravda*, 10 July 1920.
97. *Pravda*, 10 March 1921.
98. R Leviné-Meyer, *Inside German Communism*, London 1977, page 18.
99. See G.L. Smirnov, introduction to N.I. Bukharin, *Chelovek, politik, uchenyi*, Moscow 1990, page 5.

Chapter 4: The Bridge of Philosophy and Culture
1. V.I. Lenin, *Collected Works*, Vol. 36, Moscow, n.d., page 595.

2. See S. Cohen, *Bukharin and the Bolshevik Revolution*, Oxford 1971, page 109, and N. Bukharin, *Historical Materialism*, New York 1925, pages 260 and 261.
3. N.I. Bukharin, *Chelovek, politik, uchenyi*, Moscow 1990, page 352.
4. Bukharin, *Historical Materialism*, page 29.
5. Bukharin, *Historical Materialism*, page 31.
6. Bukharin, *Historical Materialism*, page 51.
7. K. Kautsky, *The Road to Power*, Chicago 1909, page 50.
8. Bukharin, *Historical Materialism*, page 98.
9. Bukharin, *Historical Materialism*, page 51.
10. K. Marx, 'The 18th Brumaire of Louis Bonaparte' [1852], in K. Marx, *Surveys from Exile*, Harmondsworth 1973, page 146.
11. A. Gramsci, *Selections from Prison Notebooks*, London 1971, page 438.
12. K. Marx, 'Theses on Feuerbach' [1845], in K. Marx, *Early Writings*, Harmondsworth 1975, page 421.
13. K. Korsch, *Marxism and Philosophy*, London 1970, page 56.
14. See for example *Ataka: sbornik teoriticheskikh statei*, Moscow 1924, page 121, or N. Bukharin, *Proletarskaia revoliutsiia i kultura*, Petrograd 1923, page 37.
15. A. Zanardo, 'Bukharin as a Marxist Theoretician', in S. Bertolissi (ed.), *Bukharin: Tra rivoluzione e riforme*, Rome 1982, page 101.
16. Lenin, *Collected Works*, Vol. 32, page 95.
17. *The Bolsheviks and the October Revolution. Minutes of the Central Committee of the Russian Social-Democratic Labour Party (Bolsheviks) August 1917–February 1918*, London 1974, page 158.
18. E.H. Carr, *The Bolshevik Revolution*, Vol. 1, Harmondsworth 1966, page 210.
19. K. Tarbuck, *Bukharin's Theory of Equilibrium*, London 1989, page 169.
20. Bukharin, *Historical Materialism*, page 72.
21. Bukharin, *Historical Materialism*, page 73.
22. U. Stehr, *Vom Kapitalismus zum Kommunismus*, Hamburg, 1973, page 24.
23. Bukharin, *Historical Materialism*, page 74.
24. For a development of this criticism see G.A. Wetter, *Dialectical Materialism*, London 1958, pages 143–9, and Stehr, pages 15–30.
25. Bukharin, *Historical Materialism*, page 74.
26. Bukharin, *Historical Materialism*, page 74.
27. N. Bukharin, *Izbranniye trudy*, Leningrad 1988, page 9.
28. Bukharin, *Historical Materialism*, page 79.
29. Bukharin, *Historical Materialism*, page 150.
30. K. Marx, *A Contribution to the Critique of Political Economy*, London 1970, page 21.
31. Bukharin, *Historical Materialism*, page 112.
32. Bukharin, *Historical Materialism*, page 233.

33. G. Lukács, 'N. Bukharin's Theory of Historical Materialism' [1925], in A. Deborin and N. Bukharin, *Kontroversen über dialektischen und mechanistischen Materialismus*, Frankfurt-am-Main 1969, page 285.
34. Lukács, page 286.
35. This is a point which was recognised by Lukács, who praised Bukharin for attempting to rescue the Marxist tradition from revisionists like Bernstein and Cunow, but condemned him for distorting that which he was defending. Lukács, page 283.
36. Cohen, page 108.
37. A. Rosmer, *Lenin's Moscow*, London 1971, page 43.
38. N. Bukharin, 'The Proletariat and Questions of Artistic Policy', in *Krasnaya Nov'*, 1925, No. 4.
39. N. Bukharin, 'Autobiography' [1926] in *Izbranniye trudy*, page 9.
40. Quoted in G. Gorzka, *A. Bogdanov und der russische Proletkult*, Frankfurt 1970, page 92.
41. Quoted in Gorzka, page 90.
42. Quoted in Gorzka, page 83.
43. Bukharin, *Historical Materialism*, page 233.
44. N. Bukharin, 'Posing the Problem of Historical Materialism', in *Ataka*, page 120.
45. For a recent defence of Bogdanov see A.A. Belykh, 'A.A. Bogdanov's Theory of Equilibrium and the Economic Discussions of the 1920s', in *Soviet Studies*, July 1990.
46. N. Bukharin, *Building up Socialism*, London 1926, page 17.
47. V.V. Gorbunov, 'Lenin's Critique of Proletkult's Theory of Cultural legacy' in Voprosy istorii KPSS No. 5, page 91, *Soviet Studies*, April 1987; see also J. Biggart, 'Bukharin and the Origins of the 'Proletarian Culture' debate', in *Soviet Studies*, 1987.
48. Quoted in Gorzka, page 131.
49. Quoted by Lenin in *Collected Works*, Vol. 27, page 342.
50. Bukharin, *Historical Materialism*, page xi.
51. L. Trotsky, *Literature and Art* [1924], New York 1970, page 50.
52. T. Cliff, *Trotsky, Sword of the Revolution*, London, 1990, pages 105–10.
53. L. Trotsky, *How the Revolution Armed*, Vol. 1, London 1979, page 38.
54. Quoted in Gorzka, page 207.
55. *Pravda*, 16 December 1919.
56. K. Marx, *Collected Works*, Vol. 5, Moscow, n.d., page 47.
57. *Pravda*, 7 November 1922.
58. *Pravda*, October 24 and 25, 1923.
59. Lenin, *Collected Works*, Vol. 31, page 287.
60. Trotsky, *Literature and Art*, pages 44 and 46.
61. Quoted in S. Fitzpatrick, 'The Bolsheviks' Dilemma: Class, Culture and Politics in the Early Soviet Years,' *Slavic Review*, Vol. 47, No. 14, Winter 1988, page 602.

62. Z.A. Sochor, *Revolution and Culture*, Ithaca, NY, 1986, page 155.
63. Details in A.M. Ball, *Russia's Last Capitalists*, Berkeley and Los Angeles 1987, pages 8–9.
64. M. Dobb, *Soviet Economic Development since 1917*, New York 1966, page 112.
65. Lenin, *Collected Works*, Vol. 33, page 288.
66. Iu.V. Emel'ianov, *Zametki o Bukharine*, Moscow 1989, pages 156–7.
67. V.A. Koslov, *Kul'turnaia revolutsiia i krest'ianstvo, 1921–1927*, Moscow 1983, page 426.
68. Koslov, pages 75–6.
69. Bukharin, 'The Proletariat and Questions of Artistic Policy'.
70. N. Bukharin, 'Bourgeois Revolution and Proletarian Revolution' [1922], in *Put' k Sotsialismu v Rossii*, ed. S. Heitman, New York 1967, page 162.
71. Bukharin, *Proletarskaia revolutsiia i kul'tura*, pages 20, 22.
72. Bukharin, 'Bourgeois Revolution and Proletarian Revolution', page 169.
73. Bukharin, *Proletarskaia revolutsiia i kul'tura*, page 33.
74. Bukharin, *Proletarskaia revolutsiia i kul'tura*, page 45.
75. Cohen, page 42.
76. Lenin, *Collected Works*, Vol. 5, page 249.
77. Gramsci, *Selections from Prison Notebooks*, page 16.
78. *Pravda*, 18 December 1918.
79. *Protokoll der Konferenz der Erweiterte EKKI, 12–23 Juni 1923*, Hamburg 1923, pages 156–7.
80. A. Gramsci, 'The School of the Party', in *Scritti Politici*, (P. Spriano, ed) Vol. 3, Rome 1973, page 115.
81. Bukharin, *Historical Materialism*, pages 305–6.
82. Bukharin, *Proletarskaia revolutsiia i kul'tura*, pages 36–7.
83. Bukharin, 'The Proletariat and Questions of Artistic Policy'.
84. L. Trotsky, *The Challenge of the Left Opposition, 1928–1929*, New York 1981, pages 203–4.
85. Quoted in T. Cliff, *Lenin*, Vol. 1, London 1975, page 270.

Chapter 5: The New Economic Policy
1. Details in R. Conquest, *The Harvest of Sorrow*, London 1986, pages 51–2.
2. W.J. Chase, 'Moscow and its Working Class, 1918–1928. A Social Analysis', Boston College PhD thesis 1979, page 52.
3. Bukharin played no role in the Kronstadt affair. Getzler notes: 'There is not a shred of evidence to support the oft-repeated story that Bukharin, at the Third Comintern Congress, referred to the Kronstadters with sorrow as "erring ... true brothers, our own flesh and blood" whose revolt the Communists had reluctantly been "forced to

suppress".' I. Getzler, *Kronstadt, 1917–1921*, Cambridge 1983, page 257.
4. Interestingly only M.I. Frumkin, who turned out to be one of the most vociferous defenders of the continuation of the NEP on Bukharinist lines in the late 1920s, defended continuing requisition. *X S'ezd RKP(b)*, page 433.
5. *Dekreti Sovetskoi Vlasti*, Vol. 13, page 204.
6. *Dekreti Sovetskoi Vlasti*, Vol. 13, page 283.
7. *Dekreti Sovetskoi Vlasti*, Vol. 13, page 285.
8. V. Serge, *Memoirs of a Revolutionary*, London 1984, page 147.
9. A.M. Ball, *Russia's Last Capitalists*, Berkley and Los Angeles 1987, pages 20–2.
10. E.H. Carr, *The Bolshevik Revolution*, Vol. 2, London, 1966, page 303.
11. M. Dobb, *Soviet Economic Development since 1917*, New York 1966, page 151.
12. Details in Ball, pages 20–2.
13. N. Boukharine, 'La nouvelle orientation économique de la Russie des Soviets', in *La Phare*, Nos 21–2, 1920–1.
14. *Pravda*, 15 April 1921.
15. N. Bukharin, *Izbranniye Proizvedeniia*, Moscow 1988, page 24.
16. V.I. Lenin, *Collected Works*, Vol. 32, Moscow, n.d., page 187.
17. *XI Konferentsiia RKP(b)*, 19–22 December 1921, pages 49–50.
18. N. Bukharin, 'Anarchism and Scientific Communism', in *The Poverty of Statism*, Minneapolis 1981, page 3.
19. Lenin, *Collected Works*, Vol. 33, page 301.
20. *XI Konferentsiia RKP(b)*, page 50.
21. See for example his article on 'The New Course' in N. Bukharin, *Izbranniye Proizvedeniia*, page 32.
22. *Bericht über den IV Kongress der Kommunistischen Internationale*, Hamburg 1923, page 103.
23. *Cinquième Congrès de l'Internationale Communiste, 17 Juin–8 Juillet 1924*, Paris 1924, page 165.
24. *Cinquième Congrès de l'Internationale Communiste*, page 170.
25. *Dekreti Sovetskoi Vlasti*, Vol. 13, page 251.
26. Lenin, *Collected Works*, Vol. 32, page 344.
27. Lenin, *Collected Works*, Vol. 32, page 345.
28. Lenin, *Collected Works*, Vol. 32, page 330.
29. Lenin, *Collected Works*, Vol. 32, page 345.
30. Iu.P. Bokarev, *Sotsialisticheskaia promyshlennost' i melkoe krest'ianskoe khoziaistvo v SSR v 20-e gody*, Moscow 1989, page 174.
31. Lenin, *Collected Works*, Vol. 33, pages 95–7.
32. Lenin, *Collected Works*, Vol. 33, page 63.
33. Lenin, *Collected Works*, Vol. 33, pages 62 and 94.
34. Lenin, *Collected Works*, Vol. 33, page 115.

35. Lenin, *Collected Works*, Vol. 33, page 219.
36. Lenin, *Collected Works*, Vol. 33, page 279.
37. N. Bukharin, *Put' k Sotsialismu v Rossii*, ed. S. Heitman, New York 1967, page 400.
38. N.I. Bukharin, *Chelovek, politik, uchenyi*, Moscow, 1990, pages 94–5.
39. Quoted in Bukharin, *Put' k Sotsialismu v Rossii*, ed. Heitman, xiv–xv.
40. Lenin, *Collected Works*, Vol. 33, pages 470–1.
41. Lenin, *Collected Works*, Vol. 33, page 468.
42. Lenin, *Collected Works*, Vol. 33, page 470.
43. Serge, page 200.
44. See for example the comments of Iu.C. Borisov in V.C. Lel'chuk, ed., *Istoriki Sporiat: Trinadtsat' besed*, Moscow 1989, page 256.
45. L. Trotsky, 'The Fundamental Questions of Food and Agrarian Policy (A Proposal made to the Central Committee of the Party in February 1920)' in L. Trotsky, *The Challenge of the Left Opposition, 1923–1925*, New York 1975, page 109.
46. L. Trotsky, *First Five Years of the Communist International*, London 1974, pages 231–2.
47. *Arkhiv Trotskogo*, Vol. 1, Moscow 1990, page 155.
48. Trotsky, *First Five Years of the Communist International*, page 233.
49. Trotsky, *The Challenge of the Left Opposition, 1923–1925*, page 322.
50. L. Trotsky, 'The New Course' in Trotsky, *The Challenge of the Left Opposition, 1923–1925*, page 129.
51. L. Trotsky, 'Towards Capitalism or Socialism?', in Trotsky, *The Challenge of the Left Opposition, 1923–1925*, page 322.
52. Trotsky's speech to the Fourth Comintern Congress [1922], quoted in L. Trotsky, *The Third International after Lenin*, London 1974, page 32.
53. Bokarev, page 238.
54. M.P. Kim, *Ekonomicheskaia politika sovetskogo gosudarstvo v perekhodnyi period ot kapitalizma k sotsializmu*, Moscow 1986, page 224.
55. N. Bukharin, *Partiia i oppozitsionnyi blok*, Moscow 1926, page 7.
56. Quoted in Carr, *The Bolshevik Revolution*, Vol. 2, page 313.
57. Dobb, page 151.
58. Carr, *The Bolshevik Revolution*, Vol. 2, page 310.
59. T. Cliff, *Lenin*, Vol. 4, London 1979, page 147.
60. *Izvestiia*, 13 June 1924.
61. C. Bettelheim, *Class Struggles in the USSR. Second Period, 1923–30*, Hassocks 1973, page 249.
62. G. Meyer, *Studien zur sozialökonomischen Entwicklung Sowjetrusslands 1921–1923*, Pahl-Rugenstein Verlag n.d., page 501.
63. Bokarev, page 196.
64. Meyer, page 382.
65. Serge, page 198.

66. Serge, page 147.
67. Serge, page 198.
68. Serge, page 79.
69. Lenin, *Collected Works*, Vol. 32, page 100.
70. S. Cohen, *Bukharin and the Bolshevik Revolution*, Oxford 1971, pages 270–2.
71. *Pravda*, 14 October 1922.
72. *Pravda*, 25 January 1923.
73. Bukharin, *Izbranniye Proizvedeniia*, page 32.
74. *Pravda*, 14 October 1922.
75. *XI Konferentsiia RKP(b)*, page 50.

Chapter 6: The Russian Peasantry
1. S. Cohen, *Bukharin and the Bolshevik Revolution*, Oxford 1971, page 159.
2. K. Marx, *Theories of Surplus Value*, Part 1, London 1969, page 407.
3. Quoted in K. Marx, and F. Engels, *Selected Correspondence, 1846–1895*, London 1934, page 355.
4. Marx and Engels, *Selected Correspondence*, page 508.
5. *N.I. Bukharin: Selected Writings on the State and the Transition to Socialism*, ed. R.B. Day, Nottingham 1982, page 162.
6. N. Bukharin, *K voprosu o trotskizme*, Moscow 1925, page 123.
7. M. Lewin, *Russian Peasants and Soviet Power*, London 1968, page 28.
8. R.W. Davies, *The Socialist Offensive. The Collectivisation of Soviet Agriculture, 1929–1930*, London 1980, page 10.
9. M. Gorky, 'On the Russian Peasantry', in R.E.F. Smith (ed.), *The Russian Peasant*, London 1977, page 17.
10. Gorky, page 12.
11. L. Trotsky, *Terrorism and Communism* [1935], Ann Arbor, Mich. 1972, page 111.
12. Trotsky, *Terrorism and Communism*, pages 111–12.
13. V.M. Selunskaia, *Sotsial'naia Struktura Sovetskogo Obshchestva*, Moscow 1987, page 14.
14. Stepniak, quoted in M. Dobb, *Soviet Economic Development since 1917*, New York 1966, page 44.
15. See for example details of pre-revolutionary famines in R. Conquest, *The Harvest of Sorrow*, London 1986, page 56.
16. V.P. Danilov, *Rural Russia under the New Regime*, London 1988, page 59.
17. R. Luxemburg, 'The Russian Revolution', in M.A. Waters (ed.), *Rosa Luxemburg Speaks*, pages 375–6.
18. V.I. Lenin, *Collected Works*, Vol. 30, pages 116 and 113.
19. Lenin, *Collected Works*, Vol. 26, page 456.
20. Lenin, *Collected Works*, Vol. 27, page 177.

21. Lenin, *Collected Works*, Vol. 33, page 501.
22. Lenin, *Collected Works*, Vol. 27, page 232.
23. Lenin, *Collected Works*, Vol. 27, page 300.
24. Lenin, *Collected Works*, Vol. 27, page 298.
25. Lenin, *Collected Works*, Vol. 33, page 277.
26. Seliunskaia, page 48.
27. Lenin, *Collected Works*, Vol. 32, page 404.
28. N. Bukharin, *Programme of the Communists (Bolsheviks)*, Moscow 1919, page 15.
29. Bukharin, *Programme of the Communists (Bolsheviks)*, pages 37–8.
30. Bukharin, *Programme of the Communists (Bolsheviks)*, pages 38–9.
31. *Pravda*, 2 February 1919.
32. *VIII S'ezd RKP(b)*, 18–23 March 1919, page 108.
33. Lenin, *Collected Works*, Vol. 29, page 169.
34. N. Bukharin, *Partiia i oppozitsionnyi blok*, Moscow 1926, page 19.
35. Bukharin, *Partiia i oppozitsionnyi blok*, page 37.
36. Bukharin, *Partiia i oppozitsionnyi blok*, page 10.
37. *Pravda*, 22 February 1920.

Chapter 7: The Hammer of Trotskyism

1. Introduction to N.I. Bukharin, *Put' k sotsializmu*, Novosibirsk 1990, pages v–vi.
2. N.I. Bukharin, *Chelovek, politik, uchenyi*, Moscow 1990, page 6.
3. M. Lewin, *Political Undercurrents in Soviet Economic Debates*, Princeton, NJ, page 12.
4. E.H. Carr, *The Bolshevik Revolution*, Vol. 3, London 1966, page 459.
5. V.I. Lenin, *Collected Works*, Vol. 33, Moscow, n.d., page 458.
6. *XII S'ezd RKP(b)*, 17–25 April 1923, Moscow 1968, page 613.
7. See Trotsky's speech to the plenum on 26 October 1923, reprinted in *Voprosy Istorii KPSS*, No. 5, 1990, page 34.
8. A.G. Löwy, *Die Weltgeschichte ist das Weltgericht*, Vienna 1969, pages 214–15.
9. He reported this to Boris Nicolaevsky, a Menshevik, who met Bukharin in Paris in 1936. See B.I. Nicolaevsky, *Power and the Soviet Elite*, Ann Arbor, Mich., 1975, pages 12–13.
10. *Arkhiv Trotskogo*, Vol. 1, Moscow 1990, page 56.
11. *Pravda*, 18 December 1918.
12. Quoted in S. Cohen, *Bukharin and the Bolshevik Revolution*, Oxford 1971, page 154.
13. *Pravda*, 7 June 1923.
14. L. Trotsky, *The Challenge of the Left Opposition, 1923–1925*, New York 1975, page 149.
15. N. Bukharin, *K voprosu o trotskizme*, Moscow 1925, page 11.
16. Bukharin, *K voprosu o trotskizme*, pages 12–13.

17. Bukharin to January plenum 1924, quoted in D. Volkogonov, *Triumf i Tragediia*, Moscow 1989, Book 1, Part 1, page 197.
18. M. Eastman, *Since Lenin Died*, London 1925, page 77.
19. G. Meyer, *Studien zur sozialökonomischen Entwicklung Sowjetrusslands 1921–1923*, Pahl-Rugenstein Verlag, no date, page 521.
20. Ia. Ossovskii, 'The Party on the Eve of the 14th Congress', in *Bol'shevik*, No. 14, 1926, page 59.
21. E.H. Carr, *Socialism in One Country*, London 1966, Part 1, page 173.
22. V. Serge, *Memoirs of a Revolutionary*, London 1984, page 136.
23. L. Trotsky, *The Third International after Lenin*, London 1974, page 264.
24. Quoted in Carr, *Socialism in One Country*, Part 2, page 143.
25. *XV Konferentsiia VKP(b)*, 26 October–3 November 1926, page 601.
26. N. Bukharin, *K itogam XIV S'ezda VKP(b)*, Moscow 1926, page 5.
27. Quoted in Trotsky's letter to Bukharin of 9 January 1926, in L. Trotsky, *Challenge of the Left Opposition, 1926–1927*, New York 1980, page 35.
28. Bukharin's summing up at the extended plenum of the Central Committee and Central Control Commission of the Communist Party of the Soviet Union in *Kommunistische Internationale*, Vol. 41, 12 October 1927, pages 2005–6.
29. Report in *Pravda*, 8 December 1927.
30. N. Bukharin, *K voprosu o trotskizme*, page 49.
31. L. Trotsky, *1905* [1908–9], Harmondsworth 1971, page 53.
32. Trotsky, *1905*, page 66.
33. L. Trotsky, *Results and Prospects* [1906], London 1962, page 195.
34. Trotsky, *Results and Prospects*, page 237.
35. Lenin, *Collected Works*, Vol. 9, pages 56–7.
36. Lenin, *Collected Works*, Vol. 9, pages 236–7.
37. Lenin, *Collected Works*, Vol. 9, page 100.
38. N. Bukharin, *Izbranniye trudy*, Leningrad 1988, page 444.
39. N. Bucharin, *Vom Sturz des Zarismus bis zum Sturze der Bourgeoisie*, Berlin 1919, page 7.
40. Trotsky, *Third International after Lenin*, page 67.
41. Bukharin, *K voprosu o trotskizme*, page 114.
42. Bukharin, *K voprosu o trotskizme*, page 115.
43. J.V. Stalin, *The Theory and Practice of Leninism*, London 1925, pages 45–6.
44. J.V. Stalin, *Works*, Vol. 6, Moscow 1953, page 10.
45. Bukharin, *K itogam XIV S'ezda VKP(b)*, page 16.
46. Bucharin, *Vom Sturz des Zarismus bis zum Sturze der Bourgeoisie*, page 7.
47. Bucharin, *Vom Sturz des Zarismus bis zum Sturze der Bourgeoisie*, page 104.
48. Bukharin, *K itogam XIV S'ezda VKP(b)*, page 28.

49. N. Bukharin, *Tekushchi moment i osnovy nashei politiki*, Moscow 1925, page 9.
50. Bukharin, *Tekushchi moment i osnovy nashei politiki*, page 10.
51. Bukharin, *K itogam XIV S'ezda VKP(b)*, page 24.
52. Lenin, *Collected Works*, Vol. 26, pages 465 and 470.
53. Lenin, *Collected Works*, Vol. 22, page 474.
54. For a closely argued textual analysis of Lenin's last articles see Trotsky, *Third International after Lenin*, pages 23–7.
55. N. Bukharin, *V zashchitu proletarskoi diktatury*, Moscow 1928, page 194.
56. Trotsky, *Challenge of the Left Opposition, 1926–1927*, page 158.
57. *Leningradskaia Pravda*, 22 December 1925.
58. G. Zinoviev, *Leninizm*, Leningrad 1925, page 254.
59. Bukharin, *K itogam XIV S'ezda VKP(b)*, page 34.
60. *Records of the [US] Department of State Relating to the Internal Affairs of the Soviet Union, 1910–1929*, Reel 112, Memorandum dated 22 October 1925.
61. The term 'iron cohort' was a favourite of Bukharin and the title of an article he wrote in 1922.
62. See for example his letter in *Voprosy Istorii KPSS*, November 1988, pages 44–6.
63. N. Bukharin, 'Cultural Tasks and the Struggle with Bureaucratism' [1927] in *Problemy teorii i praktiki sotsializmu*, Moscow 1989, page 183.
64. Trotsky, *Challenge of the Left Opposition, 1926–1927*, page 67.
65. *XI Vserossiiskaia Konferentsiia RKP(b)*, December 1921, pages 49–50.
66. Bukharin, *Problemy teorii i praktiki sotsializmu*, page 186.
67. Lewin, *Political Undercurrents in Soviet Economic Debates*, page 41.
68. Lenin, *Collected Works*, Vol. 32, page 331.
69. L. Trotsky, *Writings*, 1929, New York 1975, page 81.
70. L. Trotsky, *Writings*, 1930, page 85. When Trotsky wrote these lines in 1930 they were out of date, but they were certainly valid in the period up to Stalin's counter-revolution.
71. Trotsky, *Writings*, 1930, page 85.
72. Trotsky, *Writings*, 1929, page 122.
73. Trotsky, *Challenge of the Left Opposition, 1926–1927*, page 404.

Chapter 8: 'Enrich Yourselves'

1. L. Trotsky, 'Programme of the Opposition', in *Challenge of the Left Opposition, 1926–1927*, New York, page 322.
2. N. Bukharin, *Tri rechi: k voprosu o nashikh raznoglasiiakh*, Moscow and Leningrad 1926, page 1.
3. *N.I. Bukharin: Selected Writings on the State and the Transition to Socialism*, ed. R.B. Day, Nottingham 1982, page 149.
4. Trotsky, *Challenge of the Left Opposition, 1926–1927*, page 336.
5. *N.I. Bukharin: Selected Writings*, page 197.

6. S. Bertolissi (ed.), *Bucharin: Tra rivoluzione e riforme*, Rome 1982, page 42.
7. N.I. Bukharin: *Selected Writings*, page 245.
8. Iu.P. Bokarev, *Sotsialisticheskaia promyshlennost' i melkoe krest'ianskoe khoziaistvo v SSSR v 20-e gody*, Moscow 1989, page 171.
9. *Istoriki sporiat: Trinidtsat' besed*, Moscow 1989, page 159.
10. V.P. Danilov, *Rural Russia under the New Regime*, London 1988, page 259.
11. Bokarev, page 180.
12. *Ekonomicheskaia zhizn*, 1 June 1923.
13. G. Meyer, *Studien zur sozialökonomischen Entwicklung Sowjetrusslands 1921–1923*, Pahl-Rugenstein Verlag, no date, page 418.
14. Bokarev, page 242.
15. N.I. Bukharin: *Selected Writings*, page 119.
16. A.M. Ball, *Russia's Last Capitalists*, Berkley and Los Angeles 1987, page 104.
17. 'He Who Suffers "Furious Enemies"', article probably by V.M. Smirnov, in *Arkhiv Trotskogo*, Vol. 3, Moscow 1990, page 35.
18. Trotsky, *Challenge of the Left Opposition, 1923–1925*, New York 1975, Vol. 1, page 54
19. N.I. Bukharin: *Selected Writings*, page 131.
20. Bukharin, *Tekushchi moment i osnovy nashei politiki*, Moscow 1925, page 14.
21. N. Bukharin, *Partiia i oppozitsionnyi blok*, Moscow 1926, page 6.
22. N.I. Bukharin: *Selected Writings*, page 187.
23. N.I. Bukharin: *Selected Writings*, page 172.
24. Bukharin, *Partiia i oppozitsionnyi blok*, page 31.
25. N.I. Bukharin: *Selected Writings*, page 209.
26. Bukharin, *K voprosu o trotskizme*, Moscow 1925, page 10.
27. Bukharin, *Tri rechi*, page 48.
28. V.N. Baliazin, *Professor Aleksandr Chaianov*, Moscow 1990, page 195.
29. R. Pipes, *Russia under the Old Regime*, Harmondsworth 1974, page 13.
30. Trotsky, *Challenge of the Left Opposition, 1923–1925*, page 118.
31. Trotsky, *Challenge of the Left Opposition, 1923–1925*, page 301.
32. Trotsky, *Challenge of the Left Opposition, 1923–1925*, page 118.
33. N.I. Bukharin, *Izbranniye trudy*, Leningrad 1988, page 306.
34. F. Engels, *Anti-Dühring* [1878], Peking 1976, pages 361–2.
35. *Pravda*, 3 July 1926.
36. Meyer, page 422.
37. Bokarev, page 214.
38. B. Kagarlitsky, 'Stenogramme vystupleniia na Bukharinskikh chteniiakh Borisa Kagarlitskogo, Saratov 9 oktiabr 1988', page 8.
39. Kagarlitsky, page 7.
40. See table in *Arkhiv Trotskogo*, Vol. 2, page 218.

41. Trotsky, *Challenge of the Left Opposition, 1923–1925*, page 301.
42. Trotsky, *Challenge of the Left Opposition, 1926–1927*, pages 309–10.
43. *N.I. Bukharin: Selected Writings*, page 142.
44. E.H. Carr and R.W. Davies, *Foundations of a Planned Economy*, London 1969, Vol. 1, Part 2, pages 456–7.
45. Carr and Davies, Vol. 1, page 468.
46. *Torgovo- promyshlennaya gazeta*, 24 November 1925.
47. Quoted in S. Bezborodov, *Vreditel u stanka*, Leningrad 1930, page 50.
48. Trotsky, *Challenge of the Left Opposition, 1926–1927*, page 54.
49. *Arkhiv Trotskogo*, Vol. 3, page 150.
50. *KPSS v rezolutsiiakh i resheniiakh s'ezdov, konferentsii i plenumov TsK*, Moscow 1953, Vol. 2, page 620.
51. M. Lewin, *Russian Peasants and Soviet Power*, London 1968, page 176.
52. Quoted in O. Narkiewicz, *The Making of the Soviet State Apparatus*, Manchester 1970, page 73.
53. Lewin, *Russian Peasants and Soviet Power*, page 123.
54. Bukharin, *Tekushchi moment i osnovy nashei politiki*, page 20.
55. Bukharin, *Tekushchi moment i osnovy nashei politiki*, page 25.
56. *N.I. Bukharin: Selected Writings*, pages 196–7.
57. N. Bukharin, *V proletarskoi zashchitu diktatury*, Moscow 1928, page 147.
58. Bukharin, *Tekushchi moment i osnovy nashei politiki*, page 19.
59. Quoted in *Izmeneniia sotsial'noi struktury Sovetskogo obshchestva*, Moscow 1979, page 67.
60. A. Larina 'Bukharina', *Nezabyvaemoe*, Moscow 1989, page 220.
61. J.V. Stalin, *Works*, Vol. 6, Moscow 1953, page 322.
62. Details in Trotsky, *Challenge of the Left Opposition, 1926–1927*, page 304, and Bokarev, pages 262–3.
63. See E.H. Carr, *Socialism in One Country*, Vol. 1, London 1966, page 256.
64. *N.I. Bukharin: Selected Writings*, page 196.
65. *Izmeneniia sotsial'noi struktury Sovetskogo obshchestva*, page 73.
66. Carr, *Socialism in One Country*, Vol. 1, page 257.
67. N. Bukharin, *K itogam XIV S'ezda VKP(b)*, Moscow 1926, page 47.
68. A. Ciliga, *The Russian Enigma* [1938], London 1979, page 18.
69. Quoted in 'The Tragedy of Impatience', *Kommunist* 1990, No. 5, page 81.
70. This was in constant roubles. Calculated from Ball, page 101.
71. Ball, page 41.
72. Quoted in G.D. Jackson, *Comintern and Peasant in East Europe, 1919–1930*, New York 1966, pages 60–1.
73. L. Trotsky, *Writings, 1929*, New York 1975, pages 119–20.
74. L. Trotsky, *Third International after Lenin*, London 1974, page 207.
75. L. Trotsky, *Writings 1930*, page 112.
76. Bukharin, *Tri rechi*, page 20.

77. Trotsky, *Challenge of the Left Opposition, 1923–1925*, page 106.
78. *Arkhiv Trotskogo*, Vol. 4, page 225.
79. Danilov, page 257.
80. M. Lewin, *The Making of the Soviet System*, London 1985, page 126.
81. Other sources give a similar picture: Ia. Osokina, *Sotsialisticheskoe stroitel'stvo v derevne i obshchina*, Moscow 1978, and *Izmeneniia*, page 72.
82. R.W. Davies, *The Socialist Offensive. The Collectivisation of Soviet Agriculture, 1929–1930*, London 1980, page 24.
83. Carr, *Socialism in One Country*, Vol. 2 page 335.
84. Quoted in T. Cox, *Peasants, Class and Capitalism*, Oxford 1986, page 199.
85. N. Bukharin, *Doklad na XXIII Chrezvychainoi Leningradskoi gubernskoi konferentsii VKP(b)*, Moscow-Leningrad 1926, page 14.
86. N. Bukharin, *Programme of the Communists (Bolsheviks)*, Moscow 1919, page 37.
87. *N.I. Bukharin: Selected Writings*, page 204.
88. V.I. Lenin, *Collected Works*, Vol. 33, Moscow, n.d., pages 474–5.
89. Baliazin, page 177.
90. Baliazin, page 283.
91. Unfortunately there is no opportunity to deal with Bukharin's theory of capitalist crisis here. For this see his *Imperialism and the Accumulation of Capital*, New York 1991. Other details can be obtained from Tarbuck and N.N. Kozlov, 'Bukharin, Eugen Varga, and the Comintern Debate on the Stabilization of Capitalism', in N.N. Kozlov and E.D. Weitz (eds), *Nikolai Ivanovich Bukharin: a Centenary Appraisal*, New York 1990, pages 29–58; J. Salter, 'N.I. Bukharin and the Market Question', in *History of Political Economy* Vol. 22, No. 1, 1990; J. Salter, 'On the Interpretation of Bukharin's Economic Ideas', in *Soviet Studies*, Vol. 44. No. 4, 1992.
92. *Pravda*, 30 June 1923.
93. *N.I. Bukharin: Selected Writings*, page 205.
94. G. Strel'tsov, '"Lenin's Political Testament" as Portrayed by Comrade Bukharin', in *Bolshevik*, 1929, No. 19, page 27.
95. *N.I. Bukharin: Selected Writings*, page 409.
96. Trotsky, *Challenge of the Left Opposition, 1926–1927*, Vol. 2 page 329.
97. Carr and Davies, Vol. 1, Part 1, page 155.
98. Lewin, *Russian Peasants and Soviet Power*, page 99.

Chapter 9: *The Market and Transition to Socialism*
1. N. Bukharin, *Ataka: sbornik teoriticheskikh statei*, Moscow 1924, page 69.
2. N. Bukharin, *The Politics and Economics of the Transition Period*, London 1979, page 57.
3. *Pravda*, 3 July 1926.

4. Bukharin to 1929 April plenum, in *Problemy teorii i praktiki sotsializmu*, Moscow 1989, page 281.
5. K. Marx, *Theories of Surplus Value*, Part 2, London 1969, page 397.
6. E. Preobrazhensky, *The New Economics*, Oxford 1965, pages 146–7.
7. Preobrazhensky, page 148.
8. Preobrazhensky, page 146.
9. *N.I. Bukharin: Selected Writings on the State and the Transition to Socialism*, ed. R.B. Day, Nottingham 1982, page 157.
10. Preobrazhensky, page 111.
11. However, Lenin had strongly rejected the analogy, writing 'Ugh!' when he met it in the *The Economics of the Transition Period*.
12. Preobrazhensky, pages 39–40.
13. *Arkhiv Trotskogo*, Vol. 1, Moscow 1990, page 225.
14. Quoted in introduction to Preobrazhensky, page xv.
15. Introduction to Preobrazhensky, page xv.
16. Marx, letter to Kugelmann (1868), in K. Marx and F. Engels, *Selected Correspondence 1846–1895*, London 1934, page 246.
17. *Pravda*, 3 July 1926.
18. K. Marx and F. Engels, *The German Ideology*, Part 1, London 1970, page 86.
19. *Pravda*, 3 July 1926.
20. K. Marx, *Grundrisse* [1858], Harmondsworth 1973, page 173.
21. L. Trotsky, *Third International after Lenin*, London 1974, page 208.
22. *Cinquième Congrès de l'Internationale Communiste, 17 Juin–8 Juillet 1924*, Paris 1924, page 168.
23. K. Marx, 'Critique of the Gotha Programme', in K. Marx, *The First International and After* [1875], Harmondsworth 1974, page 346.
24. See *Istoriki Sporiat: Trinadtsat' besed*, Moscow 1989, and N.I. Bukharin, *Chelovek, politik, uchenyi*, Moscow 1990.
25. L. Trotsky, *Challenge of the Left Opposition, 1923–1925*, New York 1975, page 301.
26. L. Trotsky *Challenge of the Left Opposition, 1926–1927*, New York 1980, page 336.
27. Quoted in I. Deutscher, *The Prophet Unarmed*, Oxford, 1959, page 314.
28. Deutscher, *The Prophet Unarmed*, page 314.
29. A. Nove, 'The Bukharin Alternative', in S. Bertolissi (ed.), *Bucharin: Tra Rivoluzione e riforme*, Rome 1982, page 45.
30. Trotsky, *Challenge of the Left Opposition, 1926–1927*, page 198.
31. Trotsky, *Writings, 1929*, New York 1975, page 48.

Chapter 10: The Comintern and Disaster: World Bukharinism
1. Memo from Swett in *Records of the [US] Department of State Relating to the Internal Affairs of the Soviet Union, 1910–1929*, Reel 112.
2. A. Ciliga, *The Russian Enigma* [1938], London 1979, page 4.

3. Details in E.H. Carr, *The Interregnum*, London 1954, page 186. Löwy interviewed two key German Communists – Brandler and Leviné-Meyer, neither of whom recalled Bukharin contributing to events. (A.G. Löwy, *Die Weltgeschichte ist das Weltgericht*, Vienna 1969, page 208). It should be noted that in later years, in order to divorce himself from Trotsky's criticisms of the Comintern in 1923 Bukharin pointedly referred to the period 1919–21 (that is, not beyond the March Action) as Europe's revolutionary period. See for example, N. Bukharin, *Kapitalisticheskaia stabilitizatsiia i proletarskaia revoliutsiia, Doklad VII rasshirennomu plenumu IKKI*, Moscow, n.d., page 5.
4. Bukharin, *Kapitalisticheskaia stabilitizatsiia*, page 50.
5. Bukharin, *Kapitalisticheskaia stabilitizatsiia*, pages 50–6.
6. N. Bukharin, *Building up Socialism*, London 1926, page 6.
7. *International Press Correspondence*, 6 January 1927.
8. L. Trotsky, *Third International after Lenin*, London 1974, page 16.
9. *Bericht über den IV Kongress der Kommunistischen Internationale, Petrograd-Moskau vom 5 November bis 5 Dezember 1922*, page 103.
10. *Cinquième Congrès de l'Internationale Communiste, 17 Juin–8 Juillet 1924*, Paris 1924, page 164.
11. *Cinquième Congrès de l'Internationale Communiste, 17 Juin–8 Juillet 1924*, page 93.
12. *XIII S'ezd RKP(b)*, 23–31 May 1924, page 316.
13. *VIII S'ezd, RKP(b)*, 18–23 March 1919, page 111.
14. *Kommunistische Internationale*, Vol. 14, 5 April 1927, page 664.
15. *Bericht über den IV Kongress der Kommunistischen Internationale, Petrograd-Moskau vom 5 November bis 5 Dezember 1922*, pages 103–4.
16. *Protokoll der Erweiterte EKKI*, 21 March–6 April 1925, Hamburg 1925, page 237.
17. V.I. Lenin, *Collected Works*, Vol. 33, Moscow, n.d., page 431.
18. N. Bukharin, 'The Significance of Agrarian-Peasant Problems', in *Bol'shevik* 1924, Nos. 19–20.
19. Bukharin, 'The Significance of Agrarian-Peasant Problems'.
20. Bukharin, 'The Significance of Agrarian-Peasant Problems'.
21. Bukharin, 'The Significance of Agrarian-Peasant Problems'.
22. Trotsky, *Third International after Lenin*, page 46.
23. *Pravda*, 6 December 1919.
24. *Pravda*, 26 May 1921.
25. See N.N. Kozlov and E.D. Weitz (eds), *Nikolai Ivanovich Bukharin: a Centenary Appraisal*, New York 1990, page 66.
26. Trotsky, *Third International after Lenin*, pages 63–4.
27. Bukharin drafted a number of programmes for the Comintern. The first, at the Fourth Congress in 1922, was remitted for discussion with other alternatives. The Fifth Congress set up a commission to prepare a new draft for the Sixth. This version was drafted by Bukharin and,

after various amendments, finally adopted. Much of Trotsky's *Third International after Lenin* is a detailed critique of it.
28. *International Press Correspondence* 1928, No. 30, page 550.
29. *Bol'shevik*, 1924, Nos. 5–6.
30. *Protokoll der Erweiterte EKKI*, 21 March–6 April 1925, Hamburg, 1925, page 228.
31. *International Press Correspondence*, 1928, No. 30, pages 560–1.
32. *International Trade Union Unity*, London 1925, page 18.
33. *Pravda*, 26 June 1926.
34. L. Trotsky, *Writings on Britain* [1926], London 1974, Vol. 2, pages 138–9.
35. Trotsky, *Writings on Britain*, Vol. 2, page 122.
36. Trotsky, *Writings on Britain*, Vol. 2, page 136.
37. N. Bukharin, 'Theses on the Lessons of the British General Strike', in *Communist Review*, Vol. 7, 1926, page 128.
38. Bukharin, 'Theses on the Lessons of the British General Strike', page 127.
39. Bukharin, 'Theses on the Lessons of the British General Strike', page 127.
40. *Pravda*, 26 June 1926.
41. *Pravda*, 26 June 1926.
42. *Pravda*, 26 June 1926.
43. Bukharin, 'Theses on the Lessons of the British General Strike', pages 131–2.
44. See H. Isaacs, *The Tragedy of the Chinese Revolution*, Stanford, Calif., 1951, page 58.
45. *Second Congress of the Communist International*, London 1977, Vol.1, pages 181–2.
46. Quoted in W. Chai (ed.). *Essential Works of Chinese Communism*, New York 1969, page 7.
47. Isaacs, page 63.
48. Isaacs, page 64.
49. Chai, pages 8–11.
50. *Kommunisticheskii internatsional i kitaiskaia revolutsiia*, Moscow 1986, page 67.
51. *International Press Correspondence*, 7 January 1926, quoted in N. Harris, *The Mandate of Heaven*, London 1978, page 4.
52. *International Press Correspondence*, 4 February 1927, Vol. 7, No. 14, page 281.
53. *International Press Correspondence*, 4 February 1927, Vol. 7, No. 14, page 283.
54. N. Bukharin, *Die Probleme der chinesischen Revolution*, Hamburg 1927, page 10.
55. Bukharin, *Die Probleme der chinesischen Revolution*, pages 9–11.
56. *Protokoll der Erweiterte EKKI*, 21 March–6 April 1925, page 228.

57. *Kommunisticheskii internatsional i kitaiskaia revolutsiia*, page 100.
58. Isaacs, page 117.
59. *International Press Correspondence*, 4 February 1927, No. 14, page 282.
60. *International Press Correspondence*, Vol. 7, No. 11.
61. *Pravda*, 21 January 1927.
62. L. Trotsky, *Problems of the Chinese Revolution* [1927], London 1969, pages 62–3.
63. Trotsky, *Third International after Lenin*, page 166.
64. *Kommunisticheskii internatsional i kitaiskaia revolutsiia*, page 76.
65. Isaacs, page 105.
66. Isaacs, page 98.
67. Quoted in Isaacs, page 103.
68. Isaacs, pages 105–6.
69. Isaacs, page 117.
70. *International Press Correspondence*, 3 February 1927, Vol. 7, No. 11.
71. 'Perspektiven der chinesischen Revolution', *Kommunistische Internationale*, Vol. 8, No. 14, 1927, pages 663–79.
72. 'Perspektiven der chinesischen Revolution', page 672.
73. Isaacs, page 111.
74. Isaacs, page 153.
75. *International Press Correspondence*, No. 14, Vol. 7, page 282.
76. *International Press Correspondence*, No. 14, Vol. 7, page 282.
77. Isaacs, page 118.
78. *Kommunistische Internationale*, Vol. 14, 5 April 1927.
79. Quoted in Isaacs, page 161.
80. Trotsky, *Problems of the Chinese Revolution*, page 98.
81. *China Press*, quoted in Isaacs, page 175.
82. Ch'en Tu-hsiu, quoted in Isaacs, page 163.
83. Quoted in Isaacs, pages 184–5.
84. Bukharin, *Die Probleme der chinesischen Revolution*, page 58.
85. *International Press Correspondence*, Vol. 7, No. 50, page 126.
86. I.E. Gorelov, *Nikolai Bukharin*, Moscow 1988, page 163.
87. Isaacs, pages 269–71.
88. *International Press Correspondence*, Vol. 7, No. 44.
89. *International Press Correspondence*, 14 July 1927, Vol. 7, No. 41, page 898.
90. Details in Isaacs, page 296.

Chapter 11: The NEP in Crisis
1. A. Ehrlich, *The Soviet Industrialization Debate, 1924–1928*, Cambridge, Mass., 1960, page 105.
2. A. Nove, *An Economic History of the USSR*, Harmondsworth 1969, page 117.
3. N. Bukharin, *V zashchitu proletarskoi diktatury*, Moscow 1928, page 158.

4. 'Platform of the Opposition', in L. Trotsky, *Challenge of the Left Opposition, 1928–1929*, New York 1981, pages 332–3.
5. Ehrlich, page 106.
6. Iu.P. Bokarev, *Sotsialiticheskaia promyshlennost' i melkoe krest'ianskoe khoziaistvo v SSSR v 20-e gody*, Moscow 1989, page 247.
7. N.I. Bukharin, *Put' k sotsializmu*, Novosibirsk 1990, page 216.
8. *Pravda*, 5 March 1926.
9. Party resolution quoted in *Pravda*, 5 January 1926.
10. V. Popov and N. Shmelev, 'At the Parting of the Ways. Was There an Alternative to the Stalinist Model of Development?' in Kh. Kobo (ed.), *Osmyslit' kul't Stalina*, Moscow 1989, pages 284–6.
11. Popov and Shmelev, 'At the Parting of the Ways', page 288.
12. While official statistics showed that the gross output of industry by 1927 was near prewar levels, as Trotsky pointed out per capita it was much lower. Trotsky, *Challenge of the Left Opposition, 1928–1929*, page 154.
13. A.F. Khavin, *U rulia industrii*, Moscow 1968, pages 20–2.
14. E.H. Carr and R.W. Davies, *Foundations of a Planned Economy*, London 1969, Vol. 1, Part 1, page 445.
15. *Pravda*, 21 January 1927.
16. Bukharin, *V zashchitu proletarskoi diktatury*, page 226.
17. *Pravda*, 11 October 1927.
18. *Pravda*, 18 October 1927.
19. 'Platform of the Opposition', in Trotsky, *Challenge of the Left Opposition, 1928–1929*, page 331.
20. Bukharin, *Put' k sotsializmu*, page 339.
21. R.W. Davies, *The Socialist Offensive. The Collectivisation of Soviet Agriculture, 1929–1930*, London 1980, page 28.
22. Details from Bokarev, page 247–50, Davies pages 28–9; and D. Atkinson, *The End of the Russian Land Commune, 1905–1930*, Stanford, Calif., 1983, page 266.
23. Bokarev, page 260.
24. Details from Bokarev, pages 258–60; Davies, page 30; Atkinson, pages 266–7, C. Bettelheim, *Class Struggles in the USSR, Second Period, 1923–30*, Hassocks 1973, page 96.
25. M. Reiman, *The Birth of Stalinism*, London 1987, pages 43–4.
26. *Pravda*, 12 June 1927.
27. Reiman, pages 12–13.
28. Details in N.I. Bukharin, *Uroki Khlebozagotovok, Shakhtinskogo dela i zadachi Partii*, Moscow 1928, pages 15–16.
29. Davies, page 11.
30. Atkinson, page 267.
31. M. Lewin, *The Making of the Soviet System*, London 1985, pages 92–3.
32. Davies, page 26.

33. 'Platform of the Opposition', in Trotsky, *Challenge of the Left Opposition, 1928–1929*, page 330.
34. K. Marx, *Capital*, Vol. 1, London 1954, page 714.
35. *Pravda*, 18 October 1927.
36. Trotsky, *Challenge of the Left Opposition, 1928–1929*, page 337.
37. Bukharin, *Put' k sotsializmu*, pages 160–1.
38. *Pravda*, 13 April 1926.
39. D. Filtzer, *Soviet Workers and Stalinist Industrialization*, London 1986, page 26.
40. *Pravda*, 13 April 1926.
41. *Pravda*, 28 May 1926.
42. M. Dobb, *Soviet Economic Development since 1917*, New York 1966, page 189.
43. Quoted in H. Kuromiya, *Stalin's Industrial Revolution*, Cambridge 1990, page 98.
44. *Oktiabr*, 29 April 1929.
45. Carr and Davies, Vol. 1, Part 2, pages 488–92.
46. Felix Dzerzhinskii, head of the Supreme Council of National Economy, quoted in a 'Confidential Report' dated 20 January 1925, in *Records of the [US] Department of State Relating to the Internal Affairs of the Soviet Union, 1910–1929*, Reel 112.
47. *Pravda*, 25 May 1926.
48. *Pravda*, 25 May 1926.
49. *Direktivy KPSS i Sovetskogo pravitel'stva po khoziaistvennym voprosam*, Moscow 1957, Vol. 1, page 672.
50. 'Platform of the Opposition', in Trotsky, *Challenge of the Left Opposition, 1928–1929*, page 311.
51. Decree of Council of People's Commissars, Central Committee and Central Control Committee of the Communist Party on 'The Successes and Insufficiencies of the Campaign for a Regime of Economy', 16 August 1926, in *Bor'ba KPSS za sotsialisticheskuiu industrializatsiiu strany i podgotovku sploshnoi kollektivizatsii sel'skogo khoziaistva, 1926–1929, Dokumenti i materialy*, Moscow 1960, page 154.
52. *Pravda*, 2 February 1927, and Bukharin, *Put' k sotsializmu*, page 183.
53. Bukharin, *Put' k sotsializmu*, page 183
54. Bukharin, *Put' k sotsializmu*, page 217.
55. Bukharin, *Put' k sotsializmu*, page 219.
56. 'Platform of the Opposition' in Trotsky, *Challenge of the Left Opposition, 1928–1929*, pages 311–12.
57. Carr and Davies, Vol. 1, Part 1, page 504.
58. The figures for wage levels in the USSR at this time are highly suspect because it was common for wages to be in serious arrears and because statistics were based on workers buying goods at official prices. Very often the goods they needed were not available and had to be purchased

on the more expensive black market. Carr and Davies, Vol. 1, Part 2, page 507.
59. Carr and Davies, Vol. 1, Part 2, page 507.
60. One was between agricultural and industrial capital in Britain from the 1780s until the abolition of the Corn Laws in 1846. Another was shown in the US civil war, where northern industrial capital confronted slave plantation capitalists in the south.
61. Bukharin, *Put' k sotsializmu*, page 227.
62. M. Lewin, *Russian Peasants and Soviet Power*, London 1968, page 204.
63. *Pravda*, 18 October 1927.
64. Excerpt from speech in Appendix to Reiman, page 136.
65. Reiman, page 102.
66. Bukharin, *Put' k sotsializmu*, page 299.
67. Bukharin, *Put' k sotsializmu*, page 300.
68. Bukharin, *Put' k sotsializmu*, page 315.

Chapter 12: Was Bukharin the Alternative to Stalin?

1. *Istoriki sporiat: Trinadtsat' besed*, Moscow 1989, page 255.
2. *Istoriki sporiat*, page 270.
3. G.A. Bordyugov and V.A. Kozlov, 'Man in History; History in Man. Nikolai Bukharin, Episodes of a Political Biography', in *Kommunist*, September 1988, page 105. Recent political journals have carried articles bearing titles like 'The Turning Point of 1929 and the Bukharin Alternative', and 'The Choice of History and the History of Alternatives (Bukharin Versus Trotsky)'.
4. S. Cohen, *Bukharin and the Bolshevik Revolution*, Oxford 1971, page 277.
5. M. Lewin, *Political Undercurrents in Soviet Economic Debates*, Princeton, NJ, 1974, page 69.
6. L. Trotsky *Challenge of the Left Opposition, 1928–1929*, New York 1981, page 184.
7. Quoted in M. Lewin, *Russian Peasants and Soviet Power*, London 1968, pages 202–3.
8. The letter has not been published but its contents can be gleaned from Stalin's reply to it in J.V. Stalin, *Works*, Vol. 11, Moscow 1953, pages 121–32.
9. Stalin, *Works*, Vol. 11, page 179.
10. Cohen, page 286.
11. Trotsky Archive, deposited at Harvard University, Document T 1835, page 3.
12. Trotsky Archive, Harvard, Document T 1901, page 2.
13. Trotsky Archive, Harvard, Document T 1901, pages 5–6.
14. Trotsky Archive, Harvard, Document T 1901, page 9.

15. N. Bukharin, *Problemy teorii i praktiki sotsializmu*, Moscow 1989, page 298.
16. Trotsky Archive, Harvard, Document T 1901, page 9.
17. Quoted in H. Kuromiya, *Stalin's Industrial Revolution*, Cambridge 1990, page 70.
18. Bukharin, *Problemy teorii i praktiki sotsializmu*, page 291.
19. Trotsky Archive, Harvard, Document T 1901, page 8.
20. N.I. Bukharin, *Put' k sotsializmu* Novosibirsk 1990, page 400.
21. Bukharin, *Problemy teorii i praktiki sotsializmu*, page 273.
22. *N.I. Bukharin: Selected Writings on the State and the Transition to Socialism*, ed. R.B. Day, Nottingham 1982, pages 309–11.
23. Bukharin, *Problemy teorii i praktiki sotsializmu*, page 273.
24. O. Latsis, *Vyiti iz kvadrate*, Moscow 1989, page 250.
25. *N.I. Bukharin: Selected Writings*, page 307.
26. *N.I. Bukharin: Selected Writings*, page 306.
27. *N.I. Bukharin: Selected Writings*, page 318.
28. *N.I. Bukharin: Selected Writings*, page 319.
29. *N.I. Bukharin: Selected Writings*, page 324.
30. N. Bukharin, *Put' k Sotsializmu v Rossii*, ed. S. Heitman, New York 1967, page 403.
31. Quoted in Trotsky, *Challenge of the Left Opposition, 1928–1929*, page 379.
32. Kuromiya, page 49.
33. N. Bukharin, 'Nekotorie problemy sovremennogo kapitalizma i teoretikov burzhuazii' in *Organizovannyi kapitalizm; diskussia v Komakademii*, Moscow 1930, page 174.
34. L. Trotsky, *Writings, 1929*, New York 1975, page 365.
35. Trotsky, *Writings, 1929*, page 115.
36. Bukharin, *Problemy teorii i praktiki sotsializmu*, pages 302–3.
37. Trotsky, *Writings, 1929*, pages 403 and 86.
38. Trotsky, *Writings, 1929*, page 183.
39. Quoted in L. Shapiro, *The Communist Party of the Soviet Union*, London 1960, page 364.
40. Bukharin, *Put' k sotsializmu*, page 373.
41. Trotsky, *Writings, 1929*, page 402.
42. Trotsky, *Writings, 1930*, page 136.
43. *N.I. Bukharin: Selected Writings*, page 316.
44. Bukharin, *Put' k sotsializmu*, page 393.
45. Bukharin, *Put' k sotsializmu*, page 371.
46. The proportion of production of means of production to industry as a whole was 33.3 per cent in 1913 and 39.3 per cent in 1928. *Izmeneniia sotsial'noi struktury Sovetskogo obshchestva*, Moscow 1979, page 36.
47. Quoted in R.V. Daniels, *Conscience of the Revolution: Communist Opposition in Russia*, Cambridge 1960, page 351.

48. Though he was wrong to include Uglanov. Daniels, page 323, and Trotsky, *Challenge of the Left Opposition, 1926–1927*, New York 1980, page 116.
49. Trotsky, *Writings, 1929*, page 211.
50. Trotsky, *Challenge of the Left Opposition, 1928–1929*, page 98.
51. Trotsky, *Challenge of the Left Opposition, 1928–1929*, page 99.
52. Trotsky, *Writings, 1929*, page 48.
53. Trotsky, *Challenge of the Left Opposition, 1928–1929*, page 138.
54. Quoted in R. Medvedev, *O Staline i Stalinizme*, Moscow 1990, page 153.
55. Bukharin, *Problemy teorii i praktiki sotsializmu*, page 293.
56. Quoted in Kuromiya, page 8.
57. Quoted in Daniels, page 348.
58. A. Ehrlich, *The Soviet Indistrialization Debate, 1924–1928*, Cambridge, Mass., 1960, page 173.
59. Ehrlich, pages 173–4.
60. Trotsky, *Challenge of the Left Opposition, 1928–1929*, page 296.
61. Trotsky, *Challenge of the Left Opposition, 1928–1929*, page 318.
62. Bukharin, *Put' k sotsializmu*, page 380.
63. Bukharin, *Put' k sotsializmu*, page 380.
64. Bukharin, *Put' k sotsializmu*, page 408.
65. Bukharin, *Put' k Sotsializmu v Rossii*, ed. Heitman, page 407.
66. Bukharin, *Put' k Sotsializmu v Rossii*, ed. Heitman, pages 412, 413 and 414.
67. *N.I. Bukharin: Selected Writings*, pages 339 and 338.
68. *N.I. Bukharin: Selected Writings*, pages 346–7.
69. Details in M. Reiman, *The Birth of Stalinism*, London 1987, pages 57–66.
70. N. Bukharin, 'The Lessons of the Grain Collection Campaign, the Shakhty Case and the Tasks of the Party', in Bukharin, *Put' k sotsializmu*, pages 261–94. It should be said that others were taken in by the elaborate staging of the trial, Trotsky included.
71. Trotsky, *Challenge of the Left Opposition, 1928–1929*, page 379.
72. Lewin, *Political Undercurrents in Soviet Economic Debates*, page xi.
73. See *Sotsialisticheskii Vestnik*, 8 March 1929, and quote from Boguslavsky in C. Merridale, 'The Reluctant Opposition: the Right "Deviation" in Moscow, 1928', in *Soviet Studies*, 1989, No. 3, pages 395–6.
74. N. Shimotomai, 'Defeat of the Right Opposition in Moscow Party Organization: 1928', in *Japanese, Slavic and East European Studies*, Vol.4, 1983, page 16.
75. A. Avtorkhanov, *Stalin and the Soviet Communist Party*, London 1959, page 115.
76. Trotsky, *Challenge of the Left Opposition, 1928–1929*, page 381, and *Third International after Lenin*, London 1974, page 222.

77. This was confided to Angelo Tasca by Bukharin himself in a clandestine meeting in January 1929 and recorded in Tasca's diary. 'Incontro tra Bucharin, Humbert-Droz e Tasca', in *Annali Feltrinelli*, page 658.
78. See Reiman, pages 95–100.
79. Interview with Paul Scheefer, in *Records of the [US] Department of State Relating to the Internal Affairs of the Soviet Union, 1910–1929*, Reel 110.
80. Daniels, page 362.
81. See *Pravda*, 21 and 24 August 1929.
82. Bukharin, *Problemy teorii i praktiki sotsializmu*, pages 300–1.
83. Bukharin, *Problemy teorii i praktiki sotsializmu*, page 299.
84. F.M. Vaganov, *Pravyi uklon v VKP(b) i ego razgrom (1928–1930)*, Moscow 1970, page 29.
85. Vaganov, page 150.
86. Vaganov, page 5.
87. A. Larina, 'Bukharina', *Nezabyvaemoe*, Moscow 1989, page 88.
88. Trotsky, *Challenge of the Left Opposition, 1928–1929*, page 379.
89. Bukharin, *Problemy teorii i praktiki sotsializmu*, and 'Incontro tra Bucharin, Humbert-Droz e Tasca', page 658.
90. *Borba KPSS sotsialisticheskuiu industrializatsuiu strany i podgotovku sploshnoi kollektivizatsii sel'skogo khoziaistva, 1926–1929 gody*, Moscow 1960, page 310.
91. E.D. Weitz, 'Bukharin and Bukharinism in the Comintern', in N.N. Kozlov and E.D. Weitz (eds), *Nikolai Ivanovich Bukharin. A Centenary Appraisal*, New York 1990, page 66.
92. S. Wolikow, in S. Bertolissi, *Bucharin: Tra Rivoluzione e riforme*, Rome 1982, page 83.
93. Bukharin, *Problemy teorii i praktiki sotsializmu*, page 241.
94. Cohen, page 293.
95. Trotsky, *Challenge of the Left Opposition, 1928–1929*, page 379.
96. 'Incontro tra Bucharin, Humbert-Droz e Tasca', page 657.
97. Quoted in Daniels, page 335. The classic discussion of this complicated problem is to be found in T. Draper, 'The Strange Case of the Comintern', in *Survey* 18:3 (1972). See also Kozlov and Weitz.
98. Daniels, page 335.
99. Stalin, *Works*, Vol. 11, page 270.
100. Stalin, *Works*, Vol. 11, pages 234 and 245.
101. Trotsky, *Writings, 1929*, page 68.
102. Stalin, *Works*, Vol. 11, page 332.
103. The wisdom of providing Stalin with such damaging material is doubtful, but it was logical given the view that Bukharin represented a greater danger than Stalin.
104. Trotsky, *Challenge of the Left Opposition, 1928–1929*, page 67.

105. O.B. Nebogin and A.G. Samorodov, 'Discussions in the Moscow Party Organisation in the Years 1928–1929', in *Kommunist*, No. 6, 1990, page 71.
106. Trotsky Archive, Harvard, Document T 2852.
107. *Moskovskii Bolshevikii v borbe s pravym i levym' opportunizmom*, Moscow 1969, page 253, mentions a district meeting of five to six in one case and 13 in another.
108. E.H. Carr and R.W. Davies, *Foundations of a Planned Economy*, London 1969, Vol. 2, page 61.
109. Carr and Davies, Vol. 2, pages 62–3.
110. Quoted in I. Deutscher, *Soviet Trade Unions*, London 1950, pages 77–8.
111. *Borba KPSS sotsialisticheskuiu industrializatsuiu strany i podgotovku sploshnoi kollektivizatsii sel'skogo khoziaistva, 1926–1929 gody*, page 311. He used the same phrase in conversation with Tasca, 'Incontro tra Bucharin, Humbert-Droz e Tasca', page 656.
112. Quoted in N.I. Bukharin, *Chelovek, politik, uchenyi*, Moscow 1990, page 115.
113. Quoted in Bukharin, *Chelovek, politik, uchenyi*, page 113.
114. Quoted in Vaganov, page 118.
115. Reiman, pages 27–8.
116. Shimotomai, page 32. There is also a mention of this same incident in Vaganov, page 242.
117. A. Ciliga, *The Russian Enigma* [1938], London 1979, page 166.
118. Bukharin, *Problemy teorii i praktiki sotsializmu*, page 253.
119. Bukharin, *Put' k sotsializmu*, pages 253–4.
120. *Pravda* and *Izvestiia*, 26 November 1929.
121. Accounts of these meetings are contained in 'An Interview with Boris Nikolaevsky' and 'Letter of an Old Bolshevik' in B. Nikolaevsky, *Power and the Soviet Elite*, Ann Arbor, Mich. 1975, and L. Dan, 'Bukharin on Stalin', in *Novyi Zhurnal*, No. 75, 1964, pages 176–84. For discussions on the authenticity of these documents see R. Medvedev, *Nikolai Bukharin: the Last Years*, New York, 1980, pages 116–19, Larina, pages 250–7 and J.A. Getty, *Origins of the Great Purges*, Cambridge 1985, pages 215–17.
122. Dan, page 182.
123. Medvedev, *Nikolai Bukharin: the Last Years*, page 100.
124. N. Bukharin, 'Marx's Teaching and its Historical Importance', in R. Fox (ed.), *Marxism and Modern Thought*, London 1935, page 1.
125. *Etiudy*, Moscow 1932.
126. See C. Rakovsky, 'The Five Year Plan in Crisis', in *Critique*, Pamphlet Series, No. 13, Glasgow 1981.
127. Shapiro, page 384.
128. Kuromiya, page 38.

129. Kuromiya, page 46.
130. *Profsouizy Moskvy: ocherki istorii*, Moscow 1975, page 199.
131. Trotsky, *Writings, 1930*, page 79.
132. Cohen, page 351.
133. Kh. Kobo (ed.), *Osmyslit' Kul't Stalina*, Moscow 1989, pages 621–3.
134. The full text is in R. Medvedev, *Let History Judge*, London 1976, pages 183–4.
135. Larina, page 263.
136. Quoted in Bukharin, *Chelovek, politik, uchenyi*, pages 155–6.
137. Quoted in Bordyugov and Kozlov, page 105.
138. Quoted in Trotsky, *Writings, 1930*, page 200.
139. Bertolissi, page 180.
140. *XVII S'ezd VKP(b)*, 26 January–10 February 1934, Moscow 1934, page 129.
141. G. Katkov, *The Trial of Bukharin*, New York, 1969, page 192.
142. Letter No. 1 to F. Dzerzhinsky [1924], in *Voprosy Istorii KPSS*, November 1988, page 43.
143. Quoted in Medvedev, *Nikolai Bukharin: the Last Years*, pages 97–8.
144. Letters in *Voprosy Istorii KPSS* [1933], November 1988, pages 48–9.
145. *Report of the Court Proceedings in the Case of the Anti-Soviet 'Bloc of Rights and Trotskyites'*, Moscow 1938, page 5.
146. *Report*, page 370.
147. *Report*, page 379.
148. *Report*, page 423.
149. Medvedev, *Let History Judge*, pages 183–4.

Index

1905 revolution, 20

accumulation, 133, 139, 142–3, 159, 167, 210, 227, 230, 234, 242
Adler, F, 18
agrarian-cooperative socialism, 96
agricultural labourers, 145, 150
agricultural tax, 145
agriculture, 20, 98, 132–3, 136, 202, 204, 207, 214ff, 222
anarchism, 38, 127
Anglo-Russian Trade Union Committee, 182, 184–5, 190
Antonov rebellion, 78
army, 22, 24, 32, 34–5, 45–6, 53, 55, 68, 80, 87, 104, 236
Austria, 13, 18, 35
Avtorkhanov, A, 236

base and superstructure, 12–13, 44, 64–5, 77
Baugy Group, 15
Bavaria, 54
Bernstein, E, 123
Bogdanov, A, 66–8, 76
Böhm-Bawerk, 4
Bolshevik party, 4, 23, 25, 27, 35, 37, 38, 48, 72, 91, 101, 102, 113, 143, 169, 193
  7th Congress, 21
  8th Congress, 38, 52
  9th Congress, 47, 49
  10th Congress, 61, 78
  11th Congress, 71, 81, 85, 89, 103
  12th Congress, 111, 130, 132, 147

Bolshevik party *continued*
  13th Congress, 112
  14th Congress, 114, 124, 200, 219
  15th Congress, 115, 200, 219
  17th Congress, 248
  Byrne Conference (1915), 15–16
  11th Conference, 81, 127
  14th Party Conference, 145
  15th Conference, 115, 141
  party democracy, 112, 128, 199, 226
  party leadership, 39, 56, 91, 113
  party programme, 23, 106
Borodin, M, 187, 192
Brest-Litovsk treaty, 22–5, 27, 32, 34, 36, 45, 47, 54, 61, 113, 171, 181
Britain, 13, 108, 138, 172, 178, 206
British General Strike, 171, 181–4
'Buffer Platform', 50–1
Bukharin, N,
  ABC of Communism, 14, 27, 106, 156
  Bourgeois Revolution and Proletarian Revolution, 71
  Economic Theory of the Leisure Class, 4
  Economics of the Transition Period, 39, 41–2, 45–6, 48, 59, 66, 68, 80, 113, 123, 159, 162, 224
  Down with Factionalism, 112–14, 121
  Draft Programme for the Sixth Comintern Congress, 180

Bukharin, N *continued*
  From the Overthrow of Tsarism to
    the Fall of the Bourgeoisie, 121
  Historical Materialism, 58, 60, 62,
    65–8, 75, 222
  late articles, 245
  Imperialism and World Economy, 4,
    7–12, 14, 28, 73, 118
  'Lenin's Political Testament', 85,
    111, 223, 232, 234, 240
  *The New Course of Economic
    Policy*, 80, 94
  'Notes of an Economist', 222,
    239
  'Organised Economic Disorder',
    234
  'Perspectives for the Chinese
    Revolution', 192, 194
  'The Present Period and the Basis
    of our Policies', 122–3
  Programme of the Communists, 21,
    27, 104–5, 107
  'Proletarian revolution and
    culture', 72, 76, 110, 126
  'The Russian Revolution and its
    Destiny', 20
  'To a Future Generation of Party
    Leaders', 247
  Speech to Conference of
    Worker/Peasant Correspon-
    dents, 226–7
  'Towards a theory of the Imperi-
    alist State', 10
  accuses Trotsky of being a
    'super-industrialiser', 139
  capitulates to Stalin, 237, 244
  and Chinese revolution, 190,
    193, 197
  on collectivisation, 151, 216
  critique of bureaucratism, 109,
    126ff, 223, 229, 233, 235
  on culture, 126ff
  and degeneration of revolution,
    199, 230, 233

Bukharin, N *continued*
  on 'democratic dictatorship', 189
  denies bloc with Trotsky, 1929,
    225
  denies connection with Riutin,
    247
  disagrees with Lenin on state
    capitalism, 23, 30, 106
  dismisses role of working class on
    world scale, 178, 188
  economic drain caused by inef-
    fective administration, 127
  expected to back Trotsky in
    1923 faction fight, 111
  ideologically disarms working
    class, 169
  on law of value, 161
  as Marxist theorist, 66–7, 76ff,
    166
  meetings with Kamenev, 238,
    240
  on 'national types of socialism',
    177, 185
  on the NEP, 79ff, 94, 121, 229
  and new programme of 1928,
    210ff
  on offensive against the kulaks,
    209, 215–6, 232
  on permanent revolution, 20,
    118
  and the peasantry, 104ff, 120
  on planning, 136–8, 160, 204,
    234
  political rehabilitation of, 1988,
    251
  as populariser of Marxism, 27
  and 'primitive socialist accumula-
    tion', 158–9, 161
  proposes a shorter working day,
    14
  on rationalisation, 212
  on regime of economy, 211
  relations with Stalin, 114, 194,
    199, 214, 227

Index

Bukharin, N *continued*
  sacked from leading positions, 244
  and scissors crisis, 133
  on socialism in one country, 121ff, 124
  on Stalin's extraordinary measures, 216
  supports rich peasants' cause, 144, 147
  on tempo of industrialisation, 136, 140, 151, 203–4, 209
  and 'theory of the offensive', 53, 56, 179
  and transition to socialism, 165
  on united front, 175
  and worker-peasant alliance, 104
Bukharinism, 48, 94, 111, 129, 149, 171, 196, 218, 249, 251
bureaucracy, 38, 70, 73–6, 91–2, 96, 124, 126, 127–9, 148, 167–9, 182, 199, 203–4, 211, 228–9, 214, 216, 221, 231–2, 243
bureaucratically deformed state, 50, 70, 122, 210, 213
bureaucratism, 74, 112, 126

Canton, 191, 194, 197
capitalism, 5–6, 30, 38, 40–1, 42
Carr, E H, 90, 110, 114, 141, 155
Central Committee (Bolsheviks), 18, 23, 25–6, 32, 34, 48, 61, 111, 201, 215, 219, 222, 231, 236–8, 240–3, 245–6, 251
centrism, 228–9
Chaianov A, 150, 153
Cheka, 38
Ch'en Tu-hsiu, 187
Chiang Kai-shek, l91–4, 196–8, 206
China, 8, 172, 175–6, 187, 189–90, 198, 239
Chinese Communist Party (CCP), 186–8. 190–4, 196–97
Chinese revolution, 119, 171–2, 185ff, 206

Ciliga A, 146, 243
civil war, 23, 25, 31–4, 38, 42, 44, 46–7, 49, 53, 70, 78, 84, 90–1, 96, 101, 169
Clausewitz, K von, 77
Cliff T, 15, 44
Cohen S, 4–5, 8, 10–11, 27, 40, 58, 65, 73, 171, 218–19, 239, 246
collectivisation, 4, 32, 98, 100, 105, 109, 139, 161, 208–9, 215–16, 221, 230, 237, 246–7
colonies, 52, 178, 180
Comintern, 8, 52, 54, 56, 63, 66, 124, 147, 171–3, 180, 184–6, 188, 192, 195, 197, 201, 239, 242, 249
  1st Congress, 52
  3rd Comintern Congress, 45,
  4th Comintern Congress, 81, 87, 175, 181, 187
  5th Comintern Congress, 32, 165, 175–6, 182
  Executive Committee of the Communist International (ECCI), 185
  6th ECCI Plenum, 188
  7th ECCI Plenum in December 1926, 190
  Comintern programme, 181, 238
Communist Party of Great Britain, 182–5
Conquest, R, 34
Constituent Assembly, 18–19, 119
cooperation, 86, 151–5
cooperative-agrarian socialism, 98
'costs of revolution', 41–2
Council for Labour and Defence, 47
Council for National Economy, 35, 215
culture, 58, 66–76, 124, 153, 212, 223

Dan, F, 245
Daniel, R V, 236
Danilov, V P, 149
Davies, R W, 141, 205, 207
declassing of proletariat, 37, 44, 70, 78, 91
degeneration of revolution, 5, 27, 32, 38, 44, 57, 66, 72–5, 77, 88, 95, 129, 131, 151, 160, 216, 227
democratic centralism, 73–4, 92, 112–13, 121
democratic dictatorship, 117–20, 189–90
determinism, 59–61, 64–5, 67
Deutscher, I, 168
dialectics, 48, 58–63, 65–6, 74, 178
Dobb, M, 89

Eastman, M, 113
Ehrlich, A, 232
Engels, F, 25, 61, 98, 101, 138
'Enrich yourselves', 94, 130, 139, 144, 170, 219
equilibrium, 43, 62–5, 222, 226

famine, 34, 79
feudalism, 20, 72
Feuerbach, L, 60
First International, 53
First Soviet Congress, 23
First World War, 4, 13, 48
five year plans, 109, 168, 202, 219, 246–7
forced industrialisation, 4, 32, 139, 208
France, 19, 53, 174
Frumkin, M I, 219

General Strike, 172, 183–5, 185
Georgia, 110, 143, 145–6
Germany, 13-14, 22–5, 34, 52, 54, 56, 61, 79, 121, 171–3, 177, 238

German Social Democracy, 123, 245
goods famine, 205
Gorbachev, M, 5
Gorelov, I E, 171
Gorky, M, 99
GPU, 220, 236, 249–50
Gramsci, A, 59, 60–1, 74–5, 245
'growing into socialism', 154, 199, 214
Guizot, F P G, 144–5

Hayes, M, 20
Hegel, G W F, 63
Hilferding, R, 5
Hitler, A, 238, 248
Hobson, J A, 5
Hong Kong, 187
Hungary, 54–5, 79

imperialism, 5, 13–15, 17, 21–2, 53, 66, 106, 173, 180–1
imperialist state, 9–10, 13–14
industrialisation, 110, 140, 142, 159, 200–1, 205, 208, 211–12, 214, 221, 226, 230, 237, 242
  snail's pace progress of, 57, 139, 153, 199–200, 205
industry, 86–8, 90, 110, 132–4, 132, 158, 199–203
internationalism, 15, 52, 57, 122, 173, 177, 188
investment plans, 200, 204, 206, 222
Isaac, H, 187, 194
Izvestiia, 244–5

Joffe, A, 187

Kaganovich, L, 219, 228, 241
Kagarlitsky, B, 138
Kalinin, M, 145, 236
Kamenev, L, 18, 111, 124, 147–8, 217, 223, 235, 238–40, 242, 249–50

Index

Kautsky, K, 4, 5, 7, 10, 39, 59–60, 65
Kirov, S, 228, 249
Kommunist, 28
Korsch, K, 59–60
Kritsman, L, 33, 36, 150
Kronstadt, 52, 55, 61, 78, 242–3
Krupskaia, N, 10, 70, 85, 144
Khrushchev, N, 224
Kuibyshev, V, 215, 227, 231
kulaks, 100, 102, 142–3, 147–51, 154, 208, 215–16, 218, 220–22, 232
Kun, B, 55
Kuomintang (KMT), 186–8, 190–91, 193–6

labour aristocracy, 180
land distribution, 100, 105, 119, 152
Larina, A, 145, 238, 251
law of labour expenditure, 162–3
law of primitive socialist accumulation, 156–7, 160–1, 164
law of uneven development, 174
law of value, 156–7, 162–4
leasing of land, 146
Left Communism, 18, 22–3, 25–27, 29, 31, 34, 44, 47, 68, 74–5, 83, 126, 235
Left Communist Theses, 28, 31, 167
Left Opposition, 4, 6, 57, 109, 111, 115, 129, 133, 142–3, 154, 160, 168, 172, 175–6, 198, 204, 209, 212–13, 218, 225, 228–9, 235, 249
  for industrialisation, 208
  on collectivisation, 209
  destroyed 1927, 242
  Opposition Platform, 130, 142, 200, 204, 210, 213
Lenin, V I, 4, 6, 8, 10, 15–16, 21–4, 26–7, 29, 31, 37, 39, 43, 46–52, 55, 57–8, 61, 63, 66, 68, 71, 73, 77–8, 81, 83–8, 94, 102–6, 111, 113, 116–18, 120, 127, 148, 152–4, 169, 177, 189, 197, 223, 235, 251
  'On Co-operation', 85–6, 124, 152
  April Theses, 18, 119
  Imperialism the Highest stage of Capitalism, 8
  "*Left-wing*" *childishness and the petty-bourgeois mentality*, 27
  notes on *The Economics of the Transition Period*, 41
  The State and Revolution, 10
  The Tax in Kind, 83
  'Testament', 58
  accuses Bukharin of representing profiteers and petty bourgeoisie, 110
  on cooperatives, 152, 154
  against freeing foreign trade, 110
  on national liberation, 176
  and the NEP, 82ff
  and the peasantry, 102ff
  and permanent revolution, 119
  'against socialism in one country', 124
  on 'state capitalism under the dictatorship of the proletariat', 29
  on uneven capitalist development, 174
  on withering away of state, 223
Leningrad, 243
Leon, M, 4, 127, 143, 149, 155, 218
Liebknecht, K, 54
Lodestone group, 238
Lukacs, G, 59, 65
Luxemburg, R, 4, 6, 11, 15, 54, 101

management of industry, 37, 46, 50, 71, 90

'March Action', 52, 56, 171
market, 57, 86, 889, 134–5, 137–8, 104, 156, 162–4, 199, 230–1, 234
market socialism, 5, 19, 40, 161, 234
Marx, K, 5, S, 10–12, 25, 60–4, 68–9, 77, 97, 159, 122, 161–2, 169, 180
  Communist Manifesto; 53, 105, 172
  Capital, 64
  on commodity production, 107
  on the peasantry, 96ff
  on planning, 208
  Provisional Rules of First International, 53
  theory of the state, 10
  on transition period, 163, 166
Marxism, 5, 27, 59, 60, 62–3, 65–6, 131, 185, 245
Medvedev, R, 245
Menshevism 18, 38, 54, 108, 113, 115, 117–19, 190
middle peasantry, 99, 102, 105–6, 142, 142, 144, 149–51, 214
militarisation of labour, 47–8, 53, 113
mir, 97–9
monopolistic degeneration, 135–36, 164, 224, 234
Moscow, 18, 27, 35, 71, 78, 90 144, 147, 221, 236, 240–1, 243

Narodism, 97, 153
national question, 4, 15, 52, 54, 176, 189
nationalisation, 10, 28, 31, :35, 37, 126
New Economic Policy, 31, 47, 56–7, 59, 64, 70–1, 74, 78–9, 81–2, 84, 86, 88–92, 104, 110 128, 134, 156, 168, 172, 202, 221
  and the class balance, 88, 169

New Economic Policy *continued*
  and pluralism, 92
  as strategic retreat, 82, 84, 86, 93, 95–6
  second wind, 145, 147
  accorded universal status, 177
Nepmen, 92, 133, 210, 214
New Opposition, 124
new programme of 1928, 218, 221, 224, 231
Nogin, V, 35
Northern Expedition (China), 193, 197
Nove, A, 4, 161, 168
Novy Mir, 18

Ordzhonikidze, S, 250
Ossinskii, N, 47

parliamentarism, 19, 40
peasantry, 8, 19–21, 26, 33–4, 36, 47, 71, 78–9, 84–6, 90, 95–7, 101–2, 106–7, 110, 128, 132–3, 138, 153–4, 178, 207, 231, 235
  differentiation, 97, 99–100, 104, 146, 148, 150, 153, 214, 231
  unable to act as autonomous force, 148, 242
permanent revolution, 116–17, 119, 178, 188, 195
Petrograd, 25, 27, 30, 33, 70
petty-bourgeoisie, 21, 28, 83–4
Piatakov, Iu, 250
Pilsudski, J, 54, 84, 195
planning, 28, 41, 87, 134–5, 137, 164, 199, 209
'Platform of the Ten', 49, 51
Poland, 15, 54–5, 206
Politburo, 47, 49, 110–11, 217, 219, 225, 236–8, 240, 242–3, 247
poor peasants, 22, 97, 100, 102, 108, 130, 140, 142, 149–150, 208

Pravda, 4, 51, 55, 66, 68–9, 79, 111–12, 143, 171, 196, 201, 210–12, 222, 236, 241, 243–5, 252
Preobrazhensky, E, 14, 27, 156–9, 161, 163, 165, 168, 199, 229, 242
prices, 133–4, 222 (*see also* scissors crisis)
private trade, 133, 147
Proletkult, 68
Provisional Government, 20, 189
pumping over of agricultural resources, 219, 221

Radek, K, 27, 55, 187, 190, 229, 242, 250
Rakovsky, C, 115, 246, 250
rationalisation, 212–13, 216, 227
red imperialism, 52–4
Red Professors, 236, 241
regime of economy, 210, 212–13, 227
Reiman, M, 206, 215, 229
requisitioning, 34, 78, 104
restoration period, 134, 199
revolutionary war, 23, 35, 62
rich peasants, 21, 57, 92, 94, 97, 99, 140, 143, 159, 203 (*see also* kulaks)
right-wing Bolshevism 27, 58, 106, 172, 218, 221–2, 226, 228–30, 236–7, 239–43, 247
Riutin, M, 247–8
Rosmer, A, 66
rural Soviets, 143, 151
Russian revolution, theories of, 115ff
Rykov, A, 35, 93, 219, 221, 228, 231, 236, 238, 241, 243, 246–7, 250

scissors crisis, 131–134, 137, 143, 158, 205

Second International, 4–5, 10, 17, 39, 65, 116
Serge, V, 79, 86, 91, 114
Shakhty case, 234
Shanghai, 194, 196
Shliapnikov, A, 89
Shmelev, N, 30
show trials, 234
Smirnov, V M, 159
Smith, A, 135
social democracy, 71, 180, 239
social fascism, 180, 238–9
social Revolutionaries, 38, 189, 242
'socialism in one country', 57, 76, 120, 123, 130, 147–8, 167–8, 170–4, 177, 181, 200, 210, 213, 221, 230, 242
Socialist Workers' Party, 29
Sokolnikov, G, 110
soviets, 18–20, 30, 38, 43, 46, 75, 91, 128–9
Spartakists, 35, 54, 171
stabilisation of capitalism, 128, 179–80, 201
stages theory, 22, 116–18, 188, 193, 197
Stalin, I V, 4, 18, 22, 24, 32, 49, 54, 68, 82, 92–3, 105, 109–11, 114–15, 128, 134, 143–4, 160–1, 198–9, 208, 214–15, 217, 219, 222, 224, 226, 228–30, 233, 237–9, 241, 245, 247
Foundations of Leninism, 120
calls for industrialisation, 208
calls for 'self-criticism', 126
and Chinese revolution, 191–2
destroys the NEP, 230
'duumvirate' with Bukharin, 114, 124, 191, 197, 218
fights the Right, 208, 236–41
and Georgians, 111
and grain crisis, 215

Stalin, I V *continued*
  on growth of class struggle in the approach to socialism, 223
  invents 'socialism in one country', 120
  leads counter-revolution, 5, 73, 151, 161, 168, 172, 234
  Lenin advises removal as General Secretary, 111
  liquidates kulaks, 215
  voluntarist planning of, 142, 204, 208
Stalinism, 4–5, 12, 32, 127, 154, 196, 219, 224, 227, 248, 211, 228
  thaw in 1933, 247
Stalinist apparatus, 125, 145, 170, 204, 229, 235, 243, 246,
state capitalism, 5, 7–8, 10–11, 13–14, 17, 21, 28–31, 54, 63, 66, 73, 81, 83–4, 124, 161, 167, 198, 216, 224–5, 231
state capitalism under proletarian dictatorship, 31, 29–30, 58, 67, 80, 83, 86–7, 166
subbotniks, 35, 37
Sun Yat-sen, 186–7
Supreme Council of National Economy, 37, 245
Supreme Economic Council, 49

Tambov, 20
Tasca, A, 239
theory of the state, 12
Thermidor, 218, 232
third period, 180, 238–9
Tomsky, M, 46, 93, 141, 219, 228, 231, 236, 239, 241, 243, 246–7
trade union debate, 51, 61
trade unions, 35, 37, 43, 48, 50, 91, 211, 231, 236, 241, 246
transition to socialism, 39, 42, 63, 82, 88, 93, 101, 151, 162–3

trial of 1938, 115, 245, 249
Trotsky, L D, 4, 6, 8, 18, 20, 22, 24, 26, 36, 39–40, 46–50, 52, 55, 57, 61, 68–9, 71, 76–7, 82, 88, 94, 99, 110–14, 117, 119, 124, 130, 139, 147–8, 161, 168, 178, 190, 195, 199, 204, 217–19, 222, 228–30, 232, 235–6, 239, 242, 250
  Lessons of October, 116
  'Towards Capitalism or Socialism?', 88
  War and the International, 4
  accuses Bukharin of paving way to capitalism, 165
  accuses Bukharin of 'tailism', 136, 149
  attitude to kulaks, 148
  on bureaucracy, 126–8
  begins campaign for party democracy, 111
  on China, 190
  contrasts fate of Rights and Lefts under Stalin, 246
  critique of Bukharin's Draft Comintern Programme, 174
  and economic debate before 1929, 168ff
  on equilibrium, 226
  exiled, 115
  keeps alive revolutionary tradition, 249
  misjudges Stalinism, 129, 227ff
  on NEP, 48, 58, 87ff, 137
  opposition to Stalin, 5, 110, 224–5, 230
  on permanent revolution, 116–18
  on planning, 168
  on possible alliance with Stalin or Bukharin, 168–70, 225
  on regime of economy, 212
  rejects alliance with Bukharin, 225

Trotsky, L D *continued*
  and scissors crisis, 133
  on stabilisation of capitalism, 179
  warns against misinterpreting
    Preobrazhensky's law, 160
Trotskyism, 109, 130, 172, 177,
  188, 222–3, 238, 242–3, 245
Tsarism, 13, 18, 30
Tsarist officials in Soviet
  Government, 38, 70–1

Uglanov, N, 141, 221, 236, 240, 246
ultra-imperialism, 5–7
ultra-leftism, 17, 27, 179
unemployment, 90, 141
united front, 175, 182, 239
United Opposition, 238

Vaganov, N, 237
vanguard party, 46, 73
voluntarism, 26, 52, 57, 61, 82,
  204, 238
Voroshilov, K, 220, 236, 247
Vyshinsky, A, 250–1

wages, 89–90, 142, 211–12
War Communism, 31–2, 35–6, 39,
  41, 44, 46–9, 52–3, 56–8, 61,
  70, 74–5, 79–80, 84, 86, 38,
  90–2, 94, 113, 167, 171, 232
war panic 1927, 207
White armies, 32
worker-peasant alliance, 102, 104,
  115, 130, 137, 142, 148–9,
  159, 219
workers' control, 27, 46
workers' democracy, 49–51, 112,
  129, 230, 235
Workers' Opposition, 50–1
workers' state, 4, 10–11, 29, 31,
  43–4
working class, 5, 14, 25, 33, 36, 38,
  44, 90, 96, 140, 231
world economy, 5–6, 15, 173
world revolution, 20, 22, 24–5, 29,
  36, 53–4, 61, 76, 96, 117–19,
  121–3, 136, 152–3, 164, 169
  173–6, 179, 181, 199, 227

Yeltsin, B, 5

Zetkin, K, 55
Zinoviev, G, 18, 49, 52, 55, 91,
  111, 115, 124–5, 147–8, 171,
  182, 187, 205–6, 217, 238,
  242, 249-50

Published by Pluto Press

The Serge-Trotsky Papers

Edited by David Cotterill

Leon Trotsky and Victor Serge represent the great and tragic oppositional figures to Stalin's dictatorial grip on the Soviet Union in the late 1920s and 1930s. Written during this period, letters exchanged between these two friends, published here in translation for the first time together with other material from both the Trotsky Archive at Harvard and the Serge Archive in Mexico, present a unique first-hand account of the alternatives and arguments of the Trotskyist opposition in exile. The correspondence chronicles Trotsky's attempts to found a new Fourth International, as well as casting new light on the trajectory of the Russian revolution from Lenin to Stalin and the long term effects of Stalinism for the revolutionary movements in the West.

A remarkable insight into the lives of two prominent thinkers of the twentieth century, these papers also help us to understand an important relationship during a critical period in European politics. The editors provide clear introductions which contextualise and clarify the documents.

ISBNs hardback: 0-7453-0515-6 softback: 0-7453-0516-4
March 1994
Order from your local bookseller or direct from Pluto Press
(phone 081 348 2724 for prices and availability)

Pluto Press 345 Archway Road, London N6 5AA

Published by Pluto Press

Socialist History
The Journal of the Socialist History Society

Editor: Willie Thompson

Socialist History is a new departure in historical journals. Appealing to those within the historical profession as well as readers with a general interest in the subject, each issue will include articles, reviews and other material on a broad range of topics – often by leading writers in the field – as carefully researched and closely argued as those found in mainstream counterparts.

1: A Bourgoise Revolution? Seventeenth century England.
Brian Manning: Corporal Thompson and the Crisis of the English Revolution / *Willie Thompson*: Samuel Pepys and the Emergent Bourgoisie   0-7453-0805-8   Spring 1993

2: What was Communism? I *Kevin Morgan*: The CPGB and the Comintern Archives / *Janos Jemnitz*: Labour and Politics   0-7453-0806-6   Summer 1993

3: What was Communism? II *Mike Squires*: The CPGB and 'Class Against Class' / *Steve Parsons*: A Tragedy of the Purges   0-7453-0807-4   Autumn 1993

Each issue is 64 pages, and there are three issues per year.

Order from your local bookseller. For a subscription telephone 081 348 2724.

Pluto Press 345 Archway Road, London N6 5AA

Published by Pluto Press

The Good Old Cause
British Communism 1920–1991

Willie Thompson

I take my hat off to Willie Thompson ... He has done something I shouldn't have believed possible ...
Peter Fryer, Worker's Press

How could a political group with overtly revolutionary aims and a strong commitment to a faraway country find a place inside a society which is both markedly conservative and decidedly insular? *The Good Old Cause* is a unique attempt to answer this question.

ISBNs hardback: 0 7453 0578 4   softback: 0 7453 0579 2

The Long Death of British Labourism

Willie Thompson

Willie Thompson argues that the hierarchical and disciplined structure of organisations within the British labour movement prevented it from ever becoming a real threat to the Establishment. And for this reason it prospered. At the same time, he suggests, it was its willingness to accommodate the status quo that led to its slow decline in the second half of the twentieth century. Willie Thompson concludes that it is time to recognise that the labour movement has brought about its own demise.

ISBNs hardback: 0 7453 0580 6   softback: 0 7453 0581 4

Order from your local bookseller or contact the publisher on
081 348 2724.

Pluto Press 345 Archway Road, London N6 5AA

Celebrating a rich history of over twenty years of political and cultural publishing, Pluto Press are re-issuing classic works by authors such as Frantz Fanon, Noam Chomsky, Susan George and Peter Fryer

Pluto Classics

Eamonn McCann: War and An Irish Town
New edition, ISBN 0-7453-0725-6

Augusto Boal: Theatre of the Oppressed
ISBN 0-86104-080-5

Noam Chomsky: Necessary Illusions
ISBN 0-7453-0380-3

Frantz Fanon: Black Skin, White Masks
ISBN 0-7453-0035-9

Peter Fryer: Black People in the British Empire
ISBN 0-7453-0342-0

Peter Fryer: Staying Power
The History of Black People in Britain
ISBN 0-86104-749-4

Susan George: The Debt Boomerang
How Third World Debt Harms Us All
ISBN 0-7453-0594-6

Peter Sedgwick: Psychopolitics
ISBN 0-86104-352-9

Michael Barratt-Brown and **Pauline Tiffin**:
Short Changed: Africa and World Trade
ISBN 0-7453-0699-3

Pluto Press 345 Archway Road, London N6 5AA